RESEARCH IN
FAMILY INTERACTION

RESEARCH IN
FAMILY
INTERACTION

Readings
and Commentary

Edited by William D. Winter
and Antonio J. Ferreira

382357

SCIENCE AND BEHAVIOR BOOKS, INC.
Palo Alto, California: 1969

Second Printing, 1971

Library of Congress Catalog Card number 68-54536.

ISBN 0-8314-0022-6.

Preface

The general purpose of this collection of readings is to present an extensive but detailed coverage of the problems involved in studying family interaction, the methodologies devised to handle these problems, and some representative findings in interaction research.

The study of interaction among family members is a relatively new area of endeavor. However, because of its obvious mental health implications, it has already excited many professional people and produced a rapidly growing body of research. This research is just beginning to gain the attention of curriculum molders, and we can expect work on family interaction to become increasingly represented in the graduate studies of psychologists, psychiatrists, social workers, and sociologists. Thus, this anthology of articles is intended to be an introduction to this important field of research, an introduction which we believe will be useful and inviting to graduate students as well as to professional people who work with families.

The articles in this volume are divided into three sections. Section I deals with the general methodological issues and problems encountered in doing family interaction research, some suggested solutions to these problems, and a framework for analyzing the adequacy of research designs.

The remainder of the book comprises selected research reports which illustrate a variety of approaches to the study of family interaction and also present important content on family dynamics for interested clinicians. These reports are grouped according to the general technique employed by the investigator to study families. Each section is composed of a few main articles from which major portions are presented, and some articles from which only a brief description of the investigatory technique used is excerpted. These brief excerpts will give the reader an introduction to the variety of interesting techniques available, although these generally have not led as yet to any substantial body of data.

The first group of research reports (Section II) illustrates the usual attempt to understand the family environment by studying one or more of its members separately and trying to determine family structure by inference from the attitude of these members. The rest of the articles deal more centrally with actual family interaction. Section III deals with the decision-making process, a major theme of interaction research. Section IV illustrates findings from interaction studies which focus on the emotions, feelings, attitudes, and dominance relationships in a family. Section V focuses on studies of behavioral interaction, both verbal and nonverbal, and also deals with the question of whether this interaction is the same in a family and in a group of unrelated strangers. The book concludes with a selection of articles on communication within the family, a concept which runs across and integrates the previous topics.

Having described the general structure of this volume, the editors hasten to add that the rationale for grouping the articles this way and the choice of where to place a given article was quite arbitrary. Most articles could have fitted nicely into more than one part or section, and other classification schemes would have worked equally well. The final classification shown in the Table of Contents is largely a matter of convenience or a reflection, perhaps, of the editors' aesthetics.

Books of readings are easy to edit when articles are reprinted in full. We have chosen the more risky route of boldly editing many of the selections in order to bring out only that portion which carries forth the particular theme we are illustrating, sometimes, no doubt, omitting the content which might have been the original author's very *raison d'etre* for writing the article. In our abridgements, major omissions are indicated by asterisks, and minor omissions of a few words, sentences, or footnotes are left unmarked, so as to make for smoother reading. Tables and figures have been renumbered in some instances. The interested reader is urged to consult the primary sources to find a more complete description of the author's findings and point of view.

The editors wish to stress that this particular selection of articles reflects their own long-established preference for interactional studies that produce hard data. The final selections made were those that we felt would best achieve the overall goals of this book. This means that many fine articles could not be accommodated for a variety of reasons unrelated to their quality. In addition, to illustrate a point, we sometimes selected articles which may not represent the most sophisticated work of the author.

It is our pleasure to publicly express our gratitude to the many authors and publishers who granted permission to reprint the journal articles included in the present collection. We owe a special debt to the authors who, despite ego hurts, granted us permission to edit their works to the extent we did.

Contents

SECTION I. METHODOLOGICAL ISSUES IN FAMILY
            INTERACTION RESEARCH   1

1. The Patient's Family: Research Methods   5
   Leslie Y. Rabkin
2. Supplementary Methods in Family Research   18
   George Levinger
3. Familial Etiology of Schizophrenia: Is a Scientific
   Methodology Possible?   24
   Alan F. Fontana

SECTION II. STUDIES OF INDIVIDUAL FAMILY MEMBERS   37

4. The Family Relations Indicator: A Projective Technique for
   Investigating Intra-Family Relationships Designed for Use
   with Emotionally Disturbed Children   39
   John G. Howells and John R. Lickorish
5. Family Socialization Techniques and Deviant Behavior   50
   Frances E. Cheek
6. Thought Disorder and Family Relations of Schizophrenics   63
   Margaret T. Singer and Lyman C. Wynne
7. The Role of Psychological and Social Factors in the Onset
   of Somatic Illness in Children   76
   Arthur Z. Mutter and Maxwell J. Schleifer
8. Nonlexical Speech Similarities as an Index of Intrafamilial
   Identifications   87
   Joseph Becker and Judy McArdle
9. Conflict in Families of Schizophrenics as a Function of
   Premorbid Adjustment and Social Class   95
   James C. Baxter and Sonya C. Arthur

SECTION III. STUDIES OF FAMILY INTERACTION:
             DECISION-MAKING   99

10. The Family as a Three-Person Group   101
    Fred L. Strodtbeck
11. Family Interaction and Decision-Making   110
    Antonio J. Ferreira and William D. Winter
12. Family Interaction: A Social-Clinical Study of Synthetic,
    Normal, and Problem Family Triads   125
    Arthur M. Bodin
13. Married Couples' Responses to Disagreement   128
    Robert G. Ryder and D. Wells Goodrich

14. Measurement of Family Relationships and Their Effects   137
       Amerigo Farina and Richard M. Dunham
15. An Application of the Rorschach Test in Family
    Investigation   148
       Joshua Levy and Nathan B. Epstein
16. A Structured Family Interview   150
       Paul Watzlawick

SECTION IV. STUDIES OF FAMILY INTERACTION:
             FEELINGS, ATTITUDES, POWER   153

17. Interpersonal Perceptivity among Family Members   155
       Antonio J. Ferreira
18. Hostility Themes in the Family TAT   162
       *William D. Winter, Antonio J. Ferreira, and
       Jim L. Olson*
19. Laboratory Measurement of Parental Behavior   168
       *Robert E. Schulman, Donald J. Shoemaker, and
       Irvin Moelis*
20. Interaction Testing in the Study of Marital Dominance   177
       Gerald Bauman and Melvin Roman
21. Family Interaction Patterns and the Emotionally Disturbed
    Child   187
       J. Glenn Hutchinson

SECTION V. STUDIES OF FAMILY INTERACTION:
            BEHAVIOR   193

22. Family Experiments: A New Type of Experimentation   195
       Jay Haley
23. Consistency, Rigidity, and Power in the Interaction of
    Clinic and Non-Clinic Families   203
       Stanley A. Murrell and James. G. Stachowiak
24. Research on Family Patterns: An Instrument Measurement   213
       Jay Haley
25. Some Interactional Variables in Normal and Abnormal
    Families   222
       *Antonio J. Ferreira, William D. Winter, and
       Edward J. Poindexter*
26. Interaction Process Analysis of Family Decision-Making   232
       William D. Winter and Antonio J. Ferreira
27. Some Dynamics of Laughter during Family Therapy   242
       *Gerald H. Zuk, Ivan Boszormenyi-Nagy, and
       Elliot Heiman*
28. Family Functioning as an Index of Need for Welfare Services   245
       Ludwig L. Geismar

29. Family Interaction Associated with Child Disturbances:
    Assessment and Modification   250
        Barclay Martin
30. Family Interaction Scales   254
        Jules Riskin

SECTION VI. STUDIES OF FAMILY INTERACTION:
              INTRA-FAMILY COMMUNICATION   261

31. Communicator-Communicant Approach to Family
    Interaction Research   263
        Gilbert Levin
32. Information Exchange and Silence in Normal and Abnormal
    Families   272
        Antonio J. Ferreira and William D. Winter
33. Experiment with Abnormal Families: Testing Done in a
    Restricted Communication Setting   285
        Jay Haley
34. An Experimental and Clinical Study of Family
    Decision-Making Processes   302
        *Robert A. Ravich, Morton Deutsch, and
        Bert Brown*

Bibliography   304

Methodological Issues in Family Interaction Research

In The Art of Scientific Investigation, *William Beveridge states that it may be unwise to study closely the literature dealing with the particular problem on which one is going to work, because ". . . reading what others have written on the subject conditions the mind to see the problem in the same way and makes it more difficult to find a new and fruitful approach [1957, p. 4]." The difficulty of which Beveridge speaks is quite evident in the area of family interaction, to which most of us come encumbered by the prejudices, conceptual schemata, and operational techniques instilled in us by years of training in the study, diagnosis, and treatment of individuals or, a somewhat happier circumstance, the study of unrelated groups of strangers (group dynamics or therapy).*

Until very recent times, most clinicians were concerned only with the individual patient as a unit, as if his life space were encapsulated by his skin. The nature of the clinician's interest varied with his predilection, but the locus was the isolated individual. The psychiatrist was concerned with his patient's mental status and diagnosis, the psychoanalyst with the fantasies or real-life events underlying his oedipal complex, the psychologist with his intelligence, etc. The patient's family was of interest only as a source of genetic material, life history data, or as the shadowy figures grappled with on the analytic couch.

Perhaps the most significant shift of focus from a purely individual frame of reference occurred when clinicians suddenly discovered that schizophrenic patients had real, live mothers, whose active influence helped determine the patients' condition. This influence was generally thought to be destructive, and the descriptions of such mothers (by predominantly male clinicians) as "schizophrenogenic" or "ice-box" mothers became quite popular. Still, most hospitals continued to treat only the individual patient, while child guidance clinics, although recognizing the living importance of the parents of a given child patient, limited themselves to offering individual interviews to the mother, and not even that to the frequently inaccessible father.

So, despite the broadening of the frame of reference to include the mother of the identified patient, she was often seen in stereotyped terms, as a bad person who had a bad effect on her passive offspring. The process was not viewed, at first, as a reciprocal interaction, and only within the last decade or two has the clinician discovered that the patient has a

1

father, a wife, and other relatives who exert an influence on him, as well as being influenced by him. But interest in the family as a unit of interacting individuals was not a simple, direct end-product of the historical process described above. Even while psychiatry, for example, was overwhelmingly involved with individual diagnosis and treatment, pioneer scientists from other fields, such as Burgess (1926) and Baldwin, Kalhorn, and Huffman (1945) were describing family interaction patterns and the general psychological atmosphere of the home, while others like Lewin (1946) and Redl (1945) were giving us new insights into group dynamics and group methods of treatment. However, although these men were influential in drawing our attention to interactional factors, the clinical Zeitgeist was against them; and it has only been recently, through the catalytic efforts of men like Bell (1961), Ackerman (1958), Jackson (1957), and Bateson and his co-workers (1956) that clinicians have begun to conceptualize the patient as one nexus in a family that is an interacting, stable system of roles and communications, with a transmitted culture of its own. Mottola (1967) presents a brief review of the development of this approach.

Although many clinical investigators were willing to accept this new look and to see the value of conceptualizing families as units or communities, with their own appropriate levels of analysis, they approached this new area with the armamentarium and thinking developed in learning how to deal with individuals or with therapy groups, plus perhaps some leftover vague uneasiness engendered by the hoary controversies over the existence of the group mind and gestalt phenomena in psychology. It seemed obvious that the easiest way to study families was to apply the techniques with which we were already familiar in individual and group work. This approach has not been successful, as will be pointed out later in this book.

Even the knowledge we have gained from group dynamics research cannot be directly applied to families. As Haley (1962) points out, group dynamics experimenters typically do research with unrelated groups of strangers and attempt to eliminate any effect due to prior acquaintance on the experimental variables they are measuring. Yet it is precisely the area of prior history which is of interest to family researchers. We want to know how a family typically reacts, each member to the other, regardless of the effect of the particular laboratory set-up, rather than how the members react to the independent variable, regardless of their relationship to one another.

We open this book with an article by Rabkin which critically reviews some of the major methodologies which have been used to study families, ranging from case histories to observational studies of family interaction. Despite their methodological difficulties, these latter methods offer great promise if their designs can be improved. In his article, Levinger presents evidence for the value of combining objective observational methods and subjective reports, and points out that in his study the observational methods showed gross correspondence with the judgment of clinicians. Fontana presents a rather detailed critique of the assumptions and methodological difficulties underlying the typical family interaction studies of schizophrenics. In particular, his series of factors which should be taken into account in a good interaction study might serve as a useful checklist for the reader as he analyzes the research studies in the remainder of this volume. In the portion of Fontana's article not reprinted here, he reviews the empirical results obtained in a number of investigations of families of schizophrenics, and the interested reader is again urged to examine the original sources for material not included in the present anthology.

The Patient's Family: Research Methods*

Leslie Y. Rabkin

* * * The purpose of this paper is to extend general criticisms of family research to more specific methodologies. In addition, we hope to present some guideposts for further research which will allow for a new approach to understanding the family of the psychiatric patient. The methodologies to be examined below are: (1) the case history, (2) psychological testing, (3) psychotherapeutic observation, (4) interviewing, (5) attitude and rating scales, and questionnaires, (6) observational studies. Specific examples will be utilized but no attempt will be made to be comprehensive in our coverage of the literature.

Case History Studies

In this category fall those studies in which the authors, having access to a large number of hospital or clinic records, make a *post-hoc* investigation of the backgrounds of a specific clinical group, seeking to find significant events or patterns of occurrences which can be said to be characteristic of the group in question. Such factors as parental rejection and/or overprotection (e.g., Kasanin, Knight, and Sage, 1934), the incidence of broken homes (e.g., Madow & Hardy, 1947), or patterns of family relationship and the home environment (e.g., Ellison & Hamilton, 1949), have been particular focal points. Other studies, fewer in number, like that of O'Neal and Robins (1958), have been entirely empirical in nature, seeking simply to sift the case records with no preconceived ideas as to what they might find, tabulating all data which showed a noteworthy trend.

Case history studies have always appealed to researchers in institutions with a large patient population. The material is readily available, the collating of data can be done by a secretary or graduate student, and this method of data gathering can claim to avoid the pitfall of subjective clinical impression, so notoriously unreliable. There appear, however, to be glaring methodological problems in studies utilizing this material.

---

*Abridged from *Family Process*, 1965, *4*, 105–132, with permission of the author and *Family Process*.

The first difficulty is that these histories are not gathered for research purposes but are generally part of the clinical evaluation of the patient. Thus, only certain items tend to get tabulated, those considered by the social worker to be relevant to the etiology of the patient's disorder. This means that certain theoretical notions intrude into what gets recorded. For example, we know that Freudian theory postulates that the vicissitudes of sexuality play an overwhelmingly important part in personality development. Within this orientation, then, many questions may be asked about the patient's sexual development and behavior, and their findings later interpreted to show how sexual disturbances played a key role in the patient's pathological development. However, Hovey (1959), for one, has shown that many self-referent items pertaining to sex (e.g., "I have had sexual experiences that make me feel ashamed") fail to significantly discriminate psychiatric patients from controls. Thus, incidence in the patient population and prevalence in the general population are not compared. Without this check, the results cannot be clearly interpreted.

Not only are histories collected for clinical purposes, but their source itself raises many questions as to their validity for research. For the most part, life history data is collected from a single informant, usually the mother of the patient. The exigencies of hospital and clinic time being what they are, little effort is made to cross-check and in some way to validate this historical data. This means that the patient's past life and his behavior soon begin to be • described via the categories and phraseology of the informant. No wonder, then, as Goffman (1961) points out, the patient in a mental hospital often imagines a "conspiracy" existing between his family and the medical staff. Note should also be made of the well-documented inability (Yarrow, Campbell, & Burton, 1964; Haggard, Brekstad, & Skard, 1960) of mothers to accurately report on behavioral and developmental events, even when the report concerns their small child. Factors of conscious and unconscious forgetting and distortion enter here.

An example of the errors possible with this method of data collection, and one particularly pertinent to the results reported by many researchers concerned with the etiology of schizophrenia, concerns the phenomenon which Kasanin et al. (1934) pointed out many years ago—the "overprotective" mothers, because of this very trait, tend to remember and give the fullest amount of history material. Thus, if incomplete and inadequate records are discarded from the sample, as has invariably been the case, we will find ourselves left with just those records given by overprotective mothers. Reasoning from case material to etiology then becomes rather indefensible.

Once the records are chosen for analysis, what of control groups or some base-line for comparison? There has been an unfortunate tendency to choose control groups, if they have been used at all, more on the basis of their availability rather than their relevance to the study. Often these controls are staff personnel at the hospital where the patients are confined, an occasional attempt being made to match them with the patients on a number of "easy," demographic variables. The sometimes inappropriateness of such a group can be vividly seen in a study by Oltman, McGarry, and Friedman (1952), who sought to gauge the significance of broken homes and parental loss in schizophrenia. They chose, as a control group, hospital employees, and concluded that the incidence of broken homes in schizophrenia was no higher than in the control group. However, analysis of their data shows these controls to have an incidence of parental loss which is *twice* that of the population at large. This can hardly be said to be a normal control.

Having chosen a control, the researchers may then seek to rate certain aspects of the history—for example, the extent of parental rejection. While bare demographic data (age, sex, etc.) are straightforward enough to be reliably coded, this reliability often falls quite low when what is to be classified are more subtle behaviors. McKeown (1950), for example, found an inter-rater reliability among four judges of only 67.2 percent when their task was to set parental behaviors into the following categories: demanding-antagonistic, superficial, protective, indulgent, and encouraging.

Nor is any cognizance taken of the factors of degree and timing of these occurrences, certainly not in any comparative way. The importance of this specification is pointed up by Despert (1942), who writes, concerning schizophrenic children:

> Various degrees of rejection and ambivalent behavior are also frequently noted in parents of neurotic children. However, there again the factor of severity must be considered. The profound and complete rejection on the part of the mothers of these children was a conspicuous factor [p. 201].

It may be just such variables as degree and timing of occurrences which can help reconcile the confusing finding that certain parental traits (e.g., rejection) crop up in the life histories of patients with all types of diagnoses. An approach based on such a "critical periods" notion of socialization should lead to a series of refined hypotheses.

Finally, all the data having been assembled and analyzed, results are reported and evaluated—a procedure which should be reasonably scientific and objective, but which tends to be strongly influenced by the clinician's theoretical point of view. Bender (1955), for example, takes the view that:

> ...schizophrenia is a maturation lag at the embryonic level in all areas which integrate biological and psychological behavior; an embryonic primitivity or plasticity characterizes the pattern of behavior disturbances in all areas of personality functioning. It is determined before birth and hereditary factors appear to be important [p. 512].

Within this framework, a study was carried out by Bender and Grugett (1956) which purposed to show that while the home and family environment of neurotic and asocial children is the specific etiological factor in their problems, schizophrenic children do *not* seem to come from such uniformly bad environments. This statement is not only counter to the findings of most other case history studies, but seems to belie the results which Bender herself obtained in a previous study (1955). As Sanua (1961) points out, an analysis of this earlier study shows that 42 percent of the sample of schizophrenic children *did* come from disturbed homes, where they were abused, or lived in foster homes during infancy.

Interviewing Studies

These studies involve interviews of varying degrees of structure and intensity with the mothers of psychiatric patients (Tietze, 1949), both parents (Nuffield, 1954), or the patients themselves (Kohn & Clausen, 1956). The usual report is a composite of clinical impressions and quotes from an interview schedule. For the most part, these interview studies are conducted in the clinic or hospital where the patient is being treated, and only occasionally do they utilize a control group.

Assessing interview studies presents us with problems similar to those met in evaluating the case history method, as well as several new ones. An important point concerns the data which is not reported or, if reported, not clarified. Sometimes the interview focuses on specific aspects of the life history. An example is the well-designed study of Kohn and Clausen (1956), which had carefully matched schizophrenics and controls focus their reports on family experiences occurring during their thirteenth year. This is an intentional narrowing of the data gathered. Often, however, the disregard for other historical and ecological variables (particularly social-class and sex differences) simply leaves us with many unanswered questions.

In Tietze's (1949) study, for example, in which she interviewed the mothers of 25 schizophrenic patients and characterized them all as over-anxious, obsessive, frigid, and domineering, she buttressed her clinical hypotheses about the parent-child relationship, as Gerard and Siegal (1950) pointed out, with examples drawn only from the backgrounds of *female* patients. No attempt was made to spell out possible sex differences in background.

We are also faced, once again, with the problem of the validity of these accounts. There is every reason to believe that social desirability factors will operate in a situation so emotionally loaded for the participants, as well as the associated factors of blocking, selective recall, denial, etc. As Kohn and Clausen (1956) noted about their interview material:

> We must assume that to some degree these reports must be inaccurate. Both patients and parents have undoubtedly failed to see significant aspects of their relationships; their reports are un-

doubtedly colored by the experience of psychosis, and by the changes in the relationships since the period of childhood reported on [p. 311].

Nor do the descriptions of the usual maternal informant (e.g., in Tietze), laced as they inevitably are with words like "narcissistic," "manipulative," "self-centered," offer much hope that the reports offered are accurate or even relatively unbiased accounts. Of course, the countertransference elements exemplified by the very choice of these adjectives must also be weighed. Expectancy and need-perception are powerful factors!

In the case of the interview, as with all clinical studies of patients and/or families, we have the distortion involved in what can be called "self-selection" of cases, our sample always being limited to those individuals who offer themselves for treatment or survey. The differential rates across social classes and ethnic groups in seeking this help (Hollingshead & Redlich, 1958; Srole, Langner, Michael, Opler & Rennie, 1962) impose another source of bias on the data gathered.

Psychodiagnostic Studies

This method of research has been the special domain of psychologists, who have used various batteries of tests to unearth patterns of family behavior or the personality characteristics of the family members. For the most part, they have used those best-known projective techniques, the Rorschach and the Thematic Apperception Test. The testees have sometimes been only mothers (Prout & White, 1950; Toms, 1955), other times the patients themselves (Singer, 1954), and occasionally the entire family group (Morris & Nicholas, 1950; Fisher & Mendell, 1956). The more frequent type of psychodiagnostic study, however, has been in the nature of a "content analysis" approach to the records of patients drawn from the various diagnostic groupings, focusing on their individual psychodynamics and attempting to reconstruct some early relations with significant others.

The chief criticism which can be levied at the use of psychological tests to assess family interaction is our lack of knowledge concerning the connection between the material elicited and any sort of "real" behavior. This is true, of course, of some of the other techniques reviewed (e.g., how are attitude scale results related to behavior?), but interpretation of psychologicals involves an even higher order of inference because of their greater indirectness. Weinberger (unpublished manuscript, 1962), for one, has critically discussed the problem of the relationship between psychological test analysis and behavior, concluding that " ... test reports generally stress intrapsychic dynamics and either ignore completely their relationship to overt behavior or else make tentative connections which are often unverifiable [p. 6]."

Perhaps the work of such researchers as Jackson and Weakland (1961), in the area of the "schizophrenic family's" interaction patterns, will help to verify some predictions made from psychological test data. In any

event, the controversy over the usefulness of psychodiagnostics for prediction has raged for many years (Meehl, 1954), and the problems of validity
are manifold (Harris, 1960).

There is also the interpretation bias involved in the use of tests, leading to the focusing on the pathological and conflictual areas of personality
functioning, with little concern for signs of psychological health, defensive
strength, or growing maturity. Family members assessed from this frame
of reference naturally tend to appear in a rather negative light. Since the a
priori bias of the investigators is usually toward uncovering parental
pathology, a "freezing" of opinion takes place (Sperber, 1962; Dailey,
1952) which can only lead to a distortion in interpretation.

Alongside these more theoretical problems is the problem of inadequate control groups. This is exemplified in a study by Prout and White
(1950), comparing the Rorschachs of the mothers of 25 schizophrenic
patients and 25 normal young adults. As expected, the mothers of the
schizophrenics were portrayed in negative terms, such as their excessive
ambitiousness for their sons. The control mothers were seen as more
energetic and maternally warm, as well as more accepting of their sons as
individuals. What is important here, however, is that this control group
consisted of a more intelligent and socially-minded group of mothers
(such as hospital volunteers) than one could expect to find in the general
population.

Thus, while interesting hypotheses often emerge from these studies,
the great amount of overlap between groups which plagues the attempts
to utilize psychological tests to describe family environments or parental
personalities, lessens the research usefulness of this tool, at least as it has
been used to this point.

Attitude Scales, Rating Scales, and Questionnaire Studies

These methods, exemplified by the Parental Attitude Research Instrument (PARI), developed by Schaeffer and Bell (1958), and the University
of Southern California Parent Attitude Survey, devised by Shoben (1949),
attempt to elicit the attitudes of parents through a series of scales each of
which is theoretically relevant to the child's personality development. The
items used are generally in the form of opinions ("children should be
shown lots of affection") with which the parent is asked to agree or
disagree along a four-point scale of intensity. To make these statements
less threatening and avoid distortion, the items are usually presented in
the form of a cliche or truism. Originally designed to measure the attitudes of the mothers of normal children, they were quickly taken over to
help assess the child-rearing attitudes of the mothers of deviant groups of
children and adults.

The proponents of this type of research have pointed to the greater
objectivity of such measures, and they have administered them in various
ways, both in person and through the mails. Although most of these
studies have sought to assess the attitudes of parents towards their children, occasional attempts have been made to unearth the child's attitude
towards his parents (Cass, 1952).

The most important factors which tend to vitiate the validity of the questionnaire studies are (1) that what is measured here is present attitudes, with unknown historical continuity; and (2) that little is known about the relationship of expressed attitudes to actual behavior even concurrently, much less retrospectively. What is known (Zunich, 1962; Greenbaum, 1954) suggests that these relationships are at best tenuous, and more likely non-existent.

Because these are present attitudes, they are very much influenced by present circumstances. And these present conditions tend to be that one member of a family has been labeled as "sick," and another member, often in the very clinic or hospital where the "sick" one is being treated, is asked to tell of his or her attitudes towards child-rearing or of incidents which occurred in the life history of the patient, particularly those in which the informant was involved.

It seems inevitable that such a situation will lead to defensiveness on the part of the respondent. Much of this will stem from guilt feelings called forth out of a sense of responsibility for the illness of the patient. In addition, those parents whose conceptions of the origin of the patient's illness fall into what Korkes (1959) calls the "dissociative-organic" or the "dissociative-social" groups, will parade out a wide series of ingenious defensive maneuvers. This defensiveness can take many forms—suppression of information, justification of actions and beliefs, repression of what actually occurred. Add to this the problem of actual forgetting and the acquiescence (Bass, 1955) and social desirability sets (Cowen & Tongas, 1959) which color any such rating scale, and you have a vast array of distorting factors. It would appear that present attitudes, as reported, would have doubtful validity as an index of what actually occurred during the period of early childhood training.

Even if we assume that currently expressed attitudes can be valid indices of real behavior, the work of Gordon (1957) and Leton (1958), among others, casts doubt on the usefulness of the currently most widely used measures, the Shoben scales and the PARI. These researchers have found little relationship between what attitudes parents profess to have, as measured by these instruments, and what behavior they can be observed to engage in.

Two other problems which plague all studies utilizing such measuring instruments are those of "drop-outs" and demographic variables. Goldstein and Carr (1957), for example, were unable to differentiate the child-rearing attitudes of the mothers of catatonic schizophrenics from those of the mothers of paranoid schizophrenics. What they found was that the mothers of the catatonics were more often unable or refused to fill out the questionnaire, and when they did so, left out answers. The problems of who volunteers for a study and the depletion of the experimental group through drop-outs are as important in the area of attitude studies as they are in that of interviewing. The results of research such as that of Lubin, Levitt, and Zuckerman (1962) on the differential personality patterns of responders and non-responders to a questionnaire, should be carefully considered. They found, for example, that while responders were significantly higher (on the Edwards Personal Reference Schedule) for *n*-order and on the dependency ratio, non-responders were significantly higher on *n*-aggression.

In line with the problem of demographic variables, it has consistently been found (Zuckerman, Ribback, Mouashkin, & Norton, 1958) that obtained differences among various groups probably have little to do with the normalcy or deviance of the patient, but are a reflection of social-class, religious, and age differences among the parents. Thus, unlike the other methods of study reviewed in this paper which purport to find startling differences among groups, even the most ardent attitude scale and questionnaire researcher has been hard put to unearth any significant and replicable group differences which cannot be readily interpreted as artifacts of these methodological problems.

Psychotherapy Studies

The many articles which fall under this rubric are generally the result of many years' work with one or another group of patients and consist of a series of clinical impressions. The descriptions of patients and parents are usually couched in a language different in quality from that which is used in the more "objective" studies. What one gets here is generally a psychodynamic formulation, sometimes based on therapy of the patient alone (Despert, 1951), sometimes on therapy conducted with both parent and child (Sperling, 1951), and, more recently, on some form of "conjoint" family therapy (Jackson & Weakland, 1961), in which all available family members are seen together by a single therapist.

There have, of course, been many criticisms leveled at psychotherapy itself, from Eysenck's (1952) complaint that it "doesn't work" to Astin's (1961) slightly tongue-in-cheek view of therapy's "functional autonomy." As a research tool there have been found an equal, though not so dramatic, number of difficulties inhering in this method.

First of all, the literature on the phenomenon of operant conditioning leaves us with some confusion as to the exact role of the therapist in influencing the production of material which arises in the course of psychotherapy. It would seem risky to lend complete credence to what is observed and collated out of this situation for the purposes of research until we can better understand the role of the therapist-observer, his influence and biases. When a patient's therapy is the specific focus of a research program, there is always the danger that simply collecting the data will distort the process and confound the results. This is the classic analytic argument against psychotherapy research, and it remains a moot point.

More specifically, in terms of research design, none of these therapy write-ups are based on a comparison with control groups and, more often, little is specified about the patient beyond his or her age and sex. As Bateson (personal communication, 1961) has pointed out, for example, the exact importance of the "double-bind" (Bateson, Jackson, Haley, & Weakland, 1956) in the family of the schizophrenic cannot be elucidated until this phenomenon is studied in other groups such as the families of delinquents. Nor can we overlook the ethnic variations, Bateson continues, considering the prevalence of this mode of communication in, for example, the middle-class Jewish family.

Finally, considering the importance of social-class factors in the establishment of family behavior patterns (Spiegel & Bell, 1959), the fact that the majority of psychotherapy studies have been carried out on middle- and upper-class patients means that the results probably have an important class bias. Little has so far been done in this direction with Hollinghead and Redlich's (1958) Class V group.

Observational Studies

These ambitious studies, grounded in a concern with the family as an ongoing, communicating group, involve, in intent, a radical departure from past investigations of family functioning. Theoretically, as Haley (1964) notes, they have "shifted their focus to the family as a unit of study, as a system in itself, with an attempt to differentiate one type of family from another rather than an attempt to determine how a family influences a member."

The basic paradigm has been to bring together two or more family members, present them with a task of more or less structure to be worked out conjointly, and have observers classify and rate their behaviors (Loveland, Wynne, & Singer, 1963; Goodrich & Boomer, 1963; Schulman, Shoemaker, & Moelis, 1962; Garmezy, Clarke, & Stockner, 1961; Farina, 1960). The tasks presented in these sessions have included standardized questions or tasks (Levinger, 1963); projective test stimuli (Loveland, et al., 1963); and questionnaires to be filled out and the different responses reconciled (Stabenau, Tupin, Werner, & Pollin, 1965; Titchener, D'Zmura, Golden, & Emerson, 1963). The behaviors measured (primarily verbal, but including non-verbal) have usually been rated along dimensions of conflict, dominance, intrusion, and influence patterns, and more rarely, those of support, encouragement, or other integrative behavior. Primarily, these studies have been content rather than process oriented, emphasizing the amount, for example, of maternal domination or parental conflict, rather than the ongoing "who-does-what-to-whom, when" sequence, although this latter type can also be found.

There are many problems in interactional, observational research, some specific to the study of families, others inherent in the methods themselves. On the general level are such factors as observer inference concerning the behavior being coded, of particular moment when using such methods as the Bales system (Bales, 1950) where the observer's judgment of primarily verbal interaction is all-important; the representative nature of the situations observed; the relationship of observer to observed; the reliability of judgments, etc.

For the most part, experimental family interaction studies have not only failed to solve adequately these general problems but have demonstrated methodological difficulties of their own, such as the interference of preconceptions concerning the family of the psychiatric patient carried over from single-member studies; a focus on part-process, mainly of a negative valence; and only scattered attempts at utilizing control groups or a variety of families.

Most studies seem also to straddle the fence between examining what individual family members do and what the family does as a unit. For example, in a study carried out at the National Institute of Mental Health, with families of normals, delinquents, and schizophrenics, Stabenau et al. (1965) utilized a combination of projective and cognitive test devices administered individually to family members and a Revealed Differences technique in which the members performed conjointly. The family task revealed no significant differences between the groups, and the investigators were forced back to examining the individual protocols to assess parental perceptions of family relationships while making "global" judgments (apparently with preknowledge of which families were which) about family transactions.

Another problem concerns the tasks presented to the families. Judging by the methods used so far in these studies, the realm of generalization of results would appear to be quite limited. A task like the color-matching technique of Goodrich and Boomer (1963) is one, as they are quick to point out, which "is relatively simple, which involves judgments about physical reality rather than social reality, and which contains only one ambiguity [p. 19]." One might hazard a guess that, in reality, the conflicts which these couples will be forced to cope with as time goes on will be complex, concerned more with social reality, and quite ambiguous. The fact that theirs is a longitudinal study of family formation will result in some answers as to the connection between this laboratory task and reality tasks.

The inferential process in family interaction studies should be commented on. The categorization of family interchanges has been found to be highly reliable when observers are trained in a certain method. Yet, as Haley (1964) cogently notes,

> ... [the use of several observers] is thought to be more scientific, and yet even if several raters agree, which is unusual unless they have been trained to look at the data in the same way, there is still doubt whether the family is actually doing that something or whether raters are merely making the same inference because they have a common point of view [p. 44] .

Given, for example, the backlog of "knowledge" concerning the schizophrenic's mother and her dominance, confused communication, etc., it is likely that raters' predispositions will interfere with their raw observational power. And, as noted above, most studies have had to end up relying on "qualitative" descriptions, since attempts to order families in some other manner have failed.

Perhaps Haley's (1964) demonstration of the viability of mechanical recording devices to take the most simple measurements of family interaction will lead to further adoption of this methodology. In its own way, this admittedly crude measure of family patterns is no more primitive than the kinds of evaluations being carried out by observers whose capacity for apprehending the intricate totality of interaction leaves much to be desired. How, after all, is an observer to be able simultaneously to evaluate verbal messages on the informational and symbolic level, vocal inflections, bodily movements, and the temporal relationship of events?

If the methodology of this important type of research is to be improved, two steps are of the utmost importance. First of all is the development of a language of interaction, a conceptual system which can encompass the behavior of two or more people simultaneously, rather than in a cause and effect sequence. Second is the further use of the complex experimental techniques suggested by Haley (1962) for testing the hypotheses drawn from observational research, which should, in turn, refine our observational abilities.

SOME GUIDEPOSTS FOR FUTURE RESEARCH

In the preceding pages, I have presented a résumé of the most popular methods used to study the family of the psychiatric patient. These methods can be broadly classified as:

1. Those which rely on the report of others, of varying degrees of relationship to the patient—examples are the sampling of maternal attitudes through the PARI and the interviews held with relatives and friends—designed to gather a psychiatric history or to allow the clinician to assess the personality, attitudes, and behavior of these "significant others."

2. Those which require a retrospective account from either patient or family, such as Kohn and Clausen's (1956) request that the patients try to recall their early-adolescent family experiences. These studies often make the same explicit assumption as do the "report" ones: that reported attitudes or behaviors are rigidly fixed and have not changed over time, through maturation, or under the impact of the patient's illness. Nor do these studies usually allow for the inevitable distortions of memory, both simple forgetting and the more psychologically determined repressions which color any retrospective account.

3. Those which rely on present observation of the family. These observations have generally been made in the course of psychotherapy, although more recent studies have relied on observational analysis of family interaction. In these studies, too, behavior has been classified according to a priori categories which portray, for example, "domination" as bad, "sharing" as good, with little concern for how these behaviors *appear to the participants*. Also, as these studies are concerned with cause and effect relationships, to reason backward from what is presently observed in the family interaction appears to be an arbitrary dismissal of the all-too-real effect which the disturbed member's illness has on the present situation. In light of the literature on the reorganization of the family which occurs after some member has been identified as the "sick"

one (Clausen & Yarrow, 1955), it may be too early in family research to assume that any bit of reported or observed behavior is a causative element in the patient's disorder and not an effect of this very fact.

Quite often, in making statements concerning cause and effect from these data, researchers have fallen victim to what Benjamin (1959) has called "predictive contaminants." These are the "possible determinants of a successful prediction which lie outside the inductive or deductive theoretical framework on which the prediction is presumably based and which, therefore, could partially or wholly destroy whatever validating significance might otherwise be attributed to the success of the prediction [p. 27]."

Some possible "contaminants" of family studies are easy to specify. For example, we may predict that a certain constellation of parental traits will lead to a certain pathological outcome, disregarding the possibilities that: (1) these attitudes may be the parental *response* to the patient's behavior and not its cause, or (2) the end result may be mental illness, but the cause may lie in genetic transmission, biochemical factors, etc. And this hardly exhausts the possible alternative explanations.

Even more pertinent is the "contaminant" which resides in the possibility that these "pathological" parental attitudes and behaviors lead to a certain outcome not as a *cause sui*, but because they are perceived and reacted to in a certain way by the child, a way perhaps unrelated to the manner in which both parents and researcher construe them.

There is, indeed, reason to believe that the influence of parental attitudes and behavior depends more on the *child's perception* of them than on what they "really" are.

* * * On the basis of these various theoretical propositions, it seems highly important to assess the child's view of his parents and family life. An examination of these perceptions, utilizing different methods, should provide us with many leads for future family research and help clarify the effects of different family attitudes and "environments" on various types of children.

We have carried out some research (Rabkin, 1962, 1964) as a first step in this direction. Utilizing a series of direct and indirect questions and a picture method on groups of normal, neurotic, schizophrenic, and behavior disorder children, it was found that the disturbed children differed from normals in their family role perceptions. Schizophrenic children, for example, tended to see mother as more dominant and punitive, father as more passive and less competent, than did normals, while children with behavior disorders saw father as far more hostile than did normals or any other group. Neurotics perceived a family environment akin to that of the schizophrenics, but with father a stronger, more assertive and competent figure than he was for the psychotic children. These differing perceived family role constellations were interpreted in terms of their effect on the children's identifications and symptomatic behavior. Presently, we are engaged in assessing the role perceptions of *all* family members, with an eye toward discovering the key areas of disagreement and conflict in each type of family.

Another area of relevant inquiry, still untapped, is this: assuming that there is, indeed, a communication of family pathology and that the child learns faulty habits of coping and distorted modes of thinking within this context, the question remains as to *how* this communication is carried out, *what* exactly is learned, and *how* this learning takes place.

The recent work of Wynne and Singer (1963a, 1963b), focusing on the links between differing patterns of family transactions and types of schizophrenic thought disorders in the offspring, is a beginning approximation toward understanding these problems. The type of common concern around which their research centers can be understood from the following statement (Wynne & Singer, 1963a):

Although the isolated statements of individuals [in families of schizophrenics] may even appear "normal," nevertheless, viewed from beginning to end, the over-all transactional disorder in a family's communication sequences may be comparable stylistically to that found in the vagueness or fragmentation of a severely impaired schizophrenic. That is, the form or structure of these family-wide transactions is comparable to that of individual schizophrenic thought disorder [p. 194].

This type of research, examining the entire family communication network, focusing on *structure* rather than *content*, is far more meaningful for our understanding of psychopathology than the multitudinous "trait" studies reviewed earlier. After all, as Bruner (1964) has recently pointed out, the behaviors and modes of thought of humans "reflect the routines and subroutines that one learns in the course of mastering the patterned nature of a social environment [p. 2]." So far, we know all too little about the different patternings which characterize the family environments of disturbed individuals, or for that matter, normal ones.

The problem is, of course, even more complex than this. We don't know, for example, how the child learns to "read" his parents; what cues he uses to assess mood, attitude, feeling; nor what effect these perceptions have. The child, despite our theoretical language, does not have access to the parents' "unconscious" attitudes and feelings, except as they are expressed in behavior; and as metacommunication studies have shown, this behavior may have a variety of relationships to the conscious messages being presented in any context. If this is the case, how does the child learn his own family signals, and how does he come to cognize their meaning?

Supplementary Methods in Family Research*

George Levinger

Progress in both theoretical and empirical understanding of family relationships will be speeded through the use of a combination of research methods in the same study—specifically, direct behavioral observation together with indirect report by family members or other respondents. This thesis will be presented by reviewing the use of these kinds of techniques in family research, discussing the advantages and limitations of each used singly, and illustrating their combined use in a recently completed study. * * *

SUBJECTIVE REPORT AND OBJECTIVE OBSERVATION

The two general methods available to the scientific researcher are those of indirect report and of direct observation. The first set of methods employs the subjective orientation of the respondent to filter the raw facts of his experience. He may give information via an impersonal questionnaire or via a personal interview. The second set of methods is aimed directly at the overt behavior of the subjects, avoiding reliance on second-hand reports. We shall examine the strengths and weaknesses of these methods and then describe a study in which they were used jointly.

The advantage of the questionnaire or the interview is that it is both economical and focused. It affords the most immediate route toward the subject's introspection about his behavior or feelings. To quote Gordon Allport: "If we want to know how people feel, what they experience and what they remember, what their emotions and motives are like, and the reasons for acting as they do—why not ask them? [Selltiz, Jahoda, Deutsch, & Cook, 1959, p. 236]." Of course, introspective report has a long history of being criticized. Its data are susceptible not only to willful but also to unwillful distortion, and there is much evidence to support such charges. Furthermore, such data are inadequate when the investigator is concerned with behavior of which the respondents are not clearly aware (e.g., amount of family conflict or evenness of influence distribution).

---

*Abridged from *Family Process*, 1963, 2, 357–366, with permission of the author and *Family Process*.

To avoid the distortions of self-report, one might employ "competent judges" who know the respondent well and are able to make objective judgments about him. Particularly when more than one such judge is available, valuable data can be obtained by such a procedure. Of course, it is hard to find such accommodating acquaintances, particularly those who can answer the kinds of questions frequently asked in family research.

Until now, in systematic research on family interaction and behavior, most data have been derived from questionnaires or interviews typically addressed to mothers. Almost the entire literature on social class and child-rearing patterns is founded on such evidence. Occasionally in such studies, fathers and children are also included, but it is uncommon for these studies to use several members of the same family as respondents.

Behavioral observation as a technique has a different sort of advantage. While it does not yield rich introspective reports, the observer is able to gain a first-hand sample of the interaction that prevails. He avoids the obvious distortions noted above and gains an insight on the functioning of the total group. He can record action as it occurs and predict more directly to future interaction. Problems of the respondent's unawareness of, or unwillingness to report, the critical behavior are reduced. On the other hand, one must consider the biases stemming from subjects' reactions to being observed and from the unrepresentativeness of the observed situations.

Family interaction is not frequently studied through direct observation. Perhaps this has had to do with the privacy of the home, with the high cost, with the fact that observation must deal with present history and does not delve into the past, and with other factors. The observations of developmental psychologists such as Baldwin, Kalhorn, and Huffman (1945), who dimensionalized parent-child behavior, or Barker and Wright (1954), who observed children in their natural habitat, are conspicuous partly because they are so unusual. Looking closely, though, one discovers that such views of the "family" have usually been confined to the interaction between mother and child, rather than among all family members. Studies of ethnographers or of sociologists such as Koos (1946) or Blood (1958) have avoided this limitation, but in turn they have suffered from a lack of standardization. A "new look" in family research is seen in controlled observational studies of decision-making processes, exemplified in the work of Strodtbeck (1954), Kenkel (1957), Farina (1960), Cheek (1962), Goodrich and Boomer (1963), or Vidich (1956). These studies have all used artificial situational tests which aimed to provide a standard milieu for revealing and comparing family interaction.

The situational test has both its favorable and its unfavorable aspects. Certainly it brings family research closest to the usual model of scientific method. Science is not interested in the natural phenomena alone. It is equally concerned with the construction of laboratory analogues to nature in which one's hunches may be tested more rigorously. Thus situational tests can provide a relatively constant backdrop on which family interaction can be pictured and observed. Tests can elicit infrequent behavior, unlikely to occur in the typical natural situation. And when there exists a standard for comparison, even when subjects distort their usual behavior, they will reveal a great deal more than they realize.

Obviously, behavioral observation also has important disadvantages. Direct observation is more costly in time per subject than any other method; it may influence the very process being studied. and, used without introspective report, it may give a misleading or unrepresentative impression of family patterns. One paper, by Vidich (1956), made specific criticisms of the situational test. Vidich asserts that such a standard situation is likely to produce artificial behavior: where subjects are unmotivated to participate, play atypical roles almost to mock the researcher, and even may try to seduce the observer into taking part in their own decision-making. Vidich implies that these methodological problems are insuperable and that such standardized techniques should never be used. His evidence, however, is limited to his own admittedly unsatisfactory study of eleven couples, with few external criteria to support these strong charges. The experience of other investigators would not agree with Vidich's conclusions.

From our own exploratory study, which used several methods, the writer would agree with many criticisms of behavioral observation. It is costly and it does give a somewhat artificial picture of family life. However, by constructing one's situations properly, one can ensure that families will reveal important information about their internal relationships. In our study, we presented families with various kinds of problems—such as planning a Fourth of July outing to a new spot—where we cared more about the *manner* of the answer than about the answer itself. It appeared much harder for families to distort the *process* than the *content* of their interaction. For example, one family reached the unlikely decision of going ice-skating on the Fourth of July, but revealed at least as much about their interaction as did the less imaginative groups who decided on picnics.

AN ILLUSTRATIVE STUDY

Whatever the strengths or weaknesses of the various techniques, the present purpose is to suggest that they can be used as *supplements* to one another, rather than as mutually exclusive devices. To illustrate this point, we shall present selected aspects of the writer's recent study of family triads. One aim was to obtain exploratory data about variables such as influence distribution, conflict, support, and the parents' satisfaction with spouse and child, as well as comparing so-called abnormal with normal families. A second aim was to examine the correspondence among three different sources of data: standardized behavioral observation, parental descriptions of family members, and outside judges' descriptions.

Procedure. Before turning to the findings, let us briefly look at the procedure. Subjects were 31 families, consisting of father, mother, and one eleven-year-old child—regardless of the actual number of children in the family. Seven of these families came from a children's psychiatric clinic where they were being seen during their diagnostic study. The other 24 families had children in the sixth grade of a suburban school.

Each family was scheduled for an interview of about an hour and a half. During the first part of this period—varying from 30 to 45 minutes—each family engaged in a series of ten tasks presented by the observer, who remained in the room. The tasks included such items as: deciding where to go on a holiday; how to spend $10,000; what to do in several unclear disciplinary situations involving a parent and child; and telling stories to TAT pictures. In each instance the problem was briefly described, each member was asked to think of his own choice, and then the total group was asked to arrive at a family solution.

Observation. The performance session was observed according to Bales' Interaction Process Analysis (Bales, 1950), which emphasized both the task-relevant and the social-emotional actions of the members. Each distinguishable action was tallied in one of 12 categories according to Bales' scheme. The reliability of the observations ranged from .74 to .91 in different sessions where it was checked.

Verbal Report. After the performance part, the child was excused and the parents asked to complete two forms. The first was the Interpersonal Check List, constructed by Leary. Each parent described himself, spouse, child, own father, own mother, and ideal self, ideal spouse, ideal child. The 128 adjectives and phrases in the list are so arranged that it is possible to compute a "dominance" and a "love" score for each person described. Next, each parent spent a final few minutes answering other questions about his family.

External Judgments. In the clinic, the two staff members having the closest contact with each family also filled out some forms. They described father, mother, and child on the Interpersonal Check List, and rated both the total family triad and each individual member on a series of additional scales. In the school, we obtained ratings and descriptions of the children from the teachers.

Biases of These Methods. All measurement techniques are subject to a certain degree of error. In the study under discussion, the observation procedure appeared to be relatively reliable, although it was of low reliability in the infrequently coded categories. More serious was the relative unrepresentativeness of the interaction situations created by the ten problems administered by the researcher. This issue occurs in almost all observation procedures. One cannot obtain an entirely representative sample of all possible interaction situations, either in the family or in any other natural groups. Even such minor matters as the openness of the response categories affected the amount of interaction. "Open-ended" tasks, allowing free choice of responses, induced significantly more interaction than did "closed-ended" tasks where family members could select from only a limited number of alternative answers—as in Strodtbeck's "revealed difference" interaction technique.

The method of inquiry also had its limitations. Regarding the ratings of selves and others made on the Interpersonal Check List, it was found that the parents' responses were highly charged with "social desirability" (Levinger, 1961; Edwards, 1957). That each subject's perceptions were only "part of the truth" is borne out by considerable differences between the ratings of the parents and those of clinicians and teachers. Both in the clinic and in the school, parents saw their children more favorably than did the more neutral professional judges.

Nevertheless, reliance on the external judges alone would have been unsatisfactory. Both the clinicians and the teachers expressed low confidence in certain ratings, since they too had unrepresentative contacts with these families. Not only were their observations based on contacts in unstandardized situations, but their sample of contacts was as biased as that of the research situation.

Due to the exploratory nature of the study under discussion and the limitations in the methods employed, the correspondences among the different methods can be compared in only a few areas. Contrasts will be discussed between the observation and report methods with reference to the areas of "dominance" and of "love."

Regarding marital dominance, there was a relatively gross correspondence between the observation and the report data. Judges' ratings were obtained only from the clinic sample of seven families, but these agreed almost perfectly with the observation findings. (In six cases there was exact agreement, and in the seventh the clinicians rated husband and wife "equal" in dominance versus the former's slight observed superiority in influence.) The Check List data corresponded only grossly with the observation data in total group comparisons between the clinic and the school samples. In other words, the *average* husband in the latter sample was reported *relatively* more dominant than his wife, and observation showed that 81 percent of the school husbands, but only 29 percent of the clinic husbands (17/21 versus 2/7) exercised greater influence in the performance session. More refined comparisons revealed little further correspondence.

Regarding the area of "love" or cooperativeness, there were also some rather crude correspondences. The couples who on the Check List expressed the highest satisfaction between the partners had the least overt conflict in the performance session ($r = -.45$, $p < .05$). Furthermore, the school wives, who were described by their husbands as more supportive than were the clinic wives on the Check List, were observed to show significantly more agreement and positive social-emotional behavior than their clinic counterparts. More precise analysis *within* either sample, though, did not yield further significant associations.

Essentially, it appears that our measuring instruments in this study showed some crude correspondence in their results. By and large, the observations made during the standard session agreed better with the judgments of clinicians than with those of the parents themselves. In part, this lack of correspondence can be attributed to error in the measuring instruments. Also, it may be a function of true lacks of correspondence: i.e., the real difference in families' behavior between public interview (whether with researcher or clinician) and the private home. Only further studies can determine the extent of these lacks in true correspondence.

ADVANTAGES OF COMBINING OBSERVATION AND REPORT

One final substantive finding should be presented which illustrates the advantages of interlinking systematically the use of objective observation and subjective report. One hypothesis of the study was that the more demanding the parents' reported standards for their child, the greater would be their overt demands on him during the performance session. Parental dissatisfaction with the child's dominance was considered an index of the former, while asking him to participate during the performance session was a measure of the latter.

The hypothesis found strong support. Thus the clinic parent, who was of course more displeased with the child, actively demanded his participation more than did the school parents. The data went even further, though. Considering the school sample alone, there remained a striking negative correlation (−.54) between satisfaction with child dominance and the parents' frequency of actively soliciting his participation in the problem-solving tasks.

Such a correlation has both theoretical and methodological implications. On the theoretical side, one may look beyond the apparent correspondence between the child's passivity in the eyes of parents and of the observer. Given children of *equal* observed passivity, the greater the parental dissatisfaction, the higher the frequency of solicitation. One would wonder to what extent such parental actions are instrumental in furthering and maintaining a child's passivity in more general situations. This is an example of a circular pattern between parental expectation and behavior, and child behavior, typical of many other interactions one would find in studying family processes.

On the methodological side, such a finding requires the use of at least two *independent* techniques. It is impossible to investigate such circular processes without recourse to *both* subjective and objective records of family relationships. Seen in this light, introspection and external inspection appear to supplement one another in a useful way. While each by itself has its weaknesses, together they should serve to further the systematic understanding of family interaction.

Familial Etiology of Schizophrenia: Is a Scientific Methodology Possible?*

Alan F. Fontana

The functional role of the family in the development of schizophrenia has been the subject of intensive investigation. Researchers have reported that several personality characteristics differentiate between parents of schizophrenics and non-schizophrenics, and that several aspects of family interaction patterns differ in the families of schizophrenics and non-schizophrenics. However, reviewers (Frank, 1965; Meissner, 1964; Rabkin, 1965; Sanua, 1961) have not shared the optimism and conclusions of the majority of researchers. The recent review by Frank (1965) states that in the last forty years of research, *no* factors have been found which differentiate either between the families of psychopathological and normal members, or among families of pathological members who are classified according to different diagnostic categories. That author's pessimism extends to the more general issue concerning the applicability of the scientific method to the study of human behavior: "Apparently, the factors which play a part in the development of behavior in humans are so complex that it would appear that they almost defy being investigated scientifically and defy one's attempt to draw meaningful generalizations from the exploration which has already been done [p. 210]."

Frank is quite correct in raising the issue of methodology. It is a truism that any body of scientific facts must rest upon a scientifically sound methodology. The conclusions from any study not so based cannot be considered scientific, no matter how scholarly they may be. Some of the previous reviewers have paid insufficient attention to the methodology of individual studies. Rather, their approach has been to tabulate positive and negative results without evaluating the methodological adequacy of individual studies. This approach may have obscured some consistent empirical trends which can be found in well-designed studies.

The purpose of this paper is to examine the scientific status of the three major research approaches, first methodologically and then in terms of empirical results. The sources of data for the approaches to be consid-

---

*Excerpted from *Psychological Bulletin*, 1966, 66, 214–227, with permission of the author and the American Psychological Association.

ered are: (1) clinical observations and psychiatric impressions of family members in treatment, (2) retrospective accounts of child-rearing practices and attitudes obtained from family members' responses to interviews and questionnaires, and (3) current patterns of interaction among family members directly recorded and systematically coded by the investigator. The present analysis will focus on issues concerning the scientific appropriateness of the methodology per se.

CLINICAL OBSERVATIONAL STUDIES

The major limitation inherent in the methodology of clinical observational studies is that the theoretical biases of the therapists tend to become inextricably interwoven with the recording and obtaining of data. Since there is no mechanical recording of the data, the therapist becomes the recording instrument. The therapist typically makes notes after the therapy session has been completed. Thus not only are his perceptions of the moment colored by his biases, but his recollections are subject to primacy-recency effects. Acquisition of the data is also likely to be affected by the therapist's preconceptions. Verbal conditioning studies have demonstrated that people's verbal productions can be shaped to a marked degree by the listener's expressions of interest. Therapists are likely to be unaware that they are selectively reinforcing certain aspects of their patients' behavior.

There is some evidence that many of the theoretical concepts that serve as a framework for therapists' descriptions of the familial characteristics of schizophrenics are not accurate (Jackson, Block, Block, & Patterson, 1958). Jackson et al. asked 20 well-known psychiatrists, who had had considerable experience with schizophrenics and their families, to perform two Q sorts on 108 statements according to their conceptions of the schizophrenic's mother and father. Factor analysis produced three factors for each parent. The six factors were considered to represent the conceptions of mothers and fathers of schizophrenics most widely held in the field of psychiatry. The conceptions were correlated with descriptions of the parents of 20 autistic and 20 neurotic children which had been made by Q sorts of the same 108 items. None of the conceptions showed even a trend toward differentiating the two groups of parents. The results of the Jackson et al. study provide an empirical example and documentation of the inadequacies of this method. Whereas the clinical observational method is valuable as a source of provocative hypotheses and potentially fruitful insights, intrinsic difficulties make it unsuitable as a firm basis for a scientific methodology.

RETROSPECTIVE STUDIES

The validity of interviews and questionnaires for ascertaining the actual parental child-rearing practices and attitudes during the subject's childhood rests upon several assumptions: (1) that people conceptualize their lives in terms of the language used by the investigator so that their understanding of the questions is similar to that of the investigator; (2) that people can accurately recall events and feelings of many years past with minimal forgetting; (3) that people will report unpleasant events without selective forgetting, defensive distortion, and justification of actions by inaccurate elaboration; and (4) that people will report past events unaffected by social desirability or other response sets. Fortunately, there is a substantial amount of empirical data available for evaluating the tenability of these assumptions. McGraw and Molloy (1941) interviewed mothers twice concerning their retrospective accounts of the developmental history of their children. The first time, they conducted the interviews in the usual manner of an intake interviewer. One month later they interviewed the mothers again with more detailed and specific questioning, including pictorial representations of many of the developmental skills involved in the questions. The accuracy of the reports, when compared to staff examination of the children during their development, increased markedly from first to second interview for many questions, particularly for those accompanied by pictorial representations. These results demonstrate the considerable lack of commonality of meaning between investigator and subject when questions are phrased in their typical, unelaborated form. Moreover, questions dealing with feelings and attitudes are not amenable to the pictorial specificity possible in other areas.

The ability of people to recall past events and feelings reliably has been investigated in wider, longitudinal research projects. Haggard, Brekstad, and Skard (1960), Robbins (1963), and Yarrow, Campbell, and Burton (1964) have compared retrospective parental reports to historical parental reports; and Jayaswal and Stott (1955), McGraw and Molloy (1941), Pyles, Stolz, and Macfarlane (1935), and Yarrow et al. (1964) have compared parental recollections to observational material obtained by a research staff during the children's development. All these studies found considerable unreliability in retrospective reports, as well as large intrasubject variability in accuracy across items.

Content of the material to be recalled has an important effect on accuracy of recall. Questions asking for recall of quantitative information and concrete events are answered more reliably than inquiries about attitudes and feelings (Haggard et al., 1960; Yarrow et al., 1964). Haggard et al. (1960) have reported, further, that the greater the initial anxiety associated with an attitude, the less accurately the attitude is recalled. In fact, recall of attitudes originally associated with great anxiety is almost completely unreliable. Kohn and Carroll (1960) found that the picture of past events varied considerably depending upon the member of the family doing the reporting. Heilbrun (1960) found no difference between the way the mothers of schizophrenic and of normal daughters described their child-rearing attitudes, but did find that schizophrenic daughters described their mothers as more pathological in their attitudes than did normal daughters. On the other hand, Jayaswal and Stott (1955) reported that young adults and their parents showed high agreement in their descriptions of the young adults as children. However, neither set of descriptions bore much relation to teachers' descriptions of the young adults obtained when they were children.

Many empirical studies have shown that social desirability and other response sets affect subjects' responses to questionnaire items. There are some data to indicate that responses to questions in an interview are subject to similar biases. McGraw and Molloy (1941) and Pyles et al. (1935), have shown that maternal inaccuracies in recall tended to be made in the direction of precocity in their children; that is, mothers tended to underestimate the age at which their children acquired developmental skills and the time taken to acquire the skills. Robbins (1963) has reported a variation on this finding: inaccuracies tended to reflect the recommendations of a noted contemporary child-rearing expert.

The results of studies evaluating the reliability of retrospective reports make the assumptions underlying the method untenable. Kasanin, Knight, and Sage (1934), Rabkin (1965), and Sanua (1961) have pointed out additional weaknesses in this method. Two are peculiar to the use of interview material from case history folders. These records vary widely in their completeness, with the result that many are rejected because of missing data. Overprotective mothers give more information about their children's background, so that a selective bias influences the characteristics of the records accepted. Offspring of such mothers are very likely over-represented in samples drawn on the basis of completeness. Another bias derives from the manner in which the case histories are obtained. The intake interviewer asks questions and records the data according to his theoretical biases. This same limitation was discussed in connection with the clinical observational method. There is one reservation peculiar to questionnaire data. A high and consistent relationship between current attitudes and current behavior has not yet been empirically demonstrated. It would seem to be an almost insurmountable task to demonstrate a high and consistent relationship between past attitudes and past behavior. For all the above reasons, the retrospective report method is judged to be an inadequate foundation for a body of scientific facts.

FAMILY INTERACTION STUDIES

A criticism that has been applied to each of the preceding methods of investigation is that, in many cases, the data are not recorded and coded objectively and systematically. Haley (1964) and Rabkin (1965) have extended this criticism to family interaction studies, pointing out that high interjudge reliabilities may occur as a result of two or more judges coding within the framework of the same theoretical biases. Thus, one could not be sure that the data were free of inferences from the observer. Haley has suggested and used automatic recording and tabulating of interactional indices by electronic instruments (Haley, 1962, 1964). This insures highly reliable coding, but is purchased at a high price. In one study, Haley (1964) used a machine to tabulate automatically the number of times one person followed another in conversation. However, it is impossible to tell from the data whether the second person interrupted, asked a question, answered a question, disagreed, agreed, said something irrelevant, or was even talking to the first person. The meaningfulness of the data is questionable when they are stripped of such categories. It should be possible, however, to make increased use of instrumentation without sacrificing most of the content of the interaction. Even at best, instrumentation would not solve the problem completely, since the investigator must still program his instruments to code selected aspects of the interaction. A balance must be reached between unchecked observer contamination and such rigid control of possible contamination that essential aspects of the phenomenon under investigation are obscured. At the present time, establishment of high interjudge reliabilities seems to be a workable solution to the dilemma.

Family interaction studies that seek to discover factors which are etiologically relevant to the development of schizophrenia necessarily assume that the causal factors lie in the characteristics of the family interaction pattern. Many people have made the opposite assumption that it is the schizophrenia of the child which has caused the family to develop certain interactional characteristics. Thus, if family interaction studies could demonstrate differences between families of schizophrenics and nonschizophrenics, the question would still be moot as to the locus of cause and effect. At the present time, one assumption is as valid as the other. The assumption that the family interaction patterns are the causal factors in the development of schizophrenia is important for present purposes because it implies several other assumptions concerning methodology. The first is that the interaction patterns in the experimental setting are the usual family patterns and the subjects' usual behavior is not altered by the knowledge that they are being studied by professional experts. This assumption is particularly dubious for those studies in which a hospitalized schizophrenic group is compared to a non-hospitalized control group. The two groups of families undoubtedly have different perceptions of the meaning of the experimenter's request for participation. For the families of schizophrenics, participation is probably perceived as a way of helping their children, while for the families of non-hospitalized controls it may well be seen as a test of their psychological health or normality. Each family's perception of its role in the research program would probably affect its mode of interaction. For example, Cheek (1964a) has found that mothers of normals were significantly more ego-defensive than mothers of schizophrenics. A similar trend was also obtained for fathers (Cheek, 1965). The problem of differential defensiveness can be largely circumvented by utilizing families of other institutionalized and stigmatized groups as controls so that all are recruited on the same basis and are likely to share the meaning of the request for participation. People could still be expected to react to being studied, but the groups would not be differentially affected. The possibility (and probability) that people's behavior will be affected by the knowledge that they are being observed is present in all areas of psychology.

A second assumption, related to the first, is that current interaction patterns are unchanged from their characteristics before the child became a patient. This means that the way family members interact is unaffected by the hospitalization and consequent change in status. It is particularly unlikely that this assumption would be valid for chronic patients. If a person has been hospitalized for a long time or for a large number of times, the family is likely to incorporate his status as a mental patient into its image of him. Likewise, the person could be expected to modify his self-concept to include the attributes of the chronic mental patient. Institutionalization effects can be lessened by using only families of acute patients, for whom hospitalization would more likely be perceived as transitory. An even more desirable group would be families of persons on outpatient or trial visit status.

A third assumption is that current interaction patterns are essentially unchanged from their characteristics at the time the child was becoming schizophrenic. In order for this assumption to be valid, there must have been no essential change over time due to aging of the parents and maturation of the child. The crucial aspect of this position revolves around the word "essential." The extent to which basic personality and interactional characteristics are modifiable beyond the first few years of life is still an issue of considerable dispute.

A fourth assumption is also made that the task around which the interaction is organized does not alter the pattern in some unique way so that it is specific to that task and a circumscribed group of similar tasks. Rather, it is assumed that the families react to the experimental task as they characteristically react to most tasks.

A fifth assumption is that family interaction patterns are the same when some members are absent as they are when all members are present. This assumption appears of dubious validity, but whether different groups of families are affected differentially by missing members is unknown. Siblings of the patients or control subjects could be included in the interactions in order to investigate this possibility.

Consideration of these five assumptions highlights the tentativeness of etiological conclusions that might be drawn from family interaction studies. Nevertheless, the study of family interaction holds promise for providing valuable guidelines for the design and hypothetical formulations of longitudinal studies, from which appropriate cause and effect statements can be made. If the inconclusiveness of the etiological assumption is granted and accepted, then there are no apparent intrinsic methodological inadequacies to the study of family interaction which would disqualify it as a scientific endeavor. The possible limitations of method arising from the etiological assumption can be largely circumvented or minimized by careful attention to specific controls. With this in mind, let us proceed to an examination of family interaction studies, first from a methodological viewpoint and then from the perspective of empirical results from the better designed studies.

DIFFICULTIES OF INTERPRETATION AND EVALUATION

Studies employing the direct recording and systematic coding of actual family interactions have been few in number and recent in origin. This reviewer is aware of only 20 reports subsequent to the year 1950 which fall into this category, with the earliest published in 1958. The paucity of such studies is primarily due to two factors: (1) the recent interest in the study of interpersonal relations, and (2) the difficulty in conducting such studies. In view of the latter factor, it is unfortunate that the results of the labor and effort invested in the majority of studies have been negated by insufficient attention to essential controls. On the basis of considerations arising from the etiological assumption and from data demonstrating the possible confounding effects of certain variables, nine criteria were selected for evaluating the methodological adequacy of studies in this area. This reviewer's judgments of the methodological status of family interaction studies are summarized in Table 1.

It is apparent from the table that there is great variability among the studies, and that much desired information is unavailable from the published reports. It is important that control and experimental groups be comparable on as many demographic variables as possible, but particularly on ages of parents and children, sex and birth order of the children, family size, and social class of the family.

Different rates of interaction and patterns of participation could be expected between parents and offspring, depending on the ages of both. All parents might plausibly be expected to be more indulgent of a small child than of a young or middle-aged adult. Similarly, adult patients and control subjects could be expected to relate somewhat differently to their parents if the latter were middle-aged than if they were close to retirement age.

The importance of keeping the sexes separate in the data analysis has been demonstrated in a number of studies. Cheek (1964b) found that schizophrenic women were more active in family interactions than were normal women, and schizophrenic men were less active than normal men. In addition, women were higher than men in acknowledgements, tension release, giving opinions, and asking for opinions. Ferreira (1963a) reported a difference in frequency of coalitions with each parent in normal families, depending on the sex of the child. Same-sex coalitions were more frequent than opposite-sex coalitions. This same relationship was found in a subsequent study (Ferreira & Winter, 1965) in terms of the initial private agreement between parents and children, and observed to increase with increasing age of the children. Again, this relationship only occurred in normal families. Baxter, Arthur, Flood, and Hedgepeth (1962), found that families of male and female schizophrenics differed in amount of conflict, depending on whether conflict was coded from the extent of initial, private agreement among members or from disagreements arising during family interaction. Also, families of male patients tended to have more mother-father conflict, while mother-patient conflict tended to be greater in the families of female patients. Investigators in most studies using the families of both male and female subjects have not equated their

TABLE 1

METHODOLOGICAL SUMMARY OF FAMILY INTERACTION STUDIES

Author	Demographic comparability of control and schizophrenic groups	Sex of subjects[a]	Hospital status of schizophrenic group	Subdivision of schizophrenic group	Control group	"Blind" coding of data	Reliability of coding	Members in interaction[b]	Task characteristics
Baxter et al. (1962)	No control group	m & f	Acute	Poor premorbid[d]	—	Ns	Good	F,M,C	Joint interview
Baxter & Arthur (1964)	No control group	m	Acute	Poor & good premorbid	—	Ns	Good	F,M	Joint interview
Behrens & Goldfarb (1958)	Questionable	m & f	Ns	—[e]		No	Fair	F(u)	Home interactions
Caputo (1963)	Good	m	Chronic		Maladjusted persons[g]	Ns	Vs	F,M	RDT[j]
Cheek (1964a)	Fair	m & f[b]	Convalescent		Normals[g]	Ns	Vs	F,M,C	RDT
Cheek (1964b)	Fair	m & f[b]	Convalescent		Normals	Ns	Vs	F,M,C	RDT
Cheek (1965a)	Fair	m & f[b]	Convalescent		Normals	Ns	Vs	F,M,C	RDT
Farina (1960)	Fair	m	Acute	Poor & good premorbid		Ns	High	F,M	RDT
Farina & Dunham (1963)	No control group	m	Acute	Poor & good premorbid		Ns	High	F,M,C	RDT
Ferreira (1963a)	Questionable	m & f	Ns		Normals, maladjusted persons	Ns	Ns	F,M,C	RDT
Ferreira & Winter (1965)	Good	m & f	Ns		Normals, delinquents, maladjusted persons	Ns	Ns	F,M,C	RDT
Fisher et al. (1959)	Good	m	Ns		Neurotics,[g] normals,[g] normals	Yes	High	F,M	Family discussion, TAT story construction
Haley (1962)	Fair	m & f	Ns		Normals	Mt	High	F,M,C	Game
Haley (1964)	Questionable	m & f	Ns	—[e]	Normals	Mt	High	F,M,C	RDT, TAT story construction
Lennard et al. (1965)	Fair	m	Ns	—[e]	Normals	Ns	Ns	F,M,C	Family discussion
Lerner (1965)	Good	m	Ns[c]		Normals[g]	Ns	High	F,M	RDT
McCord et al. (1962)	Good	m	Prehospitalization	High & low genetic level[f]	Maladjusted persons	Yes	Good	F,M,C	Home interactions
Meyers & Goldfarb (1961)	Fair	m & f	Ns	—[e]	Normals	No	Ns	F(u)	Home interactions
Morris & Wynne (1965)	Questionable	m & f	Ns	Organic & nonorganic	Neurotics[g]	Yes	Unobtained	F,M[i]	Joint therapy
Stabenau et al. (1965)	Good	m & f	Ns		Delinquents, normals	Ns	Ns	F,M,C,S	RDT

Note.— Ns = not stated, Vs = vaguely stated, Mt = machine tabulated.
a m = male, f = female.
b Analyzed separately.
c Included unspecified psychotics.
d Premorbidity rated according to the Phillips' (1953) scale.
e Schizophrenic and control groups were equated on length of current hospitalization.

f According to Becker's (1956) system of Rorschach analysis.
g Hospitalized.
h F = father, M = mother, C = child, S = sib F(u) = family (unspecified).
i Patient present but not a verbal contributor.
j Modification of the Revealed Difference Technique, after Strodtbeck (1951).

experimental and control groups for the number of each sex, while, at the same time, they have summed their interaction indices across sex. It is impossible to tell how much confounding this procedure may have introduced into the data analysis.

A control related to sex effects, which no study has considered, concerns the possible effects of birth order on interaction behavior. Schooler has used birth order as an independent variable in several studies of schizophrenia. He found that female schizophrenics disproportionately come from the last half of the birth order regardless of social class, while lastborn male schizophrenics disproportionately come from middle-class families and firstborns from lower-class families (Schooler, 1961, 1964). In two other studies, female schizophrenics born in the first half of the birth order were found to be more sociable than those born in the last half (Schooler & Scarr, 1962), and firstborn male schizophrenics were observed to perform better than middleborns who in turn performed better than lastborn patients on a task where their performance was seen as helpful to another person (Schooler & Long, 1963). These findings parallel those of Schachter (1959), obtained with normal women.

Closely allied with birth order is the issue of family size. It seems reasonable to expect that parents might have more contact with each of their children, the fewer of them there are. Also, the number of children in the family might reflect differences in parental attitudes and behavior toward their offspring.

Schooler (1964) and Cheek (1964b) have identified an important qualification which must be applied to all studies using hospitalized persons as subjects. It is most appropriate to generalize only to hospitalized schizophrenics and not to all schizophrenics. Schooler noted that latter-born female schizophrenics manifested more noticeable symptomatology, such as hallucinations and suicidal tendencies, than did their counterparts born in the first half of the birth order. He has suggested that the florid character of their symptoms might lead to latter-borns being hospitalized more readily, therefore being disproportionately represented in hospitals. In a similar vein, Cheek has suggested that overactive females and underactive males manifest interaction patterns deviant from societal norms, which may result in their being hospitalized more readily than those whose activity patterns are congruent with socially normative behavior. If many symptom characteristics turn out to be epiphenomena of a more basic, common schizophrenic process, the search for schizophrenic-specific factors will be somewhat confounded by society's attitudes toward different symptoms.

Social class embodies many attitude, value, knowledge, and social-skill differences between people and, for this reason, is an extremely important variable to keep comparable among groups. Baxter and Arthur (1964) have provided striking evidence of how social class can interact with an independent variable to confound the results of the unwary investigator. These authors found that social class interacted with the premorbid adjustment of their male schizophrenic patients, so that middle-class parents of patients who had made a relatively adequate premorbid adjust-ment showed more conflict in interaction than did middle-class parents of patients who had made an inadequate premorbid adjustment, with the reverse results obtaining for lower-class groups of parents. All differences disappeared when the data were analyzed by social class or premorbidity alone. These results also argue for a subdivision of the schizophrenic sample according to some criterion such as good-poor premorbid adjust-ment or the process-reactive distinction. Both of these subdivisions have been empirically demonstrated to have prognostic validity (Becker, 1959; Phillips, 1953), to reduce the heterogeneity of schizophrenic performance (Garmezy & Rodnick, 1959; Herron, 1962), and to be highly interrelated (Solomon & Zlotowski, 1964). Thus, either subdivision makes an empirically meaningful distinction within schizophrenia and holds promise of indicating a fruitful theoretical distinction as well.

Religion and ethnicity are two interrelated variables which have rarely been controlled. Sanua (1961) has argued that reports of contradictory results in the literature might be reconciled by closer consideration of differences in the subjects' religion and ethnicity. In an exploratory study (Sanua, 1963), he found that parental characteristics differed widely according to the religion and social class of the families. These data are only suggestive, however, since some essential methodological controls were not employed. A well-controlled study in this area has been reported by McClelland, de Charms, and Rindlisbacher (1955). These investigators questioned Protestant, Jewish, Irish-Catholic, and Italian-Catholic parents about their expectations concerning their children's mastery of several independence skills. In addition to main effects for sex of parent, level of parental education, and religion, they found a complex triple interaction of these variables with the expected age of mastery. There also tended to be a difference within religion between the expectations of Irish and Italian parents. The available evidence is sufficiently strong to warrant attention to the religious and ethnic composition of the subject sample. Certainly, it would be hazardous to ignore sizable religious and ethnic differences between experimental and control groups by assuming on an a priori basis that such differences are irrelevant to the style of family interaction.

A minority of studies specify the characteristics of their hospitalized samples in terms of the acuteness-chronicity dimension. In view of one of the assumptions of the method and the unknown effects of institutionali-zation on relatives and patients, it would seem to be a highly relevant variable.

Most studies have utilized some mechanical means of recording data, yet some have relied on an interviewer to record manually the interaction as it occurs, or even after it has occurred. Most reports do not state whether the data were coded in a "blind" fashion or not, that is, with the coder unable to identify the group membership of the families. In many cases, the reliability of the coding procedure is not stated or is so vaguely stated as to be of unknown value.

DIFFICULTIES OF COMPARISON

Aside from differing degrees of methodological adequacy among studies, there are two factors which complicate direct comparison of results. One is the differing group membership comprising the "family." In some cases only parental interaction has been measured, while in other cases, interaction has included the contributions from the parents and the patient or control child; and in one case assessment was made of the interaction among parents, patient or control child, and another child of the family. It is difficult to assess the possible differential effects of group size, role diversity, and other factors which accompany variation in the number of members in interaction.

A second factor is the difference in task characteristics utilized in the studies. The majority have used modifications of the revealed difference technique (RDT) initially developed by Strodtbeck (1951). The RDT essentially consists of having each member of the family privately state his solutions to a number of problem situations. Then the experimenter asks the family to discuss each problem and to arrive at a group solution. The family discussion is recorded and coded for interaction indices such as agreement, yielding, interruption, and compromise. In studies employing the RDT, however, the range of problem situations extends from highly loaded interpersonal situations involving parent-child conflict to rather trivial, neutral situations. The focus of attention on the structure of family interaction has led to a neglect of the content, around which the interaction is organized, as a factor worthy of systematic study itself. It is not readily apparent that family reactions to situations involving parent-child conflict are structurally indistinguishable from reactions to differences among members concerning trivial preferences, such as choice of colors for an automobile or choice of food from a restaurant menu.

Instead of the RDT, other investigators have used joint interviews, family discussions, joint construction of TAT stories, home interactions, game playing, and joint therapy sessions. Haley (1964), using both the RDT and the construction of stories in the TAT, found that each task yielded somewhat different results, though each individually was inferior to the two combined in differentiating families of normals from those of psychiatric subjects. One must conclude that task characteristics do affect results, but that the extent of influence is currently undetermined. * * *

CONCLUSIONS AND RECOMMENDATIONS

Studies obtaining data by clinical observation or by retrospective recall are unsuitable bases for a scientific body of etiological facts, since the data are confounded by intrinsic methodological inadequacies. Interpretation of data acquired from direct recording and systematic coding of family interactions is subject to the cautions and tentativeness necessitated by the etiological assumption. *If the etiological assumption is granted and if the behavior sample is characteristic of the families' usual behavioral repertoire*, there are no apparent, intrinsic methodological inadequacies which disqualify this approach as unscientific. The greatest value of current studies of family interaction seems to lie in the guidelines the findings might provide for longitudinal research. Truly appropriate etiological conclusions can only be drawn from careful longitudinal studies. This reviewer doubts that sufficient knowledge is currently available to warrant the great expenditure involved in longitudinal research at the present time.

Future research on family interaction and schizophrenia would seem to require (1) use of families of recently institutionalized persons only; (2) comparability of control and experimental groups on social class, religion and ethnicity of the family, and sex, birth order, and premorbidity of the patients and control subjects; (3) inclusion of other institutionalized and stigmatized groups as controls, for example, non-schizophrenic psychiatric patients, tubercular patients, and prisoners; (4) investigation of the interaction of parents of schizophrenics with their non-schizophrenic children as a control condition; and (5) objective data recording, "blind" coding, and attainment of high interjudge reliabilities.

Haley (1962) and Handel (1965) have argued that it is premature to attempt to differentiate between the families of normal and pathological subjects or to attempt to differentiate among the families of pathological individuals. In their opinion, before such differentiation is attempted, a typology of families according to dimensions and characteristics peculiar to intimate groups is needed. This reviewer believes that the most fruitful approach would direct attention to the two goals concurrently. Certainly the typology and classification of individuals according to traits and motives, independent of theoretical concerns, has not been very effective in the more traditional realms of psychology. A similar approach to family psychology could not reasonably be expected to have a different history.

Studies of Individual
Family Members

Research studies relevant to family patterns can be roughly ordered on a continuum reflecting the degree to which they deal with the actual face-to-face interactions among family members. At one end of this continuum are the studies which concentrate entirely on the psychological structure of an individual, who irrelevantly happens also to be a member of the family. (Studies of this type are not represented in this collection.) Further along this continuum are studies of an individual from whose responses an attempt is made to understand the family from which he comes. This may be quite indirect, as when we assume that a passive man must have had at least one domineering parent, or somewhat more direct, as when we ask the subject to describe his own phenomenological picture of his parents. Our knowledge of the individual may be correlated with certain knowledge we have of the family, such as his parents' having been divorced, but the subject himself is not seen in an actual interaction with his parents; rather, they are described in their absence.

Perhaps the third point along the continuum is represented by those studies which obtain responses from several family members as individuals and from which the investigator tries to form an integrated picture of typical interactions. For example, the parents and the child might all fill out an attitude questionnaire, and from their three separate scores a meaningful family diagnosis is attempted. Further along, at point four, these three scores might be summed in some manner to obtain an average score representing the family. However, it is only when the family members are actually brought into a face-to-face situation and asked conjointly to cope with some situation that interaction research can begin—at point five. The behaviors evidenced may be scored for each individual member, which is the somewhat inappropriate application of individual methods to a transactional situation, or the individual scores may be combined to form a family score, or the behavior of the family group itself may be the primary source of data, which is what we would term true interaction research. These data can, of course, be simple counts of button pushes, or represent quite complex interactions of who did what to whom and for what reason, related to the history of the family and the roles and self-concepts of its members.

Our intention is not to deny the importance of the tremendous amount of information that has been gathered on the psychology of the individual. Obviously, it is of utmost value to understand how individuals think, feel, behave, and perceive the world. Our reservation is simply that inferences drawn from how a person behaves or from how he describes his family may have little or nothing to do with the reality of how his family functions. Practitioners of family therapy are well aware of the drastic changes in behavior and perception of family power patterns which can occur in patients as a result of the insights associated with therapy. We only ask that the family unit itself become the locus of investigation when we are trying to understand the family pattern, and, where relevant, even when we are attempting to understand any individual member of the family. Just as we cannot attain full insight into some people unless we have seen them drunk or in a position of authority, so we cannot understand some others until we see them with their families.

Most psychological research has consisted of studies of individuals from which inferences about families have sometimes been drawn, and only a few samples of these are presented in this section. The paper of Howells and Lickorish is representative of the second point of the continuum mentioned above, in which inferences concerning a child's family are made from the child's phenomenological picture of that family, as presented on a projective test. Frances Cheek takes the same general approach, using a perception-of-parent-behavior questionnaire filled out by the child. Her paper is unique in that she tests a detailed theory of socialization developed by an academic theoretician, Talcott Parsons.

Singer and Wynne ably represent the third point on our suggested continuum in that projective test responses are obtained from patients and their families individually, and the investigator integrates these into a pattern from which predictions are made as to which patient belongs to which family. Mutter and Schleifer show how changes in the psychosocial setting of the child and his family are involved even in the development of physical illness in the child. Here, data obtained from individual interviews and observations of parents and child were integrated by the clinician and correlated with the child's diagnosis. Becker and McArdle report that normal family members resemble each other in the average action length of their private free speech more than do clinic families. Interestingly, Winter and Ferreira (in press) found directly opposite results when they analyzed talking time for interactional speech in which the family members were talking to each other. The article by Baxter and Arthur represents a bridge with the next section, in that the premorbid ratings of schizophrenics and the social class of their parents were used as variables which were related to the conflict shown by the parents in a conjoint interview. Thus, the interactional behavior of two family members was correlated with a characteristic of the third, which would qualify this as a family interactional study, depending on how many people we would insist be included in our operational definition of a family.

The articles in this section are also valuable in giving us insight into the complex interrelations among the personality characteristics of family members, the structure of the family, and the social milieu in which the family operates.

The Family Relations Indicator

A Projective Technique for Investigating
Intra-Family Relationships Designed for
Use with Emotionally Disturbed Children*

John G. Howells and John R. Lickorish

It is generally agreed that a child's behavior is largely determined by his relationships with his family and, in particular, by his relationships with his parents. Hence, an assessment of the child's neurotic or delinquent behavior should include a thorough investigation of his family relationships. For young children, a picture-projective method of investigation may be used, since interviews and techniques requiring written answers are usually impracticable.

* * * The Family Relations Indicator was evolved to assess the child's general relationship with his family and, in particular, to explore the parent-child relationships. [A more complete exposition of the FRI has been given by Howells & Lickorish in their recent book, *The Family Relations Indicator* (1968). *Eds*.] The technique is based upon gaining "associative" responses to a series of twenty pictures portraying family scenes. The responses to the cards are not "interpreted," and it is not necessary for the child to make up a "story," which so many children find difficulty in doing. Short responses of only a sentence or two may be quite adequate. The replication of the pictures provides a rough internal check on the consistency of the child's replies, as well as providing the cumulative effect of a little information from each of three pictures. Several of the above features, so far as we know, either are found exclusively in our technique, or appear in a combination not found in other tests.

PLAN OF INVESTIGATION

Aim. The aim of the investigation was to determine whether the technique we had devised would give a reasonably accurate account of the child's relationships with his family. In particular, we wished to discover if

---

*Abridged from the *British Journal of Educational Psychology*, 1963, *33*, 286–296, with permission of the authors and the publisher.

it would give an accurate picture of the relationships between parents and child. The "association" method of responding to the pictures was adopted, since this allowed the child the widest range of verbal expression, while the pictures "channeled" his replies along the lines of family relationships.

Theory. It was assumed that if a friendly relationship were established between the child and the examiner, then the child would describe the figures in the pictures in terms of his own personal experience. It was considered possible that "wishful thinking" and fantasy might distort the descriptions of his relationships. In an attempt to minimize this distortion, we decided to encourage the child to make statements about the characters, instead of trying to compose a story. In this way we hoped that the responses would be factual and in accordance with the child's real frame of reference. We further assumed that the child's responses would reflect the actual home situation, since if a high degree of rapport were obtained with the child, he would have little hesitation in revealing what he felt about his family.

Preliminary Investigation. A considerable number of pictures was tried out in the preliminary investigation; many of them were taken from books and magazines, but some were drawn especially for the purpose. After a considerable amount of experiment, it was decided that *all* the pictures must be specially presented. This initial investigation continued for about three years. We were eventually able to secure the services of a professional artist, who drew the final set of pictures to our specifications. These were:

1. The pictures were to be black and white pencil drawings.
2. There was to be as little emotional expression as possible portrayed in posture, gesture, or face.
3. Clothes were not to be obviously indicative of any particular socio-economic class.
4. An age range of 8 to 11 years was suggested for the children, with an appropriate age for the parental figures.
5. Interior scenes were to have a minimum of detail, but sufficient to suggest definite rooms.
6. Furnishings were to be as socially ambiguous as possible.
7. All scenes must be reasonably familiar to children of school age.
8. Scenes should be as little "structured" as possible, and dramatic postures should be avoided.
9. The pictures were to be drawn clearly, with fairly sharp outlines; heavy shading and blurring of outlines was to be avoided.
10. Ambiguity was to be introduced by the arrangement of the figures in the pictures, not by shading or by blurring their outlines.

The drawings were photographed and mounted on twelve-sheet board for use during the experimental investigation. A specimen card is shown in Figure 1.

Material. The final set of pictures was made up as follows. Three

Fig. 1. Sample stimulus picture from the Family Relations Indicator. (Redrawn and slightly altered for this volume.)

introductory cards showing family groups were used to acquaint the child with the test procedure, while the main series shows the following basic family situations: parents; father and child; mother and child; child alone; a sibling group; and a child and a baby. Each of these six situations is replicated three times, with the figures and the environment being sufficiently altered for the child to accept the replications as three different pictures. There is a separate series of cards for boys and girls, the only difference between them being the sex of the child in the pictures. The other figures and the environment are precisely the same in both cases. The three introductory cards are presented on each occasion, together with seventeen other cards making a total of twenty for each complete test.

Sample. The subjects used in this investigation were children referred to the clinic in the ordinary way, and we took fifty consecutive cases, having omitted those in which there was some unusual family constellation, or in which little was subsequently discovered about the family. The ages of the subjects ranged from 4 to 17 years, and there were 30 boys and 20 girls. Only 30 of the 50 children were tested for intelligence, and these had a range of IQ's from 65 to 136. All the children and their families had been attending the clinic for at least six months, and some of them for as long as two and a half years.

Administration of Test. The prime requirement for the test is the establishment of the maximum rapport between the child and the examiner. This was facilitated when the test was presented on the child's second or third visit to the clinic. Since this investigation had to be carried out as part of the normal clinical routine, it was sometimes necessary to present the test during the child's first attendance. In these circumstances, extra care was taken to ensure the establishment of good rapport. The cards were introduced to the child informally by saying, "I have some pictures here of boys and girls and adults [or 'grown-ups' if the child is very young]. I would like you to have a look at them and see if you can tell me what you think they might be doing, or saying."

The introductory cards were then presented. Very often the child would say little or nothing about them, and sometimes this reticence would extend to the initial pictures of the test series. The child was simply encouraged with praise and prompted by means of straightforward questions: "What do you think they are doing?" "Where do you think they are going?" or, "What do you think they are talking about?" No attempt was made to cross-question the child or to present a formal series of questions about each picture. Anything the child said was accepted, even if it were only an enumeration of the objects in the picture. When this occurred, he was praised for what he had done, and then it was suggested to him that he might try to think what the people were doing.

The child's replies were recorded verbatim, sometimes in shorthand and occasionally on a tape. Afterwards they were typed in double-spacing to facilitate scoring.

METHOD OF SCORING AND TABULATING THE RESPONSES

The method of scoring was not mechanical, but depended upon using psychological judgment to select from the responses those words and phrases which indicated the child's relationships with, or his attitudes toward, the members of his family. In making a formal investigation of our results, we scored the responses in the following manner: They were first divided into "information units" by means of the solidus (/). These units were sentences, clauses, phrases, or even single words. Those which described the personal relationships and attitudes of the patient were underlined and called "behavioral units." Those information units which disclosed neither relationship nor attitude were simply ignored. The behavioral units were then recorded on the Behavior Item Sheet, which was compiled as follows. From the 50 sets of responses obtained during the investigation, we selected 20 at random and analyzed them. A list was made of all the expressions which were used to describe attitudes and behavior. Some of these were found to be equivalent to one another, and the redundant expressions were rejected. Forty-nine items were finally selected and grouped together as shown in the accompanying list.

Six columns were placed parallel to these items and headed *F* (Father), *M* (Mother), *B* (Boy), *G* (Girl), *Bb* (Baby), and *Spare*.

The behavioral units were recorded by entering on the Behavior Item Sheet the letter *F, M,* etc., opposite the relevant item and in the appropriate column. The letter denoted the *object towards* whom the behavior was directed. The name at the head of the column in which the letter was placed denoted the person who produced that behavior. If the behavior

BEHAVIOR ITEM LIST

ATTITUDES	VERBALIZATIONS	ACTIONS
1. Likes	15. Praises	25. Initiative
2. Dislikes	16. Refuses	26. Plays
3. Reluctant	17. Forbids	27. Shows interest
4. Tolerates	18. Rebukes	28. Helps
5. Ignores	19. Requests	29. Obeys
6. Apprehensive	20. Demands	30. Gifts
7. Jealous	21. Defiant	31. Hits
8. Suspicious	22. Treatens	32. Fights
9. Sulky	23. Blames/Accuses	33. Mischief
10. Sad	24. Argues	34. Injures/Accident
11. Angry		
12. Cross		
13. Irritable		
14. Apathetic		
DEPRIVATIONS	DELINQUENCY	GUILT FEELINGS
35. Left Behind	42. Runs away	46. Done wrong
36. Kept in	43. Steals	47. Secretive
37. To bed	44. Deceitful	48. Apologizes
38. No toys	45. Destructive	49. Amends
39. No food		
40. No money		
41. No playmates		

was repeated a "+" was added. The column headed *Spare* was used to record the behavior of anyone extraneous to the family group.

If a feeling, attitude, or action was expressed without any indication of an object, then the number of the response only was entered on the Behavior Item Sheet. When all the behavioral units had been entered in this way, it was possible, by inspection, to determine the kind of relationships which existed between the various members of the family. In everyday clinical work, this elaborate method of scoring is not necessary. After a little practice the psychologist may dispense with the Behavior Item Sheet and simply make a brief summary of the relevant items in the responses. Thus the following specimen responses may be summarized as follows:

(a) Father is verbally hostile to the boy. *F*.1.2.3.
(b) Father punishes boy by deprivation *F*.2.3. and by hitting *F*.2.

F.1.   He is setting up the table with Dad/ and going to get something./ Father comes in,/ and father asks what he was doing/ and he said nothing./ *Father said, "You were taking something off the table"/* and father said, *"Go upstairs to-day/* and *you will have no tea."/*

F.2. The little boy is standing near the fire/ and father says, "What have you been doing to-day?/ *Why are you standing near the fire?/ Did you play with it?"/* "I didn't play with it."/ *"Yes, you were; you were poking it."/ His father smacked him/* and said, "Go up to bed/ and come down when I tell you."/

F.3. The little boy has a rocket/ and father is reading his paper/ and the little boy made a pile of books/ and put his rocket on/ *and he is telling his father what he has done./* "I have put my rocket up/ and it is ready to fly."/ Father said, *"Put it outside;/ don't do it in here."/* The boy took it outside/ and fired it/ and it was lost in the woods/ *and another boy found it and took it to him./*

In order to evaluate the accuracy of our results, it was necessary to code the information on the Behavior Item Sheets so that it could be handled statistically. It is notoriously difficult to code data which consist of interpersonal relationships and attitudes. Many scales have been devised, but none seemed suited to the data in this investigation. The scaling method used by Baldwin, Kalhorn, and Breese (1949) was too refined for the data, and the numerical coding devised by Bene (1957) was too complex. It was finally decided to employ a simple "present-absent" method of coding using five types of relationship which were defined as follows: (1) *Punitive action*, including any form of physical violence or corporal punishment. (2) *Verbal hostility*, including scoldings, rebukes, "telling off," and harsh criticisms. (3) *Deprivation*, consisting of the denial or withholding of food, pocket money, pleasures, or companionship; or being sent to bed. (4) *Indifference*. This category was used when there was an indication of a cold, non-punitive, affectionless attitude between parent and child. (5) *Positive Attitude*, indicating the presence of a helpful relationship. Because we were investigating the relationships in *disturbed* families, most of the information was entered under the "negative" categories. If a sample of the normal population were being investigated, then more "positive" categories would, no doubt, be required.

EVALUATION OF THE F R I RESPONSES

The information which had been recorded on the Behavior Item Sheet was summarized, using the five categories of relationships just defined. Each of these relationships was recorded as existing or not existing between mother and child, and between father and child. A similar assessment was made by the psychiatrist from his own knowledge of each family. The accuracy of the FRI responses was then evaluated by noting the frequency with which the statements given by the FRI were substantiated by the psychiatric assessment.

This is the usual method of evaluating the results of this type of investigation, as Foulds (1955) points out. The method has been severely criticized by Eysenck (1961); and Kreitman, Sainsbury, Morrissey,

Towers, and Scrivener (1961) have shown that psychiatric assessments are not always very reliable. But we had no option but to use this method, since all the cases had been investigated by one psychiatrist only and therefore a corroborative assessment was not available. The accuracy of the psychiatric assessment was probably increased by the following factors: (1) The families had been thoroughly investigated over a considerable period, and the assessments were not made on the basis of simply one or two psychiatric interviews. (2) The information gained by the psychiatrist during his own interviews was supplemented by the following sources: social workers' reports, based on interviews with the parents and visits to the home and school; results of play diagnosis; school reports; reports from the family doctor; and in some cases information gained in interviews with the probation officer, the children's officer, or the welfare worker.

There is, however, one weakness in the psychiatric assessment which we could not avoid, since it was impossible to separate our investigation from our normal clinical practice. The children replied to the FRI as part of the clinical investigation, and the summary of their replies was in the psychiatrist's possession when he made his assessment of the families for the comparative study. It may, therefore, be argued that these results would contaminate the psychiatrist's asssessment of traits and relationships. In reply to this we may say: (1) The FRI results had been in his possession for at least six months, so that he would be unlikely to remember them individually. (2) In making his assessment, he would not, of course, refer to the psychological report. (3) The other sources of information would be sufficiently weighty to contradict, if necessary, the results of the FRI.

The agreements and disagreements between the FRI and the psychiatric assessment are shown in Table 1.

By using Table 1 we can estimate the extent to which the FRI responses provide accurate information about family relationships. It is clear that the FRI does not provide *all* the available information about parent-child relationships in the specified categories, nor should we expect it to do so. It is unlikely that the result of an investigation lasting half an hour (the time usually required to administer the FRI) would provide as much information as an investigation extending over several months or even years. The difference between the amount of correct information provided by the FRI and the total information available is indicated by Column V. These results might be criticized on the grounds that this difference is large and that the *over-all* agreements are little better than chance. But such a criticism would not invalidate the fact that the information which the FRI has actually provided is fairly accurate as shown in Column V of Table 1. So far as we can discover, no one has attempted to show that a picture-projection method will produce *all* the theoretically available information about either individuals or groups.

Some authors like Jackson (1950) and Walton (1959) have used the method to discriminate between nosological groups of children. Others have used this technique to provide a description of the subject's person-

TABLE 1

THE FREQUENCIES WITH WHICH THE VARIOUS RELATIONSHIPS WERE SCORED
'PRESENT' AND 'ABSENT' BY THE F R I AND THE PSYCHIATRIC ASSESSMENT
AND THE AGREEMENTS BETWEEN THEM

RELATIONSHIP	FATHER-CHILD RELATIONSHIPS				
	I^a	II^b	III^c	IV^d	V^e
Punitive Action	13	17	13	7	65%
Verbally hostile	28	6	8	8	78
Deprivation	14	11	20	5	74
Indifference	21	11	14	4	84
Positive Attitude	5	24	9	12	30
Totals	81	69	64	36	70%

RELATIONSHIP	MOTHER-CHILD RELATIONSHIPS				
	I	II	III	IV	V
Punitive Action	19	18	7	6	76%
Verbally hostile	39	2	6	3	93
Deprivation	23	5	20	2	92
Indifference	1	22	25	2	33
Positive Attitude	9	19	17	5	64
Totals	91	66	75	18	83%

[a]Column I—No. of cases in which the FRI and the psychiatric assessment *agree* that the
relationship is *present*.

[b]Column II—Agreement on the *absence* of the relationship.

[c]Column III—Relationship scored 'present' by the psychiatric assessment *only*.

[d]Column IV—Relationship scored 'present' by the FRI *only*.

[e]Column V—Ratio between Column I and Columns I + IV.

ality or attitudes, for example, Rosenzweig (1948), Phillipson (1955), and
Hartwell, Hutt, Andrew, and Walton (1953).

We have attempted to show that the information produced by the FRI
describes the relationships which actually exist within the family. Since
these relationships may be independently assessed with reasonable
accuracy, this assessment forms an "objective" standard (English, 1958)
against which the accuracy of the FRI results may be measured. In order
to do this we have compared the *total amount of information produced
by the FRI* with *the extent to which this information was verified by the
psychiatric assessment*. The accuracy of the FRI is represented by the
percentage ratios given in Column V of Table 1.

In addition to parent-child relationships, a considerable amount of
information concerning the child's *own* attitudes and feelings was given in
the FRI responses. The nature and accuracy of this information is shown
in Table 2.

Other information of clinical value was sometimes given but not with
sufficient regularity to make a further evaluation worthwhile. Occasionally, references to marital, sibling, or school problems provided valuable
"clinical leads" to be investigated during subsequent interviews.

TABLE 2

THE EXTENT TO WHICH THE FINDINGS OF THE F R I WERE
SUPPORTED BY THE PSYCHIATRIC ASSESSMENT WITH
RESPECT TO THE SPECIFIED TRAITS SHOWN BY THE CHILD

TRAIT	I[a]	II[b]	III[c]
Verbally aggressive	17	13	76%
Physically aggressive	27	25	92
Antisocial	24	17	71
Guilt feelings	18	11	61
Apprehensive	7	6	86
Jealous	7	4	57

[a]Column I—Frequency with which a given trait was present according to the FRI.
[b]Column II—Frequency with which the FRI result was supported by the psychiatric assessment.
[c]Column III—Percentage agreement between Columns I and II.

No attempt was made to assess the reliability of the FRI. This is a notoriously difficult undertaking with projective techniques, since comparable sets of duplicate pictures are almost impossible to produce, and any appreciable time interval between test and re-test might vitiate the reliability coefficient, since appreciable changes in the child's attitudes or relationships may have occurred during that interval. The "split-half" technique might be employed in a similar manner to that adopted by Anthony and Bene (1957). But we have already incorporated a modification of this principle in our method of scoring, since a relationship was not recorded as "present" unless it was clearly mentioned in at least two separate responses.

DISCUSSION AND CONCLUSION

The Family Relations Indicator provides information about three sectors of family life. These are: the relationships between the child and father, relationships between the child and mother, and certain personal characteristics of the child himself. The types of relationships and traits which have been evaluated were not deduced from a priori principles but were empirically derived from the results of a preliminary investigation. When the full-scale investigation was carried out, no other major relationships or traits appeared frequently enough in the responses to warrant their addition to our original list. The preponderance of "negative" relationships and traits in our results is due to the fact that the investigation was concerned only with emotionally disturbed children who had been referred as patients to the department. Naturally, not all these patients were equally disturbed, nor did they all show the same kind or number of disturbed relationships.

It is possible that some relationships did not appear in the responses because they were too painful to describe. This would agree with the theory of the repression of painful experiences, but we were not able to investigate this point.

An inspection of Table 1 shows that the "positive" relationship between father and child occurs in seventeen cases according to the FRI, but only five of these are supported by the psychiatric assessment. It is possible that this discrepancy may be due to wish-fulfillment on the part of the child, who would *like* father to show him more interest and attention but, in fact, father does not do so. The existence of a gross discrepancy between the two findings on this relationship and a fairly high agreement between them on all the other relationships tends to support this view, but there is no independent confirmation of it.

The percentage agreement for the mother-child relationships is appreciably greater than that for the father-child relationships. This may be due to the fact that most psychiatric investigations tend to be mother-child centered, with a relative neglect of father's relationship to the child. Again, there is no independent confirmation of this view.

Fantasy, which is often associated with children's projection responses, very seldom appeared in the replies we obtained. Fantasy, in the sense of an "imaginative construction" as opposed to wishful thinking, is easily detected when present because the activity described is clearly impossible. Thus, a boy of 5 years 10 months replies to card $M.2$, "He is going to tickle Dad and then tear that book. Tear that book up and kick Dad in the tummy and get a spear and kill him."

The traits listed in Table 2 were deduced directly from the replies, except that "guilt feelings" were inferred from the secretive or self-punitive actions of the child.

We have found in subsequent clinical work that it is not wise to try to extract too much information from the responses. They usually show the parent-child relationships quite clearly and frequently disclose the attitude of the child toward other members of the family. In addition, the responses often provide useful information in the form of "clinical leads," which, although not scorable in the manner we have described, might well be included in the psychologist's report interpreting the results. Thus, the tone of voice used in a reply or a dramatic gesture may be very illuminating clinically but impossible to score adequately.

We have encountered several difficulties in interpreting the responses given by the children when their family relationships were complicated by removal into foster care; the death of a parent; the presence in the home of an aunt, grandparent(s), or other relations; or the presence of a much older brother or sister who could conceivably act as a parent figure. These complicated situations were excluded from the reported results, as there was no means of telling from the responses whether the child was speaking of his actual parent—even if the parent had died—or whether he was speaking of a parent-substitute in the form of aunt, elder sibling, or grandparent.

We endeavor to make the maximum rapport with the child and never exert pressure to obtain information. It is possible that we might sometimes gain more information by systematic questioning, but we feel that information can be obtained at too high a price and that it is unwise to press the child for information that he will not freely supply, since such pressure would lead to a loss of rapport between the child and the examiner.

It seems clear to us that a projective technique used with young children will sometimes provide information which could not be otherwise obtained. It provides an assessment of personal and family relationships which could be utilized for diagnostic or therapeutic purposes. The projection technique is valuable also because it often yields information quickly and provides valuable clinical leads at the first or second interview. The technique we have described fulfills these functions over a limited area but does not pretend to give extensive personality pictures or an *exhaustive* account of interpersonal relationships.

Family Socialization Techniques and Deviant Behavior*

Frances E. Cheek

The significance of parent-child relationships for the later development of a way of life deviant from that normally expected by society has been hypothesized for many years.

* * * While many have tried to grapple with this problem, from Freud through the transactionists, it is questionable whether a systematic, experimentally testable theoretical framework capable of investigating the genesis, maintenance, or diminution of deviant behavior within the family has yet been produced.

The present paper describes the results of an exploratory testing of one such theoretical framework, that of Talcott Parsons (Parsons & Bales, 1951; Parsons, 1955), in terms of three types of deviants—alcoholics, reformatory inmates, and schizophrenics. However, the study and its findings are presented not so much as a confirmation of Parsons' theories, though they do indeed support his hypotheses, but rather to suggest a line of investigation which with further and more intensive work may prove useful in our understanding of the familial context of deviant behavior.

Let us first consider Parsons' theoretical scheme. With regard to deviant outcome, Parsons feels that there is no basic distinction between the mechanisms of normal development and pathogenic mechanisms, but that the difference relates to the balancing of system inputs and outputs in the process. While it would be impossible to present here a complete account of his theoretical scheme for the process of socialization, we will attempt to present enough to clarify his notions of deviant outcome as a function of aberrant socialization (McCord & McCord, 1956).

Parsons follows Freud in differentiating three main phases in the development of the child. Briefly, he characterizes these stages as follows: In the oral phase, in the first year or two of life, the primary focus is on the relation of the child to the mother, and the basic problem is getting the organic need system under control in the sense of integration of a system and not suppression of its parts. Integration of control is derived

---

*Abridged from *Family Process*, 1966, 5, 199–217, with permission of the author and *Family Process*.

through expressive communication, and balance between the supportive and denial phases is necessary in order to ensure appropriate internalization. In the second main stage, the fusion of the original internalized mother-child identity results in a two-unit personality system of what Parsons calls dependency and autonomy need dispositions. This is the phase in which the anal crisis occurs and the critical aspect is that of support of both the dependency and autonomy needs. The third stage is the oedipal crisis in which the relation to the father is of direct importance, and the critical problem is that of the informational input and its relation to the reactions of frustration. In order for adequate sex role differentiation to occur, adequate cues must be provided by the parents for the discrimination of the male or female role.

Parsons suggests how the familiar pathological syndromes such as compulsion, psychopathy, manic-depressive illness, paranoia, and schizophrenia can be seen as etiologically related to imbalance of system inputs and outputs at the various stages.

The *compulsive* personality is characterized by too rigorous control, too tight an integration, and he suggests that this relates to difficulties in the oral phase, namely, too severe frustration; and even more significantly, too much contrast between support and denial at the phase of internalization, though relatively strong support must be assumed in order to account for strong internalization. He feels that this points to the relatively strict and severe but basically loving mother.

Psychopathy, which he also suggests finds its origin in difficulties in this phase, is characterized by too loose control. Parsons feels that this should be associated with relatively little initial deprivation but still more with too little contrast between support and denial, which would point to a *laissez-faire* and indulgent mother.

He suggests the *manic* and the *depressive* derive from the second main stage. He feels that the manic is likely to have been over-supported at this stage and also underfrustrated. This is the overdependent child with a weak autonomy motive who is compulsively in need of gratification, which, he says, points to the "overprotective" mother. He feels that the depressive, on the other hand, must have suffered from undersupport at this stage, combined with overfrustration. This would lead to rapid development of the autonomy need, but the child is insecure because it does not meet adequate reciprocation from the mother. This type of child wants to love but is afraid of rejection, and becomes compulsively independent, which points to the "underprotective" mother.

The *paranoid-schizoid* pair, he feels, are related to the oedipal crisis, the *paranoid* type having been thus far excessively frustrated by the withdrawal of too large a proportion of earlier rewards and the holding up of a father object too drastically different from the mother to which he has been attached. Then her support is not sufficient to build a bridge to the adequate positive cathexis of the new father object. He feels that this suggests too wide a gap between the roles of the two parents.

He suggests that the *schizoid*, on the other hand, has had too little information, and that frustration results from an insufficient differentiation of the roles of the parents, so there are not adequate cues for critical discrimination.

In the present paper, we shall report some findings concerning the parent-child relationships of three types of deviants—alcoholics, reformatory subjects, and schizophrenics—and also a comparison group of "normal" (nonpsychotic) subjects. The findings were obtained with a questionnaire used originally in a study of family interaction patterns of schizophrenic and normal young adults (Cheek, 1962). In that study the questionnaire was used as a means of setting up in a standardized fashion discussion sessions between family members which were later coded with a variation of the Bales Interaction Process Analysis categories (Bales, 1950). However, it was also decided to use the questionnaire as a means of contrasting the verbal reports of the family members about their interaction with their observed behaviors together.

The questionnaire included twenty problem situations of the sort which might come up in a family where a young adult lived with his parents. Ten of the problems concerned the behaviors of the young adult toward the parents (five toward the mother, five toward the father), and three alternative solutions to each problem were offered which were based upon Parsons' types of deviant behavior (Parsons & Bales, 1951). Thus, the behaviors of the young adult might be characterized as "active rebellion," "passive rebellion," or "conformity." The other ten problems concerned the behaviors of the parents (five of the mother, five of the father) toward the young adult. The solutions were based on Parsons' mechanisms of social control (Parsons & Bales, 1951). The behaviors of the parents towards the young adult might be characterized by "support-permissiveness," "role enforcement," or "withdrawal, ignoring."

After its initial use with the families of schizophrenics and normals, the questionnaire was used to set up discussion sessions with groups of alcoholics and reformatory subjects in studies of the effects of drugs upon interaction (Cheek, 1963). It was noted that the responses of the various groups to the questionnaire seemed to follow distinct and characteristic patterns, and it was decided to attempt to collect sufficient numbers of subjects in the alcoholic and reformatory groups to make possible a comparison with the schizophrenic and normal subjects studied earlier.

Additionally, it was decided to look at the questionnaire responses of the four groups in terms of Parsons' conceptualization of the relation of the type of deviant outcome to family socialization techniques. If the alcoholics, for instance, could be regarded as suffering from a compulsion to drink, they might fit into his category of compulsives, who should, according to his theory, have strict but loving mothers. In terms of the questionnaire categories, the mothers of alcoholics should then be high on role enforcement but also on support-permissiveness.

The reformatory boys, who might fit into the psychopathic category, should, according to Parsons, have mothers who were *laissez-faire* and indulgent. In terms of our questionnaire categories, the mothers would be seen as high on support-permissiveness, low on role enforcement.

The schizophrenics would, of course, fit Parsons' schizoid category, and the theory would suggest that they might have parents who showed little role differentiation. In the American family, the father typically takes the instrumental, the mother the expressive role. We might expect then more instrumental behavior on the part of the mothers, more expressive behavior on the part of the father. Thus there might be more role enforcement response in relation to the behavior of mothers, more support-permissive response to describe the behaviors of fathers.

With regard to the three types of deviancy examined in the questionnaire, one might expect the alcoholics to be high on expectations of conformity in view of the internalized strict behavior of the mother, though perhaps also high on perceptions of active or passive rebellion. Parsons has suggested that the criminal deviant, in this case the reformatory inmates, should be actively rebellious, and hence in our terms would be high on expectations and perceptions of active rebellion, while the schizophrenics, whom he sees as withdrawing and passively rebellious, would be high on expectations and perceptions of passive rebellion (Parsons & Bales, 1951).

Of course, the deviants studied did not fit Parsons' categories perfectly, nor did we manage to include the manic, depressive, and paranoid groups, which he also placed within his theoretical scheme. Nevertheless, it seemed of value to examine what was available.

Let us now review in greater detail the research procedure, including the nature of the questionnaire, the circumstances in which it was administered to each of the four groups, the characteristics of the groups to whom it was administered, and how the data were processed and analyzed.

METHOD OF PROCEDURE

The Questionnaire. As we have said earlier, the questionnaire was designed to provide a standardized procedure with which to introduce and structure family discussion sessions in the study of family interaction of schizophrenics, and also to compare verbal report of the family members about their interaction with their observed interaction.

It consisted of 20 problem situations of the sort which might arise when a young adult lived with his parents. Ten of the problem situations concerned the behaviors of the parents toward the child (five of mother to child, five of father to child), and the three alternative solutions offered were based on Parsons' mechanisms of social control.

In his discussion of the mechanisms of social control of the deviant, Parsons describes four phases—support, permissiveness, denial of reciprocity, and manipulation of rewards. In response to our need for a threefold classification, we combined the first two to form a support-permissive category and the second two to form a role enforcement category. A third category, withdrawal from the socialization process, was added.

Thus, *Problem Situation Seven* deals with the behavior of the parent toward the child, in this case the father.

"The son has been looking for work off and on but does not seem to be very anxious about getting a job right now. However, the father is very anxious for the boy to begin work because he feels it will benefit the boy and also because the money is needed at home."

Solution One, "Let the boy take his own time about getting a job and sympathize with his feeling of unreadiness," is *support-permissiveness*. Solution Two, "Refuse to allow the boy to drift along in this way and urge him continually to play a more responsible role in the family," is *role enforcement*. Solution Three, "Just not bother himself about the boy's not working and not keep trying to get him to cooperate," is *withdrawal, ignoring*.

Ten of the problem situations concerned the behaviors of the young adult towards the parents (five toward the mother, five toward the father), and three alternative solutions to each problem were offered, which were based upon Parsons' types of deviant behavior.

Parsons describes four major directions of deviant motivation, which he derives by subdividing his basic compulsive, conformative, and alienative types according to whether the orientation is active or passive. Thus, he classifies deviancy into conformative active, conformative passive, alienative active and alienative passive. In the forced choice situation required for the study, three alternatives were necessary in order to structure the pattern of family disagreements for the family discussions, and therefore three dimensions—active rebellion, passive rebellion, and conformity—were used.

For instance, *Problem Situation One* deals with the behavior of the child toward the parent, in this case the mother.

"The son feels that his mother is always picking on him. His mother criticizes the way he dresses, the fact that he does not make his bed or keep his room tidy, and so on."

Solution One, "Argue with his mother and try to convince her that she is unfair in picking on him so much," is *active rebellion*. Solution Two, "Give in to his mother's demands and make an effort to be neater," is *conformity*. Solution Three, "Just ignore his mother's criticism and picking, and leave the room when she starts it up," is *passive rebellion*.

In order to study how well the various solutions offered fitted into six different categories, ten raters were given all the solutions and asked to fit them into six categories. This was done with 97 percent accuracy.

The questionnaire respondent was asked to check for each problem situation which solution he felt best described what *ought* to happen (normative expectation) and which solution he felt was most like what *actually* would take place in his own family situation (actual perception) when and if such a problem arose.

Thus, in Problem One the boy might check Solution Two, "Give in to his mother's demands and make an effort to be neater," as his normative expectation (what he ought to do) and Solution Three, "Just ignore his mother's criticism and picking and leave the room when she starts it up," as his actual perception (what he probably would do).

The Subjects. In the present study we are examining the questionnaire responses of 120 male adults, 30 each from four different groups—schizophrenics, normals, alcoholics, and reformatory inmates.

The 30 *schizophrenics* were given the questionnaire in the earlier study of family interaction with schizophrenics. All diagnosed schizophrenics (without organic complications), both male and female, aged 15–26, living with their natural parents (all three being literate and English-speaking), released from any one of New Jersey's state, county, or private mental hospitals during a certain time period, were invited by letter to take part in the study. About 30 percent of those suitable took part. The questionnaires were filled in by the schizophrenics (and their fathers and mothers) covertly in an interview held at the hospital at which the patient had been hospitalized. Sixty-seven schizophrenics, 40 male and 27 female, took part in the study. However, 30 of the males most like the schizophrenic group in terms of socioeconomic characteristics were selected from the larger group for the present comparison of questionnaire responses.

The 30 *normal* subjects were part of the comparison group in the family inter-action study. These were young adult males, none of whom had ever been diagnosed or treated for a mental disorder, aged 15–26, living with their natural parents, all three being literate and English-speaking. They were located in YMCA, 4-H, college, industrial, and other settings, and an attempt was made to have this group comparable to the schizophrenic group in terms of age, sex, ethnicity, religion, and social class. The normal young adults (and their fathers and mothers), like the schizophrenics, filled in the questionnaire covertly in an interview held in some neutral setting such as a school. Thirty of the 31 subjects used in the interaction study were randomly selected for the present analysis.

The 30 *alcoholics* were all patients in a six-week inpatient treatment center for alcoholism at a New Jersey state hospital. Originally 8 had filled in the questionnaire in the course of taking part in a drug interaction study, but the number was increased to 30 by group filling-out of the questionnaire at the research unit.

The 30 *reformatory subjects* were all inmates of a New Jersey reformatory, housed at a state hospital as work crews. Originally, 4 had filled in the questionnaire in taking part in a drug interaction study, but the number was increased to 30 by group filling-out of the questionnaire at the research unit.

The four groups, though similar, were not perfectly comparable in terms of socioeconomic characteristics. Only the alcoholic group deviated markedly in terms of age. They were much older than the other three groups, with a median age of 41. The reformatory, schizophrenic, and normal groups were all young adults with median ages of 24, 21, and 18 respectively.

In terms of education, the reformatory subjects were most different from the other three groups, being more poorly educated than the others. (Their median educa-tional level was completion of tenth or eleventh grade.) The alcoholics were only slightly better educated than the schizophrenic and normal groups. (The median edu-cational level for these three groups was four years of high school completed.)

The social class of each individual was calculated by means of Hollingshead's (1957) two-factor index of social position. In the case of the schizophrenics and normals, father's occupation and education were used to calculate social class because they were a younger group, some still in school. In the case of the alcoholics and reformatory subjects, own occupation and education were used to calculate social class position.

The reformatory subjects were of a lower social class (median Class 5) than the alcoholics (median between Classes 3 and 4), schizophrenics (median Class 4), and normals (median Class 3).

In terms of ethnicity (determined by nationality of father), the four groups show-ed a spread. The alcoholics had fewer German and Italian members than the other groups, and more Irish, French Canadian, and American. (However, this last category was so full because they were not carefully enough instructed to identify the original ethnic identity of their father.) Like the alcoholics, the reformatory boys had more Irish members than the other two groups. The schizophrenics were somewhat lower on Irish members than the other groups and a little higher on Italian members.

Processing and Analysis of the Data. For each subject, there was obtained the total number of choices of solutions that showed normative expectations and actual perceptions of child to mother or father of active rebellion, passive rebellion, or conformity; and mother or father to child of support-permissiveness, role enforcement, or withdrawal. Group means were calculated for the alcoholic, reformatory inmate, schizophrenic, and normal groups.

Three-way analyses of variance were used to study whether there were significant differences between the choices of the four groups of subjects, whether normative expectations differed significantly from actual perceptions of behavior, and whether responses relating to mother-subject or father-subject behavior differed significantly.

Also, in order to study whether the subject's expectations and perceptions of parental behaviors related to his expectations and perceptions of his own behaviors in different ways in the four different groups, product-moment correlations were calculated.

RESULTS AND DISCUSSION

We will first describe briefly the results of the analyses of variance and then relate the findings to the hypotheses based on Parsons' theoretical scheme.

The mean scores of the four groups on normative expectations and actual perceptions of behaviors of mothers and fathers to children in terms of support-permissiveness, role enforcement, and withdrawal, and of behaviors of children to mothers and fathers in terms of active rebellion, passive rebellion, and conformity are shown in Table 1. The results of the analyses of variance are shown in Table 2.

The groups differ significantly in responses with regard to all three categories of parent-to-child behaviors. Clearly, child-rearing techniques, as seen by the subjects themselves, have differed markedly in their families. Significant F-ratios for the parent-to-child behaviors indicate that: (1) the reformatory inmates have given most responses of parental support-permissiveness, the schizophrenics next, while the normals and alcoholics are both much lower in this dimension; (2) the reformatory inmates have given most parental withdrawal responses with the normals and alcoholics giving much fewer and the schizophrenics least; and (3) the alcoholics have given most parental role enforcement responses, the reformatory subjects least.

However, on the child-to-parent behaviors only one category shows a significant difference. It is hardly surprising in view of the deviant status of three of the groups that it is conformity on which this difference appears. Reflected in the significant F ratio is high conformity on the part of the normals, low conformity on the part of the reformatory subjects.

Normative expectations and actual perceptions of behavior differ significantly in three cases. In the responses relating to the behaviors of parent to child, withdrawal of the parents is perceived more than it is normatively expected. In the responses with regard to the behaviors of the child to the parent, passive rebellion is perceived more than it is expected, and conformity is expected more than it is perceived. However, a significant first-order interaction reflects the fact that while in the normal group the difference between normative expectations and actual perceptions of withdrawal of the parents is very slight, it is larger in the schizophrenic and alcoholic groups, and very large in the reformatory group.

TABLE 1

MEAN NORMATIVE EXPECTATIONS AND ACTUAL PERCEPTIONS BY NORMAL,
SCHIZOPHRENIC, REFORMATORY, AND ALCOHOLIC MALE SUBJECTS OF
BEHAVIORS OF PARENT TO CHILD AND OF CHILD TO PARENT IN THEIR OWN FAMILIES

	Alcoholics (N = 30)	Reformatory Inmates (N = 30)	Schizophrenics (N = 30)	Normals (N = 30)
BEHAVIORS OF PARENT TO CHILD				
Mother (Normative Expectations)				
Support-permissiveness	1.7	2.5	1.8	1.7
Withdrawal	.2	.3	.5	.7
Role enforcement	3.1	2.2	2.7	2.6
Mother (Actual Perceptions)				
Support-permissiveness	1.8	2.2	1.9	1.6
Withdrawal	.5	1.0	.4	.6
Role enforcement	2.7	1.8	2.7	2.8
Father (Normative Expectations)				
Support-permissiveness	1.3	2.1	2.0	1.6
Withdrawal	.3	.6	.2	.3
Role enforcement	3.3	2.3	2.8	3.1
Father (Actual Perceptions)				
Support-permissiveness	1.3	1.8	2.4	1.7
Withdrawal	.6	.8	.3	.4
Role enforcement	3.1	2.4	2.3	2.9
BEHAVIORS OF CHILD TO PARENT				
Mother (Normative Expectations)				
Active rebellion	1.0	1.3	1.0	.9
Passive rebellion	.3	.4	.3	.3
Conformity	3.7	3.3	3.7	3.8
Mother (Actual Perceptions)				
Active rebellion	1.1	1.6	1.0	1.0
Passive rebellion	1.2	1.0	1.1	.9
Conformity	2.7	2.4	2.9	3.1
Father (Normative Expectations)				
Active rebellion	2.1	1.6	2.1	2.1
Passive rebellion	.4	.7	.2	.4
Conformity	2.5	2.7	3.7	2.5
Father (Actual Perceptions)				
Active rebellion	2.0	1.8	2.2	1.8
Passive rebellion	.7	1.0	.7	.9
Conformity	2.3	2.2	2.1	2.3

Responses with regard to behaviors relating to the mother and behaviors relating to the father differ significantly only in the cases of active rebellion and conformity. More active rebellion responses relate to the father, more conformity to the mother. However, significant first-order interactions reflect group differences with regard to behaviors relating to the mother and behaviors relating to the fathers. Thus, in the case of active rebellion, while the whole group gives much fewer active rebellion responses toward the mother than toward the father, the reformatory inmates tend to show much less difference than the other groups in this respect. With regard to conformity, while the groups in general show more

TABLE 2

RESULTS OF THE THREE-WAY ANALYSES OF VARIANCE EXAMINING THE
SIGNIFICANCE OF THE DIFFERENCES BETWEEN THE RESPONSES OF THE FOUR
GROUPS, BETWEEN NORMATIVE EXPECTATIONS AND ACTUAL PERCEPTIONS, AND
BETWEEN RESPONSES RELATED TO THE MOTHER AND RESPONSES
RELATED TO THE FATHER

	BEHAVIORS OF PARENT TO CHILD			BEHAVIORS OF CHILD TO PARENT		
	Support–Permissiveness	Withdrawal	Role Enforcement	Active Rebellion	Passive Rebellion	Conformity
MAIN EFFECTS						
Groups	7.62**	44.4**	11.19**	ns	ns	3.32*
NE/AP	ns	8.48**	ns	ns	39.20**	69.52**
SM/SF	ns	ns	ns	68.66**	ns	123.17**
FIRST ORDER INTERACTION						
Groups X NE/AP	ns	2.7*	ns	ns	ns	ns
Groups X SM/SF	3.10*	ns	ns	3.81*	ns	4.02**
NE/AP X SM/SF	ns	ns	ns	ns	ns	10.02**
SECOND ORDER INTERACTION						
Groups X NE/AP X SM/SF	ns	ns	ns	ns	ns	ns

*Significant above the .05 level.
**Significant above the .01 level.

conformity responses toward the mother than toward the father, the
normals differ most in this respect and the reformatory subjects differ
least. With regard to support-permissiveness, the normals show no father-
mother difference, the schizophrenics show more paternal support-
permissive responses, and the reformatory subjects and alcoholics more
maternal support-permissive responses. The reformatory subjects are
especially high on maternal support-permissiveness and the alcoholics
especially low on paternal support-permissiveness.

The difference between normative expectations and actual perceptions
relates to whether behaviors are associated with the father or mother in
one case only. In general, normative expectations of conformity are higher
than actual perceptions of conformity, but the difference between the
two is greater in the case of behaviors relating to the mothers.

The interactions between groups, normative expectations and actual
perceptions, and behaviors related to the mother as opposed to behaviors
related to the father are not significant in any category.

Let us now consider how these findings relate to Parsons' theories of
the relation between family socialization techniques and deviant behavior.
Parsons hypothesized that the alcoholic must have had a strict but loving
mother. According to their questionnaire responses, the alcoholics perceive both mothers and fathers as very high on role enforcement, fathers
being seen as higher than mothers in this respect. This does indeed suggest
a strict mother but also an even more strict father. But are these mothers

also seen as loving? They are not seen as high on support-permissiveness in contrast to the other groups, but mothers of alcoholics are seen as much higher on support-permissiveness than the fathers of alcoholics, who are especially low in this respect. Low withdrawal responses for both fathers and mothers of alcoholics suggest parents who are not indifferent, though combined with the low support-permissiveness and high role enforcement, this does not necessarily suggest affection but rather attention being given to the child.

With regard to child-parent behaviors, we had anticipated that the alcoholics might expect more conforming behavior of children toward parents. However, we find that the alcoholics do not give conforming responses more than the other groups, nor are they especially high on either active rebellion or passive rebellion.

Parsons hypothesizes that the psychopath has had a *laissez-faire* and indulgent mother. The responses of the reformatory subjects show a combination of high expectations and perceptions of maternal support-permissiveness and high maternal withdrawal and low role enforcement, which support this theory. However, the fathers of the reformatory subjects are also seen as low on role enforcement and high on withdrawal, though not high on support-permissiveness like the mothers. This suggests a *laissez-faire* atmosphere in which neither parent enforces rules, both withdraw, though the mothers are somewhat more supportive than the fathers.

We had expected that the reformatory boys might be high on active rebellion responses and low on conformity. We find that they expect and perceive much active rebellion and little conformity toward the mother. Toward the father, on the other hand, they expect and perceive much passive rebellion. They tend to be low on active rebellion responses in relation to the father and not especially low or high on conformity responses toward the father.

According to Parsons, we would expect inadequate role differentiation in the family of the schizophrenic. The schizophrenics present a picture of family life in which fathers are high on support-permissiveness and low on withdrawal and role enforcement. The schizophrenics see themselves as high on expectations of conformity toward the father, low on expectations of passive rebellion toward the father, and high on perceptions of active rebellion toward the father. Somewhat surprisingly, in view of the significance usually assigned to the mother in studies of the family of the schizophrenic, the schizophrenics do not present an especially characteristic picture of maternal behavior.

In general, these findings tend to lend support to Parsons' hypotheses about the relationship between family socialization techniques and deviant behavior. The alcoholics would indeed appear to have strict mothers who are at least more loving than their fathers. The reformatory inmates appear to have permissive mothers, while in the families of the schizophrenics the high support-permissiveness of the fathers suggests that parental sex roles are not differentiated in the usual fashion.

However, in the case of the alcoholics and reformatory inmates, the role of the father would appear also to be atypical, as Parsons' scheme has not suggested. The father of the alcoholic is seen as high on role enforcement and low on support-permissiveness, while the father of the reformatory inmate is seen as low on role enforcement and high on withdrawal. Thus, our study suggests a more complex family picture—including aberrancies of the role of the father—than Parsons has hypothesized.

Let us now turn to the correlational analysis. As previously stated, product-moment correlations were calculated in order to study in each group the relation between responses relating to child-parent and parent-child behaviors. More of these correlations were statistically significant than would be expected by chance. We shall present and discuss the correlations that were significant in relation to a special purpose, that of suggesting certain possibilities with regard to the differential consequences of various parental socialization techniques for the different kinds of deviants.

The justification for this is as follows: In the previous Bales interaction study of schizophrenics, we found not only that the fathers of schizophrenics were more supportive in their interaction than the fathers of normals, but also that where the fathers were less supportive, the schizophrenics got sicker on follow-up (Cheek, 1965a). In our present correlational analysis we find that where the father is seen as high on support-permissiveness, the child is seen as high on conformity ($r = .55$; $p < .01$). Also, in the interaction study, where mothers of schizophrenics gave fewer positive sanctions in their interaction, the schizophrenics were sicker at the time of the interaction study (Cheek, 1965b). We find now a very high correlation ($r = .90$; $p < .01$) between the expectations of the schizophrenic that the mother should withdraw and the expectation that the child should be passively rebellious.

It may be then that our correlations suggest which type of behavior from father or mother would be associated with conformity or with active or passive rebellion on the part of the deviant. Let us look at the alcoholics and reformatory inmates in this way.

In correlations of parent-child and child-parent behavior for the alcoholics, we find that the more role-enforcing the alcoholic thinks the mother should be, the more conforming he thinks the child should be ($r = .57$; $p < .01$). The correlations also show that where the alcoholic thinks the mother should be support-permissive or withdrawing, he thinks the child should actively rebel ($r = .41$ and $r = .39$, both $p < .05$). Perhaps then, when the alcoholic is treated strictly by the mother (or by another maternal figure), he might conform, but where a maternal figure is permissive, he might actively rebel.

Where the alcoholic thinks the father should be high on role enforcement, he expects the child to be high on conformity ($r = .30$, not significant); where he sees the father as withdrawing, he sees the child as high on passive rebellion and low on conformity ($r = .56$ and $-.44$; $p < .01$). Similarly then, where the father (or other paternal figure) treats the alcoholic strictly, he might conform; where the paternal figure withdraws, he might passively rebel.

The correlational analysis shows the reformatory boys to be high on expectations of support-permissiveness on the part of the mother ($r = .79$; $p < .01$). With regard to the father, they are high on expectations of active rebellion where they are high on expectations of role enforcement on the part of the father ($r = .44$; $p < .05$) and high on expectations of conformity where they are high on expectations of support-permissiveness from fathers ($r = .54$; $p < .01$). It may then be that the reformatory boys might be actively rebellious where maternal figures are support-permissive or paternal figures are role-enforcing, while they might conform if paternal figures are support-permissive.

However, while these findings are suggestive with regard to the relationship between deviant behavior and family process, and perhaps with regard to the management of the deviant, let us now consider some important qualifications.

In the first place, as we have said, we have regarded our alcoholics as Parsons' compulsives and our reformatory inmates as his psychopaths. It is true that addictive behavior may in a sense be regarded as compulsive behavior; also our reformatory group might reasonably include a larger number of diagnosable psychopaths than the normal population, and their behavior might be regarded as "psychopathic." However, neither of these are perfect fits.

Secondly, our four groups are not perfectly comparable in terms of socioeconomic characteristics. The alcoholics were older, while, probably even more significantly, the reformatory boys were less well educated and of a lower social class than the alcoholics, schizophrenics, and normals. There is a large literature on differences in parental socialization techniques in relation to social class (Bronfenbrenner, 1958), and parental permissiveness and withdrawal have been said to be characteristic of the lower class. However, it may also be that this environment is specially conducive to the development of psychopathy. Additionally, the groups were not perfectly matched in terms of ethnicity, which may have produced biased results.

Also, this view of parental socialization techniques is that of the young adults; we do not include the views of the parents themselves. Nor do we include any kind of objective behavioral data with regard to family interaction. Our study is therefore open to the criticisms made of all questionnaire studies in which verbal report of subjects regarding external phenomena is utilized. However, in the case of both the normal and schizophrenic samples, observational data on the family interaction was available, and what is reported here from the point of view of the young adults is essentially an accurate, though incomplete family picture. The fathers of the schizophrenics were indeed, according to the additional data, more supportive than normal fathers, though many other dimensions were revealed in the combined observational and questionnaire study.

A fourth limitation has been the crudeness of the present measuring instrument of family socialization techniques and types of deviant behavior. The findings in the interaction study, for which the questionnaire was especially developed, made it clear that it would have been useful to separate out support from permissiveness, for, while in the mothers of the normals high support-permissiveness was associated with high interaction rates of agreement, in the mothers of the schizophrenics high support-permissiveness was associated with low interaction rates of disagreement.

Parsons' theoretical scheme for the analysis of the socialization process deals with a variety of inputs and outputs. However, the major inputs which he considers are two—support and denial—realized concretely in the strict but loving parent, the indulgent and permissive parent, etc. Psychologists have recently devoted a great deal of attention to the study of learning behavior in relation to reinforcements—positive or negative (Franks, 1964). These positive and negative reinforcements might be translated into Parsons' inputs of support and denial. It is now proposed, by one psychologist at least (Dunham, 1966), to examine schedules of reinforcement in families of schizophrenics, with the thought that schizophrenics may either be created by aberrant reinforcing schedules or may elicit such schedules from their environment. According to Parsons' theoretical scheme, if translated into reinforcement theory, each type of deviancy would be associated with certain typical and aberrant reinforcement schedules on the part of the parents.

The findings in this study do indeed suggest different parental patterns of reinforcement in relation to the various deviancies studied. However, while Parsons has hypothesized that these are etiologically significant in the development of the deviancy, the possibility remains that the deviants themselves may have elicited these behaviors from their parents.

The etiological question notwithstanding, what is now needed is careful examination of these parental reinforcement schedules in natural or experimental situations, or perhaps with questionnaires specially designed for this purpose. Also, particularly in relation to treatment, it would be valuable to investigate the effects of various reinforcement schedules on various types of deviants. Such studies should give us highly significant information about the nature of the environment of the deviant, which may also tell us how to manage the deviancy.

READING 6

Thought Disorder and Family Relations of Schizophrenics*

Margaret T. Singer and Lyman C. Wynne

In companion papers on the Family Studies research at the National Institute of Mental Health, we have indicated that our research has been focused upon links between individual schizophrenic impairment and family patterns of thinking and communicating (Singer & Wynne, 1963, Wynne & Singer, 1963a, 1963b, 1964; Singer & Wynne, 1965a).

In the study of individual offspring, we have been especially concerned with the structural or formal aspects of ego disorganization, particularly thought disorder. We have conceptualized schizophrenic thinking along a continuum based upon broad developmental principles in which relatively "amorphous" forms of thinking can be distinguished from better differentiated but still "fragmented" forms of thinking (Wynne & Singer, 1963b). In the present study we have also used a dimension of severity of ego disorganization as well as traditional diagnostic distinctions.

In the study of family patterns we have been especially concerned with those family styles of communicating and relating which help shape a growing child's forms of thinking. We have conceptualized "thinking" as a process which has begun with the focusing of attention, becomes manifest in communication, and can result in shared meaningful experience. In this research projective techniques were used as a means of sampling the transactional styles of family members, especially patterns of handling attention and meaning.

In companion papers (Wynne & Singer, 1964; Singer & Wynne, 1965a), we have presented criteria for predicting the characteristics of patient-offspring from family patterns evaluated with projective techniques. These criteria stress stylistic, formal features of the transactions of family members, rather than the content of their responses. In this study the data used by the predicting psychologist (M.T.S.) were typescripts of psychological tests obtained by other psychologists from the parents and siblings of psychiatric patients. Blind predictive diagnoses and ratings were made by the psychologist about the patients without tests or other data about the patients themselves, except their sex and approximate age.

*Abridged from *Archives of General Psychiatry*, 1965, *12*, 201–212, with permission of the authors and the American Medical Association.

Tests of from two to five families were studied as a set. Then the psychologist was given the tests from the patient members of these families and attempted to match them blindly with their families. Predictions and matchings were thus made with a series of 35 late adolescent and young adult patients and their families. The patients in these families, fully categorized in the preceding paper (1965a), were a mixed diagnostic group of amorphous and fragmented schizophrenics, borderline schizophrenics, and neurotics. In the present paper, we shall present the results with the predicting and matching procedures, and discuss a few methodological and theoretical implications.

RESULTS

Predicting Procedure Results. Four kinds of predictions were made: traditional global diagnosis, forms of thinking and communicating, severity of symptomatic ego disorganization, and narrative descriptive predictions.

1. Traditional Global Diagnosis: In predicting the characteristics of the 35 patients in this study from family test data, the psychologist first used a traditional three-level diagnostic grouping—frankly schizophrenic, borderline schizophrenic, and non-schizophrenic neurotic. The predicted characteristics of the offspring, compared with the independent clinical consensus, are summarized in Table 1.

TABLE 1

GLOBAL DIAGNOSES

		INDEPENDENT CLINICAL DIAGNOSES OF PATIENTS			
		Schiz	Borderline Schiz	Nonschiz	Total
DIAGNOSIS	S	(17)	1	1	19
PREDICTED	BS	2	(7)	1	10
FROM TESTS	NS	1	1	(4)	6
OF REST					
OF FAMILY	Total	20	9	6	35

$\chi^2 = 28.94$, $df = 4$, $p < 0.001$.

Of 20 patients clinically diagnosed as frankly schizophrenic, 17 were correctly predicted. Similarly, all but two of the patients in each of the borderline (9 patients) and non-schizophrenic (6 patients) groups were correctly predicted from the family data ($p < .001$).[1] It should be noted that there were only two "two-step" errors, with one non-schizophrenic

---

[1] Dr. Donald Morrison, Biometrics Branch, NIMH, did the statistical analysis of the data. Dr. Morrison notes that "although the χ^2 tend to be increased by the rather small expected values of some cells of the tables, Cochran (1954) has presented a justification for not combining categories in tables of such data."

diagnosed as schizophrenic, and one schizophrenic diagnosed as non-schizophrenic.

2. Prediction of Forms of Thinking: Using the dimension of form of thinking (Wynne & Singer, 1963b), ranging from amorphous (A), mixed (M), fragmented (F), and constricted (C), the predictions once again were accurate at a highly significant level ($p < .001$), as shown in Table 2. None of the amorphous patients were predicted to be fragmented, and none of the fragmented patients were predicted to be amorphous.

TABLE 2

FORMS OF THINKING AND COMMUNICATING

		INDEPENDENT CLINICAL DIAGNOSES OF PATIENTS				
		A Amorphous	M Mixed	F Fragmented	C Constricted	Total
DIAGNOSIS	A	(7)	4			11
PREDICTED	M	1	(2)			3
FROM TESTS	F		2	(14)	1	17
OF REST	C			2	(2)	4
OF FAMILY	Total	8	8	16	3	35

$X^2 = 39.03$, $df = 9$, $p < 0.001$.

3. Prediction of Severity: A third kind of prediction was made, using the dimension of severity of symptomatic ego-disorganization, with Levels 3, 4, and 5 involving different degrees of severity of frank psychosis, with Level 2 questionably psychotic (borderline), and with Level 1 neurotic. The success of the predictions is seen in Table 3. There were only three errors of more than one step in the 35 cases. Once again, these predictions were accurate at better than the .001 level.

TABLE 3

SEVERITY OF SYMPTOMATIC EGO DISORGANIZATION

		INDEPENDENT CLINICAL RATINGS OF PATIENTS					
		Psychotic					
		5	4	3	2	1	Total
PREDICTED	5	(6)		1			7
RATINGS	4		(6)	1		1	8
FROM TESTS	3		1	(3)	1		5
OF REST	2			2	(7)	1	10
OF FAMILY	1		1		1	(3)	5
	Total	6	8	7	9	5	35

$X^2 = 63.65$, $df = 16$, $p < 0.001$.

4. Narrative Predictions: Predictions were also made about each of the patients in lengthy narrative terms. The accuracy of these descriptions of the patients seemed striking, but cannot be evaluated statistically. Examples of the original protocols together with these narrative predictions will be presented in a later publication. For all except 2 of the 35 patients, central qualitative features were successfully predicted in terms of the *form* of thinking. The predictive descriptions were sufficiently detailed so that one of the clinicans, who had treated or supervised the treatment of a sample of 9 patients, was able to identify correctly which patient was being described predictively, even though these descriptions of the patients were based only upon material obtained from the rest of the family.

Matching Procedure Results. Table 4 summarizes the results of efforts to make blind matchings of offspring with their families. Out of 36 matchings (33 patients[2] and 3 siblings of patients[3]), 3 incorrect reversals were made (6 total errors[4]). Considering a perfect match for an entire set as a success and anything less as a failure,[5] by multiplication of probabilities for groups of the sizes indicated in Table 4, the overall probability that this level of predictive accuracy could be achieved by chance is .000002.

TABLE 4

OFFSPRING-FAMILY MATCHING STUDY

No. Families in Each Set	No. Sets	No. Sets Perfectly Matched
2	2	2
3	6	4
4	1	1
5	2	1

---

[2] Two families differed too much in social and cultural characteristics to be grouped with each other or with other families and therefore were studied with the preceding procedure but not the matching procedure. Thus, 33 patients were matched with their families, while the families of 35 patients were studied with the predicting procedure.

[3] In one set of three families, each family consisted of two parents and three offspring. The eldest offspring in each family was male and was the designated psychiatric patient. Each second offspring was male and free of symptomatology, and each third offspring was a daughter also symptom-free. The psychologist was first given the tests from each set of parents and the daughter, with the task of predicting the characteristics of the sick male offspring. Then the tests of the three well sons were matched blind with the three families and finally the tests of the three sick sons were matched with their families.

[4] In addition, Dr. Singer correctly matched 11 schizophrenic patients with their families from protocols made available by the Lidz group at Yale. These matchings were performed in two groups, 4 female patients and 7 male patients. Illustrative notes from these matchings have been quoted by Lidz, Fleck, Alanen, and Cornelison (1963).

[5] For example, in one set of five families, three were matched correctly and two were reversed. This is considered a "failure" for statistical purposes for the entire set.

COMMENT

Lessons from Errors

We have emphasized that content of thinking was relegated to a secondary role in making these blind differentiations. Content of family protocols may, if given undue weight, be seductively intriguing—and misleading. An early, temporary error in matching families with patients dramatized this pitfall and the importance of concentrating on structural, formal test features: when the first set of four families and patients were viewed and the actual matchings considered, the predictor was impressed by marked content similarities between certain of the patient protocols and certain parental protocols, and was initially lured from the procedural "rules" emphasizing formal features. She also noted certain *individual* similarities between a particular patient and a particular parent and neglected the overall, family-wide constellation in this family. Using this content-orientation and these individual similarities as a basis for the matchings, three out of the four matchings were incorrect. Within the hour, before hearing about this result, the psychologist reconsidered and wrote a rescinding note asking that these matchings be disregarded. She then rematched the families, this time making the matchings on the basis of form of thinking and ego functioning, and deliberately ignoring, insofar as possible, similarities in content. This time the matchings were entirely correct, and the criteria for making the matchings became better defined.

Another early instructive error occurred in the matching of two patients with families who differed markedly in verbal productivity. In one of these families, the parents were extraordinarily talkative and highly intellectual. The other family spoke relatively little, with little evidence of intellectual strength. In the more talkative family, however, the psychologist noted that there was a considerable shifting about of attention, and meanings were diffused; on the basis of these and other features of the parental tests, she correctly predicted that the patient was likely to feel intruded upon, propelled by outer forces, and would be openly schizophrenic. She also predicted correctly that the offspring of the depressed, relatively unproductive family would not be schizophrenic.

However, in the matching procedure the verbally productive family was erroneously matched with a patient who had a similar high level of verbal productivity and who also used similar flamboyant intellectualizations. The depressed, unproductive family was incorrectly matched with an apathetic "amorphous" schizophrenic. Thus, the predictions were correct but the matchings were wrong because too much weight was given in the matchings to the surface productivity. In reviewing the protocols of the verbally productive family later it was noted, as had been done in the predicting procedure, that underneath all the talk, attention and meaning were diffused, and there was a deep pessimism about ever establishing meaningful affective interactions. In the unproductive, depressed family, there were relatively few indications of attention problems, and they seemed to persist at interaction, despite depression and guilt about doing so.

This pair of mismatchings reemphasized that patient-family similarities in surface characteristics of depression, tension, verbosity, etc., even when flamboyant or striking, may be misleading, and that difficulties in focusing attention and pervasive, underlying feelings of meaninglessness and pointlessness are more significant. These are features which are discussed and illustrated in the preceding paper of this series (Singer & Wynne, 1965a).

As this example suggests, it is necessary to distinguish those parental behaviors which seem to serve as models for identification from those which elicit or provoke complementary behavior in offspring. In another family, for example, an alert and quickly responsive father was very cryptic. His wife was also responsive and alert, but elaborated her thoughts unduly. thus the son would be expected to identify with the alertness and quickness of both parents. However, the predictor expected that he would have difficulty identifying with the mystifying crypticness of the father and, indeed, be provoked to offer many alternative meanings in order to discover what the father had in mind. Thus, it was predicted that he would become diffuse and rambling like his mother rather than like his father. Using this level of reasoning, the psychologist predicted that this aspect of behavior in the son would complement the father's crypticness and simultaneously have the appearance of an identification with the mother.

A Transactional Formulation

Let us now step back from specific details of findings and methods to consider the conceptual framework within which this work can be best interpreted. Our approach to family research is broadly similar to the transactional formulation summarized by Spiegel and Bell (1959):

> Essentially a field approach, the transactional point of view postulates that the events involving the sick individual with his family occur within a total system of interdependent subsystems, any one of which—for example the individual, the family, the community, the value system—may become, temporarily, a focus of observation. The "world" being observed must include the observer and his act of observing. Within the field encompassing the interconnected subsystems, a component system, such as the individual, can be isolated and studied as an entity, but this is a heuristic device which always involves some distortion and sacrifice of precision or predictive ability.
>
> If this philosophical position is accepted, then the individual and the family are seen as subsystems which are intimately and complexly interrelated. Neither has any greater "reality" than the other, and no characteristic of one or both has any necessary priority. A somewhat similar philosophical stance has been adopted by others under the name of "general system theory." No matter what it is called, this point of view alters the concept of

causality. Viewing one entity or process as causing another, or as dependent on another is possible only if their interrelations can be isolated from total contexts. Putting variables within a total context shifts the question from "What in the family 'causes' pathology in the individual?" to "What processes occurring between the individual and the family are associated with the behaviors which are called 'pathology'?"

In our research we have been concerned primarily with the influence of the family constellation upon the personality development, schizophrenic and otherwise, of offspring. In using projective test protocols, we have not directly utilized data about the individual's biologic equipment, nor about the broader community and cultural context within which he lives. However, the research has been so designed that the reasoning process in making predictions continually used inferences about these other aspects of the overall transactional field. Let us consider, in turn, how we have conceived of the relations between the personality organization of individual offspring and three other main research areas: the nuclear family as a constellation; the extended family, social class, and cultural context; and the biological organization of individual family members.

The Family Constellation

We have stressed that all of the predictions and matchings were made by inferring how the family members were likely to fit together as a constellation. It follows then that predictions made on the basis of data from one parent should be improved by data from the rest of the family social system in which the patient grew up.

Consider, for example, two mothers who are found to be similarly disturbed when evaluated as individuals apart from their families. The psychological impact of these similar mothers in different family constellations might vary considerably—depending on differences in their "fit" with the rest of the family social system. In some families a father may augment, or at least not counteract substantially, the disturbing impact of the mother, even though he may, in other roles outside the family, or with other kinds of emotional support, be able to bring into the open another side of his nature. Hence, any corrective potentialities evident under other circumstances may not be operative and available within the family for internalization by the children.

In other families the father may not share or collusively support the wife's disturbed functioning. If his stylistic differences from his wife do not lead to utterly chaotic family disorganization, and if he can have a steady, differentiated, recognizable role in the family, he may become an alternative, effective model for identification. Predictively, his children will be conflicted, perhaps severely neurotic, but probably not with gross schizophrenic gaps in their ego functions.

This kind of formulation is difficult to evaluate systematically because the variations in the dynamics of family constellations are so numerous. As we have already indicated, parental influences are interwoven and organized over time into a dynamic whole, so that the impact or influence of an individual parent should not be evaluated only in isolation. Keeping these problems in mind, we have attempted to see if the potential influence of one parent can be compared with that of both parents.

Starting with the blind interpretations of the tests of the more disturbing parent in each pair, a psychiatrist evaluated the test descriptions of the other parent and judged whether the other parent would be likely to aggravate or to counteract the pathogenic potentialities of the first parent. In the present series, all of the parents of the schizophrenic patients were judged to have an aggravating influence, whereas the second parent in each of the families of clearly non-schizophrenic patients was judged to be likely to counteract the more disturbing parent. As one might expect, the distinction for the parents of the borderline patients was less clear.

A methodological shortcoming of this subproject was that "aggravating" versus "counteracting" influences were judged from the narrative descriptions originally written by the predicting psychologist without this specific distinction in mind. For this reason, the judgments made about the parents on the "aggravating" versus "counteracting" dimension were not equally satisfactory for all of the sample. Therefore, the ratings on this dimension are not presented as a definite finding but as a suggestion for further investigation. In Table 5, synoptic evaluations of the kind used in this evaluation are exemplified for four pairs of parents. It is of especial interest that the four mothers in Table 5 were all quite disturbed and disturbing, but when the father seemed to provide a corrective, "counteracting" influence, the offspring turned out to be neurotic or borderline rather than frankly schizophrenic. Within the present sample of parents, whenever one parent—*either* parent—was judged to have a definite "counteracting" influence, the offspring were never frankly schizophrenic, even though the other parent was sometimes quite severely disordered as an individual.

Because the siblings of the sick offspring also contribute to the nature of the family constellation, the "social system" view of family relations suggest that knowledge of the siblings should affect blind predictions about the patient-offspring. In order to see whether data about a patient's siblings appreciably altered predictions, a slightly-modified predictive procedure was used with nine of the families. Instead of working from the beginning with both parental and sibling tests, the predicting psychologist was first sent the protocols from the parents only and preliminary predictive ratings were made. Later, the final ratings were made after the sibling protocols had also been studied. Inferences from the sibling data helped in making some of the predictions more precisely accurate. For example, the prediction for one patient was shifted from borderline (Level 2 of severity) to neurotic (Level 1) on the basis of the sibling data. However, the sibling data did not in any instance lead to drastic revisions in the predictions.

TABLE 5

SYNOPTIC EVALUATIONS

MOTHER'S KIND OF PROBLEM OR FUNCTIONING	FATHER'S FUNCTIONING: AGGRAVATES OR COUNTERACTS INFLUENCE OF MOTHER	INDEPENDENT DIAGNOSTIC RATINGS OF PATIENT-OFFSPRING
Meanings are woolly and nebulous . . . exudes diffuse anxiety and inadequacy . . . remarks drift without closure	An intrusive, subtly paranoid man, who encompasses another person . . . experiences things amorphously . . . highly repetitive . . . never openly assumes a clear role as interpreter (Aggravates)	Severely disturbed amorphous schizophrenic (5-A) (Female)
Scatters attention, has many intrusive thoughts which disrupt . . . offers peculiar interpretations of ordinary percepts . . . makes efforts to reach other person in a transaction. High energy level	Misperceives, relates too intrusively and intimately; poor ego boundaries . . . dependent, moody . . . Idiosyncratic and markedly vacillating (Aggravates)	Severely fragmented schizophrenic (5-F) (Female)
Acts vague, unsure; percepts not well-defined . . . scatters attention . . . likes situations to appear "nice" (pseudomutual) . . . Insidiously controlling	Alert . . . too cryptic in his communications, but has clear percepts (Counteracts)	Borderline paranoid personality (2-F) (Male)
Has very blurry response for unstructured situations . . . searching desperately for affection from family and others	A clear-minded, somewhat literal man . . . maintains relationships at a distance . . . not prone to blur, fragment, etc. (Counteracts)	Nonschizophrenic neurotic character (1-C) (Female)

Context of Social Class, Culture, and Extended Family

Because this research was designed to focus especially upon relationships between the nuclear family and individual offspring, we attempted to select families from all social class levels. However, *within each set* of families to be matched with offspring, the social class level was held constant insofar as possible. If in a given set of families diagnosis and social class happened to be significantly correlated, a judge might inadvertently use social class cues to facilitate accurate predictions and matchings.

Each family was classified by Hollingshead's two-factor Index of Social Position (Hollingshead & Redlich, 1958). (In this index an educational score is weighted by four and an occupational score is weighted by seven.) Combining Social Classes I and II (upper and upper-middle) and combining Classes IV and V (skilled and unskilled working class), we evaluated the question of whether diagnosis of patient-offspring could have been predicted from social class. Table 6 indicates this relationship was statistically random. Similarly, the relationship between social class and form of thinking, as well as social class and severity, was not significant.

TABLE 6

SOCIAL CLASS RELATIONSHIP

| | | DIAGNOSIS | | |
	Schizophrenic	Borderline Schizophrenic	Nonschizophrenic	Total
I Upper	0	0	0	0
II Upper-middle	8	7	4	19
III Lower-middle	8	2	1	11
IV Upper-lower	0	0	0	0
V Lower	4	0	1	5
Total 20		9	6	35

$x^2 = 4.72$, $df = 4$, ns

Thus, it is unlikely that social class cues gave sufficient information to the predicting psychologist to make correct predictions. A possible exception occurred with one of the first sets of families studied in which three schizophrenic patients came from families of Classes III and IV, while a borderline schizophrenic and a non-schizophrenic patient in this particular matching group came from Class I families. Thus, in matching this one set of patients with their families, it is conceivable (though unlikely) that social class cues may have been of some assistance, although it could not have helped distinguish *among* the three schizophrenics and their families who were all matched correctly. Later, social class was strictly controlled in the selection of families for the matching sets.

In principle, we feel that the stylistic features of communication emphasized in our guidelines (Singer & Wynne, 1965a) are applicable to families of any social class. Preliminary cross-cultural data using this approach indicate that these principles also can be utilized in studying tests from families of diverse cultural origins.

Tentatively assuming that our present findings have general applicability, we hypothesize that in all social-class and cultural settings in which schizophrenic illness occurs, formal, structural features of individual schizophrenic illness, especially the variety of thought disorder, will continue to be predictably related to the form of the communication patterns and interpersonal relationships of the *particular* family in which the individual has grown up. This possibility depends upon establishing criteria, such as those used in this study, which do not hinge upon distinctive cultural or social-class characteristics, but upon stylistic, formal matters which can be found and evaluated for the schizophrenics of any culture.

Thus, the important issue here is whether our criteria for dealing with family patterns are in fact universally relevant to schizophrenic illness, wherever such illness may occur, or are merely relevant idiosyncratically within the cultural and class setting of this study. We have begun cross-cultural studies of this issue.

Additional predictive problems are posed if the patient-offspring has had important relations with members of a significant extended family organization or with persons in the community about whom no data are available. Our clinical impression is that a few of the families had important transactions with untested persons outside the nuclear family. In one family an aunt, who was not available for study, had lived in the household in earlier years and participated importantly, and confusingly, in the child-rearing. By and large, however, the families in this study had few important deviations from urban American nuclear family organization.

These families differed, nevertheless, in the clarity and stability with which they delineated their *psychological* boundaries. These differences in family boundaries were partly but not completely deducible from the projective test transactions. The psychotherapeutic studies of families at the National Institute of Mental Health have indicated that the pre-schizophrenic child grows up with confused perceptions of the psychological boundaries of his family. Wynne, Ryckoff, Day, and Hirsch (1958), have described these boundaries as a kind of "rubber fence," which is impermeable in the sense that the offspring cannot psychologically leave, but is elastic in the sense that feelings and ideas which are acceptable within the family subculture constantly and perplexingly shift. Clinical observations suggest that schizophrenics have characteristically failed in preadolescence to have relations with "chums" who are acknowledged and at least tolerated by the child's family. Such relations outside the boundaries of the nuclear family probably are especially essential in present-day urban America in assisting the normal child to learn to have intimate and emotionally meaningful experience outside of the nuclear family. The adolescent peer-culture continues this developmental process. In some other cultures the extended family provides a complex but well-delineated social structure through which the growing child makes the transition into the wider adult community.

We hypothesize that pre-schizophrenics ordinarily fail to make orderly developmental transitions from relationships within the nuclear family to relationships within the broader culture. In most of the families studied in this project, the developmental patterns of the patients had seemed distorted by an excessive absorption in nuclear family patterns. The psychological boundaries of these families appeared to have the "rubber fence" form of impermeability. However, it is possible that in disorganized, lower-class neighborhoods from which families were mostly *not* selected for the present study, nuclear family boundaries may be excessively permeable or absent. In such families a child may develop a series of fragmented identifications with a series of persons in the disorganized community and suffer from unstable starting points within the nuclear family. In both kinds of families the transition from familial to extrafamilial relationships is developmentally distorted. We regard these problems of the links of nuclear family with extended family, community, and broader culture as of great importance in a comprehensive transactional approach to schizophrenics and their families, but outside the scope of the empirical research which is reported in this paper.

Biological Factors

It should be clear that the transactional formulation advanced here is not incompatible with potential findings of biologic factors in schizophrenic illness. What kinds of biologic variation are most consistent with the findings of the present study and what kinds of biologic contribution would be at odds with these findings? This question needs to be considered from the viewpoint of how biologic and experiential factors interact and combine in successive developmental phases.

We assume that the individual's biologic capacities for focusing attention and for perceiving, thinking, and communicating gradually are shaped and modified by interchange with the environment during development. This viewpoint is *epigenetic*: the interchanges or transactions at each developmental phase build upon the outcome of earlier transactions. This means that constitutional and experiential influences recombine in each developmental phase to create new biologic and behavioral potentialities which then help determine the next phase. If the transactions at any given developmental phase are distorted or omitted, all the subsequent developmental phases will be altered because they build upon a different substrate. We hypothesize that the family environment needs to provide certain kinds of influences in each maturational phase of the individual. What is appropriate and what may have psychopathological consequences thus varies over time and must always be considered in this developmental context. * * *

Family Disturbance Secondary to Disturbance of Offspring

The question is often raised whether disturbed family relationships may not simply be the consequence of having an offspring in the family who is ill and disturbing. The transactional and epigenetic view of development postulates circular or spiral, serially unfolding processes and is in opposition to the assumption that parental influences operate continuously and exclusively only in the direction of the offspring. Clinical observations in the National Institute of Mental Health Family Studies program have provided abundant evidence that each offspring helps shape the family system, which he in turn internalizes as ego development unfolds. Our viewpoint thus differs from those exclusively environmentalist theories which have sometimes implied that particular kinds of psychological trauma have an undirectional effect upon a passively receptive child or that "schizophrenogenic" mothers or parents have one-way victimizing effects upon their offspring. * * *

The Role of Psychological and Social Factors in the Onset of Somatic Illness in Children*

Arthur Z. Mutter and Maxwell J. Schleifer

This report will examine the role of psychological and social factors in the onset of "somatic" illness in young children, focusing on data obtained in an exploratory study of hospitalized latency-aged boys and girls. * * *

EXPLORATORY STUDY

Clinical experience and a review of the literature led us to hypothesize that, given the necessary biological conditions, the onset of somatic illness is related to the child's ability to cope with changes in his psychological and social environment. Because of unresolved problems in identifying pertinent variables and in methods of data-gathering and analysis, we undertook an exploratory study, the aims of which were twofold. The first aim was to identify variables concerning the psychological and social setting at the time of onset of disease. Previous research had not systematically considered a broad range of variables; major emphasis had been given to the examination of loss, both as an event and as a psychological issue, but few studies provided guidelines for examining other variables. Past research efforts primarily utilized adults as subjects and were not readily adaptable, therefore, for assessing the functioning of children. The second aim was to develop methods for gathering relevant and comprehensive information concerning the identified variables.

Method

Study Group. In selecting a study group, we had to consider two major issues: the first concerned problems in defining illness, and the second, the selection of pertinent psychological and social variables to scrutinize.

A dynamic concept of health makes a specific identification of illness difficult. Identifying the criteria indicating the stage at which a healthy child becomes ill is a complex task. A test of our hypothesis required that there be no doubt about the existence of a somatic illness in our study

*Abridged from *Psychosomatic Medicine*, 1966, *28*, 333–343, with permission of the authors and Hoeber Medical Journals.

sample. Therefore, we utilized only children hospitalized for an acute disease process.

The biological, psychological, and social forces in the life of a child are in a state of continuous change. Our study group was restricted to a single developmental phase in order to limit the range of variables necessary to examine. Latency-aged children were utilized because they comprised the largest hospitalized group able to participate in our clinical assessment.

We studied 42 families with latency-aged boys and girls who were hospitalized on the pediatric wards of a general hospital. The children were between the ages of 6 and 12 years, and had admission diagnoses of acute illnesses other than those considered to be "psychosomatic"—e.g., ulcerative colitis, neurodermatitis, bronchial asthma, and rheumatoid arthritis. The illnesses of the children in this study group were those commonly seen in a pediatric setting; distribution was as follows:

DISEASE	NO. OF CASES
Blood and lymph (Cat scratch fever; hemophilia.)	2
Genitourinary (Pyelonephritis; sulfa crystalluria; glomerulonephritis; focal nephritis; infection; cystitis.)	10
Gastrointestinal (Peptic ulcer; shigellosis; gastro- enteritis; appendicitis; hepatitis.)	6
Cardiovascular (Rheumatic fever.)	5
Musculoskeletal (Myositis; synovitis.)	3
Nervous system (Meningitis; Bell's palsy; chorea; convulsive disorder; seizure secondary to hypoglycemia.)	8
Respiratory (Croup; pneumonia; asthma.)	3
Skin (Cellulitis; furunculosis.)	3
Unknown (Hematemesis of unknown origin; hepatomegaly-lymphadenopathy of unknown etiology F.U.O., eventually diagnosed as rheu- matoid arthritis on subsequent admission.)	3
Miscellaneous (Pharyngitis.)	1

Two children had two disease processes; hence, the total is 44.

Comparison Group. Although this was an exploratory study, we added a comparison group of well children to help clarify the meaning of the data collected from our study group. We studied 45 families with a latency-aged child who had not been ill for at least six months prior to the time of the study. These families were participants in a home medical-care program of a general hospital that adjoined the site of our investigation. Records from this home medical service were randomly selected and examined in order to find cases that met the above criteria. The absence of illness in these children was confirmed during actual interviews with the families.

The study and comparison groups were comparable with respect to their socioeconomic characteristics—i.e., race, religion, size of family, age and sex of the child, and the marital and occupational status of the parents. Statistical analysis of these variables did not differentiate the two groups. These families were predominantly white and Catholic, with an average of three children. The majority of parents were married, with two-thirds self-supporting and approximately one-third on public welfare. The husbands were typically the breadwinners of the families and skilled or semiskilled laborers.

Interview Methods. Initially, the investigators utilized clinically-oriented and minimally structured interviews to gather data considered critical in understanding the functioning of the latency-aged child. We scrutinized the six-month period that preceded the onset of overt signs and/or symptoms in the ill group because of our knowlege that the actual onset of a disease process might precede the first observable manifestations of that disease. For the well children, the six-month period preceding the first interview was investigated.

A semi-structured interview schedule was developed after an assessment of the data from the first cases in the study group. Subsequently, this schedule was flexibly applied. The first interviews were clinically oriented. The interviewer then determined how well the data covered all areas in the interview schedule. Later interviews were used systematically to fill any gaps in our information.

At least one of the parents, usually the mother, was interviewed for two to three hours in conjunction with hospital visits to the child. Children were interviewed two or three times during one-hour play sessions on the pediatric ward. These data were supplemented by a review of medical records and observations concerning the child's behavior on the ward. The families of the well children were interviewed in their homes.

In developing our interviewing method, we had to consider the following:

1. The impact of hospitalization on the child and his family tends to influence their reporting of the details of the family's life. Hospitalization requires the mutual separation of the child and his family at a time of great anxiety and uncertainty about the future health of the child. The life history of the child and his family and the nature of the disease lead to particular methods of defense that both will use to cope with a significant event. In turn, this defense may influence all aspects of reporting behavior, either past or present, by the child or his parents. Further, the character and severity of the disease are not static. The manner in which the family and the child react to and manage the illness may shift as the disease process itself changes.

2. With the absence of the ill child from the home, there is a realignment of the forces and relationships within the family. For example, visiting the child may require reorganization of the everyday household routines. Members of the family may have different opportunities and needs in dealing with one another. Thus, the impact of the illness and the hospitalization may crystallize latent conflicts within the family. The data

given may be more related to this crisis rather than to an accurate history of the somatic illness.

3. The relationship of the investigator to the child and his family is influenced by their perception of his role in the overall treatment program. This directly influenced the nature and extent of information given. For example, several parents in the study, identifying the interviewer as a psychiatrist, focused on the mental-health aspects of their relationship to the child and, as the crisis of illness subsided, further meaningful contact became difficult. Although they might still meet with the interviewer, the productiveness of these contacts became severely limited. In order to engage optimally the cooperation of the families, we indicated the relevance of the information desired to the overall care of the hospitalized child. For the well group, we discussed the relevance of the information to the future medical care of the child by the home medical service.

4. The setting of the interview also shapes its character. For example, the physical characteristics of the ward, the attitude of care-taking personnel, the character of other children and their illnesses, all affected the attitudes and behavior of the study patient and his parents.

Methods of Data Analysis. In order to organize and process our data efficiently, we made explicit our major assumptions: a stable internal and external environment facilitates the child's ability to master the tasks of growth that confront him at the various developmental stages; this stability is related to the quantity and quality of changes in his psychological and social environment and the capacity of the child to manage these; the psychosocial level of organization of the child and his family shapes the child's adaptive capacity.

Data organization: we organized the data into three main areas: psychological and social setting; child's ability to cope with change; and the psychological and social organization of the child and his family.

Psychological and Social Setting. The following categories were considered to define the psychosocial setting of the six-month period under investigation:

1. Intrafamilial

　　A. Family composition and social interaction (birth, death, shift in role or function of the various family members).

　　B. Overt social behavior (abusive behavior, antisocial behavior in community, alcoholism).

　　C. Physiological functioning (puberty, menopause, pregnancy).

　　D. Affective state (depression, irritability, anxiety).

2. Extrafamilial

　　A. School, (change of school, beginning and end of school year).

　　B. Neighborhood:

　　　　1) Structure (deterioration, cultural make-up).

　　　　2) Location (moving to new area).

　　C. Socioeconomic status (loss of income).

Child's Ability to Cope with Change. The child was assessed in terms of the following:
1. Challenge inherent in change.
2. Impact of change on functioning.

Psychological and Social Organization of the Child and His Family. Indices of the child's psychological organization and of family functioning were as follows:
1. Child
   A. Ability to function with parents.
   B. Ability to function with peers.
   C. Ability to function in a school situation.
   D. Nature and range of recreational interests and activities.
2. Family
   A. Parental functioning in terms of major roles
      1) Father or mother.
      2) Husband or wife.
      3) Breadwinner or housekeeper.
   B. Cohesiveness (based on the Glueck Scale of Social Cohesiveness, Glueck & Glueck, 1950).

Data processing: We examined the quantity, nature, and timing of change in the child's psychosocial setting. These were assessed by (1) enumerating the total number of changes occurring in all the variables of the first main area above, (2) enumerating changes in the specific variables, and (3) determining the time relationship between the most recent change and the onset of illness.

We assessed the capacity of the child to manage these changes by evaluating (1) the challenge inherent in the various changes, (2) the effect they produced in his functioning, and (3) the level of psychosocial organization of the child and his family.

Scales were developed for processing the data in these areas. The data from 15 of 87 families were coded independently by three individuals. The reliability of these scales ranged from .75 to .87. In general, where problems in judgment existed, they were due to insufficient data rather than differences in the interpretation of scale points.

Statistical methods: The chi-square technique was used to analyze the data. Significance was considered to exist at the .05 level. We utilized percentages in analysis to minimize the interdependence of the results. Where data were insufficient, they were categorized as "unknown." In general, areas in which findings did not assume the level of statistical significance are not reported.

RESULTS

The results are summarized in Table 1.

TABLE 1

RESULTS OF EXPLORATORY STUDY ON PSYCHOLOGICAL AND SOCIAL
FACTORS IN THE ONSET OF SOMATIC ILLNESS IN CHILDREN

FACTOR	STUDY GROUP $N = 42$ (%)	CONTROL GROUP $N = 45^*$ (%)	SIGNIFICANCE		
			x^2	df	p
PSYCHOSOCIAL SETTING					
Total number changes, all categories			17.23	3	$<.001$
5−7	29	1			
3−4	29	27			
1−2	42	56			
0	0	16			
Time of change			8.41	3	$<.05$
$<$1 mo.	67	68			
1−3 mo.	26	8			
4−6 mo.	7	24			
Nature of change					
Loss	67	48	3.02	1	ns
Affective state	31	11	5.20	1	$<.05$
Physiological and behavioral	71	40	8.60	1	$<.01$
School	24	4	6.83	1	$<.01$
CHILD'S CAPACITY TO COPE WITH CHANGE					
Challenge inherent in change			7.44	2	$<.05$
Low level	52	78			
Moderate level	38	22			
High level	10	0			
Impact of change on child's functioning			3.70	2	ns
Minimal	14	10			
Moderate	19	5			
Severe	14	0			
Unknown†	53	85			
PSYCHOLOGICAL AND SOCIAL ORGANIZATION OF CHILD AND FAMILY					
Child's relationship to parents			4.25	2	ns
Poor	21	9			
Fair	41	26			
Good	21	39			
Unknown†	17	26			
Mothers' roles as mothers			8.50	2	$<.02$
Poor	29	9			
Fair	34	24			
Good	34	62			
Unknown†	3	4			
Family cohesiveness			8.08	2	$<.02$
Uncohesive	17	7			
Some	25	16			
Cohesive	38	75			
Unknown†	20	2			

*Except in *Time of change, Challenge inherent in change,* and *Impact of change on child's functioning,* where n = 38.
†Not included in chi-square computation.

Psychosocial Setting

Total Number of Changes. For an index of stability during the six months under investigation, we totaled the number of changes in all categories used to define the psychosocial setting. Each ill child experienced at least one change, while 84 percent of the comparison group also experienced at least one change. Overall, the ill group experienced a greater number of changes than the well group. The number of changes for the ill group ranged from 1 to 7, with a median of 3.5. The number of changes for the well group ranged from 0 to 7, with a median of 1.5. The difference was statistically significant (Table 1).

Time of Change. We assumed that the closer in time the change in the setting was to the onset of the disease process, the more certain we could be of its direct relevance. We contrasted the time between the most recent change and the onset of disease in the study group with the most recently reported change and the time of the initial interview of the comparison group. For the entire six-month period, the intervals were smaller for the ill group at a statistically significant level (Table 1). In both groups, however, for the majority of children experiencing change in the setting, the most recent change had occurred within the previous month. Immediate recency, therefore, would not appear to be a crucial differentiating variable.

Nature of Change. Since the majority of well children also experienced change, we concluded that the existence of change is important but not sufficient in differentiating the two groups. This led us to examine the character of the change.

a. *Loss.* The issue of loss had received special attention in psychiatric studies and did differentiate our two groups. Actual or threatened loss was experienced by 67 percent of the ill children and by 46 percent of the well children. This difference was not statistically significant (Table 1).

We also characterized loss with respect to time. The categories included loss that was: (1) permanent (death); (2) temporary (a reunion expected in the near future); (3) impending (a planned vacation); and (4) "anniversary" (of a permanent loss). In these areas there was no significant difference between the two groups.

b. *Other changes.* With respect to other aspects of the psychosocial setting, the ill group experienced significantly greater change in the affective state and the physiological and behavioral aspects in the life of the family members. There was also greater change in the child's school situation (Table 1). However, changes in neighborhood social structure and socioeconomic status did not differentiate the two groups.

Since changes in different aspects of the psychosocial setting differentiated the two groups, one cannot consider any specific type of change, such as loss, by itself to be more crucial or important than any other.

Child's Capacity to Cope with Change

The findings indicated greater instability in the psychosocial setting of the ill child. The capacity of the ill child to cope with this instability was examined by assessing the challenge inherent in the changes in his life during the period under study and the effect they had on his functioning.

Challenge Inherent in Change. The adaptation of the growing child is related to his ability to master changes occurring in his life. The challenge inherent in the various changes is related to his psychosocial level of development. We characterized each change in terms of its potential stress for the average latency-aged child, and for purposes of analysis, we utilized only the change rated as most threatening for each child. A five-point rating scale was used. The extremes and midpoint of the scale were defined as follows: (1) *mild*, consisting of events seen as minimally threatening to most latency-aged children, such as going to summer camp or minor illnesses of family member; (3) *moderate*, consisting of events such as serious illness of family member, depression of mother, or departure of close friend; and (5) *severe*, consisting of events experienced as an intense threat, such as death of a parent or permanent placement of the child outside of his home.

Almost half of the ill group of children experienced moderate to severely threatening changes in their psychosocial settings. None of the well group experienced severely threatening changes, and less than 25 percent experienced moderately threatening changes. This difference was statistically significant (Table 1).

Impact of Change on Child's Functioning. Although the challenge inherent in change had differentiated the two groups, we were still interested in the actual effect it had on the child's life. As an index of the impact of change, we examined the child's functioning, subsequent to the change, in four areas considered to be critical for latency-aged children: (1) the relationship with parents; (2) the relationship with peers; (3) performance in school; and (4) the range of activities and interests. A five-point rating scale was used and three points were defined: (1) *minimal*, no appreciable change in any of the four areas; (3) *moderate*, a definite, notable change in any of the four areas; and (5) *severe*, change in two or more areas.

The impact of the changes for the majority of the ill children was in the moderate to severe range. The response of the majority of well children who experienced change was in the minimal range. None of the well children experienced severe impact and only 5 percent experienced a moderate impact. However, the lack of information for large numbers of children makes it difficult to draw definitive conclusions (Table 1).

*Psychological and Social Organization of the Child
and the Family*

Child. The child's psychological organization is one indication of his capacity to manage the events in his life. The ill children tended to function less adequately with their parents than did the well children, but the difference was not significant. (Table 1.) In the areas of relationship with peers, functioning at school, and range of activities and interests, there was no statistical difference between the two groups.

Family. In order to examine family organization, we assessed (1) parental functioning in terms of their major roles and (2) family cohesiveness. The parents of the ill children seemed to function less adequately than the parents of the well children. However, only in the mothering role were the data sufficient for drawing statistical conclusions. The mothers of the ill children functioned significantly less adequately (Table 1).

The Glueck Scale of Family Cohesiveness was utilized to examine the six-month period under investigation. The families of the ill children were less cohesive in their social organization than the families of the well children. The difference was statistically significant (Table 1).

SUMMARY AND CONCLUSIONS

In an exploratory study, the role of psychological and social factors in the setting of "somatic" disease onset in children was examined. This interest evolved from clinical experience with children whose illness developed during a period of flux in their lives. Guiding the research was the hypothesis that, given the necessary biological conditions, the onset of somatic illness is related to the child's ability to cope with changes in his psychological and social environment. A review of the literature indicated that attention had been given to the impact, meaning, and significance of illness for the child and his family, but little to the psychological and social factors involved in the onset of disease. Although theoretical conceptions of "child's ability to cope," "his psychological and social environment," and "disease process" were available, the lack of systematic methods for gathering and evaluating data to describe these variables led to the undertaking of this study.

Clinically-oriented interviews with 42 hospitalized children and their families were used to gather data for elaboration of the status of psychological and social factors during the six-month period preceding the onset of their illnesses. Variables in the psychological and social setting theoretically and empirically relevant to latency-aged children were examined. We applied the same methods to a comparable group of 45 well children. Rating scales were developed for processing the data.

The quantity, specific character, and the potential challenge of the changes in the psychological and social setting significantly differentiated the ill from the well group. Also, there was a strong indication that the impact of the changes was more intense for the ill child. For the ill children the majority of changes occurred within one month of the first observable signs and/or symptoms of illness. As for the specific character of change, loss did differentiate the groups; however, other events, such as change in affect also differentiated the ill from the well children. Change in the physical environment has been implicated in the occurrence of contagious diseases. However, in our study, less than 15 percent of the children had diseases which could be considered contagious, and in only one family did another member have the same illness. Further, moving to a new neighborhood occurred in only 17 percent of the ill cases and did not differentiate the two groups. The child's ability to cope with these changes was assessed. The ill children tended to relate more poorly with their parents. The families of the ill children were less cohesive than those of the well children, and their mothers functioned less adequately in their mothering roles.

Our study was conceptualized in the context of a multicausational theory of disease. In reviewing our findings, we became aware of how little specific consideration we had been giving to biological factors, except for the existence of the illness. We realized how difficult it is to think about a situation in multicausational terms with a specific representation of all relevant variables. This led us to describe a specific model (Figure 1) in order to consider fully the meaning of our findings and their implications.

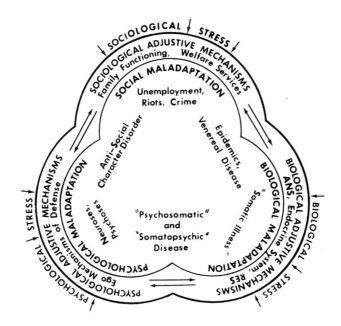

Fig. 1. Model for multicausational concept of disease.

We identified, first, three classes of variables—biological, psychological, and sociological; second, three components of each variable—stress, adjustive mechanisms, and inadequate resolutions. Professional workers have usually thought about one variable at a time: for example, interaction of biological stress and a faulty biological mechanism of the organism, leading to a somatic illness. In describing interactions between all variables, researchers have mainly focused on one kind of inadequate resolution—that is, psychological disease. For example, they have studied the role of biological, psychological, and social factors in schizophrenia.

Others have focused on the interaction between two variables, as in "psychosomatic" disease. In our own thinking, all factors have to be considered in all the inadequate resolutions.

Using our descriptive model, we can examine our own findings. We see that the families with the ill children were more poorly organized in their psychological and social functioning; they exposed their children to a wider range of more threatening social changes, thereby producing a greater psychological stress, for which the children were less prepared. Also clear are those factors on which we have limited information. The nature of the biological stress or the biological adjustive capacity of the child was not systematically scrutinized. Although we had some information on their psychological and social adjustive capacities, these were not more specifically delineated.

Despite the methodological limitations of this exploratory study, our findings indicate the importance of psychological and social factors in the onset of "somatic" illness.

Nonlexical Speech Similarities as an Index of Intrafamilial Identifications[*]

Joseph Becker and Judy McArdle

This study investigated the assumption that the social adjustment of children is related to their identification with parents who have acquired partial identifications with each other. Schematically, it is assumed that during the normal socialization process the child comes to identify with the sex-specific personality attributes of the same-sexed parent, and with the non-sex-specific attributes of both parents. The greater the non-sex-specific congruence between the parents, the more consistent the behavioral-cognitive models internalized by the child. Recent clinical and research investigations of families with severely disturbed offspring suggest a strong positive relation between highly discrepant and/or conflictual parental identification models and children's difficulty in synthesizing viable self-identitites (e.g., Erikson, 1950; Farina, 1960; Lerner, 1965; Lidz, 1963; Spiegel, 1957; Wynne, 1961).

Though folklore has taken considerable note of temporally increased personality similarities in marital partners, identification theory and research have largely ignored the phenomenon (Ackerman, 1958; Flugel, 1948; Tharp, 1963). Conditions that are reputed to facilitate identification, such as positive reinforcement for perceived similarity, vicarious identification with an admired model (Kagan, 1958), and parental control of desired reinforcers for each other and the child (Bandura, 1962), appear to be abundantly present in favorable marriages.

Most studies of intrafamilial identification have used verbal self-reports of "real" or "assumed" similarity between family members as indexes of strength of identification. The validity of these measures has been seriously questioned on several grounds, especially their susceptibility to such response biases as social favorability (Bronfenbrenner, 1958; Kagan, 1964). Very little research on identification has focused upon objectively assessed, overt, behavioral similarities within families (Hetherington, 1965). In the present study, expressive features, more particularly, non-lexical speech similarities among family members, were

[*]Abridged from *Journal of Abnormal Psychology*, 1967, 72, 408–414, with permission of the senior author and the American Psychological Association.

used as an operational index of at least the imitative aspects of identification. Justification for using expressive features as an index of identification is afforded by Parsons, Bales, and Shils's (1953) modification and explicit extension of Freud's identification concepts. Since speech is doubtless a prime medium through which identification occurs (Schreiber, 1960), speech similarities were selected as a potentially fruitful way to test the assumptions regarding intrafamilial identification and child adjustment. Nonlexical speech characteristics such as pauses and action length do not seem to be patterned by sex-specific cultural stereotypes, and they appear to be so automatized as to operate largely outside of focal awareness. Such behaviors should be ideally suited to avoiding favorability-type response biases. In addition, significant personality attributes have been associated with nonlexical speech qualities (e.g., Chapple, 1940; Goldman-Eisler, 1958; Mahl, 1959; Matarazzo, Matarazzo, Saslow, and Phillips, 1958).

In the present study, it was predicted that the nonlexical speech attributes of spouses and children in adjusted families would be more similar than those of spouses and children in poorly adjusted families. It was further predicted that in adjusted families the son's nonlexical speech would be more like his father's than like his mother's, whereas, in the poorly adjusted families this relation would not obtain. Assignment of families to the adjusted or poorly adjusted group was determined by whether their children had been referred to a psychological clinic for treatment.

These predictions regarding intrafamilial similarities were based on several suppositions. It was assumed that disturbed children are more likely to come from homes where poor marital relations prevail (Hoffman & Lippitt, 1960), and that poor marital relations tend to impede shared identifications between the spouses. The second prediction regarding similarities of sons to fathers was based on the probability that non-sex-specific identifications are only partially non-sex-specific. That is, the effects of strong identification with fathers' sex-specific characteristics would be very likely to generalize toward stronger identification with fathers' non-sex-specific characteristics as well. While this effect should also influence the poorly adjusted boys, previous findings indicate that maternal approval of the spouse is a critical determinant of the son modeling on the father (Helper, 1955). Such approval would be less likely present in a conflictual marital relation.

METHOD

Subjects. The family members who were designated as a family in this study consisted of a male child aged 6–12 years and both of his natural parents. All families had at least two children. Family members were Caucasian, non-retarded, without major physical impairment, and socioeconomically within Hollingshead's (1957) middle-class range (Groups II–IV).

Since differences in speech similarities between the clinic and non-clinic groups could be artifacts of differential residential histories, data on residential background and mobility were obtained. There were no significant differences between the groups. An overwhelming majority of parents in both groups were born and reared in the Midwest outside of major metropolitan areas. Parents of clinic children had moved somewhat more frequently, but not significantly so. While no ethnic data on the samples were sought, the surnames of both groups appear to proportionately represent the regional population's predominantly British and Germanic origins.

Clinic families consisted of consecutive male-child referrals to the University of Illinois Psychological Clinic whose families met the subject criteria. None of the children was psychotic. Typical presenting problems were thumb-sucking, daydreaming, listlessness, learning difficulties, rebelliousness, and aggressiveness. It was originally intended to subgroup the clinical cases into acting-out "behavioral" disturbances, and anxious withdrawn "personality" disorders, but this was not feasible. Both objective behavior ratings and the investigators' subjective clinical impressions of the case material indicated that most of the clinical cases were mixtures of "behavioral" and "personality" disturbances.

Non-clinic control families were obtained by writing a standard letter to a random sample of families containing school-enrolled male children of appropriate age. These control families were paid ten dollars to take part. About 25 percent of the prospective controls written to did participate. To insure that reasonably well-adjusted children were included in the non-clinic sample, school social workers were asked to screen the names of the control children for any thought to have serious enough adjustment difficulties to warrant clinic referral. Three families were eliminated from the original non-clinic sample on this basis.

Support for the assumption that the clinic families were more disturbed was afforded by their ratings of their sons on a factor-analytically derived objective Behavior Rating Scale (Becker & Krug, 1964). On this rating scale, both clinic mothers and fathers rated their sons as more withdrawn, distrusting, hostile, demanding, and unstable than the non-clinic parents at highly significant statistical levels. Furthermore, most of the clinic children were referred to the Psychological Clinic by the two local school systems. Since these systems have excellent social work staffs, only more severely disturbed children or those with unusually recalcitrant parents are generally referred to outside agencies.

The 19 clinic families for whom clearly audible tape recordings were available were group matched with 19 non-clinic families on the concomitant variables of age, socioeconomic status, and estimated IQ's of fathers, mothers, and sons. Descriptive data on the ages, socioeconomic status, and estimated verbal intelligence of the clinic and non-clinic families are presented in Table 1. Non-clinic fathers were somewhat older

TABLE 1

COMPARISONS OF THE AGE, SOCIOECONOMIC LEVEL, AND WAIS-WISC
VOCABULARY SCORES OF CLINIC AND NON-CLINIC
PARENTS AND THEIR SONS

MEASURE	CLINIC FAMILIES ($N = 18$)						NON-CLINIC FAMILIES ($N = 19$)					
	Fathers		Mothers		Sons		Fathers		Mothers		Sons	
	M	SD	M	SD	M	SD	M	SD	M	SD	M	SD
Age	35.27	3.36	34.22	3.99	9.25	1.52	39.16	7.07	35.79	4.95	8.75	1.03
Socioeconomic level	41.67	19.16	—	—	—	—	37.47	15.66	—	—	—	—
Weighted vocabulary score	11.39	2.68	11.06	3.49	11.14	2.17	12.53	3.01	12.21	2.23	11.95	3.34

than clinic fathers ($p < .05$), but paternal age was not significantly related to the dependent variables investigated. Neither mothers' nor sons' ages differed significantly between the two groups. Both groups of families averaged within Hollingshead's Social Class Level III, as indexed by fathers' educational and occupational attainments. An intelligence estimate based on vocabulary level placed group averages within the bright-normal to superior range; there were no significant differences.

Intercorrelations between the concomitant and dependent variables for all parents and all children separately are shown in Table 2. The intercorrelations in Table 2 are unremarkable for the most part. Pause frequency is negatively related to average action length and median pause length, as would be expected. Examination of the intercorrelations separately for the clinic and non-clinic samples and for the mothers and fathers yielded no significant departures from those of Table 2.

TABLE 2

PRODUCT-MOMENT INTERCORRELATIONS BETWEEN THE CONCOMITANT AND DEPENDENT VARIABLES FOR THE COMBINED PARENT SAMPLES (BELOW THE DIAGONAL) AND THE COMBINED CHILD SAMPLES (ABOVE THE DIAGONAL)

MEASURES	CHILDREN ($N = 37$)						
	1	2	3	4	5	6	7
PARENTS ($N = 74$)							
1. Age		.94**	−.11	.26	.15	−.01	−.12
2. Education	.09		−.00	.22	.09	.10	−.01
3. Estimated Verbal IQ	.02	.71**		−.49**	.22	−.04	.02
4. Socioeconomic status	−.02	−.83**	−.72**		−.22	−.11	.13
5. Pause frequence	−.07	.13	.29*	−.19		−.29	−.39*
6. Average action length	−.05	.11	.03	.10	−.53**		.04
7. Median pause length	.00	−.15	−.20	.19	−.49**	−.05	

$*p < .05$, with two-tailed tests.
$**p < .01$, with two-tailed tests.

Source and Analysis of Speech Samples. Research sessions were conducted at the Psychological Clinic of the University of Illinois. Free speech samples were obtained within the context of a larger study that sought primarily to determine whether distinguishable conflict and dominance patterns characterized clinic families with children referred for treatment of a personality or conduct disturbance. Each participant in the study was asked in private to speak extemporaneously for five minutes on any aspect of family life. These speech samples were tape-recorded on an Ampex recorder (Model 1260, Electrophone 630 microphones).

In order to obtain a more stabilized speech segment, analysis of the tapes was confined to the middle three-minute phase. The test-retest reliability of action and pausal speech phenomena has been studied over varying lengths of time. Saslow and Matarazzo (1959), in summarizing this literature, reported r's on the order of .90 for action duration and .77 for pause duration. An industrial timer, "Stop Clock" (Model SC-100, 100 volts, 60 cycles, 15 watts), scaled in hundredths of a second, was attached to the tape recorder and each tape analyzed for average action length, frequency of pauses, and median pause length. An action length was defined as a continuous segment of speech; a pause, as a speech hesitation. Because of marked variation in speech styles, action terminations were subjectively determined rather than arbitrarily defined by a specific time interval. The advantages of using human judgment rather than an automatic recording device have been discussed extensively (Matarazzo, Hess, & Saslow, 1962; Matarazzo, Saslow, & Matarazzo, 1956). Median, rather than average, pause length was used to modify the effect of an occasional prolonged loss for words in a child. Despite the subjectivity of the judgment, independent inter-rater reliability for the three speech measures averaged .91. This level of inter-rater reliability accords fairly well with that reported by Phillips, Matarazzo, Matarazzo, and Saslow, 1957 for more highly trained observers. Their trained observers with more refined equipment had inter-rater reliabilities of .99 for action durations and .98 for pausal duration.

RESULTS

To test the assumption that the nonlexical speech measures are not sex-specific, one-way analyses of variance were done on each of the three measures. The means and standard deviations are presented in Table 3. None of the F's for the analyses of variance reached the .05 level of significance. Although these analyses support the assumption that the nonlexical measures are non-sex-specific, the large heterogeneity of variance on the first and third measures should be noted. Contrary to anticipation, the variances of the clinical group tended to be smaller than those of the non-clinic group.

TABLE 3

MEANS AND STANDARD DEVIATIONS FOR AVERAGE ACTION LENGTHS, FREQUENCY OF PAUSES, AND MEDIAN PAUSE LENGTHS OF CLINIC AND NON-CLINIC PARENTS AND SONS PER 3 MINUTES OF FREE SPEECH

SPEECH INDEX	CLINIC FAMILIES (N = 18)			NON-CLINIC FAMILIES (N = 19)		
	Fathers	Mothers	Sons	Fathers	Mothers	Sons
Average action lengths (sec.)						
M	3.30	3.73	3.96	5.00	5.81	4.97
SD	0.99	1.52	2.09	4.37	3.92	2.88
Number pauses						
M	25.00	22.83	18.72	23.89	21.00	19.37
SD	7.46	8.68	8.73	9.83	7.16	8.69
Median pause length (sec.)						
M	2.22	3.01	2.51	2.83	2.19	3.28
SD	0.80	2.88	1.52	2.05	0.59	2.13

Product-moment correlations between family members of the clinic and non-clinic groups for each of the nonlexical speech measures are presented in Table 4.

Hypothesis I

The first prediction, that the nonlexical speech of non-clinic family members would be more similar to each other than that of clinic family members to each other, was supported by the intrafamiliar correlations on two of the three measures.

TABLE 4

PRODUCT-MOMENT CORRELATIONS BETWEEN CLINIC AND NON-CLINIC PARENTS
AND SONS FOR AVERAGE ACTION LENGTH, FREQUENCY OF PAUSES,
AND MEDIAN PAUSE LENGTH

NON-LEXICAL SPEECH MEASURE	COMPARISON	CLINIC FAMILIES ($N = 18$) r	NON-CLINIC FAMILIES ($N = 19$) r
Average action length	Son vs. Father	.11	.63**
	Son vs. Mother	.18	.75**
	Father vs. Mother	.23	.77**
Frequency of pauses	Son vs. Father	.17	.62**
	Son vs. Mother	.33	.42
	Father vs. Mother	.27	.55*
Median pause length	Son vs. Father	−.06	.16
	Son vs. Mother	.23	−.16
	Father vs. Mother	.01	.30

*$p < .05$, two-tailed.
**$p < .01$, two-tailed.

Average Action Length. None of the intrafamilial correlations for the clinic families approached statistical significance, whereas all three intrafamilial correlations of the non-clinic families were significantly different from zero. Furthermore, all intrafamilial correlations for the non-clinic families at least approached being significantly higher than the corresponding ones of the clinic families. Probability levels for the differences between the clinic and non-clinic groups on corresponding correlations were: son versus father, $p < .07$; son versus mother, $p < .05$; and father versus mother, $p < .05$.

Frequency of Pauses. None of the intrafamilial correlations for the clinic families was significant. While intrafamilial correlations for the non-clinic families were less strong than for average action length, they again tended to be significantly greater than chance. The non-clinic son-mother relation approached, but did not reach, an acceptable level of significance ($p < .10$). Differences between the corresponding clinic and non-clinic correlations were not significant.

Median Pause Length. The data for this measure provided no support for the hypothesis of greater similarity between non-clinic family members than between clinic family members. None of the correlations departed from chance.

Correction of Correlations for Curtailment of Heterogeneity. Interpretation of the corresponding correlations for the clinic and non-clinic families is handicapped somewhat by the heterogeneity of corresponding variances for the clinic and non-clinic groups. Tests of the variances of corresponding measures for corresponding family members within the clinic and control groups yielded four highly significant differences ($F < .01$) as shown in Table 5. For three of these four differences the clinic family members had less heterogeneity.

TABLE 5

F COMPARISONS OF VARIANCES ON SPEECH MEASURES BY CORRESPONDING
FAMILY MEMBERS IN THE CLINIC AND NON-CLINIC GROUPS

SPEECH INDEX	NON-CLINIC FATHERS vs. CLINIC FATHERS	NON-CLINIC MOTHERS vs. CLINIC MOTHERS	NON-CLINIC CHILDREN vs. CLINIC CHILDREN
Average action length	19.49*	6.65*	1.90
Number pauses	1.73	1.47	1.01
Median pause length	6.56*	23.83*	1.97

Note—df = 18 non-clinic family members, 17 clinic family members. Larger variance always used
   in numerator for F test.
*$p < .01$.

Using McNemar's (1962, pp. 144–145) correction procedure for curtailed heterogeneity, three re-analyses were performed to obtain R's for comparison with the
uncorrected r's. For average action length, the R, between clinic fathers and clinic sons
using the non-clinic fathers' standard deviation instead of the clinic fathers' resulted in
an increased correlation of .27, which was again not significant. The R for clinic
mothers and clinic sons using the non-clinic mothers' standard deviation increased the
correlation to .42 ($.05 < p < .10$). According to McNemar, correlations for double
curtailment are unsatisfactory, hence no R was computed for clinic mothers' and
fathers' average action length.

No R's were computed for the frequency-of-pause data, since the variances of the
two groups did not differ.

For median pause length, R's produced trivial increases in the correlations between
clinic father-sons (to .15) and between clinic father-mothers (to .03). Since clinic
mothers' variance was greater on this variable than the non-clinic mothers', no R was
computed for clinic mother-sons.

In summary, corrections for curtailment of heterogeneity slightly attenuated the
support for greater similarity in non-clinic families. However, several cautions are
warranted. Whether these data meet the linearity and homoscedasticity assumptions
for R could not be adequately determined because of the limited N. Also, the dearth
of normative data on the variances of the dependent variables necessitated using the
controls' variances, which may not be valid population estimates.

Hypothesis II

The prediction that non-clinic male children would tend to resemble
their fathers more strongly than would the clinic children received minimal support. On two of the three measures, the non-clinic children
resemble their fathers more strongly than their mothers, whereas for the
clinic children the reverse finding occurred. The strength of these trends
was too slight to regard them as evidence for the hypothesis.

DISCUSSION

The results were moderately consistent with the prediction of greater
nonlexical speech similarity within non-clinic families than within clinic

families. Further empirical investigation and theoretical speculation about the import of these trends appear warranted.

Lack of a meaningful pattern of correlations for median pause length may be due to children occasionally finding themselves at a loss for words. Using median rather than average pause length, only partially mitigated this effect.

The data of this study provide more direct support for the assumption that parental non-sex-specific similarities to each other are positively related to parent-child similarities and to child adjustment than for the assumption that favorable marriages foster shared parental identities. Longitudinal or cross-sectional studies relating duration and favorability of marriage outcome to temporally increased speech similarities between the spouses would afford stronger evidence for the latter assumption.

Furthermore, the discriminative utility of nonlexical familial speech similarities may be restricted to the relatively gross identification of families with schismatic versus integrated parental relations. These similarities may be less useful for more refined subdivisions such as distinguishing among integrated families that are either fused or skewed, one-spouse-dominated families, as contrasted with healthily integrated, more equalitarian ones (Lidz, Cornelison, Fleck, & Terry, 1957). That is, unsatisfactory stable families (Jackson, 1959) may well generate intrafamilial behavioral similarities on the basis of sheer repeated perceptual registration of patterns (Epstein, 1962), regardless of their reward characteristics.

It is interesting to speculate on the parental relationships which might account for high speech similarity with only one parent. It may be conjectured that the speech of very young male children, or of male inverts, would be more likely to resemble their mothers. Mowrer (1950) reports that certain talking birds are much more easily trainable by females than by males, presumably because their voices are easier to imitate. The greater exposure of the young male to his mother plus the higher pitch of the female voice would probably make it the more imitable model. Male children with a very strong defensive identification with the father as the "aggressor" would quite conceivably resemble their fathers much more strongly than their mothers.

In sum, intrafamilial speech resemblances seem to present a complex but promising avenue for investigating family integration and identification processes.

Conflict in Families of Schizophrenics as a Function of Premorbid Adjustment and Social Class*

James C. Baxter and Sonya C. Arthur

* * * The present investigation was aimed at studying patterns of interpersonal conflict in the parents of good and poor premorbid patients with the variables of social class and the family from which the patient was hospitalized controlled.

METHOD

The families used in the present study were selected from a larger sample of families identified for other purposes at John Umstead Hospital, a large state psychiatric facility in North Carolina. Sixteen sets of biological parents comprising intact families of recently admitted male schizophrenic patients between the ages of 20 and 45 years were used in the present study. In all cases, the patient had been hospitalized while living in the home of the parents. In addition, both parents had participated in an extensive evaluation program which included a joint interview conducted by psychiatrically trained social workers according to a standardized procedure.

Four balanced groups of parents were obtained by rating the premorbid personality adequacy of the patient and the socioeconomic class of the family. Premorbid ratings were made from the patients' social histories according to the Phillips (1953) Scale of Premorbid Adjustment. This scale differentiates patients along a 31-point continuum of social and sexual adjustment attained prior to the onset of the illness. Higher scores on this scale reflect greater social and sexual isolation in prepsychotic personality adjustment. Parents of the patients were then dichotomized into groups of *Goods* (scores 6–15) and *Poors* (scores 16–26.5) on the basis of their son's score. These groups were then further dichotomized into middle and lower social classes by rating the education and occupa-

---

*Abridged from *Family Process*, 1964, *3*, 273–279, with permission of the senior author and *Family Process*.

tion of the fathers. Hollingshead's (1957) two-factor index of social position was employed to distribute families along a continuum ranging from 11 to 77, with higher values reflecting lower social-class standing. Scores were found to range from 29 (Class III) to 70 (Class V) for the entire sample, and a mean difference of 6.94 for these scores between families of *Goods* and *Poors* was found to be non-significant ($t = 1.17$; $p < .10$). The ages of the parents were found to vary between 40 and 70 years, with means for the four parent groups well within chance variation (F's < 1.00). The age difference between the mothers and fathers was found to be significant ($F = 7.23$; $df = 1/12$; $p < .025$), as one would expect. The absolute size of the difference was not associated with social class ($r = .25$; $df = 14$; $p < .10$) or premorbid level ($r = .15$; $df = 14$; $p < .10$), and therefore was not considered a biasing factor.[1]

As part of a larger psychiatric evaluation, all parents had participated in an extensive joint interview which focused on historical material and which required both parents to participate in contributing information and impressions about family activities and the personality development of the patient. The material was obtained by a structured interview schedule which encouraged the parents to express themselves as freely as possible while covering prescribed content areas. The data were transcribed by the social worker who conducted the interview, as soon after the session as possible. A number of ratings were also included in the recording form to provide the social worker with an opportunity to describe various aspects of the relationship between the parents during the interview.

A rating schedule was devised for the present study which permitted quantitative evaluation of the amount of conflict observed between the parents during the interview. For purposes of these ratings, conflict was defined as "the extent to which the mother and father disagree; express opposing ideas, attitudes, values, or the like; or express disapproval or disparagement of the other's attitudes or behaviors." Thirteen specific content and behavior items from the interview were chosen for study because they were thought to be relatively productive of this type of interpersonal behavior. Care was also taken to select items which bore a general correspondence to the types of behaviors which had been used earlier by Farina (1960) in direct observations of parental interactions. Ratings were made on four-point scales reflecting the severity of the conflict present in each of the 13 topic and behavior areas. Ratings were made in all areas where sufficient information was present to rate the parental behavior with "reasonable assurance and upon rather direct inference." An indeterminate category was also provided for noting topic and behavior areas where data were insufficient for rating. Ratings were averaged over the 13 areas, providing a conflict index for each family.

---

[1] A surprising result was found, however, when absolute age differences were correlated with family conflict scores (described below). A product-moment correlation of .59 ($p < .02$) was obtained between the amount of conflict expressed by the parents and their absolute age difference.

All ratings were made by one psychologist who had had experience with similar interviews on a large number of families. A second equally experienced rater also scored eight randomly chosen interviews included in the sample, in order to evaluate inter-rater reliability. The percentage of ratings on which there was complete agreement between raters was found to range from 77 percent to 100 percent for the eight interviews, with an average agreement of 91 percent.

RESULTS AND DISCUSSION

Conflict scores for each of the parent sets were entered in a 2 x 2 analysis of variance table with the dimensions defined by Good or Poor premorbid adjustment of the patient and by middle or lower social class of the family. A summary of the analysis is provided in Table 1.

TABLE 1

ANALYSIS OF THE VARIANCE OF CONFLICT SCORES IN THE
PARENTS OF SCHIZOPHRENICS

SOURCE	df	MS	F	p
Premorbid level	1	.003	<1.00	ns
Social class	1	.018	<1.00	ns
Premorb. x soc. cl.	1	.551	6.19	$<.05$
Error	12	.089		

It can be seen that the F ratios for premorbid level and social class are both non-significant. The interaction of these variables is significant, however, producing an F ratio of 6.19 ($p < .05$). .... It can be seen that inter-parental conflict is highest in cells defined by good premorbid adjustment and middle-class status, and by poor premorbid adjustment and lower-class standing. It is interesting to note that the greatest amount of parental conflict occurs in families in which the patient's premorbid behavior has been incongruous with the subcultural norms; that is, middle-class families with socially responsive and heterosexually active sons and lower-class families with socially retiring and sexually inactive sons.

An interesting implication of these data is apparent when they are compared with the results of Farina's (1960) study. He found parents of *Poors* to be significantly more conflict-ridden than parents of *Goods* in three of his ten comparisons. In all ten comparisons, however, the direction of the difference was such that parents of *Poors* showed more conflict than parents of *Goods*. From these data he concluded that the *Poors* had been exposed to more conflict in their families than had *Goods*. The results of the present study do not support such a conclusion, apart from restrictions specifying the social class of the families.

Farina (1960) reported that his "total sample might best be described as lower middle class, and the groups appear comparable in this respect." Elsewhere in the paper, however, he reports a mean difference of 2.3 years in educational level favoring the fathers of *Poors* over *Goods*, despite the fact that the fathers of *Poors* averaged 4.7 years older than fathers of *Goods*. (In the general population, age has a negative relationship to education.) While the difference in education alone was not significant ($t = 1.54$; $p < .14$), it is suggestive of a difference in social class and raises the possibility that Farina may have inadvertently sampled from sources corresponding primarily to three of the cells represented in Table 2; i.e., sources of middle- and lower-class *Poors* and lower-class *Goods*. If this were the case, trends evident in the present study are in agreement with Farina's (1960) data. In the present sample, a comparison of families of middle- and lower-class *Poors* with those of lower-class *Goods* yielded a t of 1.63, significant at the .14 level of confidence by two-tailed test. The inclusion of families of middle-class *Goods* in this study apparently vitiated the simple effect found by Farina, however.

The present data suggest that parental conflict may not be a simple effect of premorbid level of the affected child, as Farina found, but rather varies with both premorbid level and family social position. The social-class standing of the family would seem to need careful control in future studies in family transaction patterns. * * *

Studies of Family Interaction: Decision-Making

Although we are committed to a research approach based on actual interactions among family members, we would be the first to admit that such research is exceedingly difficult to carry out successfully. In addition to the many problems of design and method pointed out in Section I, the potential researcher in this field will find a host of practical problems to beset him. Some of these have been discussed by Haley (1962) and Lennard, Braulien, and Embrey (1965). For example, it is often difficult to obtain subject families and to find a time when all members are free to be tested. Sometimes it is difficult to decide who comprises the family unit and whether children from previous marriages, aunts temporarily residing in the home, etc., are members of the family. Problems also arise in deciding how to define an abnormal family—how many members have to be abnormal, and how should abnormality itself be defined in this context? And once defined and diagnosed, what is the possible effect of being labelled normal or abnormal on the behavior of the family? At every step of research, formulating hypotheses, choosing a suitable testing instrument which validly reflects the nuances of stable family patterns, finding a language and set of concepts to describe interaction, interpreting the results in terms of the real-life behavior of the families, etc., new difficulties arise. Not enough research has been done in this area to make available to the investigator an array of pretested solutions to these problems, which would enable him to concentrate his energies on interpreting the meaning of the data he obtains.

The perfect or near-perfect study of family interaction is yet to be published. The articles in this section do not meet the rigid criteria of Rabkin and Fontana, presented in Section I. We can only admire the courage and ability of the authors who tackled new areas with vigor and creativity, and who have made the work easier for their successors. Such a pioneering work was that of Fred Strodtbeck, whose Revealed Differences Technique (RDT) has inspired much of the research on family decision-making. The importance of this area lies in the fact that in order to study family interactions in a controlled situation, we have to get the family interacting over something; and forcing the family to cope with a joint decision forces them into a somewhat natural tension system, which brings out the family patterns we are interested in observing. In Strodtbeck's RDT, each family member independently marks his alterna-

99

tives on a multiple-choice questionnaire. Then all are asked to agree conjointly on the best alternatives for certain items on which they had disagreed. Strodtbeck's original article (1951) dealt with which spouse won most of these decisions in three different subcultures. In the article reprinted here, Strodtbeck uses this technique to show that families do not behave as we would predict from group dynamics theory based on ad hoc groups, a finding congruent with those of Bodin (Article 12) and Leik (1963).

If Strodtbeck's is the technique of revealed differences, then Ferreira and Winter's can be termed the technique of "unrevealed differences." Their families are asked to complete conjointly in its entirety a new copy of the questionnaire without being limited to items on which disagreements had occurred, and so the family members can easily feign prior agreement if they wish. This technique, first developed by Ferreira (1963a), is here used to test a number of hypotheses dealing with the formal or structural aspects of the decision-making process, as manifested by normal and three groups of abnormal families. Other studies by Ferreira and Winter (1966, 1968) have shown that the variables discussed herein are stable characteristics of families, and that they also operate in two-child families (see Articles 23, 24, and 32). Bodin's paper uses this technique to assess the differences between synthetic and real families, as well as to confirm many of the findings of Article 11.

Ryder and Goodrich are not content with asking family members to resolve their naturally occurring differences. By a technique of deception, they force disagreements on a couple and present them with an insoluble task. They also make use of a factor analysis, which is rare in family work. In attempting to replicate this study with new samples, Ryder (1966) found that only the first three factors described in Article 13 showed stability, and the author discusses several reasons for this discrepancy.

Farina has done some of the key work in the study of family decision-making. By studying tape-recorded conversations among family members who are trying to reach a decision, he has been able to analyze for indicators of conflict and dominance. He has thus taken the analysis of data beyond the level of the final decisions reached to a level closer to the process used by the family in arriving at decisions. In the article reprinted here, Farina and Dunham apply their technique to the families of good and poor premorbid schizophrenics, analyzing the results both in terms of individual member scores and overall family scores (see also Becker & Siefkes, in press, and Cicchetti and co-workers, 1967, 1968).

The brief excerpts by Levy and Epstein, and by Watzlawick illustrate additional interesting techniques for stimulating family decision-making interactions, which are different from the usual questionnaire situations used in most RDT studies (see also Loveland, 1967; Rosenthal, 1968).

The Family as a Three-Person Group*

Fred L. Strodtbeck

The objective of the present paper is to test the appropriateness of certain propositions concerning *ad hoc* three-person groups by the use of father, mother, and adolescent son subject groups. Insofar as our work is carefully done, our results should contribute to the understanding of the extent to which propositions concerning *ad hoc* three-person groups may be extended to family groups, and to a more limited degree, to other groups with prior common experience and expectations of continued relations.

Our procedure for obtaining a sample discussion between a father, mother, and adolescent son was, very briefly as follows. Each family is visited at home. We explain that we are interested in the way a family considers questions which relate to the son's selection of his occupation. To help the family recall specific topics which they may have previously discussed, we ask the father, mother, and son to check independently one of two alternatives to 47 items of the following type:

1. A teen-agers' hobby club plans to enter their models in a state-wide contest. Some of the boys want to put the models up under the club's name and win honor for the club as a whole. Others want to put the models up under each boy's name so that each can gain individual honor. Which plan should they adopt?

2. Two fathers were discussing their boys, one of whom was a brilliant student and the other an athlete of great promise. In general, some people feel one father was more fortunate and some the other. Do you think the father with the *athletic* son or the father with the *studious* son was more fortunate?

3. Some people believe that a father should be prepared to speak to a son as a father and direct the son's behavior so long as the son lives, others believe the son should be accepted as completely independent of his father's direction after 18 or 21. Which would you tend to agree to with regard to a boy in his late 20's?

---

*Abridged from *American Sociological Review*, 1954, *19*, 23–29, with permission of the author and the American Sociological Association.

While our introductory remarks are being made in the home, we request permission to set up our portable tape recorder. After the 47-item questionnaire has been checked, we have the family fill out still another similar questionnaire so that we will have time to sort through their responses. We select three items which represent a potential coalition of the type in which the mother and father have taken one alternative and the son another; three with mother-son paired against the father; and three with father-son paired against the mother. We then present the family successively with these nine disagreements rotating the isolate role. They are asked to talk the question over, understand why each person chose the alternative he did, and if possible, to select one alternative which best represents the thinking of the family as a whole. While this discussion takes place, the experimenter withdraws to another room, operates the controls on the sound equipment, and tries to keep any other member of the family from overhearing or interrupting the interaction. During May and June of 1953 we obtained 48 cases in this manner.

Concerning the selection of the 48 cases, three criteria were considered: ethnicity, the families were predominantly second generation (the son, third), divided equally between Jews and Italians; socioeconmic status (SES), equal numbers of high, medium, and low; and the son's achievement, half of the boys were underachieving in school and half were overachieving, as determined by a comparison of grades and intelligence test performance. By sampling from a frame of more than a thousand 14- to 16-year-old boys in New Haven public and parochial schools, it was possible to work out a factorial design of the following type:

S E S	JEWS		ITALIANS	
	Over-achieving	Under-achieving	Over-achieving	Under-achieving
High	4	4	4	4
Medium	4	4	4	4
Low	4	4	4	4

Total 48

The recordings averaged about forty minutes in length. The interaction analysis consisted of breaking the ongoing discussion into units, or acts; identifying the originator and target of each act; and assigning each act to one of Bales's (1950) twelve categories which are identified in our discussion of the index of supportiveness below.

One primary objective of the present paper is to compare our results with those of Mills (1960), who, working with student volunteers, asked them to create from three pictures a single dramatic story upon which all agreed. The comparison requires that we utilize jointly the information concerning the originator and target of each act, as well as the category in which it is placed to form an index which reflects the tendency of a particular actor, Number 1, to give positive responses to the attempts at problem-solution by another actor, Number 2. The following steps are involved in arriving at the index of supportiveness:

(a) Sum together the acts in the following categories which have been originated by person Number 1 and directed to Number 2:

SHOWS SOLIDARITY, raises other's status, gives help or reward

SHOWS TENSION RELEASE, jokes, laughs, shows satisfaction

AGREES, shows passive acceptance, understands, concurs, complies

(b) Subtract from the above sum the number of acts originated by Number 1 and directed to Number 2 in these categories to form the numerator of the index:

DISAGREES, shows passive rejection or formality, withholds help

SHOWS TENSION, asks for help, withdraws "out of field"

SHOWS ANTAGONISM, deflates other's status, defends or asserts self

(c) Divide the above numerator by the number of acts originated by Number 2 in the following categories:

GIVES SUGGESTION or direction, implying autonomy for other

GIVES OPINION, evaluation or analysis; expresses feeling or wish

GIVES ORIENTATION or information, repeats, clarifies, confirms

ASKS FOR ORIENTATION, information, repetition, confirmation

ASKS FOR OPINION, evaluation, analysis, expression of feeling

ASKS FOR SUGGESTION, direction, possible ways of action

(d) The result, multiplied by 100, is I_{12}, the index of support by Person 1 of Person 2. Between three persons, six index values are produced. To simplify our reference to this set of values we organize it in a matrix, placing the person with the largest number of acts originated in the first row and column and the person with the least number of acts originated in the last row and column. To illustrate this convention see Table 1. To form Table 1 we have taken the median of the corresponding cells for the 48 discussions in each of the six positions. In parenthesis we show the value Mills obtained when he carried out these steps for his 48 groups.

TABLE 1

MEDIAN INDEX OF SUPPORT, FAMILIES COMPARED
WITH *AD HOC* STUDENT GROUPS*

RANK OF INITIATOR	RANK OF RECIPIENT		
	1st	2nd	3rd
1st		−6 (12)	−5 (7)
2nd	−5 (11)		−5 (4)
3rd	3 (4)	−2 (2)	

*Mills' values for *ad hoc* student groups are given in parentheses.

Mills (1953) makes the following observation with regard to Simmel's having anticipated the pattern of support which Mills found (see Von Wiese, 1932):

> The highest rates of support are those exchanged between the two more active members and the rates are very nearly the same. . . . All other distributions of rates are significantly different from these two. This is to say that, as far as exchange of support is concerned, the relationship between these two members is sharply differentiated from the other relationships. The results for this sample confirm Simmel's observation. The two more active members form the pair and the least active member is the relatively isolated third party.

For Mills the 1–2 value is 12 and the 2–1 value is 11, which are higher than the other cell values and similar. In our data the 1–2 value is minus 6 and the 2–1 value is minus 5—these do not differ significantly from the other values. By correlating the sets of medians in particular cells of Table 1, we may compare the relative magnitudes of our values to Mills's without regard for the difference in means. We obtain a *rho* of −.67. Neither the inspection of the corresponding cells of the two most speaking participants nor the correlation over the whole table can be interpreted as a confirmation of Mills's results on *ad hoc* groups. Whether the significantly lower mean level of the index of support can be accounted for by the differences in our tasks or by a lesser emphasis on polite behavior on the part of family groups we, of course, cannot say.

We are indebted to Mills for the following typology for classifying the individual matrixes. He suggests that we look at the index of support, I_{12} and I_{21}. These indexes are then compared with the medians for the I_{12} and I_{21} positions, and the experimenter indicates a plus if the value is above its corresponding median and a minus if it is below; the following results:

I_{12}	I_{21}	Support Types
+	+	Solidary
+	−	Contending
−	+	Dominant
−	−	Conflicting

For our data, $I_{1\,2}$ is minus 6 and $I_{2\,1}$ is minus 5.

Mills finds that when the two high-ranking participants have a solidary relationship, both the intake and output of support for the low man is lower than in any other circumstances. Our data are not in accord with his finding (see Table 2). The lowest value in any row would have been in the solidary (++) column if our data had corresponded to Mills's finding. It may be seen that no one of the four cells involved fulfill this requirement.

TABLE 2

MEDIAN INDEX OF SUPPORT FOR CELLS INVOLVING THE
LOW-RANKING PARTICIPANT

MATRIX CELL	SUPPORT TYPE			
	++ (17)	+− (8)	−+ (7)	− − (16)
1 to 3	−05	12	08	−11
2 to 3	03	−10	−08	−07
3 to 1	03	−02	08	01
3 to 2	00	02	−03	−05

Mills goes further to say:

> Not only is this determined position of the third party as weak as a power position can be (when the relation between the two principals is solidary), but it is likely that the power interests involved in it are inversely related to the interests of the other member. The stronger the coalition, the weaker the position of the third man, and vice versa.

Unfortunately, Mills had no measure of power other than participation. With our data, to form a "power" score, we arbitrarily give two points to each decision. If the isolated person persuades the others he is given two points and they receive none; if he holds them off and no decision is made, he is given one point and the other two get .5 each; if the isolated person is persuaded by the other two, they receive one point each and he receives nothing. Thus, for nine decisions there is a total of 18 points. Under random expectations the mean for each participant would be six.

In our experiment we find that if one attempted to predict power, as measured in this way, from participation he would account for less than three-tenths of the variation, though the correlation is significant in the .5 to .6 range. We therefore have attempted to test Mills's statement by comparing the mean power score computed by the system explained above for the first, second, and third most speaking participant for each of the four support types. It may be seen from Table 3 that the low man does not appear to be conspicuously worse off in the solidary (++) type. There is no significant gap between his power and that of the man in the

TABLE 3

MEAN DECISION-WINNING POWER BY PARTICIPATION
RANK AND SUPPORT TYPE

RANK	SUPPORT TYPE			
	+ + (17)	+ − (8)	− + (7)	− − (16)
1st	8.0*	6.3	8.0	8.3
	. . .		. . .	. . .
2nd	5.2	6.6	5.5	4.9
		. . .	. . .	
3rd	4.8	5.0	4.5	4.8

*The value 8.0 indicates that the most-speaking participants in solidary (++)
groups won on the average 8.0 of the 18 possible points. The dots in the
columns indicate significant gaps.

second position, whereas there is such a gap between the low and middle
man in the contending (+−) and dominant (−+) support types.

In three of the four support types, the most-speaking person wins the
largest share of the decisions and in all cases the least-speaking person wins
least. We have found the means for the rank positions within three of the
support types to be heterogeneous, and the gap between the first and
second most-speaking person significant at the .05 level or less. There is a
reversal of power scores between the first and second rank position in the
contending (+−) pattern.

One of the observations in Mills's article with broad implications for a
theory of group process dealt with the stability of the participation
patterns through time. His measure of stability was a comparison of the
participation rank in the first third of his sessions with the participation
rank in the last third. His conclusions are as follows:

> In summary, there is one pattern where all positions are stable;
> there is another where all positions are unstable; and in the others,
> the strongest position is stable while the others fluctuate. The
> significantly stable pattern is the *solidary* (++) one, which, as we
> have seen, tends to develop into the fully differentiated, inter-
> dependent pattern called the *true coalition*. The significantly
> unstable one is the *conflict* (−−) pattern, which is notable for its
> lack of interdetermination.

From this comment and study of other portions of the text, it is our
guess that Mills would rank the support types: solidary (++), contending
(+−) and dominant (−+) tied, and conflict (−−) lowest regarding their
implication for participation stability. For our data we have the relative
participation for three decisions each with the father, mother, and son as
isolate—a total of nine. To parallel Mills's procedure and stratify the
incidence of the isolate role, we sum the first three decisions and compare

with the sum of the last three decisions. The father, mother, and son are the isolate once in each group. By considering the rank for the first three decisions as the criterion ranking, we can compare the consistency of participation within the four support types by use of Kendall's S (see Table 4). Corresponding values from Mills's study are given in parentheses.

TABLE 4

STABILITY OF RANK BETWEEN FIRST AND THIRD PHASE[*]

	SUPPORT TYPE			
REQUIRED VALUES	+ +	+ −	− +	− −
S	344 (278)	62 (62)	0 (122)	96 (62)
M	17 (15)	8 (9)	7 (11)	16 (13)
S.05	102 (90)	48 (54)	− (66)	90 (78)
P(S)	<.05 (<.05)	<.05 (<.05)	ns (<.05)	<.05 (ns)

[*] Mills' values for *ad hoc* groups given in parentheses.

In this instance, our findings partially correspond to Mills's. Our most stable group is the solidary (++), but our least stable is not the conflicting (−−). The dominant (−+) has less stability than the conflicting, but since there are only seven cases, this apparent reversal of order must remain in doubt.

Mills includes in his paper certain observations on the temporal shifts of support patterns. He finds that the solidary (++) patterns in the first phase tend to persist into the third, whereas other patterns more frequently shift toward solidarity (++) or conflicting (−−). Mills refers to these two latter patterns as *terminal* patterns. Unfortunately, our data were not tabulated so that this comparison could be made at a modest cost. We do note, however, that one might infer from Mills's comments that primary groups with a much longer period in which to stabilize their interaction would tend to be more concentrated in the (++) and (−−) categories. While our distribution of cases is in line with this expectation, the observed differences are not statistically significant:

$$
\begin{array}{ll}
++ & 17 \ (15) \\
+- & 8 \ (\ 9) \\
-+ & 7 \ (11) \\
-- & 16 \ (13)
\end{array}
$$

The subjects we used were related in a particular and pervasive way—they were a family. There was every reason to believe that after the experimental session was over they would pick up their daily relations very much as they had been in the past. Their actions in the experimental session proceeded on a broad basis of common knowledge and their behavior in the experimental situation could very well have consequences in their interpersonal relations at a later time.

The tendency for a three-person group to break into a pair and another party, which was the central theme of Mills's analysis, would seem to run counter to certain expectations we associate with a family. Crudely expressed, parents give succor to children contingent upon the child's conforming to selected rules of behavior. This elemental aspect of the relationship becomes greatly elaborated. One is tempted to believe that by adolescence a son has moved into a position where his censure of parents may be fully as effective a control mechanism as the parents' censure of him. Competition for sexual favors is regulated by incest proscriptions. The action of one family member in the community is not without implications for other members of the family. In short, three family members may, in many important ways, reward one another and accept responsibility for one another's well-being. No member can easily withdraw from the relationship. From considerations of this order, one can form a strong common-sense basis for the expectation that the division of the trio into two and one will be attenuated in families in contrast with *ad hoc* groups, and in this way account for the disparity between our data and the expectations based on Mills's findings relative to the distribution of support.

An alternative explanation for the disparity can be based upon the task we set for our subjects. There were nine specific decisions; each person had three isolated and six coupled coalitions, and the group was instructed to try to achieve consensus. This shifting of coalitions would strike at the stability of relations which might have grown if only one task were involved; hence the task also might have caused the departure from Mills's distribution of support findings which we report in Table 1.

The effects of our using a task different from Mills's are not entirely negative. We were enabled by virtue of our decision-winning measure to test a proposition concerning the relative power of the low man in the solidary (++) group, which had not been tested with equal directness by Mills. It is plausible to believe that the members of the major coalition in a solidary (++) family would not pool their power against the low man to the same degree as would an *ad hoc* group. While the evidence we present is in line with such an expectation, the proposition at issue cannot be firmly established until it has been demonstrated, in accordance with Mills's expectations, that the low-ranking participant in *ad hoc* solidary (++) groups is in fact less powerful than the low-ranking member in groups with other support characteristics.

A point of correspondence between Mills's study and the present, which encourages one to believe that it is fruitful to think in terms of a common process underlying both primary and *ad hoc* group interaction, relates to the stability of the participation ranks. In both studies it is demonstrated that the solidary (++) pattern results in the most stable participation ranks. In this manner support type takes its place along with previously published discussions of the phase hypothesis (Bales & Strodtbeck, 1951), status struggle, and equilibrium problem (Parsons, Bales, & Shils, 1953), as one of a series of more or less cumulative increments in our understanding of factors which influence participation stability.

In conclusion, we have attempted to assess the appropriateness for families of propositions derived from the study of *ad hoc* three-person groups. We do not find in families the regularities in the distribution of support which Mills reported, nor do we confirm the tendency of solidary high-participating members to dominate the decision-making which Mills anticipated would materialize. We do find in families, like many other groups, decision-making power is associated with high participation. We confirm Mills's finding that when the two most active members are solidary in their relation to one another the stability of their rank participation is high, but we do not find that when the two most active members are in conflict, the stability is as low for families as he found it to be for *ad hoc* groups.

Family Interaction
and Decision-Making*

Antonio J. Ferreira and William D. Winter

Part of a larger research project, the study reported in this paper enlarges upon Ferreira's (1963a) previous investigation of family decision-making in normal and abnormal families. It inquiries into the conjoint behavior of the family triad (father, mother, and child) while making a family decision, that is, a decision which supposedly stems from the joint efforts of, and has impact upon, all family members in question.

METHOD

The Families. As referred to in this paper, the families were triads of father, mother, and child, who met the following criteria of acceptance: (1) they had all been living together, as a family, for at least two uninterrupted years; (2) the child in the test was at least 9 1/2 years of age; (3) they were all Caucasians, and at least second-generation Americans; (4) they were all free from any known physical illness or handicap; and (5) they were, as a family, unequivocally suited to meet the criteria for inclusion in one of the "diagnostic" groups under consideration.

Diagnostic Groups. These were defined as follows: The *normal group* (*Nor*) was composed of families of which: (1) there was no known emotional or criminal problem for any of its members for a period of at least five years prior to the testing; (2) no one had received, or been recommended to receive, any form of psychotherapy for at least the past five years; (3) the overall behavior of the family had been considered normal by the referring source. These families were referred through neighbors, friends, friends' friends, friends' friends' friends, etc., as well as from the roster of local schools. Psychiatrically sophisticated families, such as those of psychiatrist, psychologist, social worker, etc., were not accepted. The *abnormal group* (*Abn*) was composed of families where the child had been considered to have some sort of emotional problem as evaluated by an independent professional agent. These families were obtained, on a voluntary basis, through clinics, hospitals, and private

---

*Abridged from *Archives of General Psychiatry*, 1965, *13*, 214–223, with permission of the authors and the American Medical Association.

therapists. Depending on the label given to the child, the *Abn* family was placed in one of three subgroups: (1) *schizophrenia-producing* families (*Sch*), where the child in the test had been diagnosed as "schizophrenic"; (2) *delinquency-producing* families (*Del*), where the child had been involved with the law for delinquent behavior of the aggressive, acting-out type; and (3) *maladjusted* families (*Mal*), where the child, neither schizophrenic nor delinquent, received other labels, such as neurotic, maladjusted, phobic, etc.

A total of 125 families were tested in this project: 50 *Nor* and 75 *Abn*, broken down into 15 *Sch*, 16 *Del*, and 44 *Mal*. The families were tested either in the professional offices of the authors, in San Jose, California, or at the facilities of the Mental Research Institute, in Palo Alto, California. In approximately two-thirds of all families, the child tested was a boy; an exception to this was the *Del* subgroup in which there were 15 boys and 1 girl. The general characteristics of these families (Warner, 1949, scale of occupational level, educational achievement, age of the tested child, age of the parents, number of children per family) are summarized in Table 1. The chi-square analyses showed that, in the characteristics considered, there were no significant differences among diagnostic groups.

TABLE 1

GENERAL CHARACTERISTICS OF THE FAMILIES

VARIABLE	DIAGNOSTIC GROUPS				
	Nor	*Mal*	*Sch*	*Del*	Total
Father's education	15.5	14.5	14.0	14.0	14.6
Father's occupational level	1.4	1.2	1.7	1.6	1.4
Father's age	45.5	43.0	46.5	45.0	45.0
Mother's age	42.5	40.0	42.5	41.5	41.5
Child's age	16.3	14.8	16.5	16.0	16.0
No. children in family	2.9	3.1	2.7	3.3	3.1
Male children tested *	34	28	11	15	88
Female children tested *	16	16	5	1	38

*All variables except these two are expressed in median values.

Testing Procedure. After greetings and preliminary remarks to place everyone at ease, the tester (one of three assigned at random) introduced the family to the immediate task at hand, namely, the filling out of a questionnaire. The family members were told that the questionnaire contained a number of "situations" which, although improbable, they were to pretend were true and real. Accordingly, they were to indicate for every situation (among ten given alternatives) the three choices they liked the most and the three they liked the least, or not at all; the four alternatives in between were to be left blank. Once the tester was satisfied that everyone had understood the task ahead (further elucidated by means of an example), the family members were conducted to separate rooms where, in isolation from each other, they proceeded to fill out the questionnaire. When they had all terminated their individual tasks (which took roughly five to ten minutes), they were brought back together again. Before they had had a chance to talk to each other, they were informed that they had all filled out the same questionnaire and that their individual answers would remain confidential. They were further assured that these answers did not involve the notions of good-bad, right-wrong, or normal-abnormal, but simply reflected the fact that different people may have different likes and dislikes in a given situation. After this, they were told that their next task would be to fill out the same questionnaire again, but this time *as a family*. They were given another copy of the questionnaire, and it was explained that "as a family" meant that whatever they chose for each situation would apply to all three of them. They were, of course, to discuss the matter of their family choices among themselves and again to indicate on the questionnaire for every situation three alternatives they, as a family, liked the most; and three alternatives they liked the least, or not at all. The family was then left in the testing room, engaged in the process of deciding what they wanted and did not want—if they were, as a family, in the situation described in the questionnaire. The door was closed, but, with the family's full knowledge, the ensuing discussion was recorded on tape.

The Questionnaire. This was presented in the form of a booklet in which seven situations were described, each with ten possible alternatives or choices. The situations were included for their applicability to all family members regardless of sex or age, whether considered as individuals or as a family group. The alternatives given for each situation were intended to be as neutral as possible, and comparable in cultural and social desirability. The seven make-believe situations referred to (1) famous people they might want to meet if they were "going to a party this weekend"; (2) foods they might want to eat if they were "going out for dinner tomorrow night"; (3) films they might want to see if they were "going to a movie this weekend"; (4) countries they might want to go to "to live for a year"; (5) sport events they might desire to attend; (6) magazines to which they might wish to subscribe; and (7) two-tone colors they would prefer for their next car.

VARIABLES

Three aspects of this investigation were of particular interest: (1) How much agreement was there among family members as to what they liked (positive choices) and what they did not like (negative choices) prior to their getting together to interchange views? (2) How much time did the families take to reach all of the seven decisions asked for in the questionnaire? (3) How appropriate were these family decisions in terms of fulfilling the wishes of the individual family members?

These questions were translated into three measurable dimensions, or variables, defined as follows:

1. *Spontaneous Agreement (SA).* Spontaneous agreement representing the amount of agreements, or matched choices, that existed among two (in the dyad) or all three (in the triad) family members "spontaneously," i.e., before consultation with each other, as measured by comparing the individually filled-out questionnaires. One "spontaneous agreement" was counted whenever a family member's positive choice (i.e., an alternative marked as "liked") matched another family member's positive choice, or whenever a negative choice (i.e., an alternative marked as "disliked") matched a negative choice of another. Since for every situation there were three positive and three negative choices to be made by each individual, there was a possible maximum score of six matches for a dyad, and 18 matches for a triad (considered as the sum of three dyads). Therefore, given that there were seven situations in the questionnaire, the *SA* score had a theoretical range of 0 to 42 for the dyad, and of 0 to 126 for the triad.

The reliability of this *SA* variable, as measured by a split-half correlation for all the data was found to be $r = .502$ (corrected for attenuation by the Spearman-Brown formula).

2. *Decision Time (DT).* This was defined as the time in minutes spent by the family to complete the joint questionnaire. It was measured from the moment the tester left the room until the family announced (by the act of opening the door as instructed) that the task had been completed. It was regarded as a measure of the relative efficiency of the family functioning inasmuch as, other things being equal, the more time a family requires to reach decisions, the less efficient it can be said to be.

3. *Choice-Fulfillment (PP) of the Family as a Group, and of Its Individual Members.* This choice-fulfillment is a measure of the number of instances where what the individual wanted (as expressed in the individual's questionnaire) became what the family decided for (as expressed in the family's questionnaire). This individual's *PP* score[1] (Positive choices become *Positive* in the family) when summed with the *PP* scores of the other two members made up the *PP* score for the family. This *PP* score was regarded as another measure of the efficiency of the family functioning, for it represented the degree to which the family decision met the wishes of its members.

---

[1] Choice-fulfillment might have been represented by the *NN* score (*NN* refers to "the individual Negative becoming the family's Negative choice"). The results would have been essentially the same; the correlation between *PP* and *NN* was $r = .618$. However, *PP* seemed to carry a much clearer psychological meaning, and it was therefore the variable adopted to represent choice-fulfillment.

HYPOTHESES

This investigation was concerned with a number of hypotheses derived from clinical work and previous research. These hypotheses were formulated as follows.

H_1: *The SA for the whole sample of families would be greater than chance expectation, both in dyads and triads.* This hypothesis is based upon the reasoning that family members are bound to share common values and preferences, and that in their expression of likes and dislikes their shared values will direct them to similar individual choices. This hypothesis had been corroborated in a previous study (Ferreira, 1963a).

H_2: *The SA score would be greater for Nor than Abn families.* Since it has often been observed that intrafamily communication is impaired in *Abn* families, such an impairment should be reflected in decreased spontaneous agreement among family members. This hypothesis was also corroborated in a previous study (Ferreira, 1963a).

H_3: *This difference in SA scores between Nor and Abn families would affect all dyads.* This hypothesis assumes that the hypothesized decrease in *SA* in *Abn* families would be a family phenomenon, affecting all dyads and not just the expression of one individual or one pair of individuals.

H_4: *The SA scores would be the lowest in Sch families.* This hypothesis reflects the clinical impression that in *Sch* families, the impairment of communication is greater than in other kinds of families.

H_5: *The child's spontaneous agreement with the parents would increase with the age of the child.* This is to be expected from the fact that as the child lives longer with his parents he is bound to acquire more of their values.

H_6: *The child would tend to have a greater SA in the dyad with the same-sex parent.* Again, this hypothesis assumes that the usual process of identification with the same-sex parent will be translated in a spontaneous agreement with the same-sex parent greater than with the opposite-sex parent.

H_7: *In Sch families, the dyad mother-child would score a greater SA than the dyad father-child.* A common clinical impression is that in schizophrenia there is a symbiotic relationship between mother and child. The hypothesis assumes that such a symbiosis would result in a greater *SA* score in the mother-child than in the father-child dyads in *Sch* families.

H_8: *The DT would be longer in Abn than in Nor families.* It is to be expected that *Abn* families would have a lower efficiency, as measured by the amount of time required to reach family decisions.

H_9: *The Sch families would have the longest DT.* This prediction conforms with the clinical impression that schizophrenia-producing families are the most pathological, therefore the least efficient of all abnormal families.

H_{10}: *The family PP score would be smaller in the Abn than in the Nor group*. Again, the assumption here is that *Abn* families are less efficient than *Nor* families in the task of arriving at family decisions that conform with the wishes of their individual members.

H_{11}: *The family PP score would be the lowest in Sch families*. This reflects the same idea stated about H_9.

H_{12}: *A negative correlation would exist between SA and DT*. This expectation indicates that the more spontaneous agreement among family members, the faster should be the task of reaching family decisions.

H_{13}: *A positive correlation would exist between SA and PP scores*. This prediction was based upon the realization that the more "agreement" present among family members prior to any interchange, the more likely it seems that the individual choices would find "fulfillment" in the family choices.

H_{14}: *A positive correlation would exist between DT and PP*. This hypothesis is based upon the idea that the more time a family would take to reach a decision, the more likely it appears that such a decision would fulfill the wishes of the individual family members.

H_{15}: *The percentage of "chaotic" responses would be greater in Abn than in Nor families and greatest in Sch families*. The designation of "chaotic responses" was introduced in a previous project (Ferreira, 1963a). It applies to family decisions which seem to disregard, or go contrary to, the individual wishes expressed by every family member. Thus, a response was called "chaotic" if all three family members had, on their individual questionnaires, marked a certain alternative as "liked," but when filling out the questionnaire as a family the alternative in question was either left blank, or even marked as "not wanted." And, similarly, when all individuals marked an alternative "not wanted," but as a family either left it blank, or even marked it as "liked." These "chaotic" responses were considered to be an expression of extreme family malfunctioning, and to occur therefore more often in *Abn* families, and most often in the *Sch* subgroup.

H_{16}: *The outcome of "spontaneous dictatorial positions" would vary with the diagnostic groups*. The designation of "spontaneous dictatorial positions" applied to those instances where the comparison of the individual questionnaires showed that a family member had expressed his "like" (or "dislike") about an alternative which the two other family members had marked "neutral" (i.e. left blank), or even "disliked." In fact, three distinct encounters were called "spontaneous dictatorial positions": when the (say) positive choice of a member met with (1) the neutral choice of the other two, or (2) the neutral choice of one and the negative choice of the other, or (3) the negative choice of the other two. In any event, the family responses in these instances of "spontaneous dictatorial position" were regarded as an indication of the relative "dominance" of one family member in relation to the others. It was thus hypothesized that diagnostic groups would differ as to the relative number of instances when a member's spontaneous dictatorial position became, in fact, the apparent determinant of a dictatorial-looking family decision.

H_{17}: *The outcome of "spontaneous coalitions" would vary with the diagnostic groups.* The designation of "spontaneous coalitions" applies here to the occurrence of spontaneous agreement between two family members over a certain alternative. These instances of spontaneous coalition raised the question as to what decision was taken by the family over such an alternative. Specifically, did the family decision follow the spontaneous coalition? And, in this regard, which dyads succeeded the most? The hypothesis that the family decision in instances of spontaneous coalition would vary with diagnostic groups expresses the hope that in their relative "dominance" there might be further clues to understanding the features that distinguish different family groups.

H_{18}: *In Sch families, the father's and the child's PP scores would decrease steadily, as mother's scores would increase, from decision to decision through the questionnaire.* This hypothesis was derived from the results of a previous study on family decision-making where Ferreira (1963a) noticed that as schizophrenia-producing families went from decision to decision, there was a definite tendency for father and child to decrease the amount of their "participation" (a variable equivalent to *PP*) while mother increased hers.

RESULTS

For each of the formulated hypotheses, the results were as follows:

H_1. *Accepted.* Based on chance alone, the expected mean *SA* score was 12.60 for the dyad, and 37.80 for the triad. As Table 2 shows for dyads and Table 3 for triads, the observed results were much above chance expectation. The observed mean *SA* score was 17.79 for the dyads, and 53.29 for the triads.

H_2. *Accepted.* The differences in *SA* scores of triads were statistically significant among diagnostic groups (analysis of variance, $F = 4.38$, $df = 3/121$, $p < .01$). Specifically, *Nor* families had a mean *SA* score signficantly higher than *Abn* families ($F = 12.19$, $df = 1/123$, $p < .001$).

H_3. *Accepted.* As Table 2 shows, in every dyad *Nor* families had a higher *SA* than *Abn* families. These findings are significant for all three

TABLE 2

MEAN SPONTANEOUS AGREEMENT IN DYADS, BY DIAGNOSTIC GROUPS

| | SPONTANEOUS AGREEMENT IN DYADS | | | | | |
| | Father-Mother | | Father-Child | | Mother-Child | |
DIAGNOSTIC GROUPS	Mean*	SD	Mean*	SD	Mean*	SD
Normal	20.10	3.66	18.62	5.74	18.06	4.04
Maladjusted	18.74	4.87	16.22	4.74	16.81	4.69
Schizophrenic	19.00	4.26	13.93	3.24	16.20	4.93
Delinquent	18.48	4.90	15.98	5.87	16.60	5.38

*Chance expectation = 12.60.

dyads, father-mother (t = 2.61, df = 123, p < .01, one-tailed); father-child (t = 3.00, df = 123, p < .005, one-tailed); and mother-child (t = 1.78, df = 123, p < .05, one-tailed).

H_4. *Rejected.* Although, as Tables 2 and 3 show, *Sch* families did score the lowest *SA* in the triad, and in the father-child and mother-child dyads, the differences were not sufficient to accept the hypothesis. In this regard, it may be noteworthy that the *Sch* father-mother dyad scored as high as in the other *Abn* subgroups.

H_5. *Accepted* for *Nor* and *Mal; Rejected* for *Sch* and *Del.* A significant positive correlation between the age of the child and the amount of spontaneous agreement with the parents was found in normal families (Pearson's r = .435, p < .0003) and maladjusted families (r = .392, p < .005). However, the phenomenon seemed to be absent in schizophrenia-producing (r = .049) and delinquency-producing (r = .026) families.

H_6. *Accepted* for *Nor; Rejected* for *Abn.* A comparison of the *SA* scores in the dyads father-child and mother-child revealed that in *Nor* families, the child had a statistically significant tendency to have a greater

TABLE 3

MEAN SPONTANEOUS AGREEMENT IN TRIADS BY DIAGNOSTIC GROUPS

| | SPONTANEOUS AGREEMENT IN TRIADS | | | | | |
| | Positive Choices | | Negative Choices | | Total | |
DIAGNOSTIC GROUPS	Mean	SD	Mean	SD	Mean*	SD
Normal	28.12	4.88	28.66	5.28	56.78	8.53
Maladjusted	25.25	5.00	26.50	5.37	51.75	8.91
Schizophrenic	23.40	4.33	25.73	5.12	49.13	7.80
Delinquent	25.25	5.43	25.81	5.07	51.06	8.93

*Chance expectation = 37.80.

score in the dyad with the same-sex parent than in the dyad with the opposite-sex parent ($t = 2.17$, $df = 123$, $p < .025$, one-tailed). It was also observed that the spontaneous agreement with the same-sex parent increased with the age of the child ($r = .42$ for male children, $r = .37$ for female children, $p < .0006$ for both sexes). All these findings were limited to *Nor* families.

H_7. *Rejected.* The hypothesis of a symbiotic mother-child relationship in schizophrenia could not be corroborated in terms of the *SA* variable. The percentage of the dyadic mother-child *SA* (as part of the whole triadic *SA*) was found to be 32.6 percent in *Sch* families, as compared with 32.0, 32.9, and 31.6 percent in *Nor*, *Del*, and *Mal* families, respectively.

H_8. *Accepted.* On the average, *Nor* families took 18.96 minutes to reach all the decisions involved in the questionnaire, whereas *Abn* families took 24.44 minutes. The differences among diagnostic groups were statistically significant (analysis of variance, $F = 5.18$, $df = 3/121$, $p < .005$). However, when it was ascertained that there was a significant correlation between decision time and spontaneous agreement (see H_{12}), the data were recalculated to take this effect into account. The results are summarized in Table 4. The differences among the adjusted means were, again, statistically significant (analysis of covariance, $F = 3.98$, $df = 3/120$, $p < .01$). Specifically, a comparison of the adjusted means of *Nor* with *Abn* families revealed a difference to be accepted as beyond chance ($F = 8.42$, $df = 1/122$, $p < .005$).

TABLE 4

FAMILY DECISION-TIME (IN MINUTES) BY DIAGNOSTIC GROUPS: RAW AND ADJUSTED (FOR CORRELATION WITH SPONTANEOUS AGREEMENT) MEANS

DIAGNOSTIC GROUPS	DECISION-TIME	
	Raw Means[a]	Adjusted Means[b]
Normal	18.96	19.42
Maladjusted	25.54	25.32
Schizophrenic	24.60	24.00
Delinquent	21.19	20.86

[a]Analysis of variance, $F = 12.33$, $p < 0.001$.
[b]Analysis of covariance, $F = 3.93$, $p < 0.01$.

H_9. *Rejected.* The data did not confirm the hypothesis that *Sch* families as a group would have the longest *DT*.

H_{10}. *Accepted.* The findings are summarized in Table 5. Here, again, the variable Spontaneous Agreement had to be taken into consideration (see H_8 and H_{12}). Still, the differences among the adjusted means of *PP* scores were statistically significant (analysis of covariance, $F = 5.65$, $df = 3/120$, $p < .005$). The specific difference between the adjusted means of *Nor* and *Abn* groups was also considered beyond chance ($F = 9.96$, $df = 1/122$, $p < .005$).

TABLE 5

CHOICE-FULFILLMENT (THE INDIVIDUAL'S POSITIVE CHOICE BECOMES THE
FAMILY'S POSITIVE CHOICE) BY DIAGNOSTIC GROUPS: RAW AND ADJUSTED
(FOR CORRELATION WITH SPONTANEOUS AGREEMENT) MEANS

	CHOICE-FULFILLMENT				
	Raw Means				Adjusted Means[d]
DIAGNOSTIC GROUPS	Father[a]	Mother[b]	Child[c]	Family	Family
Normal	13.60	13.48	13.00	40.08	38.91
Maladjusted	12.32	12.00	12.36	36.68	37.18
Schizophrenic	12.33	12.00	10.07	34.40	35.71
Delinquent	12.38	12.50	12.69	37.57	38.31

[a]Analysis of variance, $F = 2.74, p < 0.05$.
[b]Analysis of variance, $F = 4.57, p < 0.01$.
[c]Analysis of variance, $F = 6.48, p < 0.001$.
[d]Analysis of covariance, $F = 5.65, p < 0.005$.

H_{11}. *Accepted.* A comparison between the adjusted means of *Sch* families and the remaining *Abn* group (*Mal* and *Del*) revealed that *Sch* families had the lowest *PP* scores. The difference was highly significant ($F = 16.84, df = 1/72, p < .001$).

H_{12}. *Accepted.* The correlation found between *SA* and *DT* ($r = .217$) was in the predicted direction, and statistically significant ($p < .01$).

H_{13}. *Accepted.* Between *SA* and *PP* a positive correlation was found ($r = .762$) which was statistically significant ($p < .0001$).

H_{14}. *Accepted.* For the complete data, a positive correlation was found to exist between *DT* and *PP* when the effect of the variable *SA* was partialled out (partial $r = .175, p < .05$).

H_{15}. *Accepted.* As Table 6 shows, the percentage of "chaotic" responses was significantly higher in *Abn* than in *Nor* families ($z = 2.10, p < .02$, one-tailed). Also as predicted, the *Sch* group had the greatest percentage of such responses, 11.2 percent, as compared with 3.2 percent observed in the *Nor* group, and 4.6 percent observed in the combined *Del* and *Mal* groups ($z = 2.75, p < .003$, one-tailed).

H_{16}. *Rejected.* The percentage of times when the individual family member in "spontaneous dictatorial position" actually seemed to have "dictated" the family decision was substantially the same for all diagnostic groups.

TABLE 6

CHAOTIC RESPONSES BY DIAGNOSTIC GROUPS

Diagnostic Groups	"Chaotic" Responses
Normal	3.23%
Abnormal (*Mal* + *Sch* + *Del*)	5.81
Maladjusted	5.45
Schizophrenic	11.21
Delinquent	2.21%

H_{17}. *Rejected*. The percentage of times when two family members in spontaneous coalition actually seemed to have determined the family decision was essentially the same for all diagnostic groups.

H_{18}. *Rejected*. There was no evidence for the hypothesis that in *Sch* families, or in any other diagnostic group, the *PP* scores tended to increase or decrease consistently throughout the questionnaire for any family member.

COMMENT

The results of this investigation seem to warrant the conclusion that *normal families differ, in demonstrable ways, from abnormal families*. Normal families, when contrasted with abnormal ones, were shown (1) to have a much greater agreement in what their members liked or disliked, prior to any exchange of information, (2) to spend less time in the reaching of family decisions, and (3) to arrive at more appropriate decisions in terms of a better fulfillment of the family members' individual choices.

The study followed the research technique developed in a previous study on family decision-making (1963a). A questionnaire described a number of make-believe, yet possible situations about which the family members, first as individuals, later as a group, were to indicate solutions they liked and disliked. In this manner, the contrast between individual choices and family decisions became observable by comparing their answers to the situations posed by the questionnaire. These situations (seven in the questionnaire used in this study) and the "alternatives" provided (ten in this case), were chosen for their relatively neutral content and comparability.

The families in the project were drawn according to availability, the *Nor* families through friends and schools, the *Abn* families through local psychiatric facilities. It may be important to note here that the *Nor* group was not composed of particularly unusual families already recognized for their "superior" functioning. To the contrary, the *Nor* group was composed of families that were regarded as normal only in the sense of being "average," and of meeting the diagnostic criteria of "normality" defined for this study. As a matter of fact, a number of these normal families left the investigators wondering about the sufficiency of our operational definitions. Still, as long as the criteria were met, the families were accepted and tested in a fashion that came close to randomness. In only one important way was the sample known to be biased: the *Nor* families knew that they were being tested as normal families, whereas the *Abn* families looked upon the testing procedure as a step toward the determination of their "abnormality." This bias due to knowing one's own label, unavoidable under the conditions of the experiment, might have affected the results, although it is not at all clear in what direction or manner.

The findings pertaining to the variable Spontaneous Agreement were, perhaps, the most exciting. Already in a previous study, Ferreira (1963a) had found that the amount of agreement among family members on seemingly unimportant matters, prior to any interchange, was not only greater than chance but capable of differentiating normal from abnormal families. This observation, which the present study corroborated, invites a number of speculations. The finding that spontaneous agreement is greater than chance reflects, no doubt, the fact that family members have lived together for many years, as a group, under conditions of constant interchange of information about, and accommodation to, their respective likes and dislikes. This interdependency obviously leads to a communality of views, to tastes and preferences that "agree" even on situations of make-believe. But the observation that in *Abn* families the "agreement" is significantly less than in *Nor* families (both in this and in the previous study) is not so immediately explainable. Futher evidence for the phenomenon seems to come from research on interpersonal perception which has indicated that there is a tendency for greater congruency (as an expression of broader areas of agreement) in happy, normal relationships than in unhappy, pathologic ones (Ferreira, 1964a; Tharp, 1963). Similarly, in a totally independent work, Cheek (1964a) observed that family agreement on responses to an attitude questionnaire were significantly lower in families of schizophrenics than in families of normals.

Assuming, therefore, that differences exist between normal and pathologic families in their amount of spontaneous agreement, we are led to wonder about its antecedents. Two explanations, not mutually exclusive, suggest themselves as accounting for the phenomenon: (1) The normal families—or better, the parents in these families—might have had, since the beginning of the relationship, a higher agreement with each other in their attitudes, values, etc., than that to be found in abnormal families. This would mean, of course, a greater homogamy ("likes marry likes") in the selection of a mate among would-be members of normal families than of abnormal ones. However, this explanation per se fails to account for the observation that measures of spontaneous agreement in the dyads with children are also higher in normal than in abnormal families. (2) The observed differences in spontaneous agreement reflect differences in communication, or in exchange of information among family members. This view would, indeed, conform with clinical impressions of impaired communication in psychopathology.

In light of these considerations, it is of theoretical interest to observe that the lower *SA* scores found in abnormal families were *a function of the whole triad*. As Tables 2 and 3 show, whatever the reason may be for their lower spontaneous agreement scores, it seems to affect all three dyads about equally, in both positive and negative matches—and not just the dyads formed with the child, the so-called patient in the abnormal families. The results must therefore be interpreted not as a function of the "disturbance" of the child alone, but as a product of the whole family.

Also of interest was the observation that in normal and maladjusted families, the child's spontaneous agreement with his parents increased with the age of the child, and in the direction of a greater agreement with the same-sex parent. However, these age and sex changes did not seem to occur in schizophrenia- and delinquency-producing families, an observation which may reflect problems in identification often noticed in such children by the clinician. It may be worthwhile to note that this sex difference had already been reported by Ferreira in a previous work (1963a).

A comparison of the *SA* scores obtained in this project with those obtained in the earlier study revealed that the score distance between pathologic families and normal families was pretty much the same. Calculating the average *SA* score's deviation from chance expectation for normal and abnormal families, the ratio *Nor/Abn* of these deviations was found to be 1.64 in the previous study, and 1.67 in the present one. This observation speaks well for the consistency of the results on the *SA* variable, despite the differences in method, questionnaire, and families tested in the two studies.

Just as the variable Spontaneous Agreement seemingly refers to a *static* aspect of the family group, so do the variables Decision Time and Choice-Fulfillment (*PP*) apparently refer to *dynamic* aspects of the family triad. In fact, the variables *DT* and *PP* seem to provide a measure of the family's efficiency in decision-making, with *DT* expressing input and *PP* expressing output. A family that takes a long time to reach joint decisions may be considered as handicapped in its potentiality to meet situations or events that require family decisions. Although speed of family decisions cannot be equated with normality, it seems reasonable to assume that for every situation and circumstance, there is an "average" or "normal" decision time, beyond which we could speak of wastefulness in family func-

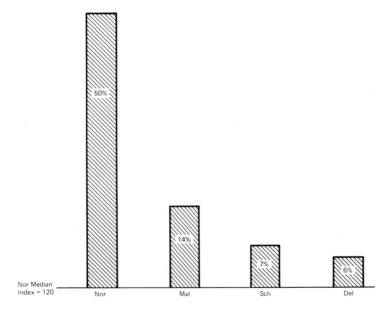

Fig. 1. Index of normality: percentage of all families above the median of the normal group (index ≥ 120).

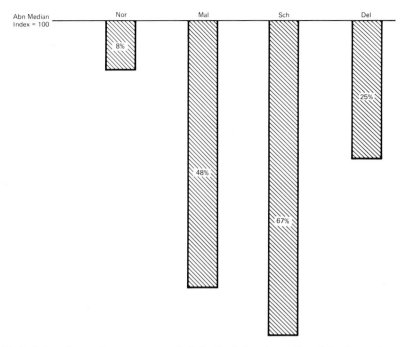

Fig. 2. Index of normality: percentage of all families below the median of the abnormal group (index ≤ 100).

tioning. This notion of wastefulness seems particularly appropriate when seen in the context of what the family might have accomplished with its decision. Since a family is not a machine, at least in the ordinary sense of the word, the idea of accomplishment here does not necessarily imply the production of "something" outside by the family, but rather the achievement of certain satisfactions inside the family boundaries. Thus, it seems that the variable *PP* as applied to the family may be a good indicator of the satisfactions that the family (as the sum total of its members) may have derived from joint decision-making. Indubitably, one of the most important ends of decision-making in a family is the fulfillment of the needs and wishes of its members. A family where more such wishes are met (couched, of course, in whatever subcultural mode might have been adopted by that family) is a family where there is bound to be a greater happiness and contentment than a family where the individual wishes of its members are much less gratified. It seems important, then, to emphasize that family decision-making in abnormal families was shown in this study to require longer time and to provide less fulfillment of individual wishes than in normal families, even when significant differences in spontaneous agreement were partialled out. Thus, the everyday conviction that abnormal families are less efficient in their functioning as a group is corroborated.

As this study shows, *abnormal families tend to arrive at inappropriate solutions to their problems (here expressed as a lower choice-fulfillment), and by rather wasteful means (here translated in a longer decision time).* This lower output/input ratio as displayed by abnormal families reached its lowest point in schizophrenia-producing families, substantiating the clinical impression that "schizophrenia" likely occupies the "sickest" end of a hypothetical normal-abnormal continuum. This conclusion becomes even more apparent when the three major variables are linearly combined in an index of normality $(SA + 2\,PP - DT)$.[2] On this index it may be observed (see Figure 1) that above the cut-off point 120 (median of the *Nor* group) only 11 percent (8 out of 75) of the abnormal families are found. But (Figure 2) the *Sch* families' marked tendency to score the worst in all three variables resulted in 67 percent of *Sch* families scoring below an index score of 100 (median of the *Abn* group), in contrast with only 48 percent of the *Mal*, 25 percent of the *Del*, and 8 percent of the *Nor* families. * * *

---

[2] A correlation between this index and the normality of families was expressed in a biserial $r = .578$, highly significant.

Family Interaction: A Social-Clinical Study of Synthetic, Normal, and Problem Family Triads[*]

Arthur M. Bodin

* * * This study arose from a recognition that traditional small-group research has rarely dealt with actual families and that family experimentation has barely begun to capitalize on the techniques of traditional small-group research. To help bridge this gap, a set of samples was selected so as to include both *ad hoc* triads of strangers and actual family triads. Moreover, the methods were drawn both from traditional small-group research and from recent family experimentation.

The 36 families investigated were of the following three types: (1) father, mother, and delinquent son; (2) father, mother, and nondelinquent son; and (3) father, mother, and nondelinquent son, each from a different family and all total strangers to one another prior to the experiment. These three triad types were called, respectively, *problem, normal,* and *synthetic* family triads. In all instances, the son was a teenager from an intact family in which neither a parent nor any sibling was a member of any of the mental health professions. All the participants were white, Christian, and closely matched on a variety of potentially relevant biographical details, including years of marriage, age, birth order, education, and occupation.

The procedure included two main tasks, the first drawn from traditional small-group research, and the second adapted from recent family research. The first task was a three-person negotiable game, played on a modified Parcheesi board. This game yielded a record of bargaining and coalition behavior under three power patterns: all equal (1–1–1), one stronger (3–2–2), and one all-powerful (3–1–1). Twenty-four games were played by each triad, in three rounds of eight games. The third round was to test family flexibility.

The second task might be called a Family Agreement Measure (FAM). It was obtained by means of a questionnaire combining elements of an

---

[*]Excerpted from a paper presented at the Western Psychological Association in 1966, with permission of the author.

"unrevealed differences" task within the format of a multiple-choice, sentence-completion test, modified to require ranking all the alternative completions. The content of the family questionnaire was adapted from recent family research and included two questions, with five alternatives apiece, on each of the following six areas of common family concern— (1) *strengths*, (2) *problems*, (3) *authority*, (4) *communication*, (5) *defensiveness*, and (6) *discipline*—in the family. Participants ranked all 60 items (12 paired sentence stems, each with five completions), first individually (in separate rooms) and then together as a family group. These two stages were designated Phase I and Phase II. Phase II, like the third round of the game, was designed to measure family flexibility by quantifying the group's success in making a requested shift in behavior.

Perceptual or motivational estimates followed each task as a basis for assessing perceptual distortions and for setting flexibility criteria.

The major hypotheses were: (1) the *authenticity hypothesis*, predicting differences between synthetic families and authentic families, and (2) the *normality hypothesis*, predicting differences between problem and normal families.

Though the results showed significant differences among family types with regard to *details* of game-playing, there were no significant *overall* differences in accommodative versus exploitative strategy. Thus, the game failed to support the hypotheses, except in specific respects, e.g., the normal families in comparison with the problem families showed: (1) less tendency to "go it alone," (2) more tendency to "share and share alike," and (3) more tendency for fathers to show benevolence by forming coalitions even when all-powerful.

However, the questionnaire results (see Tables 1 and 2) conclusively

TABLE 1

INTRA-PAIR AND TOTAL FAMILY DISAGREEMENT ON A FAMILY QUESTIONNAIRE
ACCORDING TO FAMILY TYPE AND INTRA-FAMILY ROLE

	PAIRS			FAMILY[d]
	F-M[a]	M-S[b]	S-F[c]	Σ(Pairs)
Mean Disagreement Scores				
Problem families	79.8	89.3	90.3	259.5
Normal families	72.7	81.8	81.2	235.7
Synthetic families	89.0	78.2	88.7	255.8
Analysis of Variance				
F (df = 2/33)	5.71	2.53	2.38	2.95
p	<.01	ns	ns	ns

[a]Father-Mother
[b]Mother-Son
[c]Son-Father
[d]Split-half reliability coefficient (for successive halves) = .84.

TABLE 2

INDIVIDUAL AND TOTAL FAMILY COMPROMISE[a] ON A FAMILY QUESTIONNAIRE
ACCORDING TO FAMILY TYPE AND INTRA-FAMILY ROLE

| | INDIVIDUALS | | | FAMILY[b] |
	Fathers	Mothers	Sons	$\Sigma(F+M+S)$
Mean Compromise Scores				
Problem families	49.2	52.5	73.8	175.5
Normal families	47.8	36.7	63.2	147.7
Synthetic families	55.3	66.3	72.8	194.5
Analysis of Variance				
$F\ (df = 2/33)$	0.55	9.10	2.16	7.83
p	ns	$<.001$	ns	$<.005$

[a]The "compromise" score refers to the degree to which the individual member "gave in" to the wishes of the other family members in the test situation.
[b]Split-half reliability coefficient (for successive halves) = .96.

supported both hypotheses. Findings supporting the authenticity hypothesis include: (1) consistently higher overall and parental agreement in real than in artificial families, (2) greater maternal compromise in synthetic than in normal families, and (3) more efficient joint decision-making in actual than in artificial families. Findings supporting the normality hypothesis include: (1) greater father-son agreement in normal than in problem families, (2) greater maternal influence in normal than in problem families, and (3) more perceptual distortion by mothers—overrating their husbands and underrating themselves—in normal than in problem families.

Neither task supported the flexibility hypothesis that normal families would show less rigidity than problem families.

A cross-situational comparison revealed that sons lost status from the game to the questionnaire, which had greater family import.

In sum, though the three family types differed little in overall game strategy, they produced three distinctive scoring patterns on the family questionnaire. There is evidence that task relevance is important in determining behavioral differences among family types. In this case, the questionnaire appeared to be superior to the game. Additional distinctions among family types rest on differences in individual roles (mothers showing the most distinctive behavior) and also in family rules (synthetic families functioning least efficiently probably because they lost time developing interaction norms akin to those already evolved by real families). * * *

Married Couples' Responses to Disagreement*

Robert G. Ryder and D. Wells Goodrich

* * * These particular differences of opinion were generated by Goodrich and Boomer's (1963) Color Matching Test (CMT). Unlike Strodtbeck's revealed differences technqiue (1954, 1958), which exploits previously existing disagreements, the CMT, along with the similar Stereognosis Test of Flint and Ryder (1963), generates new disagreements by using deception and therefore achieves close control over the content and past history of the disagreements. The price paid for content control is that couples discuss matters—namely distinctions among patches of colored paper—that are somewhat removed from their customary concerns.

METHOD

The Color Matching Test was administered to 49 white, middle-class couples, each of whom had been married three to four months. Couples were paid volunteers whose names had been obtained from the marriage records of the District of Columbia. Husbands ranged in age from 20 to 27, and wives from 18 to 25. Prior to the CMT, each couple had received one joint interview in their home. The interview inquired about the spouses' backgrounds and the background of their marriage. Two individual interviews, a second joint interview, six questionnaires, and other procedures were administered after the CMT was completed. The interviewers were two experienced male social workers. The questionnaires dealt primarily with husband and wife participation and decision-making, and with the relative salience of seven content areas: parenthood, relatives, friends, sex, occupation, food, and housekeeping. Interviewers' ratings and questionnaire variables will be indicated briefly as they relate to Color Matching Test findings.

For the 15-minute CMT procedure, husband and wife were seated opposite one another with a large two-sided easel between them.

---

*Abridged from *Family Process*, 1966, 5, 30-42, with permission of the senior author and *Family Process*.

Ostensibly the subjects' ability to discriminate among the slight gradations of colors on the easel was being tested. Following each of 20 color-matching tasks, the experimenter demanded that the couple discuss their choices and arrive at an agreement as to the "best possible match," stressing that "only your agreements count toward your score in this experiment." In half of the series, however, the couple was deceived: in those instances the colors were so arranged that no agreement was possible. The data consist of the couples' discussion as they searched for a mutually acceptable solution for each of the 20 color-matching tasks.

All CMT administrations were tape-recorded and subsequently typed. Typescripts were independently checked by two persons, who then prepared final corrected typescripts. The final corrected typescripts were coded independently for 47 variables by two other persons. The two raters then rerated each case after at least a three-day wait, and all four sets of ratings were pooled. Most codings apply to individual statements by the spouses, the others referring to the outcomes of individual disagreements. Median corrected rating reliability was .96 and the mean was .84. Median corrected split-half reliability was .59 and the mean was .48. For present purposes, variables were selected and combined, yielding the 17 final variables described below. For the 28 original variables, from which these 17 final variables were constructed, median and mean corrected rating reliabilities were .97 and .93. Median and mean corrected split-half reliabilities were .57 and .51.

The 17 variables on which present analyses were based are as follows:

1. *Statements* is the total number of statements made by a couple in the course of Color Matching Test administration. An individual statement is defined as any utterance by a spouse that was made between the time any other person stopped talking and the time any other person again began to speak.

2. *Husband Initiation* is the number of trials on which the husband rather than the wife made the first statement, plus the number of trials on which the husband rather than the wife was first to announce his individual color choice. It is, in other words, an index of the husband rather than the wife tending to speak first.

3. *Husband Dominance* is an additive compound of three variables, weighted roughly by their variablilities. The first is the percentage of disagreements where the husband's initial color choice, rather than the wife's, is the one finally agreed on. The second is the mean rating of the wife's degree of "submission" on disagreements where she conceded to her husband. Third, with a negative weighting, is the husband's mean "submission" rating. The percentage of cases where the husband's view prevails is combined with two other variables rather than kept by itself because of its low (.12) split-half reliability.

4 and 5. *Pre-Errors* is scored for husband and wife separately, hence provides two variables. On each trial, each spouse chooses a

color. If a person announces his choice before he hears what the other spouse has chosen, and makes a mistake, this is called an e_1 error. On the other hand, if he waits for the other spouse to state his choice first, and then announces his choice and makes a mistake, this is called an e_2 error. The e_1 errors are made without knowledge of the spouse's choice, and e_2 errors are made with this knowledge. Pre-Errors, as used here, is the total number of e_1 errors made by a spouse.

6 and 7. *Eliminating Disagreements by Error (EDE)* is also scored for the two spouses separately and is derived from e_2 errors. If, say, a husband has heard his wife's color choice, he may make the same choice and thereby guarantee the absence of any disagreement. If in so doing he makes an erroneous choice, his mistake is called an e_{2-} error. The husband may also make a mistake which involves a choice that is different from his wife's, thereby guaranteeing the existence of a disagreement. Such an erroneous choice would be called an e_{2+} error. Eliminating Disagreements by Error is the number of e_{2-} errors minus the number of e_{2+} errors.

8 and 9. *Task Discussion—Intensity (TDI)* for each spouse is the percentage of statements that include attempts to resolve disagreements by mentioning the intensity (lightness or darkness) of one or more colors. Responses of this kind adhere literally to the perceptual differences presented in the experimental task.

10 and 11. *Task Discussion—Qualitative or Metaphoric (TDQ,M)* is like *TDI* except that scored statements must include qualitative description of a color, e.g., "It's Chinese red," or metaphoric denotation, as "It's the same color as our living room rug." *TDQ,M* thus measures the extent of more articulate color description than does *TDI* and takes account of a somewhat more generous frame of reference than the specific matching task construed literally.

12 and 13. *Disapproval of Spouse (DSP)* is the percentage of statements where a subject makes critical, disapproving, hostile, or otherwise negative remarks about his spouse. *DSP* is scored for husband and wife separately.

14 and 15. *Laughter (L)* is the percentage of statements including an audible laugh. *L* is scored for husband and wife separately.

16 and 17. *Avoiding Structure (AS)* is the percentage of statements where a spouse questions the test structure, for instance by discussing possible trickery; or takes, or offers to take, some arbitrary way out of a disagreement, such as flipping a coin, or suggesting that the couple is simply unable to resolve a disagreement. This is scored for husbands and wives separately.

The means of some of these variables were examined to get at possible husband-wife differences in interaction style, and correlations among all

17 variables were computed. Principal components were computed from the correlation matrix, and the first four components, or factors, were moderately interpretable and therefore retained. Unities were left as diagonal elements in the correlation matrix, and the resulting factors were not rotated. Factor scores were to be computed from these factors. The complications in factor scoring which result from using communalities and from rotating have been shown by several writers.

Finally, factor scores and the 17 variables were correlated with data from questionnaires and interviewer's ratings of these couples.

RESULTS

Means. There may be a cultural ethic that men make decisions, or that "ladies go first"; but if so, neither of these prescriptions was reflected in average couple behavior. The percentage of disagreements where the husband's view prevailed was close to 50 percent (mean = 46.8 percent, $t = .939$). This is consistent with Strodtbeck's (1951) finding with the revealed differences technique that while Navaho wives and Morman husbands tended to win in disagreements with their spouses, Texan couples were equalitarian in the distribution of disagreement outcomes. Husband Initiation was also not significantly different from 50 percent (mean = 48.1 percent, $t = .896$).

To get at some idea of the differing styles of men and women in this situation, husbands and wives were compared on those variables where each spouse was scored separately. As can be seen from Table 1, wives tended to use a richer vocabulary in describing colors (Task Discussion—Qualitative or Metaphoric), and laughed more. Husbands, on the other hand, were apparently more likely than wives to break away from the test structure.

TABLE 1

HUSBAND-WIFE COMPARISONS

Variable	Husband Mean Score	Wife Mean Score	r_{HW}	t_{HW}
Pre-errors	1.08	.67	.02	1.546
Eliminating disagreements by error	1.45	1.43	−.13	.045
Task discussion—Intensity	2.40	2.70	.30*	.830
Task discussion—Qualitative or metaphoric	2.75	3.37	.79**	2.217*
Disapproval of spouse	.82	1.05	.18	.887
Laughter	3.58	5.76	.38**	3.991***
Avoiding structure	.18	.13	.44**	2.488*

*$p < .05$
**$p < .01$
***$p < .001$

One finding of particular interest concerns *Eliminating Disagreements by Error (EDE)*. If errors are unrelated to what one knows about his spouse's color choice, they should create disagreements (e_{2+} errors) as often as they eliminate them (e_{2-} errors). Specifically, average *EDE* should be about zero. If people tend to create conflicts by changing their color choices, then there should be more e_{2+} errors than e_{2-} errors, and average *EDE* should be negative. There is a striking tendency to distort or alter choices in order to *avoid* disagreements, as mean *EDE* was positive, and to a highly significant degree; for husbands $t = 4.43$ ($p < .001$, two-tailed), and for wives $t = 5.33$ ($p < .001$, two-tailed). The extent of the tendency to distort one's way out of disagreements might be better appreciated by noting that 25 husbands made one or more e_{2-} errors, while only 3 made e_{2+} errors. The corresponding figures for wives are 24 and 3. One is tempted to infer that lying may be a popular way of maintaining marital harmony.

Factor Analysis. Correlations among the 17 factor-analyzed variables are given in Table 2. Loadings for the first four unrotated principal components are given in Table 3. Considering the present small sample size, sampling stability of the obtained factors is uncertain. Their usefulness is therefore not in revealing some presumed underlying basis for the correlations in Table 2, but mainly in suggesting interesting dimensions for describing couple interaction process.

Factor 1 runs from affectivity (wife Disapproval of Spouse, husband Laughter, wife Laughter) to rationality (husband and wife Task Discussion–Intensity and Task Discussion–Qualitative or Metaphoric). Couples at one end apparently try to reason their way out of Color Matching Test disagreements, while those at the other end are more likely to proceed by means of disapproval and laughter. Factor 2 is clearly a verbal fluency measure. It loads high on Statements and on all variables which indicate that utterances tend to be contentful. Task Discussion–Intensity is thus assumed to reflect a rather minimal kind of statement content. Factor 3 suggests a dimension of husband versus wife leading or assertive behavior. At one end, husbands seemingly leap in first with their color choices, make higher Pre-Errors scores in so doing, and are followed by wives who make erroneous color choices in order to agree with them (Eliminating Disagreements by Error). At the other end, the reverse of these several statements seems true. Note from Table 2 that this pattern of loadings is not obviously due to direct correlations between Husband Initiation and the four error variables, which suggest that the pattern may not be a mere artifact, due to a circumstance of spouses who make their color choices first having relatively greater opportunity for e_1 errors, and less opportunity for e_2 errors. Factor 4 seems mostly to reflect style of error-making, with Pre-Errors variables loading at one end and *EDE* at the other.

The two Avoiding Structure (*AS*) variables do not seem to be in the main conceptual trends of any factors. They show up however as one aspect of verbal fluency, and wife Avoiding Structure seems high for wives who are high on leading behavior (the negative end of Factor 3). Loadings

TABLE 2

CORRELATIONS AMONG VARIABLES USED IN FACTOR ANALYSIS

	1	2	3	4	5	6	7	8	9	10	11	12	13	14	15	16
1) Statements																
2) H Initiation	-.02															
3) H Dominance	.04	-.02														
4) H Pre-errors	.00	.08	.10													
5) W Pre-errors	-.19	-.30	.22	.02												
6) H Eliminating disagreements by error	-.26	.06	-.42	-.17	.05											
7) W Eliminating disagreements by error	-.17	.27	-.18	-.04	-.13	-.13										
8) H Task discussion—Intensity	.13	-.23	.26	-.11	.10	-.07	-.28									
9) W Task discussion—Intensity	.06	-.04	.14	.07	-.08	-.25	-.18	.32								
10) H Task discussion—Qualitative or metaphoric	.53	-.13	.33	-.13	.02	-.25	-.12	.43	.16							
11) W Task discussion—Qualitative or metaphoric	.51	-.10	.25	-.01	-.19	-.20	-.21	.40	.42	.79						
12) H Disapproval of spouse	.36	-.04	-.17	-.06	-.12	-.07	-.04	-.02	-.12	.03	.00					
13) W Disapproval of spouse	.26	.02	-.33	.31	-.05	.01	-.03	-.28	-.22	-.17	-.17	.17				
14) H Laughter	.24	.03	-.17	.16	-.08	-.11	-.22	-.30	-.19	-.14	-.13	.38	.39			
15) W Laughter	.25	.03	-.16	.19	-.24	-.16	.11	-.24	-.03	-.08	-.16	.10	.29	.37		
16) H Avoiding structure	.25	-.05	.02	-.01	-.02	-.15	.03	-.08	-.20	.12	.00	-.06	.03	.30	.17	
17) W Avoiding structure	.39	-.18	-.16	.04	-.09	.22	-.08	-.09	-.30	.11	.09	.09	.20	.16	.36	.44

Note.—$N = 49$.

TABLE 3

PRINCIPAL COMPONENT FACTOR LOADINGS

	Factor			
	1	2	3	4
1) Statements	.24	.83	.02	.15
2) H Initiation	−.23	−.11	.54	.36
3) H Dominance	.57	−.05	.18	−.41
4) H Pre-Errors	−.16	.16	.38	−.54
5) W Pre-Errors	.12	−.28	−.43	−.57
6) H Eliminating disagreements by error	−.31	−.29	−.58	.35
7) W Eliminating disagreements by error	−.28	−.20	.40	.40
8) H Task discussion—Intensity	.70	.00	−.21	.00
9) W Task discussion—Intensity	.54	−.05	.38	−.08
10) H Task discussion—Qualitative or metaphoric	.72	.44	−.06	.18
11) W Task discussion—Qualitative or metaphoric	.75	.42	.08	.23
12) H Disapproval of spouse	−.15	.42	−.02	.09
13) W Disapproval of spouse	−.50	.41	.05	−.22
14) H Laughter	−.44	.55	.04	−.31
15) W Laughter	−.39	.50	.25	−.06
16) H Avoiding structure	−.11	.46	−.20	−.04
17) W Avoiding structure	−.21	.58	−.46	.16
Cumulative percent variance	18.8	35.0	44.8	53.5

for Husband Dominance are hard to interpret because of the conceptually-mixed construction of this variable. It does seem related however to the rationality end of Factor 1, and, for what it's worth, to the Pre-Errors end of Factor 4.

Correlations with Other Variables. Clearly, if dimensions derived from the Color Matching Test are to be of any use, the CMT must have some relationship with behavior occurring elesewhere. To investigate this matter, factor scores, the 17 variables used in the factor analysis, and the three variables put together as Husband Dominance (percentage of husband wins, husband "submission," and wife "submission") were correlated with a set of 50 variables derived from questionnaires and ratings by interviewers. Considering the dubious value of significance levels with this many correlations, the entire procedure must be considered tentative and exploratory, and only particularly suggestive relationships will be touched on at this time. All told, 82 correlations were significant at the .05 level, while .05 of all correlations computed would have yielded 60 significant correlations.

Wives who were apparently retiring and unassertive on the Color Matching Test tended to receive a more positive evaluation by interviewers. Concretely, wives who tended to receive positive interviewer ratings won infrequently in CMT disagreements with their husbands, had higher "submission" scores, and had higher Eliminating Disagreements by Error scores. Also, where wives were high on *EDE*, both husbands and wives reported themselves as more satisfied with their marriages.

On the other hand, it might be inferred that the interviewers preferred humorous husbands. Positive interviewer ratings of husbands tended to be correlated with *wife* CMT laughter.

None of the four factors was clearly related to overall evaluation by interviewers, but factor scores and conceptually important high-loading variables had a pattern of relationships with questionnaire variables and interviewer ratings which tended to make sense. Factor 1, for example, was associated with questionnaire variables purporting to measure conventionality, nonimpulsiveness, and reasonableness in the face of disagreements.[1]

Consideration of the correlations with Factor 2 and its highly loaded variable, Statements, suggest that taking a long time to resolve CMT disagreements was related to a general tendency toward nonacquiescent behavior, particularly on the part of the husband. Correlations with rated wife-need-for-support, and with reported wife-dissatisfaction with her marriage, suggest that a high Factor 2 syndrome included some difficulties for the wife.

Factor 3 seems to have been related to husband-impulsivity, as well it might, and also to rated wife-empathy and to differentiation of household roles between the two spouses. The high-loading variable, Husband Initiation, was significantly correlated with extent of premarital sexual activity between the two spouses (as reported by both husband and wife). Correlates of wife *EDE* have already been mentioned. Husband's Eliminating Disagreements by Error score had no significant correlates.

Factor 4 had no clearly interpretable correlates.

DISCUSSION

Can interesting dimensions be measured by the CMT? The most we can do is point to several apparently measurable dimensions which interest us. Also, "dimension" is not necessarily synonymous with "factor." A factor analysis was done in the hope that it might suggest dimensions of interest and indicate what sort of dimensions can be well measured, not in the expectation that it would reveal some kind of alleged underlying truth and hence directly indicate the dimensions we seek.

In this spirit then, *Rationality versus Affectivity* is one dimension suggested by the present results. It is a potential measure of stylistic differences between couples that is certainly measurable, coming as it seems so close to the first principal axis of the scored variables. A similar factor was also found by Flint and Ryder (1963) using Flint's Stereognosis test with some of the same couples, but after they had been married about a year. The content of this possible dimension suggests a relationship with personality measures of extraversion, or perhaps with social attitudes of romanticism or materialism. Data already in hand suggest a relationship with social conventionality.

---

[1]Nothing in these relationships suggested that high-scoring Factor 1 couples were truly more reasonable, only that they tended to use "reasons" more. "Rationality" as tapped by Factor 1 seems to reflect a style of interaction, not its adequacy in any sense.

Length of Disagreements also comes close to being a factor and is easily measurable. As noted earlier, questionnaire correlates suggest this variable is not merely idiosyncratic to the CMT situation, but may have to do with the degree to which spouses (at least husbands) generally maintain their own positions in the face of disagreement.

Husband (versus wife) Leading Behavior and Eliminating Disagreements by Error are other measures of interest. The suggestion in Factor 3 of some possible functional equivalence between these two variables warrants further exploration.

With regard to the second question, threads of commonality between Color Matching Test performance and behavior elsewhere were indeed found, as mentioned in the preceding paragraphs. The number of non-independent correlations was such that significant relationships must be treated with extreme caution, but it does seem true that each of the first three factors was sensibly related to outside measures. Also, there was a coherent cluster of individual variables which tied in with positive interviewer judgments. One might tentatively conclude then that there are some nonchance connections between CMT variables and behavior as otherwise measured.

What about the third question: how has the Color Matching Test informed us regarding central tendencies of couples' reactions to disagreement? If we take the results at face value and assume couples may approach other disagreements as they do those generated by the CMT, which of course may not be true, there is one main phenomenon we might not previously have guessed. This is the striking tendency of our subjects to avoid conflicts by giving wrong answers. Perhaps disagreement resolution in marriage is sometimes a special case of the social influence effect studied by Asch (1958) and others. Something akin to conscious or unconscious denial, distortion, misperception, or lying seems to be a common way to eliminate disagreements. A similar effect, call it denial of disagreement, has been noted informally by Moss, at the Child Research Branch, National Institute of Mental Health, and by Strodtbeck (1951), in studying revealed differences between spouses. That is, when spouses were faced with apparent discrepancies between answers, they tended to re-interpret their answers in order to demonstrate that there was "really" no disagreement. The apparent popularity of denying disagreements may be deplorable but has, as far as present data reveal, no untoward effects. In fact, wife Eliminating Disagreements by Error is related to positive interviewer ratings and self reports of high marriage satisfaction. It will be interesting to see if these findings hold up when the couples are no longer newlyweds.

Measurement of Family Relationships and Their Effects*

Amerigo Farina and Richard M. Dunham

* * * The subjects of this study were Good and Poor premorbid schizophrenic patients and their parents. The patient's score on the Phillips Scale (Phillips, 1953) determined whether the family would be placed in the Good or Poor premorbid group. The scale employed is designed to quantify the adequacy of social and sexual premorbid relationships of schizophrenic patients. The obtainable scores range from zero for excellent premorbid adjustment to 30 for dismally poor patterns of relationships with others prior to hospitalization. This dichotomy (Good-Poor) appears to be quite similar to others (such as process-reactive, dementia praecox-schizophrenia, and chronic-acute) but no distinction between the two groups regarding organic versus psychogenic etiology is implied by the present classification.

The Good and the Poor patients, as classified by the Phillips Scale, have been found to differ from each other in many important ways, although to date the research has been done almost exclusively with males. Goods, in comparison to Poors, have a more favorable prognosis; they manifest performance deficits in the presence of cues of the father, whereas Poors display such deficits in the presence of cues of the mother; and, particularly pertinent for this study, these two groups of patients appear to be reared in different kinds of families (Garmezy & Rodnick, 1959; Rodnick & Garmezy, 1957). The evidence suggests that Goods come from families dominated by the father and the Poors from homes where the mother plays the dominant role. Also, the relationships between the parents of Poors seem to be characterized by more conflict than is evidenced by parents of Good premorbid patients (Farina, 1960; Garmezy, Clarks, & Stockner, 1961). In addition to these studies which indicate a relationship between patterns of parental dominance and conflict and important characteristics of the schizophrenic son, many other studies suggest the atypicality of the relationships between parents of schizophrenic patients. These other studies have often emphasized the

---

*Abridged from *Archives of General Psychiatry* 1963, *9*, 64–73, with permission of the senior author and the American Medical Association.

excessive dominance manifested by one of the two parents and the great conflict which characterizes their relationships (Fisher, Boyd, Walker, & Sheer, 1959; Kohn & Clausen, 1956; Lidz, Cornelison, Fleck, & Terry, 1957a, 1957b; Reichard & Tillman, 1950).

The present study is closely related to the earlier study by Farina (1960), in which parents of male schizophrenic and tuberculous patients were induced to interact with each other. The current study was designed to reveal the extent to which the dominance and conflict behaviors these parents displayed toward each other in the earlier study would be directed toward the son who was included as a third member of the interacting group. The role played by the patient within the family as well as the patterns of conflict and alliance of the group was also of interest.

A second aspect of this study, which attempted to assess the effects of interaction with the parents on relevant aspects of the patient's behavior, is closely related to a prior study by Dunham (1959). In that study, Dunham presented a series of slides depicting various scenes of Good and Poor schizophrenic patients and to tuberculous patients who were free of psychiatric illnesses. Some of the scenes employed were reasonably neutral in content (a house and tree), while others contained presumably more meaningful objects (a mother scolding a boy). For each content there was a standard slide and five variations, each of which differed in increasing steps from the standard slide. The subject's task was to decide if a slide presented after the standard was the same as the standard or different. Dunham obtained some evidence indicating that the performance of the Goods was least adequate for the scene showing a father scolding a boy whereas the performance of the Poors was most deficient for the mother-son scolding scene.

A possible explanation for Dunham's findings, as well as for similar findings reported by Kreinik (1959), and by Ballantine (1962), is that patients react with decreased adequacy in the presence of cues reminiscent of past traumatic or unpleasant experiences. If this explanation is valid, a conflictful interaction with the parents might be followed by more marked inadequacy of performance by the patient if the appropriate cues are present. To test the validity of this explanation, immediately after interacting with the parents, all patients performed tasks similar to those used by Dunham, and their performance was compared to that of control patients (to be described below) who had not had very recent interactions with their parents.

METHOD

Procedure. When a patient met all of the criteria to be described in the Subjects section, his parents were sent a letter from an official of the institution in which he was hospitalized. This was the usual method employed by the hospitals in communicating with relatives of patients. The letter stated that the investigator, a clinical psychologist, was collecting information about patients hospitalized there and that the information was considered an important aid to understanding and treating their son.

The letter also requested that the parents make an appointment with the researcher at their son's hospital.

After the parents arrived at the hospital they were joined by the patient, and the routine but important nature of the information-gathering procedures was again emphasized. The entire procedure was briefly outlined to the three family members, after which the father and son were taken to another office and provided with some light reading material. Meanwhile, after some preliminary explanation, the mother was asked to provide resolutions to six hypothetical problem situations involving a son and his parents. The preliminary explanations were intended to allay the subjects' anxieties and to lead them to believe the focus of interest was centered on the content of the responses. In this way, it was hoped that recognition of the real purpose of the study, and attendant defensiveness, would be less likely.

The hypothetical situations employed were selected with a number of considerations in mind. The following were the more important ones: they should appear to be reasonably natural questions; they should be ego-involving; they should elicit specific solutions from the respondents in order to render manifestations of disagreement and aggression clearly observable; and, finally, the content of the hypothetical situations should be such that contradictory resolutions are frequently elicited, thus increasing the probability of dominance and conflict behavior. Six situations, selected from areas reported to represent particularly difficult problems for families of schizophrenic patients, were used. Two of these were as follows:

A. A 17-year-old boy wants money to go out with some friends that night. The parents do not like his group of friends and have asked him to keep away from them.

B. The school calls up the mother saying that her 12-year-old boy has gotten into trouble. He and some other boys beat up a youngster of about their own age.

In responding to these problem situations which were presented one at a time, the mother was instructed to describe what should be done if she had to make a decision without consulting with anyone. She was given unlimited time to respond, and, when she was finished, the patient and subsequently the father were similarly instructed and asked to respond to the same problem situations. After the mother, patient, and father had individually provided resolutions, they were brought back together. They were then told that although each had already given his or her opinion as to the proper way to resolve the problems, it was also important to know how the family as a whole would resolve them. They were instructed to give opinions about resolutions offered by other family members, and the same six hypothetical problem situations were read once more. As in the presentation of the situations to the family members individually, unlimited time was given for the responses. This whole procedure, including individual resolutions, was tape-recorded with high-fidelity equipment which was visible to the subjects. The taped records were later analyzed in the manner to be described.

Two precautions were taken to reduce the possibly biasing effect of the researcher's behavior on the behavior patterns of the group. The first precaution taken was to prevent the investigator from learning the group membership of the families. The subjects were selected by one investigator while the other, who was responsible for the administration of this part of the procedure, had no knowledge of the patient's premorbid history. The second precaution was that in both the individual and group administration of the hypothetical problems, the investigator's behavior was carefully standardized. The subjects were praised only after their response to the first hypothetical problem situation during the individually administered part of the procedure. The researcher's role was, otherwise, limited to calling for clarification of vague or ambiguous responses and to determining by questions when agreement did or did not exist. At least one response to each situation was elicited from each family member during the group interaction, but this was done without direct solicitation from any specific person. For example, after a hypothetical problem had been presented, the researcher waited until a response was made. After that, if necessary, he asked, "How do the others of you feel about that?"

Dominance and conflict, as displayed by these family groups, were measured in ways designed to do minimal violence to generally held connotations of these terms. The specific definition of each follows:

Indices of Dominance. These measures, as well as the conflict measures, were taken exclusively from recordings of that part of the procedure during which the family as a group responded to the hypothetical problem situations. The more dominant member of the group was assumed to speak for longer periods of time, to have his decisions accepted by the others, etc.

1. Total Number of Times Spoken: This was the sum of times for the six problem situations that each of the family members (*a*) was the first to respond after the investigator described the situation, (*b*) was the second member of the family to speak, (*c*) was the last member of the family to speak (except for unelaborated agreement, which was not considered in any of the indices).

2. Passive Acceptance of Solution: This was the number of times for the six hypothetical problem situations that each of the family members accepted a solution proposed by another by agreeing without further elaboration.

3. Total Time Spoken: This was the total time in seconds for the six hypothetical problem situations that each of the family members spoke.

4. Percentage of Total Speaking Time: For each of the family members, this was that person's *total time spoken* divided by the sum of the mother's, patient's, and father's *total time spoken*.

Indices of Conflict. These indices were intended to reflect the degree of respect and tolerance these family members had for each other and the degree to which they compromised and cooperated. It was assumed that greater conflict would be reflected by more numerous interruptions, a greater number of failures to arrive at a mutually acceptable solution, etc.

1. Frequency of Simultaneous Speech: This was the number of times for the six hypothetical problem situations during which two or all three of the family members spoke concurrently.

2. Interruptions: This was the number of occasions for the six hypothetical problem situations that a family member interrupted another. This was scored only if the person interrupting succeeded in speaking at least a phrase.

3. Disagreements and Aggressions: This was the number of times for the six hypothetical problem situations that a family member disagreed with, or was aggressive toward, another. this was scored both in terms of content of speech (such as "That's not true," "You're being foolish") and in terms of indications of hostility in the voice.

4. Failure to Agree: This was the number of times for the six hypothetical problem situations that the family members failed to arrive at a mutually acceptable solution.

These indices, as used for analyses of dominance and conflict in two-person groups, have been shown to be quite reliable (Farina, 1960). Some indices (the speaking first and last components of Total Number of Times Spoken, Passive Acceptance of Solution, and Failure to Agree) have virtually perfect reliability. For these, two judges working independently failed to agree only once in 240 judgments. The rest (excepting the speaking second component of Total Number of Times Spoken, which has not been examined) have a mean reliability of +.86, with a range from +.75 to +.96. These coefficients are actually conservative estimates of the reliability of these indices since they are derived by using hypothetical problem situations instead of families as the units of analyses.

The bulk of the patients who interacted with their parents in the manner described performed a visual discrimination task immediately following the family interaction. These patients will be referred to as the experimental groups. (Precise information about numbers and characteristics of all subjects is given in the Subjects section.) The task consisted of viewing a slide of two silhouetted figures flashed on a screen and indicating if a slide which was subsequently flashed was the same as the first or different. There were two pairs of slides, which were presented alternately, each pair consisting of a standard slide and a matching variation. One pair portrayed a mother scolding a son, and the variation differed from the standard only with respect to the angle of the mother's arm. The other pair showed a father scolding a son, and the standard and variation differed with regard to distance between the father and son. In order to insure that patients would perceive these slides as intended, they were told the slides were pictures of a mother scolding her son and of a father scolding his son. The four slides used were selected from a larger number on the basis of standardization data obtained with normal subjects. For each pair, normal subjects were able consistently to distinguish the variation from the standard in approximately 20 trials with a trial defined as one presentation of the standard slide followed by its variation or the standard slide followed by itself. A detailed description of this phase of the method may be found in Ballantine (1962).

In addition to the experimental subjects, there were groups of control subjects who also performed the visual discrimination task. In order to maximize the possibility of detecting the influence of interaction with parents on the patient's visual discrimination performance, the control subjects performed this task at a time when they had not seen their parents for at least one week.

Subjects. All patients studied were hospitalized at two of the three state hospitals serving the white population of North Carolina. All were (a) male, (b) white, (c) between their 18th and 41st birthday, and (d) diagnosed as schizophrenic with the diagnosis uncomplicated by mental deficiency or organic brain damage. However, one patient, who received a final diagnosis of anxiety reaction, was retained because his psychiatrist believed he was schizophrenic at the time he underwent the procedures of this study. Each patient (e) had lived with his biological parents in an intact family unit from birth through adolescence and (f) was not studied until his physician thought him sufficiently recovered from the illness to be considered for discharge. To determine if the groups of patients differed in level of adjustment or intelligence, each patient was rated on an adjustment scale (Ferguson, McReynolds, & Ballacky, 1953) and received the WAIS Picture Completion Test (Wechsler, 1958).

All patients were assigned a Phillips Scale score on the basis of social history data contained in the records. In accordance with previous studies, patients receiving scores of 15 and below were classified as Goods while those who obtained scores of 16 or more were placed in the Poor groups.

Information about the subjects of this study is presented in Table 1. While there are some notable differences among these groups of subjects, they seem reasonably well matched for most variables. In addition to the variables reported in Table 1, other kinds of data less amenable to tabular presentation were also obtained. These data, including occupation and place of birth of each family member, indicated these groups to be quite similar.

All patients were assigned a Phillips Scale score on the basis of social history data contained in the records. In accordance with previous studies, patients receiving scores of 15 and below were classified as Goods while those who obtained scores of 16 or more were placed in the Poor groups.

Information about the subjects of this study is presented in Table 1. While there are some notable differences among these groups of subjects, they seem reasonably well matched for most variables. In addition to the variables reported in Table 1, other kinds of data less amenable to tabular

TABLE 1

SUBJECT CHARACTERISTICS

		EXPERIMENTAL GROUPS		CONTROL GROUPS[a]	
		Goods	Poors	Goods	Poors
		N = 10	N = 8	N = 13	N = 9
Age, year — Mother	Mean	56.1	55.4		
	SD	10.0	6.5		
Age, year — Father	Mean	59.1	60.4		
	SD	9.8	4.4		
Age, year — Patient	Mean	28.8	24.6	29.8	29.3
	SD	7.4	5.6	8.5	5.5
Education in grades completed — Mother	Mean	8.7	9.0		
	SD	2.7	2.8		
Education in grades completed — Father	Mean	8.1	6.9		
	SD	2.3	2.6		
Education in grades completed — Patient	Mean	10.8	10.4	11.8	9.9
	SD	1.9	2.9	2.8	2.5
Number of siblings	Mean	2.9	2.5		
	SD	2.4	1.8		
Number years parents were married	Mean	34.3	33.6		
	SD	7.3	8.0		
Patient's score on WAIS Picture Completion Test	Mean	7.5	8.0	8.9	6.1
	SD	1.6	2.3	2.0	2.0
Duration of current hospitalization (in months)	Mean	3.1	4.3	2.8	2.6
	SD	4.1	4.3	3.5	3.4
Number of previous admissions	Mean	0.7	1.0	2.5	1.9
	SD	0.9	1.5	3.0	1.8
Hospital adjustment scale score	Mean	80.0	64.6	83.6	79.5
	SD	20.6	26.1	20.7	10.7

[a]Since parents of control subjects were not studied, information about these parents was not obtained.

presentation were also obtained. These data, including occupation and place of birth of each family member, indicated these groups to be quite similar.

RESULTS AND COMMENT

The dominance indices for families of Good and Poor patients are presented in Table 2. The indices Total Number of Times Spoken and Passive Acceptance of Solution suggest that fathers are more dominant in Good than in Poor families, whereas mothers tend to be more domineering in families of Poors than of Goods. In addition to the results presented in Table 2, for the index Total Time Spoken, the mother in each family was compared to her spouse. The results revealed that in the Poor group five of eight mothers spoke longer than their spouses while only one of ten spoke longer than the husbands in the Good group. This difference between groups is statistically significant at the .05 level according to the Fisher exact probability test (Siegel, 1956). The present finding that patients whose premorbid adjustment was reasonably good have more

TABLE 2

DOMINANCE SCORES OF FAMILIES OF GOOD AND POOR PREMORBID
SCHIZOPHRENIC PATIENTS

INDEX		GOODS (*N* = 10)			POORS (*N* = 8)		
		Mother	Father	Patient	Mother	Father	Patient
Total number of times spoken	Mean	5.5	7.5	5.5	5.75	6.5	5.75
	SD	2.3	2.6	2.3	2.4	2.4	2.7
Passive acceptance of solution	Mean	1.1	0.2	1.4	0.75	2.1	2.1
	SD	1.1	0.7	1.8	1.4	0.8	1.1
Total time spoken (seconds)	Mean	121.4	216.8	136.1	211.6	279.4	117.5
	SD	115.1	80.4	101.4	109.4	279.9	83.2
Percentage of total time spoken		26%	45%	29%	35%	46%	19%

assertive fathers than patients whose premorbid functioning was poor is in close agreement with the results of the earlier study by Farina (1960). This relationship lends itself to explanation in terms of an identification process, since it would appear to be *relatively* easy for the son of a domineering father to adopt the typical male behavioral patterns. As a child such a person has a more adequate male model to copy than the child whose father is submissive to the mother.

The index Total Time Spoken suggests, in addition, that the role played in the family by Good and Poor patients differs. The Good patients speak, on the average, 29 percent of the total time the family is verbally active, while the comparable score for the Poor patients is 19 percent. This trend does not appear to be a function of variables such as intelligence and suggests that Good patients, who by definition are more outgoing and have greater initiative, also play a more assertive role and enjoy more freedom within the family than Poor patients.

The conflict scores for these two samples of families are presented in Table 3. The scores are higher for the Poor than for the Good group. In order to evaluate the statistical significance of these results, each family's

TABLE 3

CONFLICT SCORES OF FAMILIES OF GOOD AND POOR
PREMORBID SCHIZOPHRENIC PATIENTS

INDEX		GOODS (*N* = 10)	POORS (*N* = 8)
Frequency of simultaneous speech	Mean	8.2	13.0
	SD	5.9	10.8
Interruptions	Mean	4.6	9.5
	SD	3.9	9.0
Disagreements and aggressions	Mean	11.7	23.9
	SD	7.0	14.1
Failure to agree	Mean	1.5	2.6
	SD	1.3	1.8

scores for the four indices were summed to obtain a single conflict score, and these scores were analyzed by means of a Mann-Whitney U test (Siegel, 1956). The resulting U value of 17 ($N_1 = 8, N_2 = 10$) is statistically significant ($p < .05$) and is in agreement with earlier findings in suggesting that interpersonal relationships are more conflictful for families of Poors than families of Goods.

The conflict data were also examined to determine if the patterns of conflict within the family differ for these two groups. A number of trends were found. The two indices which appear most valid, Disagreements and Aggressions and Failure to Agree, particularly seem to differentiate the conflict patterns of the groups. In Good families, 13 percent of all Disagreements and Aggressions are between the parents, whereas the comparable figure for Poors is 39 percent. For the index Failure to Agree, parents in the Good group fail to agree with each other in 27 percent of all failures to reach a unanimous family solution; the comparable score is 76 percent for Poor group parents. (The residual scores are Disagreements and Aggressions between a parent and a son and Failure to Agree in which the son is a dissenting member.)

While these trends need to be supported by additional evidence before they can be accepted, they suggest that a greater proportion of the conflict which arises in families of Poors, relative to those of Goods, is due to hostility between the parents. It may be that parents of Goods have a relatively high degree of respect and tolerance for each other and can form an alliance against a son who has his own views regarding the resolution of problems and who, moreover, is willing and able to present and maintain these views in spite of parental opposition. Parents of Poors appear less able to cooperate. Their relationship seems to be characterized by impatience with each other and a mutual lack of regard as indicated by frequent interruptions and unwillingness to compromise on the task. Their son less often holds to his own opinion and, confronted with parental dissension, tends to align himself with one of the parents. Despite this tendency of Poor group parents to display disagreement with each other rather than with the son, Poor premorbid schizophrenic patients experienced more conflict with the parents than did Goods with their parents. Poor patients and their mothers in particular displayed a high degree of conflict toward each other in comparison with the conflict between Good group mothers and sons. This difference between the groups in degree of mother-son conflict borders on the .05 level of probability ($N_1 = 8$, $N_2 = 10, U = 17.5, p < .10$).

The results of the visual discrimination task performance are presented in Table 4. The experimental group subjects underwent the hypothetical problem situations interaction with their parents immediately prior to performing the task. The control group subjects, on the other hand, had not seen their parents for at least one week prior to undergoing the procedure. The results suggest that several preliminary attempts to make the mother and father sets of pictures equally difficult to discriminate were only moderately successful. Three of the four groups required more trials to reach the criterion (five consecutive correct discriminations) for

TABLE 4

TRIALS REQUIRED TO REACH CRITERION BY EXPERIMENTAL AND
CONTROL GROUPS OF GOODS AND POORS

		EXPERIMENTAL GROUPS		CONTROL GROUPS	
		Goods $N = 8$	Poors $N = 6$	Goods $N = 13$	Poors $N = 9$
Mother picture	Mean	16.7	22.0	7.5	18.4
	SD	13.8	15.7	11.8	5.5
Father picture	Mean	20.4	23.0	14.8	17.4
	SD	10.5	14.5	12.7	13.3
Difference score (father minus mother trials to criterion)		3.7	1.0	7.3	−1.0

the father pictures than for the mother pictures; this suggested that the father pictures were more difficult to discriminate. An expected finding revealed by Table 4 is that the Poor patients tend to perform generally less adequately than the Good patients. Of greater interest is the finding, which was also expected, that the experimental group patients performed less adequately than the matched control group subjects. The difference between the groups in total trials required to discriminate both mother and father pictures is statistically significant at the .05 level according to the U test ($N_1 = 14$, $N_2 = 1.88$, one-tailed test). This finding supports the hypothesis that a conflictual interaction with the parents does interfere with the patient's performance of relevant tasks. In addition, there is a slight association between the subjects' premorbid adjustment and performance for the mother relative to the father pictures. The Good group patients have more difficulty discriminating the father in comparison to the mother pictures than the Poors as indicated by the average trials to criterion for father minus mother pictures (shown in the last row of Table 4). This trend is consistent with previous findings (Dunham, 1959; Kreinik, 1959), and suggests that Poor group patients are more disturbed by mother than father cues, whereas Good subjects show greater sensitivity to father content. Contrary to expectation, however, interaction with the parents does not appear to increase this differential sensitivity.

The performance of the experimental groups was further analyzed to establish if it was related to the characteristics of the preceding interaction with the parents. For dominance behavior, a single general score was obtained for each parent by converting the four dominance indices so that each would contribute an approximately equal weight and summing these. On the basis of this index, the patients, regardless of group membership, were dichotomized into a mother-dominated group ($N = 7$) and a father-dominated group ($N = 7$). The mother-dominated group had more difficulty discriminating the mother pictures than the father pictures and required an average of 3.6 more trials for the former than the latter. The opposite was true for the father-dominated patients who needed an average of 11.2 more trials to reach criterion for the father pictures than the mother pictures. Although the total number of patients included in the analysis is very small, the difference between the groups reaches a p level of .082 according to the Mann-Whitney U test (one-tailed). This trend suggests the possibility that dominance by a parent is related to specific behavioral deficits in the presence of cues reminiscent of that parent.

The experimental groups were also redivided into two groups of seven patients each on the basis of degree of hostility and disagreement expressed toward the patient by the father in comparison to the mother. There was no apparent difference in adequacy of visual discrimination task performance between the patients who experienced conflict with the mother and those who experienced it with the father. In a final analysis, the schizophrenic subjects were again dichotomized according to degree of conflict they experienced with their parents. In this analysis, however, the mother and father conflict scores were summed, and the performance of the high mother + father conflict group ($N = 7$) was compared to the performance of the low mother + father conflict group ($N = 7$). The high-conflict group required an average of 16.4 trials more to reach the criterion of discrimination for both sets of pictures than the low-conflict group. The difference between the groups, however, is not statistically significant, reaching a p level of .104 according to the U test (one-tailed). The trends reported suggest that conflictful interactions with either parent may interfere with the patient's general behavior in contrast to the more restricted and specific effects of parental dominance on the son's behavior. * * *

An Application of the Rorschach Test in Family Investigation*

Joshua Levy and Nathan B. Epstein

* * * In the traditional approach to the Rorschach Test the focus is on the structure and content of the individual's private world. If a psychoanalytic framework of data analysis is adopted, inferences are drawn concerning the individual's impulses, defenses, modes of coping with psychosexual conflicts, etc. These inner factors are assumed to be significant determinants of the individual's interpersonal relations. The test responses are viewed as determined by the individual's "inner life" as well as by the complex interpersonal dynamics of the testing situation, as stressed by Schafer (1954). These interpersonal and communicational aspects are accentuated during the Family Rorschach. The responses during the Family Rorschach, as we view them, are determined not only by the intrapersonal factors, interpersonal relations, and the test stimuli, but also by the complex transactional processes occurring within the family unit, e.g., the degree of mutual trust underlying family relations, individual interpretations of explicit and implicit family rules, etc. The comparison between the individual responses given alone with those given during the Family Rorschach, provides us with the opportunity of observing the stability and changes in the individual's psychological and social functioning in the presence of the family. Thus the uniqueness of the method is that it reveals the reciprocal effects between inner individual psychological factors and the familial transactions.

In our investigation so far, we have come across two recurrent findings: (1) The technique demonstrates patterns of intrafamilial transactions. (2) The technique demonstrates significant differences in individual responses to the Rorschach in the two contexts; some of the responses produced individually are different from those given by each of the members during the Family Rorschach.

---

*Excerpted from *Family Process*, 1964, *3*, 344–376, with permission of the senior author and *Family Process*.

PROCEDURE

The Rorschach Test is first administered separately to each member of the family, using the following instructions and procedures. "Here are some cards which I am going to present to you one at a time. Look at each and tell me everything it reminds you of. When you are through, please return the card." A brief inquiry follows after each card to secure the location(s) and determinant(s) of the responses(s). In our procedure, the child takes the test first, and a week later the mother and father are seen on two successive hours of the same day. Thus, the Rorschach records are obtained independently, with no member influencing the other's responses. The family is then asked to come together; each is presented with a set of Rorschach cards, and the following instructions are given: "Each of you is to see the cards you saw before. Now, look at the cards again and tell us everything they look like to you now. Then discuss among yourselves what each of you has said and come up with one response all of you agree on. When you are through, please return the card." Since these instructions are readily understood, the examiner's participation after giving them is rather minimal. The examiner is there to observe and note the nonverbal aspects of the family transactions. But when the agreed response is not reached after about five minutes of discussion, which has very rarely happened, the examiner may encourage the family to find a solution. No special inquiry is necessary since the family discussion of their responses provides us with sufficient data regarding their locations and determinants. The individual protocols are taken down verbatim, but the Family Rorschach is tape recorded. * * *

A Structured Family Interview*

Paul Watzlawick

* * * COMPOSITION OF THE STRUCTURED INTERVIEW

A. *Main Problems*

At the beginning of the interview each family member is asked individually, "What do *you* think are the main problems in your family?" He is assured that under no circumstances will his answer be divulged to the other members of his family. He is then made to wait alone in a room until all family members have been interviewed in this way and are eventually brought together again. It is then alleged to them that their individual answers have brought to light several interesting points of discrepancy, that they apparently never have discussed the problem together and that they should do so now, while the interviewer leaves the room. The family is told that they will be observed through a one-way screen and that their discussion will be recorded. They are also reminded that they are under no obligation to disclose to the others what they have told the interviewer individually. It is explained to them that their task is to reach a conclusion as to their main problems as a family.

The question "What do *you* think are the main problems in your family?" implies several things. First, it implicitly grants the subject the right to his or her own view of the family problems and shows that this view is considered important. Second, "problems" (in the plural) implies that the interviewer, who is of course expected to know the family's presenting complaint (i.e., the Identified Patient's symptom), not only does not go along with this definition of their trouble, but assumes the presence of a variety of problems. It further emphasizes that their problems are related to them as a family and paves the way for future conjoint therapy. Thus, from the very beginning, the myth is undermined that there is nothing wrong in the family except for the fact that their son or daughter happens to be "sick" or delinquent.

B. *Plan Something Together*

With all family members now together, the interviewer gives them the following instruction: "Next, I should like you to plan something together, something that you all could do together as a family. I shall

---

*Excerpted from *Family Process*, 1966, *5*, 256–271, with permission of the author and *Family Process*.

again leave you alone for about five minutes, and when I come back I want you to tell me what you have planned."

It is not so much the content of their final decision which has been found to be revealing in this task (although this too is of interest; if, for example, the family decides on accomplishing a long-postponed necessity rather than something pleasurable), but whether or not a decision is reached within the time limits, and the manner in which it was accomplished.

C. How Did You Meet?

For this part, the children are told to wait outside. The parents are then asked: "How, out of all the millions of people in the world, did you two get together?" It has been found useful for the interviewer (who remains in the room for this part of the interview) not to look at either parent while asking this question, but to point at both of them with a simultaneous gesture of both hands.

This question has been found to elicit highly significant patterns of marital interaction, so much so that experienced family clinicians are sometimes able to make highly valid predictions about the psychopathology of family members by merely listening to a tape recording of this part of the interview. In responding to this question, the spouses not only offer their sometimes very discrepant recollections of shared experiences in the past, but in doing so reveal their predominant patterns of interacting *in the present*. It is thus again not so much the *content* of their response, but the way they relate to each other in the context of the interview, which is of importance here.

D. Proverb

With the children still waiting outside, the parents are given the following instruction: "I have here [on typewritten cards] a proverb which I am sure you know. I should like you to discuss the meaning of this proverb for not longer than five minutes, while I shall again leave you alone. As soon as you have discussed the meaning, will you please call the children in yourselves and teach them the meaning of this proverb." As can be seen, the instructions do not openly state that the parents have to reach an agreement, as it was found that otherwise the interview would simply bog down at this point in the face of disagreement. Not to insist on an agreement has the additional advantage that the ensuing interaction is likely to show more clearly their typical ways of dealing with (labeled or unlabeled) disagreement.

The proverb is "A rolling stone gathers no moss." There are several interesting facts connected with this proverb, expecially in its interactional application. It shares with all other proverbs the possibility of either literal or metaphorical interpretation. It differs from most other proverbs in that it does not assign any value to what it states. Indeed, the proposition it represents is merely an equation in terms of logical syntax; it establishes a *logical relationship* between two variables ("moss" and "rolling") without introducing values for them. As far as its meaning goes, it simply means what one chooses to make it mean, i.e., either that "moss" is something desirable (roots, friends, stability, prestige, etc.), or that "rolling" is good (because it keeps a person from stagnating, makes him sharp and alert, etc.). However, once a value has been assigned to one side of the equation (either to "moss" or "rolling"), the *opposite* value *must* be given to the other side, lest the logic of the proverb be violated. It is psychologically interesting to note that most people interpreting this proverb are unaware of the fact that there exist these two perfectly valid, but mutually exclusive interpretations. The stage for disagreement is thus set (especially since either interpretation implicitly amounts to a statement of one's philosophy of life) and experience shows that it is quite rare to find two spouses who spontaneously agree on one or the other interpretation. Therefore, they are either forced to admit their disagreement—which again is very rare and is compounded by the fact that they know that they have to teach the "correct" meaning to the children—or to use special maneuvers to cover up their disagreement. * * *

E. Blame

For this task the father is made to sit to the left of the interviewer, followed at his left by the mother and the children in order of their ages (from the oldest to the youngest) in clockwise direction around the table. The interviewer then hands everyone a piece of paper (a 3" x 5" file card) and a pencil, and gives them the following instructions: "Next, I want you to write down on this piece of paper the main fault of the person on your left. Make your statement as brief as possible; don't use any names or other identifying features. When you have finished, hand your card directly to me." To the youngest child, sitting at his right, the interviewer explains that this child should write down the main fault of the father and not, of course, the interviewer. Again, the family is assured that the interviewer will not reveal the author of any statement. In addition, they are told that the interviewer will himself add two statements to the ones written by them. (These statements are always "Too good" and "Too weak"—statements known to produce controversy because of their ambiguous implications.) It is further explained to them that the interviewer's statements are made about any two family members and not necessarily about the father (who sits at the interviewer's left). After writing his statements, the interviewer shuffles the cards and begins to read them out, one after the other to the family. After reading each card he asks all family members in turn, beginning with the father and finishing with the youngest child: "To whom do *you* think this applies?" However, although the interviewer shuffled the cards in plain sight of the family, he always starts with his own two statements, and only then reads out the family's statements in the random order produced by the shuffling. (This arrangement is maintained in order to facilitate ongoing research into the scoreability of this task.) If necessary, the interviewer will insist on a forced choice and will not accept responses like "This applies to both our children" or "This does not apply to anybody in our family." Each family member is thus forced to blame somebody, and by so doing implies automatically that in his opinion this criticism was leveled by the person sitting on the right of the "victim." * * *

Studies of Family Interaction: Feelings, Attitudes, Power

The articles in Parts B and C are decision-making studies which could just as well have been placed in the preceding group. However, we feel that these articles reflect a somewhat different emphasis or focus of analysis from those of Part A. In Part B are found research studies which concentrate on family feelings and attitudes, as expressed by measures of empathy, hostility, dominance, conflict, etc.

The investigation by Ferreira (Article 17) is an interesting one, in that it represents a study of pseudo-interaction. The family members are not placed in an actual face-to-face interaction, but each is deceived into believing a fantasied interaction has taken place, namely that the other members have judged the merit of his artistic production. The discrepancy between the actual judgments and the fantasied judgments forms the basis for an empathy score.

In Article 18, Winter, Ferreira, and Olson asked their three-person families to make up TAT stories together; then they analyzed the themes for degree and overtness of hostility, using scores based on the final stories produced. Schulman, Shoemaker, and Moelis also had family triads complete imaginative stories, but their families worked on the task in a playroom filled with attractive objects which would distract the child from the task. Their interest was in the parental methods used to keep their child on the task, rather than in the content of the stories which were produced, the source of data in the previous article. They found that the parents of conduct-problem children exhibit significantly more hostility and rejection of their children than do the controls, a finding which invites comparison with that of the preceding article (18) for the delinquent subsample, and with Article 14.

Bauman and Roman present an interesting technique for measuring the results of certain interactional processes on family answers to a standard intelligence test. By comparing the individually-given answers with the conjoint answers, in a method similar to unrevealed differences mentioned earlier, dominance of one member over another can be measured and correlated with other pertinent variables. Hutchinson also investigates the interactions between sex of child and family dominance and conflict patterns; his results should be compared with those of Articles 14 and 22, and with Becker and Siefkes (in press).

In these studies, the results for family conflict and hostility seem simpler and more easily integrated than those for dominance. The concept of dominance may be of a different order than the concept of conflict. A high conflict score means that the family has engaged in certain overt behaviors which we define as conflict. But a high dominance score obtained by an individual family member may be less clear in meaning. For instance, a high father dominance score may be more complex, in that the mother may be giving him permission to win, so which one is actually dominant may be an almost meaningless question—or better, a question very difficult to handle with our present theoretical framework and research techniques.

Interpersonal Perceptivity among Family Members[*]

Antonio J. Ferreira

* * * As it is used here, "interpersonal perceptivity" means the ability an individual is said to have to guess, nonverbally and more or less accurately, the mood, attitude, and behavior of another individual. Accordingly, this experiment was designed to set up a guessing situation that would confront the guessor with the guessee and permit a numerical evaluation of an expressed guess. To keep the problem manageable, the subject's interpersonal perceptivity of only one kind of mood, attitude, or behavior was investigated; to this end, the parameter "rejection" was chosen and operationally defined. Thus a research situation was envisioned in which a pair of subjects, A and B, were to be confronted in such a way as to permit, say, the matching of a numerical expression of A's rejection of B with a numerical expression of B's blind expectancy of rejection by A.

METHOD

First, each family member was asked to color a number of flags drawn on pieces of cardboard, and each was provided with a standard box of eight crayons and a set of eleven 2" x 3" cards bearing a stamped drawing of a tri-striped flag. The subjects were instructed to try to color each flag differently, but always strive toward "the most pleasing color combinations." During this task family members were effectively isolated from each other in separate rooms. When the coloring was concluded, the subjects were instructed to place the flags in an envelope and write their first names on the outside. Thus the stage was set for the testing situation.

The testing itself consisted of two successive steps, resulting in two scores. In the first step, the flags colored by one family member were presented to another member with the statement: "These are the flags painted by your mother (or son, or husband, etc.). . . . Go through them one by one, and throw away those you do not like for whatever reason." Meanwhile, the envelope containing the flags and bearing the visible signa-

[*]Abstracted from the *American Journal of Orthopsychiatry*, 1964, *34*, 64–70, with permission of the author and The American Orthopsychiatric Association.

ture of the family member in question was placed on the table face up, together with a box bearing a conspicuous sign reading, "Bad. Throw away." The subject was instructed that this box was to function symbolically as a waste basket into which the rejected flags were to be thrown. Thus each family member was invited to throw away—that is, to reject—the productions of the other family members. The number of flags thrown away, from zero to eleven, constituted the score R, which assumedly measured the overt or explicit nonacceptance or rejection of the other family member. In a second step, aimed at determining the "expectancy of rejection," each family member was asked to make a guess, based on his or her knowledge of the other family member, as to how many of the flags that he or she had colored were being thrown away by the other family member. The number of flags the subject expected another family member to reject constituted the E score, which assumedly measured the "expectancy of rejection" for the particular relationship with that family member.

The collection of data took place from October 1960 to September 1961, in a relatively wide geographical circle centered on the city of San Jose, California. The subjects were the members of family triads. A family triad was defined as a father, a mother, and a child who had lived together as a social aggregate for at least two years; the child was to be ten or more years of age.

The families were categorized as "normal" or "pathological" according to an operational definition: A normal family was any family having no known psychiatric pathology, whose members had not been recommended for, or gone through, any form of psychiatric treatment for at least the past five years. Pathological families were those containing one or more members with identified psychopathology and undergoing, at the time of the testing, some form of psychiatric evaluation, therapy, or both. Families of psychiatrists, psychologists, or social workers were excluded from the project. Families were included as long as they were available and fit these criteria.

Normal families were obtained by scouting among neighbors, acquaintances, friends' neighbors, neighbors' friends, and so on, in progressively wider circles; for the most part they were tested in their own homes at a time suitable to all concerned (usually the evening), due precautions having been taken against any form of interruption or outside interference.

Pathological families were obtained directly through referral or indirectly in local psychiatric clinics and hospitals. Usually the child was the identified patient. In ten of these families the child had received the diagnosis of schizophrenia; most of these schizophrenic children were, or recently had been, hospitalized. The pathological families were tested in a clinic, hospital, or private office, but not in their homes. I was the sole tester.

There were 25 normal and 30 pathological families in the study. Broadly speaking, these 55 families constituted a rather homogeneous group, being Caucasian with predominantly American cultural values, and coming from the middle and upper-middle socioeconomic class. The two subgroups of normal and abnormal families did not differ significantly in the ages of their members: the overall age of the fathers ranged from 30 to 54 years, with the median at 42.5; of the mothers, from 30 to 49 years, with the median at 39.1; and of the tested children, from 10 to 21 years, with the median at 14.6. On the average, the families had 3.1 children (3.3 children in normal and 3.0 children in pathological families). Of the tested children, 30 were boys (12 in the normal and 18 in the abnormal families) and 25 were girls (13 in the normal and 12 in the abnormal families).

RESULTS AND DISCUSSION

As can be seen from the description of the testing procedure, there were four scores for each family member: two R scores representing the number of flags they rejected, and two E scores representing the number of flags they expected to be rejected. This report is concerned exclusively with the question of how well a family member guessed the rejecting behavior of another family member.

The first consideration here, of course, is that this question involves an interpersonal comparison and raises a problem similar to that posed by the concept of "utility" in game theory experiments. In terms of our data, this problem can be visualized by recognizing that given two subjects, A and B, A may express a slight rejection by throwing away all flags, whereas B may express a great deal of that "same" rejection by throwing away only a few. In this light it is apparent that the correspondence between, say, a father's expectancy of his son's rejection (score E), and the son's actual rejection of his father (score R) could be assessed only in a coarse and general way. Accordingly, the guesses were categorized simply as "good" or "bad." A guess was considered good whenever the E score of a given subject coincided, plus or minus one, with the R score of the family member whose rejecting behavior he was trying to guess; in other words, when the difference between the expectancy of rejection and the actual rejection was 0 ± 1, the guess was considered a good one, as opposed to a bad guess which, by definition, missed the target by two or more flags. In this way, it was found that the total of 330 guesses comprehended 148 good and 182 bad guesses.

On the a priori assumption that both E and R scores were random events in the full theoretical range of scores (0 to 11), the finding of 148 good guesses far exceeded chance expectancy ($p < .001$). However, the data suggested a different assignment of probabilities, inasmuch as the theoretical range of scores did not correspond with the actual events. In fact, a posteriori, it seemed that all responses had been "restricted," the great majority of scores (R and E scores as well) having fallen between 0 and 7 instead of the theoretical 0 to 11 range. This narrowing of the range of responses whereby a subject did not reject (R score) or expect to be rejected (E score) more than a restricted amount, probably represented a cultural factor. Be that as it may, it seemed that the data should be re-examined in terms of probabilities assigned on the basis of the actual

TABLE 1

ANALYSIS OF VARIANCE FOR VALUES OF EMPATHY INDEX

Source	df	MS	F
Children vs. adults	1	17.68	5.42*
Normal vs. abnormal	1	4.38	1.34
Interaction	1	1.40	
Within cells	326	3.26	

*$p < .05$.

(0 to 7), rather than the theoretical (0 to 11) range of scores. Under these new computing conditions, the number of good guesses was still significantly better than chance (binomial test corrected for continuity, $p < .05$, one-tailed). And even when the computation was based on the stringent assumption that the guessors had full (cultural?) information about not only the range but the frequency distribution of the guessee's R scores, the guesses of family members were better than chance (binomial test corrected for continuity, $p < .08$ for all individuals, $p < .04$ for children only, one-tailed).

A different approach to the hypothesis of interpersonal perceptivity was also investigated: Since each subject was requested to make a guess in regard to the other two members of the family triad, a comparison of these two scores (E_1 and E_2) would reflect the subject's view of the relative rejecting behavior of the other two members. One of the following three different situations would occur: (1) $E_1 > E_2$, (2) $E_1 = E_2$, or (3) $E_1 < E_2$. Then the question became: How often were such relative guesses correct? Again, the findings were statistically significant, inasmuch as there were 80 such correct guesses, although only 59 were expected by chance (binomial test, corrected for continuity, $z = 3.36$, $p < .0005$, one-tailed). From these results it seemed reasonable to conclude that an operative factor other than cultural was responsible for the "goodness" of the guesses and, therefore, that the hypothesis of interpersonal perceptivity had been corroborated.

At this point, an inquiry into the characteristics of the phenomenon of interpersonal perceptivity seemed appropriate. Two hypotheses appeared particularly suitable for investigation: that the phenomenon of interpersonal perceptivity is (1) more pronounced in children than adults and (2) more pronounced in normal than abnormal individuals.

The first hypothesis, that interpersonal perceptivity decreases with an increase in age, was formulated following the clinical and theoretical observations of Dunbar (1944), Ferreira (1961, 1963b), and Sullivan (1947). Accordingly, a comparison was made between children and adults (parents) in terms of their guesses; it was found that the children had made 53.6 percent good guesses, whereas the adults had made only 40.5 percent. This difference, conforming with the hypothesis, was statistically significant (chi-square, corrected for continuity, $X^2 = 5.56$, $df = 1$, $p < .01$, one-tailed).

The second hypothesis, that interpersonal perceptivity is greater in normal than in pathological individuals was formulated on the basis of observations of Ferreira (1961), Jackson and Carr (1955), and Olden (1958). By first assuming that every member of a normal family was normal, and every member of an abnormal family was abnormal, a comparison was made between normal and abnormal subjects in terms of their good guesses. In this fashion, it was found that normal subjects had 48.7 percent good guesses, while abnormal subjects had 41.7 percent. This difference, though in the predicted direction, did not reach statistical significance. In an alternative approach to the testing of both hypotheses, an "empathy index," based on the difference between the guess (E score) and the fact (R score) was computed. Table 1 and Figure 1 highlight the relevant findings.

At this point it is worth mentioning that, as a group, fathers displayed as much perceptivity as mothers, and that the children's ability to make good guesses did not seem to favor either parent.

We turn our attention now to the investigation of an important question raised some time ago by Foa (1958), namely, whether the phenomenon of interpersonal perceptivity is a property of the individual who guesses, or of the individual being guessed. Ordinarily, it is assumed that interpersonal perceptivity, often called empathy or intuition, is exclusive-

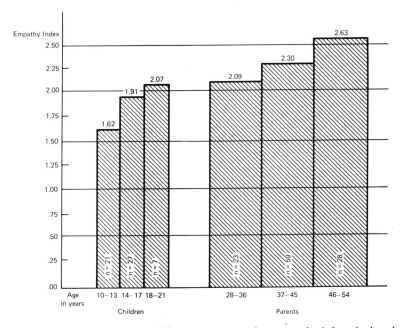

Fig. 1. Average Empathy Index for different age groups. The greater the index, the less the empathy.

ly a function of the guessor; but Foa pointed out that at least in some instances the phenomenon could just as well be interpreted as the result of a sort of behavioral transparency of the guessee. To investigate the question of empathy vs. behavior transparency, a further analysis of the data seemed appropriate.

It may be recalled that every subject made two guesses, each in relation to the other two members in the family triad. A pair of such guesses could be "good-good," "good-bad," or "bad-bad." Accordingly, it seemed reasonable to postulate that, if the phenomenon under study was due exclusively to a property of the individual who guesses (empathy), the frequency of "good-good" plus "bad-bad" pairs of guesses should exceed the frequency expected by chance, since the individual would have a tendency to be either a good ("good-good" pair of guesses) or a bad ("bad-bad" pair of guesses) empathizer. On the other hand, following the same line of reasoning, it could be expected that if the phenomenon was instead, a manifestation of the transparency of the guessee, then, having been well guessed by one family member should tend to coincide with being well guessed by the other family member with a frequency greater than chance. Grouped in these two different ways, the frequencies of "good-good," "bad-bad," and "good-bad" pairs were calculated but they did not depart from chance. The hypotheses that the phenomenon of interpersonal perceptivity was predominantly a function of the guessor (empathy) or of the guessee (transparency) were, therefore, not corroborated.

In the light of these findings, it seemed appropriate to question whether interpersonal perceptivity is an individual phenomenon and consider the possibility that it might be, instead, a relationship event. Some support for this view was to be encountered in the finding that a parent had more "good" guesses for a child of the same sex than for a child of the opposite sex (chi-square, $\chi^2 = 5.38$, $df = 1$, $p < .05$, two-tailed). But clearer evidence resulted from a surprising finding: in the dyad combinations (father-mother, father-child, mother-child), family members tended to have the same kind of guess—that is, good or bad—toward each other. Further, and of possibly great interest, was the observation that this sort of mutuality in perceptivity was encountered in normal families with a frequency much greater than chance (binomial test corrected for continuity, $z = 3.25$, $p < .001$, one-tailed), but it was apparently absent in dyads from abnormal families. In this regard, the two groups of families behaved quite distinctly.

To conclude, the results of this study seem to provide experimental evidence for the occurrence of the phenomenon of interpersonal perceptivity. In terms of this experiment, the subject's ability to make good guesses about the intensity of the rejecting behavior of a given family member was significantly better than chance. However, the data led us to consider that interpersonal perceptivity may not be sufficiently explained in terms of a property of the individual. In fact, this study suggests instead that the phenomenon may be a relationship event in which some factors or components seem to stand out:

1. A *cultural factor* that apparently determines the range within which rejection may be expected. In terms of the present experiment, this factor was seemingly responsible for the accumulation of scores (both E and R) within the range 0 to 7, instead of the theoretically available 0 to 11 range. This point conforms well, of course, with the common observation that it is much easier to be empathic about an individual of the same rather than of a different cultural background.

2. An *individual factor*, a property of the guessor often referred to as empathy or intuition, variable with age and probably also with psychopathology and other parameters of ego functioning. The part played by this factor was evidenced in the observation that children seemed to have a significantly greater perceptivity than adults, and that interpersonal perceptivity apparently varies with the age of the individual (see Figure 1).

3. A *relationship factor* that conceivably makes the phenomenon depend, at least to some degree, upon some sort of mutuality and reciprocity in the dyad. The possible importance of this factor became all the more intriguing when it was observed that its presence in normal dyads contrasted with its seeming absence in the dyads from abnormal families.

I need not emphasize that the results of this study must be taken with caution and reservation. The approach was novel and the conclusions were often reached *ex post facto*, by inspection of the data. However, it is hoped that this experiment, pioneering as it was, may have served to open new vistas and perhaps have shed some light upon the hitherto elusive phenomenon of interpersonal perceptivity.

Hostility Themes in the Family TAT[*]

*William D. Winter, Antonio J. Ferreira,
and Jim L. Olson*

In a recent study (Winter, Ferreira, & Olson, 1965), the authors described
a method of assessing family pathology by asking family triads to produce
conjointly three TAT stories based on nine cards. These stories were
scored by the Arnold (1962) system of Story Sequence Analysis, and the
scores obtained were found to differentiate between normal and abnormal
families. However, the Arnold scores did not discriminate among the
abnormal groups tested.

At that time, we speculated that this lack of discrimination might be
due to two factors: (1) the basis used for forming subgroups of abnormal
families, i.e, the diagnosis of the child, might have been invalid, and the
subgroups of abnormals might not, in fact, be different from each other;
(2) the nature of the Arnold system may mask real differences among our
groups, in that this system is based on the underlying import or emotional
meaning of the study, not on how these imports might be expressed in
specific themes. In order to investigate further these two possibilities, it
seemed worthwhile to analyze some of the presumably more superficial
themes in the stories. We chose themes of hostility, partly because of their
theoretical importance and popularity in the literature, and partly because
relatively objective methods of measuring hostility themes have been
developed (Olson, 1964; Pittluck, 1950).

METHOD

Subjects. The families tested were 126 triads of father, mother, and
child. These were divided into four groups based on the diagnosis of the
child: (1) 50 Normals (*Nor*); (2) 44 Emotionally Maladjusted (*Mal*), e.g.,
neurotics; (3) 16 Schizophrenics (*Sch*); and (4) 16 Delinquents (*Del*).
(For a fuller description of the subjects, see Article 11.)

Procedure. In this part of the research, each family was presented
with a set of three TAT cards and instructed to work together to make up
a story they all agreed upon, which would link the three cards together in

[*]Abstracted from the *Journal of Projective Techniques and Personality Assessment*, 1966, *30*,
270-274, with permission of the authors and the publisher.

the order in which they were presented, and which would describe what the characters were doing, feeling, etc. The three sets of TAT cards used were: (1) 7GF, 5, 10; (2) 13B, 4, 3BM; (3) 6GF, 3GF, 18GF. The investigator then left the room for five minutes; upon his return one of the family members, who had been chosen to be spokesman, told him the story they had agreed on. The procedure was repeated twice more with new cards and a different spokesman each time. The choice of who would be the spokesman for each story was not related significantly to the diagnosis of the family. In addition, an analysis of the tape recordings taken during the time period when the families were left alone to make up their stories revealed that the percentage of hostile themes suggested by each family member, compared to the percentages of the other two members, was not related to diagnosis, using the deviation-from-randomness measure of Haley (1964).

Variables and Scoring. The three TAT stories so obtained from each family, as told to the investigator, were transcribed and scored for the following two variables by a psychologist who had had no personal contact with the families and did not know their diagnoses:

1. Weighted Hostility (*Wt Host*). The basic score for this variable was obtained from the Hafner-Kaplan (1960) scale for the analysis of hostile content of test protocols. In this scale, specified themes are given weights according to the degree of hostility they represent. For example, themes involving a minimum of hostility, such as guilt, death symbols, or military figures, are scored "1"; on the other hand, themes involving maximum hostility, such as direct physical aggressive acts between people, are given the maximum weight of "4". However, for our study this Hafner-Kaplan hostility score appeared to require a correction, since the longer the story, the greater the opportunity for hostile (or other) themes to be introduced. Therefore, the sum of the Hafner-Kaplan scores was corrected by dividing the total number of words used in the telling of the story, to obtain *Wt Host*, expressed as a percentage.

$$Wt\ Host = \frac{\text{Total Hostility}}{\text{Total words in Story}} \times 100$$

2. Percentage of Overt Hostility (*% Overt*). The Hafner-Kaplan scale scores themes not only for degree of hostility, but also for whether they represent either overt or covert hostility. For example, of the themes receiving a weight of "4" for hostility, those involving fighting and assault are scored as overtly hostile, while those involving suicide or self-injury are scored as covertly hostile. The *% Overt* hostility consists of the number of overtly hostile themes divided by the total of the overt plus covert themes.

$$\% \ Overt = \frac{\text{Overt Hostility Themes}}{\text{Total Hostility Themes}} \times 100$$

Both *Wt Host* and *% Overt* were based on all three stories combined.

Hypotheses. The hypotheses corresponding to these two variables were that, compared to abnormal families, normal families would manifest: (1) lower *Wt Host*, and (2) lower *% Overt* hostility.

These two hypotheses were based on the reported findings of several researchers that more severely disturbed families express more antagonism and hostility (Caputo, 1963; Farina, 1960; Ferreira, 1963b); and that disturbed individuals tend to express more overt or unmodified agression (Gottschalk, Gleser, & Springer, 1963; Haskell, 1961).

Statistical Analysis. The significance of the differences between groups of normal and abnormal families was evaluated by analysis of variance and subsequent one-tailed *t* test. Due to the unbalanced ratio of male to female children in the *Del* group, two different statistical analyses were computed. For the first, the *Del* group was omitted and a two-way analysis of variance with sex of the child as the second variable was performed for the *Nor, Mal,* and *Sch* families, using a computer program which allowed for disproportional numbers of cases in the cells. For the second, a simple analysis of variance was computed for all families with male children in our sample. Preliminary analysis of variance indicated that the age of the child was not a significant variable.

RESULTS

1. *Wt Host.* The combined results for the two analyses of variance are given in Table 1. As can be seen from this table, *Wt Host* significantly differentiated the four diagnostic groups on both analyses. No sex or interaction effects were obtained.

TABLE 1

ANALYSES OF VARIANCE DATA FOR WEIGHTED HOSTILITY

CHILD'S SEX		*Nor*	*Mal*	*Sch*	*Del*
Male	Mean	6.3	8.5	5.8	8.8
	SD	3.0	2.6	3.0	4.7
Female	Mean	6.5	9.8	5.8	
	SD	2.4	3.6	2.7	

(a) Two-way analysis of variance (*Nor, Mal, Sch*)
   F Diagnosis $= 12.28$ $df = 2/104$ $p < .005$
   F Sex $= 0.60$ $df = 1/104$ *ns*
   F Interaction $= 0.52$ $df = 2/104$ *ns*
(b) One-way analysis of variance (all males)
   F Diagnosis $= 4.30$ $df = 3/84$ $p < .01$

A comparison of the means of the four groups by one-tailed *t* tests revealed no significant differences between the *Nor* and *Sch* groups on either analysis of variance (both *t*'s $< .70$). However, comparing the families with male children alone, using the one-way analysis data, we find that the *Nor* families scored significantly lower in *Wt Host* than did the

Mal ($t = 2.72$, $p < .003$) and the *Del* families ($t = 2.55$, $df = .84$, $p < .005$). Similarly, for the two-way data combining male and female children, the *Nor* families had lower *Wt Host* scores than did the *Mal* families ($t = 4.08$, $df = 104$, $p < .0001$). Two-tailed t tests for the male children showed that the *Sch* families also scored lower than the *Mal*'s ($t = 2.41$, $p < .02$) and the *Del*'s ($t = 2.38$, $p < .02$), and for all children the *Sch*'s scored lower than the *Mal*'s ($t = 3.72$, $p < .0002$). To summarize, the *Mal* and *Del* groups produced stories with significantly greater weighted hostility than did the *Nor* and *Sch* groups, a finding which partially supports the hypothesis.

It was decided to examine also whether any of the three TAT stories by itself differentiated these diagnostic groups, when scored for *Wt Host*. Since no effects attributable to the sex of the child had been found, all families in each group were combined and a one-way analysis of variance for each story was computed. Briefly, the first story did not discriminate among the four groups, but the second ($F = 5.52$, $p < .01$) and third ($F = 3.35$, $df = 3/122$, $p < .05$) did. However, since each family received the three sets of TAT cards in the same order, it is not possible to determine whether these last two sets were more effective because of the stimulus characteristics of the cards they contained, or because they were given later in the series.

Incidentally, the same F tests were computed using the total number of scorable hostile themes (unweighted) divided by the number of words in the story. The Hafner-Kaplan weights used in *Wt Host* seem to improve the differentiation among groups slightly, although the results for both variables were quite similar. For example, the one-way analysis of variance F for all male children using the unweighted themes was 3.81; using the weighted themes, it was 4.30. We would suggest, therefore, that the standard weights be used in future research.

2. *% Overt*. The data for both analyses of variance can be found in Table 2. This variable did significantly differentiate the *Nor, Mal*, and *Sch* total groups in the two-way analysis, but did not differentiate all four groups (male children only) in the one-way analysis. In the former set of data, one-tailed t tests revealed no significant differences between the *Nor* and *Sch* families, but the *Nor*'s did show a significantly lower percentage of overtly hostile themes than did the *Mal*'s ($t = 2.47$, $df = 104$, $p < .007$). For the male children only, adding the *Del* families into the analysis of variance produced overall results which were not significant. The *Del* families with male children scored almost the same as the *Nor*'s, and both of these groups were intermediate between the high-scoring *Mal*'s and low-scoring *Sch*'s. It is only between these latter two extreme groups of *Mal*'s and *Sch*'s that a significant difference is obtained ($t = 1.97$, $p < .05$, two-tailed). The hypothesis seems clearly supported only with regard to the difference between *Nor* and *Mal* families.

The first two stories, when analyzed individually, failed to differentiate the groups. However, a significant F value was found for the third story, following the procedure outlined previously ($F = 6.83$, $df = 3/122$, $p < .005$).

TABLE 2

ANALYSES OF VARIANCE DATA FOR PERCENTAGE OF OVERT HOSTILITY

CHILD'S SEX		*Nor*	*Mal*	*Sch*	*Del*
Male	Mean	24.6	30.4	18.1	26.3
	SD	17.8	16.8	15.7	19.9
Female	Mean	20.9	34.3	21.7	
	SD	12.2	14.9	21.2	

(a) Two-way analysis of variance (*Nor, Mal, Sch*)
     F Diagnosis = 4.83 df = 2/104 $p < .01$
     F Sex   = 0.12 df = 1/104 ns
     F Interaction = 0.64 df = 2/104 ns
(b) One-way analysis of variance (all males)
     F Diagnosis = 1.39 df = 3/84 ns

DISCUSSION

These results partially confirm both hypotheses. In general, the *Nor* and *Mal* families behaved according to expectations, but the *Sch* and *Del* families did not. It would be inappropriate, therefore, to treat the *Mal, Sch*, and *Del* families as a homogeneous group. Our data indicate that the *Mal*'s produced TAT stories which were more hostile in content and with themes which were more "overtly" hostile than did the *Nor*'s. Within the context of this specific testing situation, it would appear that the *Mal* families produced thematic material indicating that their motivational systems and fantasies are heavily imbued with hostile preoccupations which are somewhat primitive and outwardly directed in nature.

Perhaps our most surprising finding is that the *Sch* families produced stories with the least weighted hostility and least overt hostility present in the themes, thus differing markedly from the *Mal* families. The reasons for this difference are not clear. To say that these families are truly not hostile would not seem to conform with clinical experience. Therefore, we are led to assume that their hostility is either far removed from the level of explicit expression, or that it is conveyed in ways too subtle to be detected by our scoring system, or that these families avoid the expression of emotional antagonism by confirming themselves to nonrevealing stories as an expression of family effort to disengage emotionally when a strong negative feeling threatens to come forth.

The *Del* group seems least clearly defined. Their stories have the highest scores for weighted hostility of any group, when male children are compared. However, their percentage of overt hostility is close to that of the *Nor*'s. Compared to the *Mal*'s the hostile themes of the *Del*'s is some-what more covert in nature, which does not seem consistent with the overtly aggressive behavior which was the basis of the child's diagnosis. This discrepancy is worth further investigation. Perhaps this pattern does reflect a stable characteristic of the *Del* family triad. But another explana-tion suggests itself in the possibility that these families may be trying to give a good impression to the investigator, as a way of offsetting their

recent encounter with the law. It is not clear what personality characteristics and situational variables are affecting the unexpected responses
obtained from the *Sch* and *Del* groups.

These findings seem particularly interesting when taken in conjunction
with the scoring of these same stories by the Arnold system of Story
Sequence Analysis (Arnold, 1962), which evaluates the overall pathology
of the basic theme or import of the story. As reported above, the Arnold
scores of the three abnormal groups do not differ from one another, but
all three score as more pathological than the normals (Winter et al., 1965).
Since the present results indicate that the Hafner-Kaplan scales do differentiate the three abnormal groups of families, our conclusion is that our
previous results were due to the nature of the Arnold scoring system. Our
interpretation of our findings in both studies is that the basic value systems and ways of viewing the world of the *Mal, Sch*, and *Del* groups are
equally abnormal, but the manner in which they express hostility
differs * * *

Laboratory Measurement
of Parental Behavior[*]

Robert E. Schulman, Donald J. Shoemaker,
and Irvin Moelis

* * * An obvious alternative to the reliance on questionable data obtained in an interview is the use of a home visit. This method of obtaining information regarding parent-child interaction patterns has been used by social workers and in more intensive psychological research, but is rarely seen as a routine procedure in psychological or psychiatric clinics. The obvious reasons for its relative disuse are expense and lack of quantifiable measurement techniques.

Another alternative, one utilized as a part of a larger investigation of parent-child relations conducted by one of the present writers and other staff members of the University of Illinois Psychological Clinic, is the measurement of parent-child interaction in the clinic playroom situation. In utilizing this method, either one or both of the parents have been invited into the playroom with the child, with the instructions either to play freely with the child or to interact with the child on some predetermined task. Various measures of the observed interaction have been obtained, and attempts to relate these measures to child behavior *outside* the playroom have been made. Although this method is similar to that utilized by Bishop (1951) and Moustakas, Siegel, and Schalock, (1956), it differs in that the primary focus is on the relation existing between parent-child behavior in the playroom and child behavior in the general life situation. If such relations can be demonstrated, then the possibility arises of using the parent-child interaction in the clinic to help locate factors in the general parent-child interaction that are related to child maladjustment.

The present study focused on one aspect of child behavior (aggression) and two aspects of parental behavior (frustration and model) that, on the basis of previous research (Leton, 1958; Levin & Sears, 1956), were hypothesized to be related to aggression in children. In considering frustration, we were concerned with the parents' excessive limiting or control-

[*]Abstracted from the *Journal of Consulting Psychology*, 1962, *26*, 109–114, with permission of the senior author and the American Psychological Association.

ling of the child's behavior with resulting frustration to the child. In considering the parents as a model for agression, we were concerned with the example for aggressive behavior that the parents might present to the child in the interaction with each other in the child's presence. The hypotheses tested were (a) the parents of conduct-problem children will exhibit significantly more control over the behavior of the child than will parents of non-conduct-problem children and, (b) the parents of conduct-problem children will exhibit significantly more aggression between themselves than will the parents of non-conduct-problem children.

METHOD

Delineation of the Variables. On the basis of pilot study, nine behavior-rating categories were specially constructed for use in the present research. Four of the categories deal with the aggressive model variables; five deal with the parental control variables.

Control Variables

pd (parental domination): Parent dominates the task and restricts the child's behavior.

pr (parental rejection): Parent rejects child's behavior in the task situation.

pt (parent takes over, literally): Child stands aside while the adult goes ahead to do the task.

ph (parent hostile to child): Parent is not physically hostile, but is overcritical, forbids certain behaviors, does not reward child for his effort.

ps (parent subtle direction): Parent offers aid if child will do task a certain way and gives child information which tends to bias child in parent's direction.

Aggression Model Variables

a (parents argue): Parents disagree between themselves over how the task should be done.

d (dominance): One parent attempts to dominate and control the behavior of the other.

h (hostility between parents): One or both parents are aggressive toward the other, not physically, but through remarks and gestures.

cr (criticism): One parent criticizes and corrects other parent's behavior.

These categories were scored by two trained observers in 10-second blocks of time. An automatic timing device flashed a light every 10 seconds; at that time the observer recorded the behavior that had occurred in the preceding 10 seconds. Behavior was rated by the two observers for 45 minutes or 270 10-second blocks of time. Since the parents were engaged in many activities, and the experimenter was interested in relatively few behaviors, the pertinent behavior did not arise in every 10-second block.

In addition to the behavior-rating categories, several six-point rating scales were included to give additional information concerning the overall effectiveness of the family unit, cooperation and hostility between the parents, rejecting behavior by the parents, a love-hostility dimension, and an autonomy-control dimension. The two observers rated each family on these scales immediately after the 45-minute observation period.

The interrater reliability coefficients for each observation and rating scale (Tables 3 and 4 respectively) were determined by computing a Pearson r between the scores of the two raters for each family.

Subjects. Forty-one males, 8 through 12 years old, and their parents served as subjects. Twenty children who were exhibiting conduct problems were selected upon the recommendation of psychologists and social workers who were working with them psychotherapeutically. As further verification of a conduct problem, the mother of each child filled out the Peterson Problem Check List, which provides a measure of the conduct and personality problems seen in a child by others. The non-conduct-problem children were drawn from the public schools by having teachers select children who were not behavior problems in school. Mothers of this group also filled out the Problem Check List.

Table 1 presents basic information about these groups. As Table 1 indicates, the groups were not significantly different in any measured characteristic except their scores on the Problem Check List.

TABLE 1

GROUP CHARACTERISTICS

Variable	Conduct Problem Group ($N = 20$)		Non-Conduct Problem Group ($N = 21$)		t
Problem Check List	M	7.30	M	2.43	8.13*
	SD	2.14	SD	1.56	
Estimated IQ	M	112.80	M	113.76	
	SD	17.37	SD	17.23	
Age of child	M	124 mos.	M	119 mos.	
	SD	17.89	SD	10.49	
Fathers' occupation	M	3.23	M	3.52	
	SD	1.61	SD	1.66	

*$p < .01$, two-tailed.

To test for differences between means, t tests were used. The possible range on the Peterson Problem Check List is 0 to 10, low scores indicating absence of a problem. The estimated IQ scores were obtained by prorating the three subtests (Information, Vocabulary, and Block Design) as described by Wechsler (1949), while the social-class ratings were obtained by giving fathers' occupations a score as described by Warner, Meeker, and Eells (1949).

It was necessary to make contact with 36 families to obtain 21 non-conduct-problem (NC) subjects. Thus, 58.33 percent of those contacted agreed to serve as research subjects. In the conduct-problems (C) group only two families refused to cooperate in this research.

In order to keep the identity of a family (i.e., conduct, non-conduct) from the observers, the specific experimental appointments were made by people affiliated with the University Psychological Clinic, but not by the two observers. During the experimental session and all the ratings, the two experimenters were not informed about the group identity of any of the families.

Materials. The parent-child interaction took place in a carpeted play-room equipped with one-way mirror and microphone. Directly in front of the mirror was a table on which the experimenters had constructed a plywood garage, school, church, and house of the type normally used in play therapy. These were all one-story buildings with no roofs, so the children could easily manipulate small dolls and doll furniture in the buildings. The doll figures consisted of two adult males, two adult females, a girl, a boy, and a baby. These materials directly associated with the task were presented to the family. The room also contained numerous toys considered highly desirable by most children; these included a small wading pool with boats, a drum set, blackboard and chalk, doctor's set, Lincoln logs, beads, and a small football and baseball. These toys were chosen because they were generally much more desirable than the task materials. Through the use of these desirable toys, and the instructions to the parents (see next section) which stressed the importance of keeping the child working with the task materials, the experimenters intended to create a situation analogous to the socialization process in which the parent, reacting to social pressure, must attempt to guide the child away from activities that might be more intrinsically desirable toward activities that are more "constructive" or socially acceptable. In this way, it was hoped that the playroom situation would mirror, even if only to a mild degree, interaction situations normally occurring in the home, thus strengthening the relation between playroom and home interactive behavior. Observation suggested that the experimenters were successful in creating a mild conflict in the child as to whether to cooperate with the parents on the task or to play with the extraneous toys.

Playroom Task. The mother and father were asked to construct verbal imaginative stories using the scene set up in the playroom. The parents were given the beginnings (story leads) of ten stories which they and the boy were to complete. In making up the stories, it was the parents' job to keep the child interested in the task. The task equipment could be used in any way the parents and child wished. The following story leads are typical of those given to the parents: (1) The boy is outside playing. His parents have just called to him to come inside. . . . (2) The family is in the house getting ready to go on a picnic. . . .

Experimental Procedure. All families were treated in the same manner. At the time of the appointment, the first experimenter (E_1) met the families in a waiting room. He knew their names but not their group identity. He gave the instructions to the family, then sent the child back to another room and gave the parents the additional information that they were going to be observed. After this, the family and E_1 entered the experimental playroom. A practice story lead was then worked on in the presence of E_1, who assisted the family in getting started and spending the correct amount of time on the story. After this practice, E_1 left the room and entered the observation room, where the second experimenter (E_2) had been. Without knowing the names of the people in the playroom, E_2 started the tape recorder and timing device during the practice story. The experimenters sat at individual tables in the observation room, separated from each other by a cardboard partition. At the light signal, scoring of behavior was started.

After the observation period, E_1 took the boy and administered a short form of the WISC, while E_2 at this time obtained from the parents their occupation and the boy's birth date, and answered any questions they had. At this time, E_2 indicated that he did not know who the parents were and that they were not to tell him. In this way, E_2 was able to tally the frequency counts still unaware of the group identification of the family.

RESULTS

Before considering the results relevant to the major hypotheses, it is necessary to point out that, as the intercorrelations in Table 2 indicate, the five control variables apparently were not measuring the same thing. Parental rejection (*pr*) and parental hostility (*ph*) appear to be measuring a common variable of love-hostility and seem to be independent of the other three control variables. While the categories of parent domination (*pd*) and parent takes over (*pt*) are negatively correlated, they show a low positive relation to an autonomy-control rating scale (.19). This suggests that these two variables may be mutually exclusive or incompatible

TABLE 2

INTERCORRELATION MATRIX OF
CONTROL VARIABLES

Variable	*pr*	*ph*	*pd*	*pt*
pr				
ph	.77*			
pd	.07	−.01		
pt	−.15	−.17	−.62*	
ps	.03	.00	−.30*	−.07

*$p < .05$, two-tailed.

methods of parental control. In their reaction to the situation, parents may show *pd* or *pt* but not both. In considering the results, therefore, it is necessary to be aware that we are dealing with two dimensions, love-hostility and control, rather than a single dimension of control.

The control variables and the parent interaction variables were analyzed by use of the median test (corrected for continuity) as described by Siegel (1956). The two raters' frequency scores for each variable were combined into a joint frequency score for each family on each variable. Each rater's score for a category was actually a combination of both mother and father behavior. In rating the family behavior, each parent was rated individually, but the main interest was on the combined behavior pattern of the parents as they related to the child in the standard situation.

TABLE 3

DIFFERENCE BETWEEN CONDUCT PROBLEM (C) AND
NON-CONDUCT PROBLEM (NC) FAMILIES

Behavior Category	C	NC	χ^2	Rater Relia-bility
Parental domination			.216	.92
above[a]	9	12		
below[a]	11	9		
Parental rejection			7.077*	.93
above	15	6		
below	5	15		
Parent takes over			.216	.98
above	9	12		
below	11	9		
Parent hostile to child			7.077*	.90
above	15	6		
below	5	15		
Parent subtle direction			.026	.96
above	11	10		
below	9	11		
Parents argue			.021	.87
above	10	12		
below	10	9		
Dominance			2.061	.93
above	14	9		
below	6	12		
Hostility between parents			.026	.86
above	11	10		
below	9	11		
Criticism			.616	.85
above	12	9		
below	8	12		

*$p < .01$, two-tailed.
[a]"Above" and "below" refer to scores above or below median.

The results of the chi-square analyses are presented in Table 3. The measures of parental rejection and hostility were both significant beyond the .01 level, indicating that the C group parents were more hostile and rejecting than the NC group parents. The correlation between pr and ph was .77.

In addition to these behavior ratings, the scores on the six rating scales were divided into high (4, 5, and 6) and low (1, 2, and 3) for each scale and analyzed by use of a 2 x 2 contingency table corrected for continuity (Siegel, 1956). Two of these scales showed significant chi-squares: the rejecting behavior continuum and the love-hostility continuum (see Table 4). These results again indicated that the C group parents were more hostile and rejecting of their children than the NC group parents. These two rating scales were correlated .78.

TABLE 4

CONDUCT PROBLEM (C) AND NON-CONDUCT PROBLEM (NC)
GROUP DIFFERENCES ON RATING SCALES

Scale	C	NC	x^2	Rater Relia-bility
Rejecting behavior			13.535**	.85
high	16	5		
low	4	16		
Cooperation between parents			3.640	.78
high	3	10		
low	17	11		
Hostility between parents			.005	.66
high	4	3		
low	16	18		
Overall effectiveness			.767	.68
high	5	9		
low	15	12		
Love-hostility			7.077*	.74
high (hostility)	15	6		
low (love)	5	15		
Autonomy-control			1.389	.40
high (control)	15	11		
low (autonomy)	5	10		

*$p < .01$, two-tailed.
**$p < .001$, two-tailed.

If no scorable activity took place during a 10-second scoring period, a check mark was entered into the scoring box. This provided an indication of the general activity level in the playroom situation.

There was no differences between the average combined (for both raters) number of check marks between the two groups. The NC group had a mean of 182.95 with a sigma of 71.98 and the C group had a mean of 181.05 with a sigma of 58.15.

As an overall measure of reliability, the percentage agreement between the two raters was calculated. Agreements were counted when both raters scored the same behavior, and in the same time sequence within a box. The average percentage agreement for the C group families was 74.02 percent with a sigma of 6.86. For the NC group it was 76.79 percent with a sigma of 5.29.

DISCUSSION

The results of this study indicate that in this situation the parents of conduct-problem children exhibit significantly more hostile behavior toward their children than do the parents of non-conduct-problem children. These parents also reject their children significantly more than do parents of non-conduct-problem children.

On the basis of these results, it is tempting to assume that we have shown a cause and effect relationship, whereby rejection and hostility on the part of the parents lead to aggressive behavior in children. The results of this study, however, can only indicate what kind of parent behavior might be expected in families where there is a child who is manifesting some form of a conduct problem.

Before examining the diagnostic implication of this procedure, it is necessary to consider why several of the variables were not significant. Considering that the task of the parents was to elicit the help of the child in making up stories, a wide range of behaviors was not available to the parents, whether the child was a conduct problem or not. Thus, for C group families one way of coping with the situation was to manipulate the materials, to make up stories without the child, and to ask questions of the boy whenever possible. It was expected, however, that the NC families would give the boy more freedom. This was not the case, and in terms of three of the control variables—pd, pt, and ps—the NC families were as controlling as the C families. Coincidentally, a chi-square analysis (χ^2 = 1.95, df = 1) of the combined pd and pt scores was completed. This suggested that the NC parents may have been more controlling than the C parents. The probability level (.20 > p > .10) achieved, however, does not allow us to feel certain in regard to this relationship. It may well be that the C parents wanted to control their child, but could temper this in attempting to "look good." The C parents could not, however, control their hostile and rejecting feelings. As Becker, Peterson, Hellmer, and Shoemaker, (1959) have demonstrated before, parents of conduct-problem children are themselves more maladjusted and more freely exhibit their hostilities. However, given the problem of interesting the child in the task, both groups of families manifested similar types of behavior.

Since the variables which were significant were highly correlated in both the case of the behavior categories and the rating scales, it is possible that we are dealing with a single factor upon which hostility and rejection have high loadings.

Finally, both groups were equally active in the playroom, yet differed significantly on two major variables. This suggests, of course, that hostility and rejection are overtones which enter into the general and more inclusive relationship which parents of conduct-problem children have with their offspring.

It was hypothesized that conflict and hostilities between the parents perhaps furnished a model for the conduct-problem child's behavior. Contrary to expectations, there was no difference between the two groups of parents on the parent interaction variables. Actually, in neither group was there very much interaction between the parents. Since both parents were engaged in the task of keeping the boy interested in the job at hand, perhaps hostility that might have been felt for each other was directed toward the task and the boy. This would be particularly true of the C group parents, who seemed to have a need to express hostility in an uncontrolled fashion.

This may be exactly what happens in the home. While both parents may in their own interaction present a model of aggressive and hostile behavior for the child, when they interact with the child they direct this hostility towards the child. In one sense, the child serves as a scapegoat.

The most unique aspect of this research is the fact that in an observed situation, those aspects of parental hostility and rejection which have been talked about and studied for the most part in an indirect manner have been observed directly. Apparently, the fact of being observed does not inhibit the parents' behavior to such an extent that primary differences between parental groups disappear. This observational technique demonstrates the possibility of relating parental playroom behavior with child behavior *outside* the playroom, and therefore becomes potentially important as a diagnostic technique. * * *

Interaction Testing in the Study of Marital Dominance*

Gerald Bauman and Melvin Roman

In 1960 we described the clinical use of a technique called Interaction Testing (Roman & Bauman, 1960). Working with families and small groups ranging from two to eight members, we first administered to each member of the group a standard clinical psychological test, such as the Wechsler-Bellevue, Rorschach, and TAT. The group or family was then assembled, and the test re-administered to them *as a group*, with instructions to arrive at responses that were acceptable to the group or family.

As a result, we were presented with essentially four sources of data:

1. Each individual's test protocols, administered and scored in the standard manner.

2. One family test protocol representing a group effort, which could be scored in the standard manner (or with minor modifications).

3. The opportunity to compare family responses with individual responses, allowing for evaluation of such qualities as the family's success in optimally using its resources, i.e., the previously demonstrated abilities or responses of the individual members.

4. The interaction processes by which decisions were reached. These could be observed and/or recorded, and could yield suggestive insights, either impressionistically or through more formal scoring and coding procedures.

Our initial experiences with this approach suggested that it held promise for the study of clinically relevant aspects of marital and family functioning, and might ultimately contribute to the development of a clinical taxonomy for families and small groups.

Toward this end it became necessary to develop standardized procedures, apply them to sizeable samples, and thus begin a systematic investigation of the psychometric as well as the clinical properties of Interaction Testing.

*Abstracted from *Family Process*, 1966, 5, 230–242, with permission of the senior author and *Family Process*.

Subjects

The 50 couples who served as subjects in this study represent a random selection from among the married patients admitted to the Westchester Square Day Hospital of the Division of Social and Community Psychiatry of Albert Einstein College of Medicine. They are a representative sample of the Day Hospital population as regards diagnosis, patient gender, and age. Of the primary patients in our sample, 22 were husbands and 28 were wives. Thirty-five were diagnosed as having been psychotic on admission and 15 as non-psychotic, although all were acutely disturbed upon admission, sufficient to warrant admission to a city hospital psychiatric ward. The average age of our patient-subjects was 41 and the range was 23 to 80.

Testing Procedure

The test employed in this study was composed of the Comprehension and Similarities subtests of the Wechsler-Bellevue. Both Forms I and II were used in order to increase the number of items. Our test battery, therefore, contained 44 questions: 20 Comprehension and 24 Similarities items.

Each patient was tested individually approximately one week after his or her admission to the Day Hospital. The spouse was then tested individually, usually on the same day, always within two days. Immediately following the spouse's individual testing, the same tests were re-administered to the couple together. During this "Interaction Testing," the two members were seated at a table next to each other and facing the examiner. The test answer form and a pencil were placed before the couple, who were told that one of them was to record the couple's answers. The choice of "recorder" was made by the couple.

The first Similarities item was then administered to the couple, who discussed the question and arrived at a written response. If the couple was unable to arrive at an answer after a "reasonable" length of time, a one-minute time limit was imposed. If this limit was exceeded, the examiner proceeded to the next item and the 0 for no answer was recorded. This rarely happened. Thirty-four of the 50 couples answered all items. Nine failed to answer one item; the other 7 couples ranged from 3 to 15 "cannot agree" on the 44 items. In cases where more than one final answer was recorded, the examiner, at the completion of the entire test, asked the couple to choose the better or best response.

Scoring

Dominance is one of four interaction processes which can be inferred by a comparison of the individual and the group protocols.

The four interaction processes are Dominance, Combination, Emergence, and Reinforcement. These are operationally defined and scored with very high reliability, i.e., interscorer agreement.

Dominance is scored when the interaction response contains one member's individual response in the absence of the other's individual response. (This includes conceptual dominance as well as mere dominance in the language used.)

Combination is scored when elements of both members' responses, in whole or in part, are found in the interaction response.

Emergence is scored for the presence of a new idea in the interaction response.

Reinforcement occurs when the same response is given by each individual alone and also by husband and wife together.

The adequacy of interaction process is also scored by assigning the symbols +, −, or 0 to each process score. We thus were able to score Positive Dominance, Negative Emergence, etc. These adequacy scores were assigned operationally, simply by comparing the numerical scores obtained for each item on the three protocols, i.e., husband, wife, and interaction. . . . (E.g., all three protocols contain a 2 response, or a 1 response, or a zero response.) The minus (−) score was assigned when the interaction response score was poorer than the better individual response score.

Our clinical interests led us to this scoring system, since it records not only such categories as dominance, reinforcement, etc., but it also characterizes these processes as appropriate or inappropriate for the task at hand through the use of +, −, and 0. We expect that such a characterization may have some reference to the concept of reality testing in the small group.

Hypotheses

Our question was: Are there any systematic determinants of dominance behavior? When our married couples initially disagree and then resolve their difference through dominance—that is, by the selection of one partner's original opinion over the other's—what decides which way this dominance is going to go? It seemed to us that we might be able to predict a priori the direction of dominance on the basis of three types of variables in our study: We called them rational considerations, semirational considerations, and nonrational considerations.

Rational Considerations: Competence. We predicted that our couples would be significantly "rational" in their dominance behavior, despite the presence of at least one seriously disturbed spouse. We expected that the objectively more competent spouse (as measured in the individual pretest) would dominate more often than the less competent spouse. We anticipated, though, that this "rationality" would be less than perfect, and thus allow room for the operation of the following "semirational" and "nonrational" considerations.

Semirational Considerations: Patient Status. Patients were expected to dominate less often than their nonpatient spouses. We reasoned that psychiatric hospitalization acts as confirmation by the social institution (the hospital) of the family's designation of the primary patient. Therefore, by hospitalizing the patient, we would probably have reinforced the couple's perception of the patient as the less competent spouse, at least for the time being. (We knew from previous experience, of course, that the "official patient" is often more competent in many areas than the non-patient spouse.) We dubbed patient status only as a "less rational" rather than "irrational" determinant out of the reality considera-tion that hospitalized patients are, *ipso facto*, less competent in certain areas of living than their nonhospitalized spouses, even though these areas of incompetence may be irrelevant to the task at hand.

Nonrational Considerations: Here we thought about two vari-ables. (*a*) Husband-wife status. We expected that husbands would dominate more than wives. This would be consistent with our general understanding of cultural family roles, and is supported by research in the field. We called this a nonrational consideration since husband-wife status has no logical or direct relevance to the content of the decision required by our experiment. That is, there was no a priori reason to assume that husbands would be more competent than wives on any particular item in our battery. (*b*) Recorder versus nonrecorder. We expected recorders to be dominant more often. Aside from the possible dynamic signifi-cance attaching to this prior decision by the couple about who shall write down their final responses, we expected the "power of the pen" to play a significant part, if only through the "acciden-tal" influence of the recorder's attitudes toward his own productions.

Results

Dominance scores. The range in number of dominance responses per couple was from 12 to 36, with a mean of 26.2 dominance responses per couple out of a possible 44.

To what extent were couples consistent in their use of dominance behavior? By comparing the Wechsler-Bellevue Form I with Form II (which is a version of the split-half reliability measure), we got a corrected reliability coefficient of .54. This is statistically significant and demon-strates that our couples can reliably be characterized according to their amount of dominance behavior; that is, some couples could be char-acterized as high in dominance and other couples as low in dominance. The reliability for Husband Dominance was .76; for Wife Dominance, .84.

Choice of Recorder. Choice of recorder was typically made by the couple quickly and with little discussion. In one case, they changed recorders; this case was not included in the recorder analysis. Twenty-six husbands and 23 wives served as recorders, obviously not different from a 50–50 split. Patient recorders numbered 30 as against 19 nonpatient recorders. This is not a statistically significant difference (*p* between .10 and .20).

Negative Interaction Processes. The range of negative interactions was from 4 to 19 out of 44 responses; the mean was 9.8. The corrected split-half reliability, statistically significant, was .48. These findings are summarized in Table 1.

TABLE 1

MEANS, STANDARD DEVIATIONS, AND RELIABILITIES[1]
OF PROCESS SCORES OF 50 COUPLES
ON 44 ITEMS OF THE WECHSLER-BELLEVUE INTELLIGENCE SCALE[2]

Process Scores[3]	Total D	D_H	D_W	E	C	R	−	+	0
Mean									
Form I	13.20	7.92	5.28	5.34	1.20	3.06	4.86	6.56	10.58
(22 items)									
Form II	12.98	8.12	4.86	5.28	1.54	3.22	4.92	7.48	9.60
(22 items)									
Standard Deviation									
Form I	2.81	3.71	3.07	2.71	1.26	1.63	2.23	2.01	2.16
Form II	2.86	3.66	2.53	2.93	1.53	1.96	2.10	2.29	2.65
Reliability[1]	.54	.76	.84	.71	.68	.51	.48	.72	.57

[1] Split-half reliability with Spearman-Brown correction using alternate forms of the Wechsler-Bellevue: 22 Form I and 22 Form II items.
[2] 24 items of Similarities Subtest and 20 items of Comprehension Subtest.
[3] Qualitative Process Scores in Couple Interaction:
D_H = Husband Dominance = Interaction response contains husband's individual response in the absence of wife's individual response.
D_W = Wife Dominance = reverse of D_H.
D_{Total} = Husband Dominance + Wife Dominance.
E = Emergence = The presence of a new idea in Interaction not present in either individual response.
C = Combination = Elements of both member's individual responses are found in Interaction.
R = Reinforcement = The same response in Interaction as both individual responses.
Quantitative Process Score in Couple Interaction:
− = Negative = The Quantitative Score (2, 1, 0) was lower in Interaction than one or both individual responses.
+ = Positive = The Quantitative Score (2, 1, 0) was higher in Interaction than one or both individual responses.
0 = Same = The Quantitative Score (2, 1, 0) was the same in Interaction as both individual responses.

Dominance Analyses. Table 2 lists the point biserial correlations derived from the differences in mean number of dominance responses for four dichotomized dimensions: sex (i.e., husbands versus wives); relative competence (i.e., higher IQ versus lower IQ, as prorated from the individual protocols); patient status (i.e., patients versus nonpatients); and recorder status (i.e., recorders versus nonrecorders). All four variables were found to have the predicted, significant relationship to dominance, as follows: husbands dominated significantly more than wives; more com-

TABLE 2

DOMINANCE RESPONSES AND POINT BISERIAL CORRELATIONS
FOR FOUR DIMENSIONS:
SEX, RELATIVE COMPETENCE, PATIENT STATUS, AND RECORDER STATUS
OF 50 COUPLES ON THE WECHSLER-BELLEVUE INTELLIGENCE SCALE

	Hus-bands	Wives	Higher IQ	Lower IQ	Non-Patients	Patients	Records	Non-Records
Mean dominance score	16.04	10.14	15.66	10.52	15.12	11.06	14.88	11.24
Point biserial r	.44		.39		.30		.26	
p	<.05		<.05		<.05		ns	

petent members dominated significantly more than less competent members; nonpatients dominated significantly more than patients; and recorders dominated significantly more than those who were not recorders. The point biserial correlations for the above were .44, .39, .30, and .26, respectively. Though three are significant at the .05 level, these correlations do not differ from each other at a statistically significant level, so that we cannot rank or weigh the contributions of our four factors to dominance behavior.

Tables 3 through 8 give the cell means and 2 x 2 analysis of variance results in which each of our four variables was paired with every other for evaluating more exactly its place in determining the couple's number of dominance responses. The results of these analyses confirm the trends suggested from our point biserial correlations; that is, that each dimension

TABLE 3

DOMINANCE: SEX VS. PATIENT STATUS

	Means		
	Husbands	Wives	Mean
Patients	13.55	9.11	11.06
Nonpatients	18.00	11.45	15.12
Mean	16.04	10.14	

Analysis of Variance

Source	df	MS	F	p
Sex	1	794.44	22.32	.01
Patient Status	1	291.28	8.67	.01
Interaction	1	28.45	.85	n.s.
Within	96	33.83		

Note — N = 50 couples.

TABLE 4

DOMINANCE: SEX VS. RELATIVE COMPETENCE

	Means		
	Husbands	Wives	Mean
More Competent	17.27	12.53	15.66
Less Competent	13.65	8.91	10.52
Mean	16.04	10.15	

Analysis of Variance for Sex vs. Relative Competence

Source	df	MS	F	p
Sex	1	503.87	15.96	<.01
Competence	1	294.11	9.31	<.01
Interaction	1	−.15	−	
Within	96	31.58		

Note − N = 50 couples.

TABLE 5

DOMINANCE: SEX VS. RECORDER STATUS

	Means		
	Husbands	Wives	Mean
Recorders	17.27	12.17	14.88
Nonrecorders	14.61	8.31	11.24
Mean	16.02	10.10	

Analysis of Variance for Sex vs. Recorder Status

Source	df	MS	F	p
Sex	1	799.31	23.05	<.01
Recorder Status	1	264.45	7.63	<.01
Interaction	1	7.93	.23	n.s.
Within	94	34.67		

Note. − N = 49 couples.

as dichotomized operates significantly in determining dominance. They also demonstrate that in all cases these dimensions act independently of the others (i.e., with no significant interaction effects). This would mean, for example, that husbands dominate significantly more than wives regardless of whether husbands are more competent or less competent, are nonpatients or patients, are recorders or nonrecorders.

TABLE 6

DOMINANCE: PATIENT STATUS VS. RELATIVE COMPETENCE

	Means		
	Patients	Non-Patients	Mean
More Competent	13.04	18.28	15.66
Less Competent	9.08	11.96	10.42
Mean	11.06	15.12	

Analysis of Variance for Patient Status vs. Relative Competence

Source	df	MS	F	p
Patient Status	1	412.69	12.01	<.01
Competence	1	660.49	19.22	<.01
Interaction	1	34.21	.955	n.s.
Within	96	34.36		

Note. — N = 50 couples.

TABLE 7

DOMINANCE: PATIENT STATUS VS. RECORDER STATUS

	Means		
	Patients	Non-Patients	Mean
Recorders	12.23	19.05	14.88
Nonrecorders	8.89	12.77	11.24
Mean	10.94	15.18	

Analysis of Variance for Patient Status vs. Recorder Status

Source	df	MS	F	p
Patient Status	1	538.14	15.08	<.01
Recorder Status	1	656.30	18.39	<.01
Interaction	1	50.34	1.41	n.s.
Within	94	35.68		

Note. — N = 49 couples.

We have demonstrated, first of all, that dominance in marital decision-making, for our example, is overdetermined. It is significantly influenced by several variables.

1. Individual characteristics of the two mates. We found that the objectively more competent member, as measured by his prorated IQ, dominated or prevailed significantly more often, but by no means always.

TABLE 8

DOMINANCE: RELATIVE COMPETENCE VS. RECORDER STATUS

	Means		
	More Competent	Less Competent	Mean
Recorders	16.48	12.11	14.88
Nonrecorders	14.17	9.55	11.24
Mean	15.63	10.49	

Analysis of Variance for Relative Competence vs. Recorder Status

Source	df	MS	F	p
Competence	1	460.22	11.99	$<.01$
Recorder Status	1	135.54	3.53	n.s.
Interaction	1	.39	–	n.s.
Within	94	38.36		

Note. $- N = 49$ couples.

If it had been always, the couple might be said to be resolving their differences on this task in the most rational way, by accepting the response of the more competent partner.

2. Sex differences. Husbands dominate more often than wives. One question raised by this finding is: To what extent does this sex difference express cultural role assignments rather than some inherent phylogenetic or psychobiological sex difference in aggression or initiatory behavior, etc? Further research is called for in which dyads would vary in sexual composition as well as social-role relationships. We are nevertheless able to speculate, on two bases. First, our knowledge of comparative psychology suggests that the contributions of biological constitution, instinct, etc., become progressively outweighed by social influences as we ascend the phylogenetic scale. This suggests that observed sex difference in dominance is based more on cultural role definition of husband-wife relationships than by essentially biological male-female relationships. Further support for this position may be found in a study by Kenkel (1957), in which he used a sample of college-student married couples, performing a task quite similar to our own. He characterized his couples as husband-dominant (when the husband's response prevailed on two-thirds or more of the items), wife-dominant (when the wives had a "score" of 66.67 percent or more), and nondominant (when neither spouse reached the 66.67 percent level). We rescored our cases in this way for comparison purposes. We both found husband dominance to outweigh wife dominance, but this occurs significantly more often in our subjects. While this difference may be attributed to educational level differences between the two samples, to general socioeconomic differences, to differences in level of pathology, or to task differences, it seems very likely that one or another form of *cultural* difference, broadly conceived, accounts for the

difference observed. Since our sample is probably closer to a working-class sample than Kenkel's, the larger number of husband-dominant couples in our sample seems consistent with general expectations.

While this comparison with Kenkel's findings is not adequately controlled to reach assured conclusions, it does demonstrate the feasibility and usefulness of cross-cultural marital dominance comparisons using interaction testing, both between cultures and within societies.

3. Patient-nonpatient status. The fact that patients dominate less often than nonpatients was predicted in the hypotheses and confirmed in the study. The prediction rested on the assumption that this variable operates more as a social-role variable than a valid indicator of competence. We found the nonpatient dominating in many instances where patient dominance would have produced a better score. The dynamics of this behavior in our couples is not altogether clear. Further work might use this kind of experiment to clarify the role of patient status. We might ask, for example: Does official patient status signify to the couple that the patient is less competent in all tasks? Or, may it be that the hospitalization of one spouse emphasizes in a realistic sense the couple's dependence on the competence of the other spouse to handle, at least for the time being, the various marital tasks that need doing?

4. Recorder-nonrecorder status. We found that this prior decision by the couple on who was to be the recorder influenced the outcome, in that recorder dominance exceeded nonrecorder dominance. Our data offer no clear evidence of the basis on which the couples selected the recorder, but the data do demonstrate the significant influence of a prior decision about their *modus operandi* on the outcome of the dyad's problem-solving behavior.

From the point of view of social psychological theory of marital dynamics, our findings seem to support the following view: There is a strong tendency, even in seriously disturbed couples, when making joint decisions, to pool their resources in a constructive way so that they tend to follow the adage that "two heads are better than one."

This pooling of resources, however, is less than perfectly efficient, since the pooling decisions are influenced not only by competence considerations, but also by cultural role attitudes (in this study, those associated with husband-wife status and patient-nonpatient status). Finally, the couple's decision about the mechanics by which it will attempt to solve its problems, its decision about the assignment of responsibility (e.g., recorder versus nonrecorder) is another variable that affects efficiency in problem-solving that can be explored. in terms of its appropriateness. * * *

Family Interaction Patterns and the Emotionally Disturbed Child[*]

J. Glenn Hutchinson

Twenty white, middle-class families with ten boys and ten girls, age 14–17, previously diagnosed as "seriously disturbed" (but not psychotic or brain-damaged) at the child guidance clinic of the Institute for Juvenile Research in Chicago, were selected for study. These were matched in terms of father's occupational level, age of child, and IQ of child with twenty white families containing ten boys and ten girls with no record of diagnosed emotional disturbance and with teacher ratings of normal adjustment and satisfactory academic performance.

The following data were collected:

1. *Family questionnaire.* A 76-item questionnaire was filled out by each of the 120 subjects privately in their homes. Two major uses were made of this instrument. First, differences of opinion on questionnaire items were presented to family members with the request that they discuss these differences and try to arrive at one common opinion—the "Revealed Difference" technique developed by Strodtbeck (1951). Second, the questionnaire responses were used to determine patterns of consensus and scores on attitudinal scales, such as "adolescent autonomy."

2. *Outcome of Revealed Difference Discussions (Power Scores).* Each family was presented with a copy of a questionnaire item on which there had been a difference of opinion among the members. The original position of each member was indicated on the copy. At the end of the discussion one of the family members marked the final position of the participants. These slips, checked for accuracy against the taped discussions, were used to determine the "power score" of each participant. Power scores were determined on the basis of the extent to which an individual could persuade other family members to accept his original position as the "group" position or maintain his original position against attempts of others to change him. A total of 15 items was discussed by clinic families and a total of 17 items by control families.

---

[*]Abstracted from a paper presented at a meeting of the Society for Research in Child Development, New York City, 1967, with permission of the author.

3. *Tape Recordings of "Revealed Difference" Discussions.* Verbatim typed transcripts were prepared from these tapes, which were then coded with the Bales IPA codes (Bales, 1950). The coded transcripts provide the basis for a large number of statistical indexes relating to patterns of verbal interaction, including sequence of communication (who speaks to whom, who follows whom), participation rates of individuals, phase patterns of group discussions, amount of total interaction required to reach consensus or terminate discussion in disagreement, proportion of instrumental and social-emotional acts in each individual's total participation, ratio of positive and negative social-emotional acts, etc. Over two hundred separate IBM decks have been prepared from these data.

4. *California Psychological Inventory.*
5. *Semantic Differential.*
6. *Franck Drawing Completion Test.*

* * * Some brief remarks now about specific findings from our study. Power scores were computed for individual family members in three patterns of three-person and three patterns of two-person discussions. Analysis of variance showed no clearly significant differences in power scores of specific family members when all "boy families" were compared with all "girl families" or when all "clinic families" were compared with all "control families." The interaction of sex of child and adjustment of child, however, produced a number of significant differences.

As shown in Table 1, in the three-person group comparisons the mother in all four categories remained in a fairly constant power position (attaining approximately one-third of the points on the average in each category). Significant differences (beyond the .05 level) were found, however, among fathers and differences significant beyond the .01 level were found among the adolescents. These differences, which appear with remarkable consistency in the comparisons shown in Tables 1–4, inclusive, indicate that with respect to power structure, the family of the disturbed girl closely resembles that of the normal boy, while the family of the disturbed boy is quite similar to that of the normal girl.

TABLE 1

PERCENTAGE OF POWER POINTS ATTAINED BY FATHER,
MOTHER AND CHILD IN THREE-PERSON DISCUSSIONS

	BOY FAMILIES		GIRL FAMILIES	
	Clinic	Control	Clinic	Control
Father*	38.3	30.4	33.1	38.3
Mother**	33.9	31.3	34.7	33.8
Child***	27.8	38.3	32.2	27.9

* Interaction of sex of child and adjustment of child significant above the .05 level ($F = 3.7$).
** Interaction *not* significant at .05 level ($F = 0.6$).
*** Interaction significant above .01 level ($F = 5.9$).

TABLE 2

PERCENTAGE OF POWER POINTS ATTAINED BY FATHER
AND MOTHER IN FATHER-MOTHER DISCUSSIONS

| | BOY FAMILIES | | GIRL FAMILIES | |
	Clinic	Control	Clinic	Control
Father*	72.5	46.0	37.5	68.0
Mother**	27.5	54.0	62.5	32.0

* Interaction of sex of child and adjustment of child significant above the .01 level ($F = 11.0$).
** Identical values for mother since Father-Mother percentages total 100.0.

TABLE 3

PERCENTAGE OF POWER POINTS ATTAINED BY FATHER AND
CHILD IN FATHER-CHILD DISCUSSIONS

| | BOY FAMILIES | | GIRL FAMILIES | |
	Clinic	Control	Clinic	Control
Father*	82.5	53.3	50.0	68.3
Child**	17.5	46.7	50.0	31.7

* Interaction of Sex of Child and Adjustment of Child significant above the .001 level ($F = 11.9$).
** Identical values for child since Father-Child percentages total 100.0.

TABLE 4

PERCENTAGE OF POWER POINTS ATTAINED BY MOTHER AND
CHILD IN MOTHER-CHILD DISCUSSIONS

| | BOY FAMILIES | | GIRL FAMILIES | |
	Clinic	Control	Clinic	Control
Mother*	72.5	55.0	55.0	61.7
Child**	27.5	45.0	45.0	38.3

* Interaction of Sex of Child and Adjustment of Child *not* significant ($F = 2.7$).
** Identical values for child.

The power scores of fathers of clinic boys and fathers of control girls are identical (38.3 percent of the total), are higher than the mother's score in both instances, and considerably higher than the adolescent's score (27.8 for the boy; 27.9 for the girl). Although experimental studies have not consistently confirmed it, perhaps the most widely accepted clinical stereotype is that of the passive, ineffective father and the domineering mother, particularly where the disturbed child is a boy.

In his studies of families with a schizophrenic offspring, Theodore Lidz, at Yale, indicates that the "skewed" pattern (power reversal) is more frequently found where the patient is a male, while the schismatic, or conflict, pattern is more frequently associated with the family of a schizophrenic girl (Lidz, 1957b). Our own data show the opposite relationship with respect to family power pattern and sex of the disturbed offspring. Statistical indexes of social-emotional interaction indicate approximately equally high negative indexes in both boy and girl clinic families contrasted with relatively low negative indexes in both boy and girl control families. In our sample, then, both boy and girl families in the clinic group appear similar with respect to conflict, particularly in the three-person discussion sessions.

Table 2, showing the outcome of father-mother discussions, presents a clear picture of a rather powerful father and a relatively yielding mother in families of disturbed boys and of normal girls, with the opposite pattern of a more powerful mother in the families of control boys and clinic girls. These differences are significant at a very high level—beyond the .002 level.

Table 3, showing father-child discussions, indicates the same general pattern, with the father of disturbed boys and the fathers of normal girls winning the lion's share of the power points, while the normal boy and the disturbed girl just about break even with their fathers in terms of power scores.

Although the interaction effect is not statistically significant at the .05 level, the same general pattern is found in Table 4, showing power distribution in mother-child discussions.

Confidence in the reliability of the above findings is increased by the fact that the same direction of differences as described above for clinic families is consistently found when we examine four groups of five families each, with the ten "boy families" divided into five with a "withdrawn" boy and five with an "acting-out" boy, the same division being made for families of disturbed girls. The picture of the relatively weak and noninfluential boy is shown in both groups, with either parent, while the opposite picture of the relatively powerful, influential girl is found in both the "withdrawn" category and the "acting-out" category, with either father or mother.

These facts suggest very strongly that we are measuring fairly consistent and stable patterns of interaction within families of disturbed children, that these patterns differ significantly by the sex of the child, but not by the specific pattern of pathology of the child—that is, seriously disturbed "withdrawn" and "acting-out" boys behave quite similarly in interaction with their parents, but quite differently from each other outside the home. The same principle applies to the disturbed girls, except that the nature of the pattern within the family is different in the case of boy families and girl families.

The crucial importance of sex differences of the disturbed child with respect to family interaction patterns is further indicated by statistical indexes on social-emotional functioning, based on the Bales codes. The verbal acts of the mother of the disturbed boy, which are high in hostile and status-deflating acts in discussion with the father, and in the three-person discussions, take on a different nature in discussions involving only the son. The negative index for the mother drops from 67.9 in the three-person sessions to .43 in discussions with her son. She uses this approach to influence the boy, however, since she gains approximately three-fourths of the total power points available in the mother-son discussions. This relatively low negative index for the mother in this pattern is in contrast to the high index of .74 for the father in his discussions with the disturbed son. A comparable shift does not take place, however, in the father-daughter interaction in the clinic families. The father of the disturbed girl has an even higher negative index[1] (though not statistically significant) in his discussions with the daughter than in the three-person discussions—.66 in the three-person, and .68 in the father-daughter discussion.

---

[1]The index cited (Index of Expressive Malintegrative Behavior) consists of the sum of all negative social-emotional (expressive) acts initiated by an individual divided by this same total plus the total of all positive social-emotional acts. An individual initiating one or more negative acts and no positive acts therefore would have an index of 1.00; an individual initiating one or more positive acts and no negative acts would have an index of 0.00; while an individual initiating exactly the same number of positive as negative acts would have an index of 0.50.

Studies of Family Interaction: Behavior

These articles represent decision-making studies whose main interest lies in the motor or verbal behavior of the family members. The first, by Haley, narrows the channel of communication to button-pushing and describes the coalition and dominance patterns thereby formed by schizophrenic and normal families. Murrell and Stachowiak are interested in who talks to whom in a family interaction and use this measure to show the stability of family patterns. The authors offer interesting comments on leadership roles within the family and on the necessity for studying families as systems in their own right. Their findings on evenness of distribution of communications within families are in disagreement with those of Haley, described in the next article. Haley used as his basic measures simple frequency counts of who speaks after whom, and combined these into an index of evenness of communication within a family. These three investigations are contentless. The authors avoided becoming entangled in the assessment of what the family members say to each other; rather, they concentrated on concrete and simple measures which they hope will reflect interaction uncontaminated by the difficulties of working with speech samples, which are heavily affected by social values, metacommunication, and rater bias.

The two articles by Ferreira, Winter and Poindexter and by Winter and Ferreira represent two different levels of analysis of the speech emitted by families making up joint TAT stories. Article 18 is a content analysis of the end product of their decisions—the actual stories produced—whereas these two articles are analyses of the verbalizations of the family members in the process of working on their stories. Article 25 deals with certain formal characteristics of speech, such as percentage of silence, overlap, and talking time (see also Article 8). The latter is converted to an index of evenness of communication measure, and the obtained results should be compared to those described in Articles 18, 23, 24, and 33. Article 26 represents a detailed analysis of the content of what the family members said to each other as they attempted to reach decisions and thus cope with the problem presented. This level of analysis makes use of clinically rich and meaningful data, but is subject to many instrumentation problems, which the authors describe.

The remaining articles are brief descriptions of promising techniques in this area. To our knowledge, there has been no other systematic research investigation of the dynamics of family laughter, as suggested by Zuk, Boszormenyi-Nagi, and Heiman. (The reader should keep in mind the limited generalizations which can be made from an N of 1.) Geismar presents a system for studying broad patterns of family functioning based on a combination of interviews and social records, which reflect real life behavior. Martin describes another laboratory method for reducing complex communications to simple behavioral data and shows how such behavior can be modified by learning techniques. Of the several scales available for measuring family interaction, Riskin's has been selected as being representative of one of the interesting methods of converting speech segments into usable data (see Article 26; Michler & Waxler, 1966, 1968; Terrill & Terrill, 1965). It is encouraging that these new techniques are coming from such diverse sources as psychotherapy, social case work, and laboratory psychology.

Family Experiments: A New Type of Experimentation[*]

Jay Haley

* * * Observations of the family of the schizophrenic indicate that when any one member tries to get together with another, the other responds in a way that disqualifies that invitation. For example, should father and mother join together in an attempt to discipline their child, they typically end in a row with each other, with one saying the other is too mild or too severe. (It should follow that if the members must "disqualify" what one another says, they would have difficulty forming and maintaining coalitions in the family.)

The hypothesis that this type of family has more difficulty forming and maintaining coalitions between two members should be verifiable with an experiment, and a report of such an experiment will be given here. Several versions of an experiment designed to test this hypothesis were attempted. The final version offered family members both the opportunity to form alliances and the opportunity to communicate at two levels. Before describing this particular experiment, a few generalizations can be made about the criteria for this kind of experimentation.

1. The experiments must deal with the responses of family members to each other rather than their individual responses to stimuli from the experimenter. The measure is of the system rather than the individuals within it, and so the experiment must require family members to interact with each other.

2. At least some of the experiments must be of such a nature that any one family will behave in a consistent way in that experiment over a period of trials. If one family behaves differently each time on the experiment, it is difficult to argue that two families who behave differently are really different.

3. The experiments must be of such a nature that it cannot be argued that intelligence, education, or manual dexterity of the family members was a major determinant of the results, unless one assumes the psychopathology being measured is based upon intelligence, education, or manual dexterity.

[*]Excerpted from *Family Process*, 1962, *1*, 265–293, with permission of the author and *Family Process*.

4. The experiments must be such that it cannot be argued that because one member is a schizophrenic the results of the experiment inevitably follow. For example, it should not be a task which the schizophrenic could not, or would not, participate in so that it could be said, "No one could do that task with him involved."

5. It must be a type of experiment in which a family will participate, willingly or not. That is, the task must be something everyone in the family can do.

6. The experiment must be of such a nature that it does not impose patterns on the family by forcing them to change under duress their typical patterns, unless measurement is being made of the ability of a family system to change under stress.

7. The experimentation must involve multiple experiments to measure multiple factors in families. There are possibly no single differences between any one type of family and any other type.

8. The experiments must show extreme differences between types of families, granted the sampling problems in this sort of study.

In summary, family experiments must meet some rather complicated criteria, besides providing the usual problems of theoretical conception and problems of measurement, and there is little precedent for the required experimental designs.

A COALITION EXPERIMENT

Father, mother, and child are placed at a round table with high partitions so they cannot see each other. In front of each person there is a small box with a window in it. This is a counter, like an automobile speedometer, which runs up a score visible only to the person in that area. Also in front of each person there are two buttons which are labeled for the persons on the left and right. That is, in mother's position she has a button labeled "husband" and a button labeled "son" (or "daughter" as the case may be). Besides these two buttons, which we shall call the coalition buttons, there are two more buttons, one on each side. These are signal buttons. When pushed, the signal button lights up a small light in the area of the person on the other side of the partition. By pushing either of these two buttons, for example, mother can signal father or child. All of these buttons are connected with pens on an event recorder in the control room so that all button activity is recorded during the experiment.

The table is wired so that the counters begin to add up a score whenever two people choose each other by pressing each other's coalition button. When mother presses the button labeled "husband," nothing happens until father presses his button labeled for her. When both buttons are pressed at once, then both counters add up a score at the same speed and continue to do so (making an audible sound) as long as both buttons are pressed. Therefore each person can gain a score only if he joins another person, and then he and that person gain exactly the same amount of score. Each person can signal another with the signal button to invite a coalition. The family is asked not to talk together during the experiment so they can only communicate by button pushing.

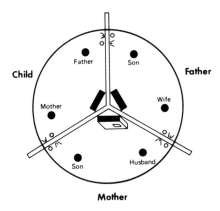

Fig. 1. Table design for coalition experiment.

Father, mother, and child are placed at this table and told this is a game they are to play together. They are instructed that they should each try to win by getting the highest score. They may push buttons one at a time or two at a time or not at all. The only rule is the prohibition against talking during the game.

The "game" consists of three rounds of two minutes each, which are begun by the experimenter and ended by him. At the end of each round, the family members are asked to read off their scores, and then the next round is begun without setting the counters back to zero so the score is cumulative.

In this situation each person must form a coalition with another to make a score, and yet he can only make the same score as the person he joins. To win, each must shift coalitions and gain score from both of the other two players. That is, if mother only joins father, she will have a high score at the end of the two-minute round but father will have the same score if he has joined only her, and neither can win.

The family members are free to signal each other to indicate they want to form a coalition; they are free to signal without following the signal with a push of the coalition button; they can signal one person while forming a coalition with the other; they can form coalitions by getting together without any signaling; and they can form one or two coalitions simultaneously. Therefore the table permits a range of family behavior and all this behavior is recorded.

In addition to the three-round game, the family is asked to have a fourth round. Before they begin the fourth round, they are asked to talk together and decide who is to win that round and who is to lose. Then they are to have another two-minute round to see if they can make the scores come out the way they planned. This conversation is recorded.

The Sample

A total of sixty families was run in this experiment. Thirty normal families were selected on the basis of a random choice of students from a high school directory. The parents of the students were telephoned, and the sample consists of those families whose members had never had psychotherapy and who were willing to come in for the experiment. The children ranged in age from 14 through 17 years, and there were 13 girls and 17 boys in the sample. The educational background of the families can be described in terms of the most educated member of the family; there were 5 high school graduates, 9 high school graduates with some additional training, and 16 college graduates or above.

Thirty families, each containing a schizophrenic child, were chosen on the basis of availability. Some families were obtained through a family therapy program, others from the records of state hospitals; and others included children actually hospitalized at the time. The children ranged in age from 11 through 20 years. The sample included one family with a stepfather who was in the home three years prior to the child's breakdown. In the sample there were 3 girls and 27 boys—a more equal distribution could not be obtained. In education, again taking the most educated member of the family, there were 4 who had completed less than four years of high school, 7 high school graduates, 7 who were high school graduates and had additional training, and 12 college graduates or above.

Of the sixty families, twenty normal families and twenty families containing a schizophrenic child were run with the instruction that they could push buttons in any way they pleased, and therefore they could form coalitions with one or two people simultaneously. This procedure is called *Experiment 1*. Another 10 normal and 10 schizophrenic families were run with the instruction that they could form only one coalition at a time and so could not score with two people at once. This is called *Experiment 2*. On certain measurements the combined totals of the two experiments are reported.

Predictions and Results

Certain predictions were made about the differences between these two groups in the experiment. These predictions will be summarized here along with a brief summary of the actual results.

1. *It was predicted that the family of the schizophrenic would have more difficulty forming and maintaining coalitions. Therefore the schizophrenic group would have a higher percent of time when no member of the family was in coalition with any other member.*

The twenty normal and twenty schizophrenic families that were run in Experiment 1, where the family members could push buttons in any way they pleased, differed significantly in the percent of time no member was in coalition with any other member. (The difference was significant at the .05 level.)

The ten normal and ten schizophrenic families that were run in Experiment 2, where the family members could only score with one person at a time, also differed significantly in the percent of time no member was in coalition with any other member. (The difference was significant at the .05 level.)

The combined results of Experiments 1 and 2, totalling 30 normal and 30 schizophrenic families, differed significantly on this measurement with a level of significance of .01.

2. *It was predicted that the family of the schizophrenic would have longer continuous periods of time when no two family members were in coalition.*

The longest periods of continuous time when there was no coalition in three rounds of the game was significantly greater in the schizophrenic than in the normal group. In Experiment 1, with twenty families in each group, the difference was significant at the .005 level. In Experiment 2, with 10 families in each group, the difference was significant at the .01 level. The results of the two experiments combined showed a significant difference at the .001 level.

3. *It was predicted that the average lengths of time in coalition would be shorter in the schizophrenic group.*

The two groups did not differ significantly on this measurement.

4. *It was predicted that the members of the schizophrenic family would be less consistent with each other than the normals, that there would be less consistency in following a signal with a press of the coalition button, and less frequent response by the person signaled.*

The two groups differed significantly in the consistency of family members only in the case of the child. The schizophrenic child followed a signal with a coalition press less often than did the normal child (significant at the .05 level). There was no significant difference between the parents of the normal child and the parents of the schizophrenic child on this measurement.

The child in the schizophrenic family was also less responsive to both parents than the normal child when his parents signaled him and then pressed his coalition button (significant at the .01 level). There was no significant difference between the parents in the two groups on this measurement.

5. *It was predicted that the members of the schizophrenic family would be less "successful" than the normal group, measured by the amount of time spent pushing the coalition button in proportion to the amount of time spent scoring with someone.*

The two groups differed significantly in the parents' "success" with the child but not in their "success" with each other. That is, if the amount of time mother and father are actually in coalition with the child is divided by the amount of time they are pressing his coalition button, the resulting percent differs significantly from the results of the parents in the normal group. (The difference is significant at the .05 level on the *t* test and the Median Test.)

Actually the parents of the schizophrenic child tended to be more "successful" with each other on this measurement than the parents of the normal child, although the difference was not significant.

6. *In the planned round, it was predicted that the schizophrenic families would have more difficulty reaching agreement on who was to win and who to lose, and it was predicted that they would have more difficulty making the round come out with the winner and loser they had agreed upon.*

The problems of classifying verbal material were such that it proved too difficult to measure whether the schizophrenic families had more difficulty reaching agreement on who was to win and who to lose than the normal families.

However, there was a striking difference between the two groups in their success at making the winner and loser come out as they agreed.

	CHOSEN TO WIN			SUCCEED	
	Normals	Schizophrenic		Normals	Schizophrenic
Child	20	20	Yes	28	15
Father	6	5	No	2	15
Mother	4	5		30	30
	30	30			

Most of the normal group could make the round come out as they planned, as far as getting the winner right, whereas half the schizophrenic group could not. (The difference was significant at the .001 level on the chi-square test.)

	CHOSEN TO LOSE			SUCCEED	
	Normals	Schizophrenic		Normals	Schizophrenic
Child	7	4	Yes	29	19
Father	16	10	No	1	11
Mother	7	16		30	30
	30	30			

Most of the normal group could make the loser come out as they planned, and they differed from the schizophrenic group at the .01 level on the chi-square test. In summary, out of 30 families in the normal group, 27 succeeded completely in doing what they planned and 3 failed. Out of 30 families in the schizophrenic group, 11 succeeded completely in doing what they planned and 19 failed.

Unpredicted Results. An unexpected result was based upon the simple measurement of who won the first three rounds of the game. The normal family members shared about equally in winning while in the schizophrenic group the father won the majority of games and the child hardly won at all. The difference was significant at the .01 level on the chi-square test.

	WON			LOST	
	Normals	Schizophrenics		Normals	Schizophrenics
Child	11	3	Child	9	21
Father	9	21	Father	7	5
Mother	10	6	Mother	14	4
	30	30		30	30

This result is similar to the measurement of how the family members divided up the total time in coalition. In the normal group the family members shared about equally in the time they were in coalition. In the schizophrenic group the mother-child coalition was significantly less than the normal (a difference at the .05 level) and the mother-father coalition was significantly greater than the normal (a difference significant at the .01 level).

If one measures the amount of time that family members were not pressing a button at all, the schizophrenic child spends significantly less time pressing buttons than the normal child (significant at the .01 level). The parents of the schizophrenic child also spend significantly less time pressing buttons than the parents of the normal child (a significant difference at the .05 level).

In signaling, the fathers in the schizophrenic group signal the children more frequently than the fathers in the normal group. The mothers signal the fathers more units of time in the normal group than the schizophrenic group. The normal child presses his parents' coalition button more than the schizophrenic child.

Summary. Although it was expected that the schizophrenic group would be more homogeneous than the normal group, the reverse proved to be the case. On almost all measurements the normal families tended to be more like one another while the schizophrenic families showed a considerable range of variability.

The family members in the schizophrenic group press their buttons less than the members of the normal group, and they spend less time scoring with each other and have longer periods of time when no one is scoring. Of the amount of time they spend in coalition together, the normal family members share coalitions about equally, while the parents of the schizophrenic get together with each other more than the normal parents do and get together with their child less than the normal parents do. The schizophrenic child tends to get together with his father more than he does with his mother. The family members of the two groups signal each other about equally, although the fathers in the schizophrenic group signal the children more, and the mothers in the normal group spend more time signaling their husbands than the schizophrenic mothers do. The child in the schizophrenic group presses his buttons less, is more inconsistent, and is more unresponsive than the normal child.

When asked to plan the winner and loser of a round of the game, the family members in the schizophrenic group tend to predict how the round will come out rather than plan it. That is, the normal family members will say, "Let's have mother win," whereas often the members of the schizophrenic family will say, "Well, father won before so I guess he will win again." They then must be re-instructed that they are to *decide* who is to win and lose, and try to make it come out as they planned. Almost all of the normal families could make the winner of the round come out as they planned, while half the schizophrenic group could not. Since it might be argued that this inability to do what they plan in the schizophrenic group is related to intelligence rather than ability to cooperate, it should be pointed out that the two groups do not particularly differ in education. There are a few with less than high school education in the schizophrenic group, and a few more in the normal group with a college education or above. There seems to be little correlation between education and inability to make the round come out as planned. (Since the question of ability to understand the procedure is at least partially relevant to this result, a group of six families with a mentally retarded child—IQ's from 60 to 90—were run in this experiment. All six chose the child to be the winner of the planned round, and all six succeeded in having the child win.) * * *

Consistency, Rigidity, and Power in the Interaction of Clinic and Non-Clinic Families[*]

Stanley A. Murrell and James G. Stachowiak

This is a study of certain non-content properties of verbal interactions as they occur among family members. Following a current research trend, these families were drawn both from "normal" and from "disturbed" populations of families. However, the referred member of the disturbed families had not, in this study, been diagnosed as "schizophrenic" as has been the case in the majority of family interaction investigations reported in the literature. Also, most, if not all, of the published family interaction studies have confined themselves to using a triad in the family, including only the father, mother, and disturbed child. In the present investigation, the scope was extended to include a sibling. Thus, all of the families were composed of the father, mother, and two oldest children.

The purpose of this study was to explore three general and related assumptions that were found to be prevalent among clinicians and researchers in the family field: (1) Patterns of interaction within families tend to remain consistent and stable over time and in different situations (Drechsler & Shapiro, 1963; Haley, 1964; Murrell & Stachowiak, 1965). (2) Patterns of interaction tend to be maintained more rigidly within disturbed families than within normal families (Bell, 1962; Haley, 1964; Jackson & Weakland, 1961). (3) The authority or power structure tends to be more autocratic within disturbed families than within normal families (Bowen, 1961; Herbst, 1954; Westley, 1958).

METHOD

To examine the validity of the above three assumptions, this study was designed to obtain simultaneously the following measures: (1) the degree of consistency with which patterns of verbal interactions in

[*]Abstracted from the *Journal of Abnormal Psychology*, 1967, 72, 265–272, with permission of the senior author and the American Psychological Association.

families occur over time and in different situations; (2) the degree of rigidity in maintaining cliques within families; (3) the amount of power held by family members relative to other family members.

Subjects. There were 22 Caucasian families who participated in the study. One group consisted of 11 families who sought psychological help for a family member at the University of Kansas Psychological Clinic. The problems for which referrals were made included a broad range of symptoms, for example, poor school achievement, hyperactivity and nervousness, enuresis, etc. In no case was there any reason to suspect that any of the referred children suffered from organic impairment, nor could any of the children be described as psychotic. In one of the families in this group the referred member was the father, who complained of tension and anxiety. Since the problem was initially presented as affecting the mother and children, this family was included. This group is referred to as the "clinic families" (*C*) group.

The second group consisted of 11 families selected from the community and invited to participate in the study. School teachers and principals were asked to recommend families in which the children were considered to be well-adjusted, normally achieving children. This group of families is referred to as the "nonclinic families" (*NC*) group.

Attempts were made to match the families on the basis of the ages, sex, and sibling position of the children, and on the level of the parents' educational attainment. [The mean age of the older child was 11.0 years in the clinic families and 11.9 in the nonclinic families; the mean age of the younger child was 7.7 years in the clinic families and 9.8 in the nonclinic families. The mean years in school for parents of clinic families was 15.9 for fathers, 14.4 for mothers; for parents of nonclinic families it was 15.2 for fathers, 13.9 for mothers.] * * *

Procedure. Upon arrival at the clinic, each family was greeted by the investigator and seated around a table in the experimental room in such a manner that each member could be observed from behind a one-way mirror. A microphone and tape recorder were present, and the family members were told that they would be observed from behind the mirror. The family was asked to participate as a group in four tasks, each of which lasted for 10 minutes. The experimenter (*E*) explained each task briefly to the family, and then left the room for the 10-minute period. When he returned, he explained the next task, and then left again, and so on.

The four tasks were selected because each offered an opportunity for interaction between the family members, and because each was somewhat different from the others. The first task consisted simply of asking the family to plan something together as a family. The second task required the family to answer a series of 11 questions about their family, and to have all members agree on their answers. In the third task, the family was asked to think of, and write down, as many adjectives or descriptive phrases as they could which would describe their family as a group. The members were required to agree on the adjectives selected. In the fourth task, all the family members were asked to participate in making up stories to seven TAT pictures. It was emphasized that all members should agree to the final form of each story, which was to be written down. These tasks proved to be quite interesting to the families, and families in both groups quickly became involved in them and seemed to be motivated to carry out the tasks successfully.

Ratings. While the families were engaged in the four tasks, two raters observed them from behind the one-way mirror. They rated the number of times that each member spoke to each other member. This was determined by: (*a*) the member whom the speaker was looking at when he or she spoke; or (*b*) the member who responded if the speaker was not clearly looking at a particular member. If the speaking member appeared to address no one in particular and no other member directly responded, his statement was scored as being directed to the group as a whole. For the 22 families in the study, the Spearman rank correlations between the two raters were at .82 or better on at least three of the four tasks. Two other families were excluded from the study, because the agreement between the raters did not meet this criterion.

Neither *E* nor the raters had any contact with any of the families outside the research situation. The *E* knew which families were *C* families, but this information was not available to the raters.

PREDICTIONS AND RESULTS

Intrafamily Consistency

It was predicted that there would be a stable pattern of frequency of "who talks to whom" in families over different situations and over time. Members were expected regularly to speak often to some members, but only rarely to others. This prediction was derived from the assumption of consistency in patterns of interactions within families. To measure the stability of frequency patterns of interaction for each family the following operations were carried out. Each possible pair of family members received a rank relative to the other pairs according to the total number of statements they exchanged on that task. Rankings were given to each of the six pairs for each of the four tasks. The correspondence between the four rankings was compared by using Kendall's coefficient of concordance (Siegel, 1956). Of the 22 families, 21 obtained positive correlations among the ranks that were significant beyond the .05 level, with 17 of these families having correlations beyond the .01 level.

To obtain a measure of the stability of these frequency patterns over time, five of the *NC* families participated again in the four tasks with the same procedure after a period of 12–14 weeks. A Kendall coefficient of concordance was used to compare the rankings of the six pairs over the eight tasks. In all five families, correlations beyond the .01 level were obtained.

Interfamily Differences

1. *Rigidity of cliques.* It was predicted that members in *NC* families would distribute their statements more equally among the other members than would members in the *C* families. This prediction was derived from

the assumption that interaction patterns are more rigidly maintained in disturbed families, with members remaining in narrow cliques from which they rarely depart. In this sense, the inference was made that an uneven distribution of "sent" statements would reflect rigidity of cliques in families.

The measure of evenness of distribution of sent statements was obtained in the following manner. The total number of statements sent by one member to the other members was divided by three. This average score was then subtracted from the actual number of statements sent to each of the three members, yielding three deviation scores (deviation from the average score). If, for example, a mother sent exactly the same number of statements to each member, the three deivation scores would each be zero. The three deviation scores were squared, the squares were totaled, and a square root was taken of this total. This square root, then, was the measure of that member's evenness of distribution of sent statements. These scores were normally distributed.

An analysis of variance was computed, comparing the 11 NC families with the 11 C families, and comparing the four member-roles (mother, father, older child, younger child). The results are presented in Table 1.

TABLE 1

SUMMARY OF ANALYSIS OF VARIANCE OF
UNEVENNESS OF SENT STATEMENTS BY
FAMILY GROUP AND MEMBER ROLE

Source	df	MS	F
Family group (A)	1	4,311.44	4.40*
Member role (B)	3	2,222.17	2.77*
A X B	3	953.04	.09
Error	80	978.48	

*$p < .05$.

The analysis revealed a significant difference between the two groups of families but in the *opposite* direction from the prediction. That is, the members of the NC families distributed their statements less evenly than did C family members. There was also an overall difference among member roles, but the only individual difference was that between mothers and older children ($p < .05$). Mothers distributed their statements more evenly than did older children. This held for both C and NC families.

2. *Power patterns.* It was predicted that the pattern of relative power or leadership in C families would differ from that of NC families. The measure of power used as each member's ratio of received verbal units. (A verbal unit refers to one complete statement made by one member to another.) Received and transmitted verbal units have been used as mea-

sures of influence by Bales and Slater (1955) and Mills (1960). Bales and Slater reported that while talking and receiving were generally highly correlated with each other, the received measure tended to be somewhat more closely associated with leadership in small groups.

Each member's ratio score for verbal units received was obtained by taking the total number of units received by that member over all four tasks divided by the total number of units received by all four family members over all four tasks. To simplify the subsequent analyses, these ratios were then multiplied by a constant (100). Figure 1 illustrates the relative differences in received ratios between *C* and *NC* families and among the member roles.

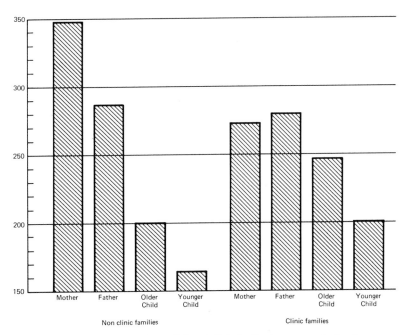

Fig. 1. Power patterns of non-clinic and clinic families in mean received ratios.

Table 2 presents a summary of the comparisons *between* the member roles of one group of families and the same member role in the other group. A separate, simple randomized analysis-of-variance design (Lindquist, 1953) was performed for each of the four member-roles.

Table 3 presents a summary of the differences in received ratios between member roles *within* the same group of families—for example, comparing mothers with fathers within the *C* families. Since the received ratios of members in the same family were being compared, these were considered to be related samples, and the Wilcoxon matched-pairs signed-ranks test (Siegel, 1956) was employed.

TABLE 2

SUMMARY OF *F* TESTS COMPARING RECEIVED
RATIOS OF MEMBERS BETWEEN FAMILY GROUPS

Comparison	*F*
NC mothers > C mothers	10.25**
NC fathers > C fathers	.59
C older children > NC older children	6.31*
C younger children > NC younger children	1.68

*$p < .025$.
**$p < .01$.

TABLE 3

COMPARISON OF RECEIVED RATIOS OF MEMBERS
WITHIN FAMILY GROUPS

Clinic Families	*p*	Non-Clinic Families	*p*
Father > mother	*ns*	Mother > father	.05
Father > older child	*ns*	Father > older child	.01
Mother > older child	*ns*	Mother > older child	.01
Father > younger child	*ns*	Father > younger child	.02
Mother > younger child	.01	Mother > younger child	.01
Older child > younger child	.05	Older child > younger child	*ns*

The results shown in Tables 2 and 3 indicate that *NC* mothers received a higher proportion of verbal units than *C* mothers, and that *C* older children received more units than their counterparts in *NC* families. Within families, *NC* mothers received more units than any other person, and both parents had higher ratios than either child. By contrast, in *C* families there was no significant difference between the parents, nor between either parent and the older child. Thus, in the case of the mothers and older children, there is a distinct difference between the two groups of families, and within their own families it is clear that *C* members have a different leadership pattern than do *NC* family members.

3. *The age factor.* As it was observed, the mean age of the older child and the younger child in *NC* families was somewhat higher than the mean age of children in *C* families. It was possible, then, that the differences found between the two groups of families on the rigidity and power measures were due to the older ages of children in *NC* families. To explore this possibility, Spearman rank correlations (corrected for ties) between age and these two measures were computed. The correlations were not significant. Since there was a possibility that substantial correlations be-

tween age and these measures might obtain at one age level and not at another, separate correlations were computed for age and these two measures for all children in the older child member-role, and for all children in the younger child member-role.

Only one significant correlation was obtained, this being between age and unevenness scores for older children (−.49, significant beyond the .05 level for a two-tailed test). That is, the older the child, if he were an older child, the more evenly he distributed his messages to other family members.

That the age factor did not contribute to the differences between the two groups of families on this measure is apparent from the finding that *NC* family members distributed their messages *less* evenly than did *C* family members. If the age factor had been strongly operative, the *NC* family members would have tended to be more even in their distributions than *C* family members, since children in *NC* families tended to be somewhat older. Also, it seems clear that there is not a general correlation between age and unevenness, since in both groups of families the children in the older child member-role tended to have the least even distributions, although this difference was significant only between mothers and older children. If there were an overall correlation between age and unevenness, the children in the younger child member-role should have had the least even distributions.

4. *Family productiveness.* ,No prediction had been made regarding differences in productiveness on the tasks between the two groups of families. After the data had been collected it seemed clear that the *NC* families were able to accomplish more on the tasks than the *C* families. Since it seemed likely that the productiveness data were related to the findings regarding leadership patterns, it was decided to test the differences between the two groups of families for the degree of significance present.

Each family received a total productivity score which included: (*a*) the number of questions answered on Task 2; (*b*) the number of adjectives listed on Task 3; and (*c*) the number of stories plus the total number of lines written in all stories on Task 4.

Since, again, the age difference between the two groups of families might have contributed to differences in productivity, Spearman rank correlations (corrected for ties) were computed for age and productivity in the older child category, and for age and productivity in the younger child category. The correlation between age and productivity was significant and positive ($t = .494$, $p < .05$, two-tailed test) for younger children. The correlation for children in the older child member-role was positive but not significant. Therefore, it seemed quite possible that the older ages of children in *NC* families might contribute to higher productivity scores. To correct for this, the two *NC* families with the oldest children and the two *C* families with the youngest children were eliminated from the analysis. The mean ages for *NC* and *C* children, respectively, were then 11.0 years for the older child, 8.8 years for the younger child, 11.5 years for the older child, 8.1 years for the younger child.

The results of a simple randomized analysis of variance showed a significant difference between the two groups of families ($F = 9.81$, $p < .01$). The difference was clearly in favor of the NC families, whose mean productivity score was 38.9 as compared to the mean score of 26.1 for the C families.

DISCUSSION

Similarities between the Two Groups of Families

Since an ultimate aim is to gain an increased understanding of the functioning of families in general, it is as important to know the commonalities among families as it is to know their differences. The present study revealed two areas of similarity among these families: (*a*) families tended to have stable patterns of "who talks to whom" over time and in different situations; and (*b*) mothers consistently sent messages equally to other members while older children regularly channeled their messages more narrowly.

The major importance attached to the finding of stable patterns of interactions in families is that it provides an empirical foundation for the current conceptualization of the family as a social system. For a family to function as a system, there must be a certain amount of regularity in its patterns of operations. Combining the present findings with the similar results reported by Haley (1964) and by Dreschler and Shapiro (1963), it may be concluded that this is a reasonable assumption to make.

The major implication of the second finding—that is, that mothers in all families distributed their messages more evenly than older children—lies not so much in the finding itself as in revealing that while mothers in these two families do appear to function differently in some areas, for example, leadership, there are other areas in which their behaviors are similar. This commonality would support the idea that certain role functions operate independently of the particular style or quality of functioning of a family in influencing some behaviors of family members; also the finding of a significant and negative correlation between age an unevenness for older children suggests that perhaps position in the family overrides age factors in some areas of behavior.

Differences between the Two Groups of Families

1. *The rigidity assumption.* The finding that NC family members sent statements less equally to other members than did C family members is at variance with the findings of Haley (1964) and with the general assumption that "disturbed" families are more rigid than "normal" families. This finding suggests the requirement of greater caution in applying the rigidity assumption and of greater specification of the situations in which rigidity appears, as well as the consequences of the rigidity. In this study, for example, the unevenness of the statement distributions may have been a function of the relatively greater prominence of the mother as a recipient of statements in NC families. A further inference could be made that the leadership patterns in NC families were related to their greater productiv-

ity on the tasks. From this view, the unevenness in NC families could be construed as adaptive or even flexible in the broad sense, while being rigid in a more narrow sense.

2. *Leadership.* The leadership pattern in the NC families fits well with Parson's (1955) description of family roles: Power is ascribed to the parents, not to the children. Father's role is an instrumental one, in that he provides for the family and is the primary link with organizations outside the family; mother is primarily engaged in the internal affairs of the family, and serves to maintain and regulate relationships and interactions within the family. Within this framework, it seems quite appropriate that the mother was the more influential member in this experimental setting, for many of the functions of the leader seemed to be concerned with encouraging the children to remain focused upon the tasks and with maintaining harmonious interactions.

The general pattern observed was as follows: In NC families the mother would take the lead, with father helping and supporting her in the leadership role. She drew the children into participation by asking questions and making suggestions. She was the primary focus of the interaction, with the other three members directing most of their statements to her. The situation was quite different from the C families. Here, there was either a shift back and forth between the two parents in attempting to provide or avoid leadership, or the two parents were both unable to motivate and control the group so that they would remain focused upon the tasks. A much greater proportion of time was spent in these families in searching for a mutually agreeable approach to the tasks, and each parent seemed unable or unwilling to provide support to the other.

It would appear, then, that the primary difference in the power structure of the two groups of families is not in terms of the NC families functioning with a "democratic" structure and the C families functioning within an "autocratic" structure. Rather, the difference is between cooperative and effective leadership versus an ineffective leadership which results from a lack of support and cooperation on the parts of the parents. Effective family leadership seems to require that the *parents* have the greater influence, and that one parent take the more dominant leadership role, with the other parent cooperating and supporting this leadership.

3. *The importance of ordinal position.* In the C families, the older child was the referred child in only half the cases. Thus, his relatively higher received ratios could not be simply attributed to his being the "problem member" in the family. This is somewhat surprising. Since the referred child could be considered the focus for problems in the family, it would not have been surprising if the referred child had regularly received the higher (or lower) received ratio of the two children.

The general implication of this finding is to encourage the further study of the disturbed family as a system, rather than focusing upon the individuals in isolation or upon the parents– disturbed-child triad. The present findings suggest that whether or not the older child is the referred member, he occupies a different position in his family system from his counterpart in an NC family system. It can be inferred, at least, that the differences in the ordinal position in these two groups of families are related to differences in the respective family systems. This raises the question, then, of the extent to which a "disturbed" family system may lead the member in the older child role to function differently than the older child in a "normal" family system.

A further implication is that symptoms manifested by an older child may serve different functions for the family system than similar symptoms in a younger child. Moreover, a "problem" older child may require other members to deal with him in a way that would be different from their dealings with a "problem" younger child. To understand the relationship between ordinal position and symptom manifestation, studies of disturbed families will need to include siblings of the disturbed child. It may well be that further work in this problem area, through studying complete family systems, will eventually provide answers to the very thorny question of why one child, rather than another in the family, manifests the symptoms.

Research on Family Patterns: An Instrument Measurement[*]

Jay Haley

This is a report of an investigation to determine whether, and on what dimensions, the patterns of interaction between members in one family can be differentiated from those in another family. Can it be shown, for example, that the interchange in a family where one or more members suffers from some form of psychopathology is different from that in a family without evident psychopathology? * * *

The Sample

A group of 80 families was selected and interviewed. This group included 40 "normal" families, primarily selected at random with the use of a high school directory. The parents were asked to come in with one child of their own choosing for an interview. The children ranged in age from 10 to 20 years, and were living at home with their natural parents. Those families which contained a member who had contacted, or been advised to contact, a psychotherapist, or who had been arrested, were excluded from the normal category. The "disturbed" group consisted of 40 families and included families in which some member (*a*) was suffering from schizophrenia; (*b*) had committed a delinquent act; (*c*) had a school problem which brought him to the attention of the authorities; as well as families in which some member (*d*) sought treatment for some neurotic problem; and families where parents (*e*) had sought marriage or family therapy. By definition a "disturbed" family was one which had not been able to contain its difficulties and had become involved in community attention. The children ranged in age from 10 to 20 years, but four children older than 20 were included. In the "disturbed" group, if the child was the identified patient the parents were asked to bring in that child. Some of these families were tested both before and after family therapy. Additionally, there was a group of six families with a gifted, or outstanding, child according to the school authorities. When these families had not come in contact with authorities because of a problem, they were

---

[*]Excerpted from *Family Process*, 1964, *3*, 41–65, with permission of the author and *Family Process*.

classed in the normal group. The families were largely middle class and were at least second-generation American.

The Procedure

For purposes of this research, it was essential that the families have a conversation in which all three members had a right to speak about the subject of conversation posed for them. A pilot sample of families was asked to "plan something to do together" on the assumption that if they all were to do it together they would all have a right to speak about the subject. However, long runs of conversation were needed, and a more structured situation was sought. At this point, the writer discovered that a research project being conducted by Ferreira and Winter (1965, 1966; Ferreira, Winter, & Poindexter, 1966; Winter, Ferreira, & Olson, 1965, 1966; Winter & Ferreira, in press) provided the sort of situations that seemed to be well suited for the kind of measurement under consideration. In their project, family triads were being studied while interacting towards a family decision over relatively neutral items on a questionnaire and during the telling of a story based upon TAT cards. The procedure promoted two different sorts of conversations: the questionnaire discussion and the TAT discussion. In the questionnaire discussion the families were speaking about precise items on a list, while in the TAT story-making the conversation ran more freely. This seemed to meet the specific purpose of the measurement reported here, since it provided long runs of conversation among family members where each family member had an equal right and opportunity to enter the discussion. Accordingly, the sharing of families was instituted between the two projects.

The Theoretical Approach

When we examine a series of family conversations and wish to make a measurement which is as noninferential as possible, there is only one set of observations of which we can be certain. We cannot be sure what the family members are saying, what they mean by what they are saying, or even to whom each is speaking, but we can be reasonably certain that each family member speaks. In fact, one can be sure of which one is speaking by placing on each person a microphone which only fires if that person makes an audible sound.

Taking a conversation of mother, father, and one child and recording the order in which the members speak, one obtains a stream which looks like this: $MCFMCFCFMFMFCFM$ . . . and so on. (At times the family members speak simultaneously, and a set of categories could be added for that; but in this research it was decided to break down simultaneous speech into who spoke first and who last, and so put the speeches in sequence. It was also decided that no person would follow himself; and so if a person spoke and was silent for a period and spoke again, this was counted as one speech.) Examining this stream of conversation, one finds a variety of frequency counts are possible. One could total how often mother speaks, or father speaks, or child speaks. Such a count would not help us compare families; we would only be comparing how an individual in one family contrasts with an individual in another family. The most elementary count which measured an *interchange* would be of sequences of two persons speaking. Examining this stream and making this most simple family count, one can note the possibilities. Father can be followed by child or mother (*FC* or *FM*), mother can be followed by father or child (*MF* or *MC*), and child can be followed by either father or mother (*CF* or *CM*). That is, this most elementary frequency count of who follows whom provides six possible categories.

To compute the frequency of use of these six categories a "Family Interaction Analyzer" was devised by the Alto Scientific Company of Palo Alto, California. Each family member at the table has a lavalier microphone which is connected to the "analyzer," a small box with six windows in it. In each window is a counter which runs up a score as the people talk. When father speaks, nothing happens until mother follows him, and then a count is made on the *FM* counter. Then when child follows mother, a count appears on the *MC* counter, and so on. Therefore, as the family has a conversation, the sequence in which they speak is immediately ordered by the machine so that totals appear automatically in each of the six categories. In addition, each microphone fires a pen on an event recorder so that a visual record of the conversation is obtained. * * *

RESULTS

The data from the interviews with 80 families was processed, and a variety of frequency counts were made: the frequency with which each individual spoke, the frequency with which one person followed another, and the frequency of longer sequences of speech, i.e., sequences of three, four, five, six, and seven speeches. The results will be presented in relation to the hypotheses being tested.

1. To answer the question whether we can demonstrate that families follow repetitive patterns, it was hypothesized that if the order in which family members speak differs from that order which would occur with random behavior, then the family is following patterns which repeat themselves.

When we compute the frequency with which father speaks after mother and child, mother speaks after child and father, and child speaks after mother and father, we can arrive at a percentage of the use by each family of the six possible categories: *MF, CF, CM, FM, MC, FC*. If the family members were behaving randomly—for example if three robots were tossing coins to see who spoke next—all of these six categories would occur equally on an infinite run. That is, each category would occur 16.66 percent of the time on an infinite run, because it would be equally likely that any one person would follow any other. Shorter runs of random responses would not all show a distribution of one-sixth in each category but would fluctuate. If we take the equal use of the six categories, or a distribution of one-sixth each, as a zero point, then nonrandomness would be indicated by a fluctuation away from that zero point. If the actual count of a sample of families distributed near that zero point, or the equal use of the six categories, it could be said that family members were speaking randomly and not following patterns. When the actual distribution of the 80 families in this study is plotted, as shown in Figure 1, it can be seen that they compose a fairly normal curve around a mean deviation from equal use of the six categories of 24.31.[1]

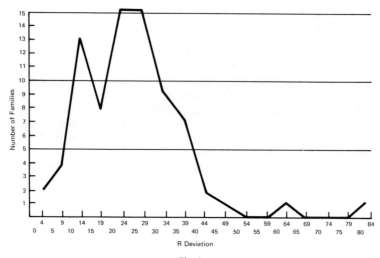

Fig. 1.

2. The second hypothesis suggested that if one created a scale with the zero point being a random distribution, then every family will deviate from that zero point, and any one family can be contrasted with any other on this common base line.

When the 80 families are ranked in order of deviation from an equal use of the six categories, it can be seen that any family can be contrasted with any other family in reference to a point common to them both.

3. The third hypothesis proposed that normal families would use more of the possibilities more often and therefore would tend toward

---

[1] This deviation from an equal use of the six categories can be computed in several ways. A particular way was used in this study, and throughout this report an index score of deviation from random, or equal use, of the six categories will be used. This will be called the R deviation score of a particular family and the means and medians discussed will be based upon these R deviation scores. This index is computed by taking as "zero" the equal use of the six categories, or 16.66 percent frequency of use of each category. When a count is made of a particular family, the deviation in frequency of use of each category from 16.66 percent when totaled (ignoring the sign) provides the R deviation score for that family. In this way a scale is established with a common zero point for all families. As a simplified example, if a family exhibits a 1 percent difference from 16.66 percent in each category, their R deviation score would be 6.00 computed as follows:

$$FC \quad 17.66 - 16.66 = 1.00 \qquad MC \quad 15.66 - 16.66 = 1.00$$
$$FM \quad 15.66 - 16.66 = 1.00 \qquad CM \quad 17.66 - 16.66 = 1.00$$
$$MF \quad 17.66 - 16.66 = 1.00 \qquad CF \quad 17.66 - 16.66 = 1.00$$

randomness on this scale, and disturbed families would use some possibilities more often than others and so tend away from randomness.

The results with 80 families show that the normal group tends toward the random end of the scale, using each of the categories more equally, and the abnormal group tends away from the zero point, showing a more skewed distribution of the six categories. The two groups differ significantly at the .00003 level and the hypothesis is supported. Figure 2 diagrams the differences between the two groups.

Examination of the data shows that 10 abnormal families fall below the median family, or in the "normal" range, and 10 normal families fall above that point in the "abnormal" range. One would expect to find normal families falling in an abnormal range on almost any measurement because of the way these families are selected. The criterion does not exclude abnormality, it merely excludes abnormality which has come to the attention of the community. Many of the normal families might contain an undiagnosed disturbed member, and many might ultimately develop a disturbed member but have not as yet. It is of interest that of the 10 abnormal families falling in the "normal" range, 4 of them contain a psychotic member while the remaining 5 families with a psychotic member fall in the abnormal range.

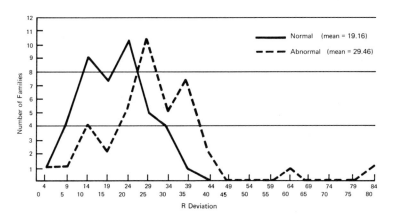

Fig. 2.

When this approach was conceived, it was assumed that this simple count of six categories would show differences between normal and abnormal families, but that counts of larger patterns would show greater differences. Therefore the family data was processed for computer analysis. Interestingly, this elementary count of sequence of two speeches differentiates abnormal from normal families more sharply than more complex counts. A count of three speeches, such as *FMC*, *FMF*, and so on, where there are twelve possible sequences, reveals less difference, but a significant difference, between the two types of families on this scale. Similarly, patterns of 4, 5, 6, and 7 speeches provide significant but less differentiation. Table 1 shows the mean differences of these various sequences.

TABLE 1

R DEV MEANS

	Normal	Abnormal	Difference	C. R.
Individual speeches	9.27	14.47	5.20	3.82*
Sequence of two	23.24	38.39	15.15	4.42*
Sequence of three	64.18	83.15	18.97	3.64*
Sequence of four	126.97	171.42	44.45	4.40*
Sequence of five	283.09	364.00	80.91	4.39*
Sequence of six	677.05	837.36	160.31	3.87*
Sequence of seven	1803.63	2103.43	299.80	3.20*

$*p < .001$.

It would appear that the two-count provided by the Family Inter-action Analyzer offers sufficient answers to the questions posed without the elaborate work necessary for computer preparation.

4. The final hypothesis suggested that if a family falls in the abnormal range on this scale and then is successfully treated with family therapy, the family will move toward the normal range on this scale.

Sufficient data is not yet available to test this hypothesis. Six families were tested before treatment and then were given exactly the same test with the same interviewer six months later. The first four families were treated by training therapists, and their supervisor reported independently that he felt none of these families had undergone any basic change. The results here support that conclusion; all the families moved toward the normal range of the scale, but only slightly. Family A, a family with a formerly psychotic mother, originally fell in the normal range and changed only from an R deviation score of 6.32 to one of 5.06. Families B and C also appear to have changed only slightly and remain in the abnormal range. Family D moved thirty points toward the normal range but remained abnormal (the change apparently represented father partici-pating more in arguments with mother). The fifth family, Family E, was treated by a more experienced therapist, and therapy was being recessed but not completed at the time of the second test. (The parents were going to Europe and leaving their 23-year-old son behind, a change which would seem represented in the higher mother-father pairing on the second test.) Family F fell in the "normal" range originally, and was also treated by a more experienced therapist. The child has improved sufficiently to leave the hospital, but little change is shown on this measurement; the family moved only three points on the R deviation scale. Until families with more clearly successful treatment are measured, this hypothesis cannot be adequately tested.

To determine whether families change with therapy, it is necessary to consider how normal families change on test and retest without the intervention of a therapist. At this point six normal families have been retested. The families change only slightly less than the group of treated families. Taking the mean percentage change in each category, the normals change 2.36 percent and the treated families 3.15 percent. The change in R deviation score shows the normal mean change to be 5.64 and the treated families 9.64. Whether this difference is significant is difficult to determine on so small a sample. It is also possible that normal families represent a different "species" from abnormal families, and therefore their fluctuation on test and retest might not be comparable to the results with abnormal families, who might be more rigid. Ideally, one should compare abnormal treated families with abnormal families who have not been treated. This raises the sampling problem of finding abnormal families who are not undergoing treatment. However, the test and retest results on these few families indicate the possibility of measuring therapeutic change in families with an instrument and therefore with high reliability.

We do not know as yet whether families which have undergone "successful" therapy will change on this measurement, but it does appear that the measurement picks up a family pattern which is surprisingly consistent over time. Three of the normal families and two of the abnormal families do not change on retest more than two points on this scale, and the percentage change in each category is slight for several of the families. As a group the 12 families change only 2.75 percent in each category, and the mean change in deviation from random is 5.73. One would expect greater fluctuation on the basis of error, chance, or the disposition of family members on those particular days.

Other Computation

When this research was begun it was predicted that abnormal families would show an unequal distribution of six categories, but it was not expected that they would show any particular pattern for a type of family. For example, it was not assumed that there would be a greater frequency of mother-child interchange in abnormal families because the mothers are said to be overprotective and the fathers passive. The differences in interchange between the two groups is shown in percentages in Table 2.

In the normal group the mother-child interchange is highest and father-child is least, while in the abnormal group the mother-father interchange is highest and the father-child is least.

A similar distribution occurs if one merely counts the dyads which have the greatest frequency of speeches, as shown in Table 2.

The father-mother interchange in the abnormal group is the most frequent, occurring twice as often as the father-child interchange. Although this means that in the abnormal group father and mother talk following each other more often than father and child, just what this difference means is difficult to determine. It might mean that father and mother are "closer" than father and child, or it might mean quite the

TABLE 2

FREQUENCY OF "SPEECHES" IN DYADS

	FC	CF	FM	MF	MC	CM
Normal	14.95%	15.34%	16.91%	15.58%	18.15%	17.94%
Abnormal	14.99%	14.74%	19.34%	19.59%	15.55%	15.78%

	Normal	Abnormal
Father-child	9	9
Mother-child	17	12
Father-mother	14	19

opposite. Insofar as the families are assigned a task in the interview and talk until that task is accomplished, it could be argued that frequency of pairs of speeches indicates disagreement, because with agreement the task and the conversation end. Therefore a more frequent interchange between two people could mean greater disagreement between them. Lacking a noninferential measure of "disagreement," we can only note the difference at this point.

Individual Participation

It might be argued that the significant differences found between the two groups on the interactional measurement are merely a result of an abnormal member participating less in the conversation. Even if the disturbed member did speak less than someone in the normal group, and granting that individual participation influences group participation, the individual emphasis does not seem to be the most useful way to examine this kind of data. The argument that individual behavior should be given the important emphasis is usually either a product of past tradition or a belief that individual behavior is the result of some innate, perhaps organic, characteristic.

Yet it is equally possible to argue that what the individual does is a response to what the other individuals are doing. The muteness of a disturbed child can be seen as a product of the ways the parents deal with him and he with them, and so a measure which includes his muteness is measuring the habitual operational patterns in that family. What one individual does is not separable from what the other two individuals are doing, and so a measurement which implies independent individual behavior is doubtfully legitimate. As an exaggerated example, one might note that the mother speaks less often in a particular family and hypothesize that this is a result of her character or personality. Yet when one examines the conversation in which she speaks, it could be noted that whenever father turns to speak to her, the child cuts in and speaks to father; and when child turns to speak to her, father cuts in and speaks to child. When the frequency of mother's speech is totaled, it could appear that she is more unresponsive than father or child, but to measure her "unresponsiveness" as if it is independent of the behavior of the others is a distortion of the situation.

However, in response to the argument that the behavior of the identified patient "causes" the difference between the two groups of families, two sorts of computation can be presented. Table 3 shows the percentage distribution of individual speeches.

TABLE 3

PERCENTAGE DISTRIBUTION OF INDIVIDUAL SPEECHES

	Father	Mother	Child	Total Speeches
Normal	31.87	34.85	33.28	37,502
Abnormal	34.32	35.14	30.52	35,932

In the normal group the mother speaks most often and the father least often, while in the abnormal group the mother speaks slightly more often than the father and the child least often. The two groups do not differ significantly on this measurement since the child in the abnormal group does not speak significantly less than the father in the normal group.

A further breakdown shows that, of the 36 families in which the presenting problem was one member who was considered the identified patient, that person spoke an average of 29.80 percent of the time, speaking least in 20 out of the 36 cases (52.94 percent). In the 33 families where the child was the identified patient, he spoke an average of 30.05 percent of the time, speaking least in 18 out of the 33 cases (54.55 percent). In contrast, the person speaking least often in the normal group was the father, and he spoke least in 18 out of the 40 cases (45.00 percent). It would appear that the identified patient tended to be the person who speaks least in the abnormal group, but in about half the cases the person who spoke least was not the identified patient.

In summary, if one raises the question whether there is a more unequal distribution of frequency of speech by individuals in the abnormal group than there is in the normal group, the answer is yes. Taking as a base line a random distribution of speech, or each of the three family members speaking 33.33 percent of the time, the normal and abnormal groups of families differ significantly (as shown by the "individual speeches" in Table 1). However, this difference does not seem attributable to the behavior of the identified patient. It would appear that whatever the measurement, individual or interactional, if one approaches the data from the point of view of a deviation from the equal use of all possibilities, then normal and abnormal families will differ. As individuals the abnormals participate less equally; as dyads they show an unequal distribution, and larger frequency measurements show a similar skewness. * * *

Some Interactional Variables in Normal and Abnormal Families*

Antonio J. Ferreira, William D. Winter,
and Edward J. Poindexter

* * * A total of 126 families were tested in this project. There were 50 normal (*Nor*) and 76 abnormal (*Abn*) families, broken down into 16 schizophrenic (*Sch*), 16 delinquent (*Del*), and 44 maladjusted (*Mal*). (For a fuller description of this sample, see Article 11.)

The families were presented with three standard TAT cards and instructed to discuss, and if possible reach agreement on, a story that would tie the three TAT cards together in the given order (see Article 18). They were further informed that they would have five minutes to talk about it, at which time the tester would return to the room and listen to the story as told by whomever the family would elect as spokesman. Five minutes later the tester came into the testing room to hear the story as told by the family-elected member. After listening to the whole story, the tester gave the family three other TAT cards with similar instructions about the story to be made up, except that for this second story the spokesman would have to be someone else—that is, one of the other two family members. In this fashion, all three family members were ultimately spokesmen for the family. * * *

For the purpose of this study, only that portion of the testing session devoted by the family to the actual process of arriving at the stories was analyzed (Winter, Ferreira & Olson, 1965, 1966). These five or more minutes (per story) of verbal interaction among family members as recorded on tape were studied with a view to measuring a number of variables, such as how much each family member speaks, how much their speaking overlaps, and how much the family stays silent.

To answer these and related questions, four research assistants were trained to listen to the tape-recorded protocols. Provided with a stopwatch, each assistant was assigned to time one of the four quantities: the number of seconds the father spoke; the number of seconds the mother spoke; the number of seconds the child spoke; and the number of seconds of overlapping conversation, i.e., two or three family members speaking

---

*Abstracted from *Family Process*, 1966, 5, 60–75, with permission of the authors and *Family Process*.

simultaneously. The period of family interaction to be so measured was limited to the period of time when family members interchanged views about the TAT cards in order to arrive at a story they all (more or less) agreed upon. Accordingly, for each story the timing began at the moment the tester left the testing room, signaled by the noisy closing of the door, and ended with the return of the tester, signaled again by the noisy opening of the door. In the event of prolongation of the allotted five minutes, the timing continued through the extended periods in the same manner. Overlap was timed whenever two or three voices were heard simultaneously, regardless of whose voices they were. In timing the speaking of an individual family member, the research assistant was instructed to continue to time the assigned voice even through periods of overlap. The amount of silence was measured indirectly by subtracting from the total time (five minutes or more) the sum of the time spoken by the father, mother and child, less the time when two or three voices were heard to overlap.

FINDINGS

The factors of age and sex of the child did not seem to influence any of the variables under consideration.

Five hypotheses concerning differences among all four diagnostic groups and, more specifically, between normal and abnormal families, were formulated and tested as follows:

Hypothesis 1 was derived from another aspect of this research project in which it was demonstrated that *Abn* families require significantly more time than *Nor* families to make family decisions (Ferreira & Winter, 1965). Thus it was hypothesized here that *Abn families require more time than Nor families to perform the family task of arriving at a TAT story.* As may be recalled, the tester gave each family a five-minute period of time to discuss the TAT cards and arrive at a story based upon them. At the end of the five minutes, the tester returned to the testing room, and asked to be told the story. However, it happened many times that at the end of those five minutes, the family had not yet reached general consensus as to what story to tell. In these instances, the tester left the room again, allowing the family "one or two more minutes" of discussion and effort to get a story. An investigation of the occurrence of these extensions of the initially allotted five minutes disclosed differences among diagnostic groups which proved to be statistically significant. Thus, *Nor* families necessitated extension of the given five minutes time much less often than *Abn* families. ($\chi^2 = 11.94, df = 1, p < .001$). In this respect, as Table 1 shows, there were no statistically significant differences among *Mal, Sch,* and *Del* subgroups.

Hypothesis 2 refers to the question of "who talked the most," and "who talked the least," stating that *there would be differences among diagnostic groups or between normal and abnormal families as to the relative amount of time spoken by family members for all three stories combined.* The hypothesis was not corroborated, except for *Sch* families

TABLE 1

NUMBER OF FAMILIES THAT DID, AND DID NOT, REQUIRE AN EXTENSION
OF THE ALLOTTED FIVE MINUTES FOR STORY-MAKING

STORIES	Nor	Mal	Scb	Del
On time	34	14	7	8
With extension	16	30	9	8

where the child was shown to talk much less than children from other family groups ($F = 4.95$, $df = 3/122$, $p < .005$). The values observed are given in Table 2 as percentages in order to permit an intuitive comparison of the relative amount of talking done by the different family members in the four groups.

TABLE 2

MEAN TALKING TIME OF INDIVIDUAL FAMILY MEMBERS,
AS PERCENTAGE OF TOTAL FAMILY TALK IN ALL THREE TAT STORIES

FAMILY MEMBERS	DIAGNOSTIC GROUPS			
	Nor	Mal	Scb	Del
Father	32.2	35.7	37.2	32.6
Mother	35.5	32.9	40.3	35.3
Child*	32.3	31.4	22.5	32.1

*Analysis of Variance, $F = 4.95$, $df = 3/122$, $p < 0.005$.

It was interesting to observe here that there was a great tendency for an individual family member to talk more when he was going to be the spokesman for the family, as Table 3 shows. This finding was observed with remarkable consistency in all three stories and for all three story-tellers, although in very many instances, as the tapes revealed, there was no explicit mention in the course of the family discussion of who would be the story-teller. There was only one exception, namely, the Scb child, who on the average spoke less than either parent even when it was his turn to tell the story.

It must be noticed here that a frequency breakdown of who told which of the three stories (that is, the first, second, or third stories) did not reveal any significant differences among diagnostic groups, even when taking into consideration the sex of the child in the test. There was a certain tendency for Nor families to have the child become the spokesman for the first or second story, in contrast with Abn families where such a tendency did not seem to be present. However, these observations could easily have resulted from a chance effect ($\chi^2 = 2.45$, $df = 1$, $p < .20$).

TABLE 3

MEAN TALKING TIME OF INDIVIDUAL FAMILY MEMBERS, AS PERCENTAGE OF
TOTAL FAMILY TALK AND AS A FUNCTION OF THE STORY TELLER

DIAGNOSTIC GROUPS		STORY TELLER		
		Father	Mother	Child
Nor	Father	38.6	29.7	28.6
	Mother	32.0	41.6	32.3
	Child	29.4	28.7	39.2
Mal	Father	41.7	34.2	32.0
	Mother	30.2	36.9	31.2
	Child	28.1	28.9	36.8
Sch	Father	44.3	38.8	30.9
	Mother	36.1	46.8	38.7
	Child	19.6	16.5	31.4
Del	Father	39.4	28.3	30.3
	Mother	33.8	39.9	32.6
	Child	27.2	31.8	37.1

Hypothesis 3 was inspired by the work of Haley (1964) on "who speaks after whom." Haley observed that "normal" families had a count much closer to randomness (that is, to the situation where all combinations of "who speaks after whom" would have the same degree of probability) than "abnormal" families, and that this difference was statistically significant. Similarly, it was hypothesized in our study that _there would be differences among diagnostic groups or between Nor and Abn families, when the amount of talk done by the family members was measured as a deviation from equal participation._ Thus, it was assumed that participation in the family conversation, if randomly distributed, would permit each family member to talk 33.33 percent of the total talking time for the family. Any deviation from this percentage of 33.33 was considered as a deviation from randomness for the particular family member; the sum total of these deviations, in absolute values, for all three members of a family was regarded as a measure of the deviation from random participation for the whole family, and designated as R_{dev}. It was, therefore, hypothesized that _Abn_ families would have a greater R_{dev} than _Nor_ families. But the hypothesis tested for the three stories combined was not corroborated by the data. The only group that supported the hypothesis was the _Sch_ group, which displayed a family R_{dev} greater than the other diagnostic groups—a difference which was not, however, statistically significant.

Hypothesis 4 referred to the amount of overlap, that is, to the amount of time when two or three voices were heard on the tape simultaneously. This hypothesis stated that _there would be differences among diagnostic_ groups, or between normal and abnormal families, in regard to the percentage of overlap. The results, however, were entirely negative. Calculated as a percentage of the total talking time for the respective family, the amount of overlap, as shown in Table 4, did not seem to have any differentiating power among diagnostic groups.

TABLE 4

"OVERLAP," AS PERCENTAGE OF FAMILY
TALKING TIME, BY DIAGNOSTIC GROUPS

DIAGNOSTIC GROUPS	OVERLAP*	
	Mean	SD
Nor	5.06	3.21
Mal	4.23	2.82
Sch	4.04	2.76
Del	4.49	3.47

*Analysis of Variance, $F = 0.68$, $df = 3/122$, ns

Hypothesis 5 stated that an investigation of "silence" in the family would disclose significant differences among diagnostic groups, and greater silence in Abn than in Nor families. The results for all three stories combined, summarized in Table 5, fully supported the hypothesis while revealing differences among diagnostic groups which were statistically significant ($F = 5.24$, $df = 3/122$, $p < .005$). The specific difference between Nor and Abn families was, as hypothesized, in the direction of a greater silence in Abn families ($t = 3.61$, $df = 122$, $p < .001$). In this respect it is interesting to note that the Sch and Del groups of families consistently scored a high percentage of silence. The consistency of these findings is illustrated in Figure 1, which indicates the percentage of silence during the three stories by diagnostic groups. As this figure shows, the percentage of silence remained approximately constant within each diagnostic group

TABLE 5

"SILENCE," AS PERCENTAGE OF TOTAL
INTERACTION TIME, BY DIAGNOSTIC GROUPS

DIAGNOSTIC GROUPS	SILENCE*	
	Mean	SD
Nor	35.7	11.3
Mal	39.2	12.4
Sch	46.1	16.1
Del	47.7	12.8

*Analysis of Variance, $F = 5.24$, $df = 3/122$, $p < 0.005$.

through all three stories, a finding which seems to add importance to the concept of silence as a differentiating variable among diagnostic groups. Also of particular interest here was the observation that an association seemed to exist between "extended story time" and a greater percentage of silence, indicating that families which required more time to arrive at a story tended to be the families that spent more time in silence. This association, although weak, was nevertheless statistically significant (biserial r = .188, p < .05).

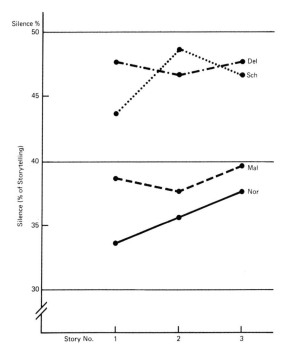

Fig. 1. Percentage of silence by diagnostic groups, as function of story number 1, 2, and 3.

DISCUSSION

The study reported in this paper investigates the possible importance of some rather simple variables as a first approach to the elucidation of significant parameters in family interaction. The investigation inquired into the group behavior of four diagnostic categories of families in the process of making up three stories based upon an ordered presentation of three TAT cards. From the tape-recorded protocols, measurements were obtained of how much time family members spoke, how much time they were silent, and how much they overlapped when they talked.

The *relative amount of talk* done by a family member, as well as the twin issues of "who talks the most" and "who talks the least" in a family, did not appear to relate to diagnostic categories. These negative findings are of likely interest to investigators concerned with basic variables in family interaction, for it has been assumed that one could count on such measures to draw inferences, for instance, about who is the "dominant" family member. Farina (1960), for example, in an investigation of parents of schizophrenic patients, used the speaking time of one parent relative to the other as an index of dominance. But only in the comparison of the relative amount of time spoken by the children did we find statistically significant differences. Yet, paradoxically, this positive finding is of limited interest, since it rests on the observation that *Sch* children spoke less than children in other family groups. This is an almost tautologic observation for, as it may be recalled, criteria used to form the *Sch* subgroup demanded that the child in the test had been diagnosed "schizophrenic," a diagnosis which often implies the observation that the child talks less than the average. Thus, the statistical significance of the discrepancy in the amount of talk done by children from the *Sch* group when compared to children from other diagnostic groups does not seem to add anything to what we had already built into the data. The finding must, therefore, be regarded not as a discovery but simply as a confirmation of the child's diagnosis. And since the child speaks relatively less, the parents must speak relatively more. Still, when we look at the time spoken by the parents, it could not be said that there was a "dominance" by either parent, or that *Sch* parents were in that respect different from parents in other diagnostic groups.

When the family talking time was partitioned among the three family members and measured in terms of their deviation from equal participation (R_{dev}), no statistically significant differences were found among diagnostic groups, although schizophrenia-producing families displayed a consistently (in all three TAT stories) greater R_{dev} than other families. In this regard, it may be worth pointing out a peculiarity of R_{dev} scores as measurements of family interaction. R_{dev} scores reflect departures from equal partition of the variable in question, and grow in size, in our use of it, whenever one individual family member talks relatively less than the other two. Indeed, if one family member is or becomes "withdrawn," the R_{dev} score shows an increase corresponding to the departure from equal partitioning of the variable involved. Thus, in this respect, differences in R_{dev} scores among diagnostic groups may be argued to be an expression of individual differences (for instance, the "schizophrenic" child who talks less, or the "manic" mother who talks more) rather than a documentation of anything peculiarly characteristic of the family as a unit.

Rather thought-provoking was the finding that, with remarkable consistency, the would-be story-teller talked more than the other two family members, although on many occasions, as the recorded tape revealed, it was not made explicit during the discussion who would become spokesman for that particular story. The finding raises the speculative possibility that when these families engaged in their discussion over the TAT cards, there might have been a tacit agreement as to who would speak for the family. Again, in this regard, the outstanding exception was provided by the *Sch* group where the child, as a story-teller, talked less, not more, than either parent. But the comments made above about the children in the *Sch* group would apply here with equal force. At any rate, the observation that any family member in the position of would-be spokesman tends to speak more than the other two family members seems to pose some meaningful questions for future research, and is of particular interest to the student of group dynamics.

The investigation of how much family members tend to talk at the same time (*overlap*) yielded results that did not differentiate among diagnostic groups. Since we could safely assume that overlapping of voices represents a measure of the degree to which family members tend to interrupt each other, our findings appear to contradict Farina's observations of parents of schizophrenics (Farina, 1960). In these parents (as compared to "control" parents) Farina demonstrated a higher number of "interruptions," which he considered as an index of their greater conflict. It must be observed, however, that our measurements do not directly replicate Farina's, for in this study we measured the percentage of timed overlap, when two or three voices were heard simultaneously, whereas Farina only counted the number of "interruptions" between parents. Here another distinction is to be noted, namely, that Farina conducted this investigation on the father-mother dyad, while we explored the triad of father-mother-child.

But our data also seem to contradict the observations of Lennard, Beaulieu, and Embrey (1965) on "intrusions" in family triads with a schizophrenic child. Lennard defined "intrusion" operationally as a statement made by a family member whose entrance into interaction is not requested, that is, where the statement-maker is "neither the target nor the initiator." He observed that the number of such intrusions tended to be smaller in schizophrenic families than in controls. So, although Lennard's "intrusion," Farina's "interruption," and our "overlap" may have a common denominator—the degree to which family members verbally interfere with each other through colliding (intruding, interrupting, overlapping) statements—they are, in fact, different variables.

The measurement of *silence* as an aspect of family interaction provided most valuable results, inasmuch as statistically significant differences were found between normal and abnormal families. As hypothesized, normal families spent relatively less time in silence than abnormal families. It may be noteworthy that the subgroups of schizophrenia-producing and delinquency-producing families had the greatest percentage of silence, a finding which would permit the placing of these families on the "sicker" end of a hypothetical normal-abnormal continuum.

It should be noted that this relative amount of silence appeared to be related to the diagnostic category rather than to the specific set of TAT cards used to elicit interchange. As Figure 1 shows, the amount of relative silence remained essentially constant from story to story for each diagnostic group. The stability of these measurements of silence was, in fact, quite remarkable. In all diagnostic groups, the percentages of silence in any one story correlated highly with the percentages in any other story. Thus, product-moment correlation between percentages of silence in Story 1 and Story 3 was $r = .710$ for the total sample. By diagnostic groups the correlation was $r = .576$ for *Nor*; $r = .691$ for *Mal*; $r = .858$ for *Sch*; and $r = .731$ for *Del* families. These findings emphasize the importance of silence as an interactional variable sensitive to, and associated with, family pathology; for as may be noticed, these correlations seem to increase with pathology: *Sch* and *Del* families had the highest correlations, *Nor* the lowest, and *Mal* a value in between. Incidentally, the correlations between percentages of silence in Stories 1 and 2, or 2 and 3, were roughly the same as those between Stories 1 and 3 reported above, which had been chosen a priori on the assumption that they would provide a more conservative estimate of the stability of these measurements. As it happened, the differences in correlations among stories were negligible within diagnostic groups. On the other hand, the differences in correlations among diagnostic groups reached statistical significance particularly in the comparison between *Nor* and *Abn* families ($z = 1.73$, $p < .05$), and between *Nor* and *Sch* ($z = 2.03$, $p < .03$). These observations suggest that abnormal families, when compared with normal ones, tend to operate with greater rigidity in regard to some important interactional variables such as silence. This notion of rigidity in pathologic family systems seems to conform well with clinical impressions that pathologic families may be quite handicapped in their ability to change their ways in the face of new situations or events. The subject deserves further inquiry.

As the results of this study indicate, the relative amount of silence seems to be a valuable indicator of family functioning. But the significance of this finding may not be fully realized until it becomes apparent that *families that spent more time in silence were often the same families that required extensions of the five-minute period* allotted to discuss and make up a story on the TAT. This association between silence and inability to perform the required task quickly is most noteworthy, notwithstanding its expression in a rather low (but statistically significant) correlation. For this association, in fact, points to a possible cause of the abnormal families' lower efficiency: these families are prevented from arriving at a story in the allotted period because they spend too great a time in silence, i.e., they talk less and interchange less information per unit of time than normal families. Indeed, considering that a family is involved in a task which requires the verbal participation of all family members, the time spent in silence appears as a likely "waste" which tends to decrease the overall efficiency of the family group. In this regard, it is interesting to note that in another phase of this research project (Ferreira & Winter, 1965), it was also found, by independent means, that "abnormal" families required a much longer time than "normal" families to perform a task of family decision-making over make-believe items on a questionnaire. Thus silence appears as an important interactional variable which reflects the relationship, not so much the specific individuals. Silence in a family, as in any other relationship (Ferreira, 1964b), is an occurrence which all members must share in authorship.

Concerning the sample, it must be noted that these families were tested in accordance with availability, and every effort was made to insure a random selection. But this effort had a limitation. The "normal" families were tested knowing of their "normality," whereas the "abnormal" families looked upon the testing procedure as a step toward the determination of their assumed "abnormality." This bias due to knowing one's own label was unavoidable under the conditions of the experiment; it must be admitted that, indeed, it might have affected the results, although it is not immediately apparent in what direction and manner. * * *

Interaction Process Analysis of Family Decision-Making*

William D. Winter and Antonio J. Ferreira

* * * The families tested were 90 triads of father, mother, and child. These were divided into four groups, based on the diagnosis of the child: (1) 35 normals (*Nor*); (2) 33 emotionally maladjusted (*Mal*), e.g., neurotic; (3) 10 schizophrenic (*Sch*); and (4) 12 delinquent (*Del*). (See Articles 11 and 18 above for further information on the characteristics of the families and the TAT procedure.) These and other variables describing the *S*s are found in Table 1. Chi-square analyses revealed no significant differences among groups on any variable except age of the child ($\chi^2 = 9.20$, $df = 3$, $p < .05$), reflecting the greater age of the *Sch* and the lesser age of the *Mal* children.

Procedure

In this part of the research, each family was presented with a set of three TAT cards and instructed to work together to make up a story they all agreed upon, which would link the three cards together in the order in

TABLE 1

GENERAL CHARACTERISTICS OF THE FAMILIES

| VARIABLE | DIAGNOSTIC GROUP | | | | TOTAL |
	Nor	Mal	Sch	Del	
Male children*	28	29	8	11	76
Female children*	7	4	2	1	14
Father's education	15.6	14.1	14.5	13.0	14.5
Father's occupational level	1.8	1.7	1.8	2.3	1.9
Child's age	15.6	13.8	17.0	14.5	15.0

*All variables except these two are expressed in median values.

*Abstracted from *Family Process*, 1967, 6, 155–172, with permission of the authors and *Family Process*.

which they were presented. The examiner left the room for five minutes, and upon his return one of the family members, whom they had chosen to be their spokesman, told him the story they had agreed on. The procedure was repeated twice more with new cards and a different spokesman each time. The choice of who would be the spokesman for each story was found to be unrelated to the diagnosis of the child.

Scoring

The discussions of the families while they were making up their stories, which took place in the absence of the examiner, were tape-recorded. These protocols were later scored in accordance with the Bales IPA system by two psychologists who had had no personal contact with the families and who did not know their diagnoses. The two scorers underwent an extended period of training and helped develop a scoring manual for this project, which we hoped would make the scoring more objective. To clarify the classification of certain task area items, IPA Categories 4 and 9 were limited to suggestions concerning how the group should proceed, e.g., "You tell the story to Dr.____" or "Shall we pass the pictures around?" Categories 5 and 8 were reserved for opinions about the TAT stories themselves, e.g., "Could it be a mother and daughter on those cards?" Categories 6 and 7 were used for statements dealing with orientation to the general task and the examiner's instructions, e.g., "Do they have to be in this sequence?" Except for these changes, the 12 categories used were exactly those of the Bales IPA (see Table 2). Since it proved impossible to determine to whom remarks were directed, the data analysis deals only with the scoring of the originator's remarks.

Variables Scored

To bring the amount of data into manageable proportions, the material was limited to only the first 105 scored IPA comments for each story, making a possible maximum of 315 comments per family triad. The scored statements of each of the three family members were tabulated into the 12 categories, making a total of 36 basic scores. These scores were combined into several indexes, which formed the major variables dealt with in this paper (the letters and numbers in the list refer to the categories in Table 2):

(*a*) *Total Interaction.* The total number of scored comments, (A + B + C + D), i.e., the sum of all 12 categories.

(*b*) *A%.* The number of positive social-emotional comments divided by the total interaction score.

(*c*) *B%.* The number of attempted answers to the demands of the task, divided by the total interaction score.

(*d*) *C%.* The number of questions related to the task, divided by the total interaction score.

(*e*) *D%.* The number of negative social-emotional reactions, again divided by total interaction.

(*f*) *D/D + A.* The proportion of social-emotional statements which are negative in content, called an index of expressive-malintegrative behavior (Bales, 1950; Caputo, 1963).

TABLE 2

IPA CATEGORIES USED IN PRESENT STUDY
(Adapted from Bales)

A. Social-Emotional Area: Positive Reactions	1. *Shows solidarity*, raises other's status, gives reward 2. *Shows tension release*, jokes, laughs, shows satisfaction. 3. *Agrees*, shows passive acceptance
B. Task Area: Attempted Answers	4. *Gives suggestion*, direction (how group should proceed) 5. *Gives opinion*, evaluation, feeling (concerning TAT stories) 6. *Gives orientation*, information, clarifies (concerning general task)
C. Task Area: Questions	7. *Asks for orientation*, information (general task) 8. *Asks for opinion*, expression of feeling (about TAT stories) 9. *Asks for suggestion*, possible ways of action (group procedures)
D. Social-Emotional Area: Negative Reactions	10. *Disagrees*, shows passive rejection, withholds help 11. *Shows tension*, withdraws out of field 12. *Shows antagonism*, defends or asserts self, deflates others

A + B + C + D = Total Interaction.

(*g*) $B + C/A + D$. The ratio of task-oriented responses to social-emotional responses.

(*h*) $2/Total$. The proportion of antagonistic comments in the total interaction.

(*j*) $7/7 + 6$. The proportion of requests for orientation to the total requests plus giving orientation comments, an index of difficulty of communication regarding the general task at hand (Bales, 1950).

(*k*) $8/8 + 5$. The ratio of requests for opinion to requests plus giving opinion, an index of difficulty in evaluation of the TAT stories (Bales, 1950).

(*l*) $9/9 + 4$. The ratio of asking for suggestions to asking plus giving suggestions, an index of difficulty of control over the group process (Bales, 1950).

(*m*) $4 + 5/4 + 5 + 6$. The ratio of giving task-relevant suggestions and opinions to the total of this behavior plus giving general orientation, which has been termed an index of directiveness of control (Bales, 1950).

(*n*) $7 + 8 + 9/4 + 5 + 6 + 7 + 8 + 9$. The ratio of asking for help to asking plus giving help (Caputo, 1963), which serves as an index of dependency.

(o) R_{dev} F − M/C. This index was derived to measure the evenness with which the mother or the child responded to, or followed a remark by the father. To obtain this score, each scorable comment by the father was examined, and a determination made of whether the mother or the child followed father's comment by one of their own. The total number of times mother followed father was divided by the total number of times mother and child followed him, and this percentage was subtracted from 50% disregarding sign, to obtain an index of equality in responding to father. The R_{dev} measures follow Haley (1964).

(p) R_{dev} M − F/C. The above procedure was used to determine to what extent father and child participated equally in following mother's remarks with one of their own, or whether they deviated from the expected 50% participation.

(q) R_{dev} C − F/M. This index measures the degree to which mother and father followed a child remark equally, or whether either one followed the child more or less than the 50% participation expected by chance.

(r) R_{dev} Total. This was a simple sum of the three R_{dev} measures, and gives an overall indication of equality of participation in the family, as defined above.

Variables (a) and (o) to (r) were computed for the entire family; the remaining variables were computed for the entire family and also for each of the three members separately. Since the age of the child differed for the four diagnostic groups, the analysis of these variables made use of analysis of covariance to measure the significance of the difference among means for the diagnostic groups, with the effect of the child's age controlled.

RESULTS AND DISCUSSION

Scoring Reliability. Two raters independently scored 300 statements taken from five different stories according to the 12 IPA categories. The percentage of disagreement for each story and the median of these values for the five stories were computed. These medians ranged from 0 percent disagreement in Categories 1, 2, 7, and 9, to 5 percent disagreement in Category 3, and 13 percent in Category 5. It is difficult to construct an overall measure of agreement, but a rough idea of scoring reliability may be obtained by summing the medians. The sum for our data is 33 percent disagreement, which is somewhat higher than the sum of medians (24 percent) obtained by Waxler and Mishler (1966) using the tape-typescript method, but it is in the same general range. If these figures are meaningful, the difference between them may reflect error, scorer skill, sample differences, or the influence of the availability of a typescript. In any case, it is clear from our study and that of Waxler and Mishler that the levels of agreement found are relatively low in comparison to the usual levels required of a test, and this has "an important bearing on the confidence that may be placed in findings about group interaction where IPA categories are used." The raters in our study found it easier to agree on what a family member had said, specifically, than on its interpretation, i.e., the IPA categorization to be given. For example, an S might say, "I think it is a mother and son picture." One rater might score it as a simple "giving of an opinion," Category 5; the other might be impressed with the inflection and tone of voice, and score it as a 10 or 12, "disagrees" or "shows antagonism." The divergent interpretations by the scorers may make clinical sense, but it is a monumental stumbling block to this type of research. This low reliability undoubtedly affects the results presented below, which should therefore be evaluated with caution.

Effects of Sex and Age of Child. Before analyzing the broad ratios and indexes listed earlier, the effects of the sex and age of the child on the 12 category scores for each family member and the R_{dev} scores were investigated by t tests. Of the 40 t tests run for male versus female children (12 category scores for each of three family members plus 4 R_{dev} scores), only two were significant. When the child was a male, he showed less tension release behavior ($t = 2.14$, $p < .05$), and his father was more likely to ask for opinions regarding the TAT stories ($t = 3.07$, $p < .01$). These results seem trivial when one considers the large number of tests run, and we are forced to conclude that no major sex differences were found. However, the number of girl children was small, and because of this fact one cannot conclude that significant results would or would not occur with a larger sample of girls. As mentioned earlier, Cheek (1964b) did find that the sex of the child was related to the child's own behavior on IPA. Our finding that girls show more tension release confirms one of Cheek's results, but this probably only reflects the girls' socially learned pattern of giggling and laughing more easily.

Age differences were analyzed in a similar fashion, by dividing the children into an older group (16+) and a younger group (9½−15). Again, the overall results were minimal. Only one comparison was significant: when the child was younger, his mother showed a greater incidence of disagreements ($t = 2.49$, $p < .01$). So we may conclude that, in terms of our findings, the age and sex of the child had no major direct effect on the category scores of the three family members or the R_{dev} scores of the family.

Total Interaction. The effect of the diagnostic classification of the family on their total interaction score was determined separately, since previous studies have shown this to be an important factor (Cheek, 1964a; Lennard, Beaulieu, & Embrey, 1965), and since a significant difference in this score was part of the justification for using broader indexes which control for total interaction. The results for this variable, including the means adjusted for the effect of the child's age, may be found in Table 3. As can be seen from this table, total interaction is significantly associated with diagnosis, with the *Nor* and *Mal* families having the highest interaction score, the *Sch*'s the lowest score, and the *Del*'s scoring in between.

TABLE 3

RESULTS FOR VARIABLES FOR FAMILY TAKEN AS A WHOLE (df = 3/85)

VARIABLE	ADJUSTED MEANS				F
	Nor	Mal	Scb	Del	
(a) Total Interaction	270.5	278.6	230.6	254.0	4.1 *
(b) A%	14.3	13.8	14.3	12.7	0.30
(c) B%	59.3	58.4	55.6	59.4	0.52
(d) C%	9.2	9.3	13.7	11.1	4.43**
(e) D%	17.0	18.3	16.3	16.6	0.32
(f) D/D + A	.53	.56	.53	.57	0.34
(g) B + C/A + D	2.40	2.33	2.32	2.65	0.37
(h) 2/Total	.03	.02	.01	.02	1.44
(i) 12/Total	.05	.04	.02	.04	1.87
(j) 7/7 + 6	.22	.23	.25	.18	0.27
(k) 8/8 + 5	.12	.13	.17	.15	2.75*
(l) 9/9 + 4	.18	.13	.33	.13	4.73**
(m) 4 + 5/4 + 5 + 6	.95	.92	.89	.78	2.93*
(n) Dependency	.14	.14	.20	.16	3.77*
(o) R_{dev} F – M/C	12.1	16.3	27.1	15.8	3.72*
(p) R_{dev} M – F/C	11.6	11.2	25.6	13.6	5.17**
(q) R_{dev} C – F/M	12.6	13.4	21.0	17.7	1.88
(r) R_{dev} Tot.	36.1	40.9	64.5	46.7	4.78**

*$p < .05$
**$p < .01$

It would appear necessary, then, to analyze group differences using ratios, rather than total scores in each category, since the latter would be related to total interaction.

Significant Family Variables. As can be seen in Table 3, nine variables, including total interaction, significantly differentiated among our four groups of diagnosed families. Three of the four R_{dev} measures are significant, indicating that the families differ in the evenness of their participation. Inspection of Table 3 will show that this deviation from equal participation is greatest in the *Scb* families. However, it is particularly instructive to note that the R_{dev} measures which are significant all involve an inequality between the child and one of his parents, and that there is no significant inequality between parents alone. In other words, the significant R_{dev}'s seem to occur because the *Scb* child does not talk much, which is confirmed by inspection of the means for total interaction for each family member. For example, the mean for the *Scb* children is approximately 46 points below that of their mothers, whereas for the other groups the difference is 11 points (*Del*) or 0–1 points (*Nor, Mal*). The significant R_{dev}'s, then, are of limited interest, since they seem merely to reflect the fact that the diagnosis of schizophrenia in the child implies that the child talks less than average. Very similar findings were obtained by Ferreira, Winter, and Poindexter (1966), using as their basic measure an R_{dev} score based on the amount of time each member spoke relative to the speaking time of the others.

One finding of interest is that $C\%$ differentiated the groups, with Sch and Del families asking a greater percentage of questions than did the Nor's and Mal's. It may be recalled that Lennard et al. (1965) found that Sch mothers and fathers asked more questions than did the Nor's, and these writers interpreted this as an attempt by Sch parents to control the situation. Excessive questioning may, of course, also be an attempt to avoid sticking one's neck out by not voicing one's own opinions but asking the opinions of others instead. $C\%$ may, then, represent a variable of interest which merits further investigation to determine, perhaps, how questions are used in these families.

In three other statistically significant variables, the Sch families obtained the highest scores. The Sch families showed the greatest difficulty of control over the group process (9/9 + 4), tending to ask for suggestions rather than giving them. They also showed a higher index of difficulty in evaluation of the TAT stories (8/8 + 5), asking for opinions rather than giving them. The Sch's also were higher on the index of dependency (7 + 8 + 9/4 to 9), asking for help rather than giving it. All three indices show that the Sch families are more passive and dependent in these situations, either unwilling or unable to express their opinions in a forceful, clear, forthright manner, preferring to ask others to express their opinions first.

On the index of directiveness of control (4 + 5/4 + 5 + 6), the Nor and Mal families scored highest, perhaps reflecting the fact that these families tended to concentrate on the task at hand and use a direct problem-solving orientation. The Del families, in particular, devoted relatively more remarks to E's instructions and the general task, as if they were uncertain how to proceed or wanted to avoid committing themselves. The Sch families scored closer to the Nor's than did the Del's on this variable, but on all the other significant indexes, the Sch's were the most abnormal group.

Variables Applied to Family Members. Variables (b) to (n) were also computed for each family member, and the significant results are presented in Table 4. It should be pointed out that the smaller number of scores in the 12 IPA categories when dealing with individual members makes these indexes somewhat less stable than when they are computed for the entire family. In addition, all ratio scores present many problems of interpretation, especially when small numbers are involved. For example, for index (j) 7/7 + 6, receiving no scores in Category 7 will produce the same zero score for the index, whether the value of Category 6 is one or one hundred; and a shift of a single point in 6 may shift the ratio greatly (1/1 + 0 versus 1/1 + 1). Therefore, perhaps more attention should be paid to the differences obtained using the whole family than to the findings of Table 4.

The data of Table 4 indicate that the fathers of Sch and Del children had a higher percentage of questions and requests for help, indicating perhaps dependent, passive behavior, with the questions reflecting help-

TABLE 4

SIGNIFICANT FINDINGS FOR VARIABLES (b) TO (n) FOR EACH FAMILY MEMBER

VARIABLE	ADJUSTED MEANS				F
	Nor	Mal	Sch	Del	
I *Father*					
(d) C%	9.4	9.0	13.9	15.2	3.23*
(n) Depend.	.14	.13	.19	.21	2.88*
II *Mother*					
(l) 9/9 + 4	.14	.12	.30	.28	3.43*
(m) 4 + 5/4 + 5 + 6	.93	.79	.59	.54	6.05**
(n) Depend.	.17	.19	.24	.14	2.29
III *Child*					
(b) A%	.15	.16	.24	.15	2.68
(c) B%	.61	.58	.41	.56	5.23**
(d) C%	.06	.06	.05	.11	3.22*
(e) D%	.18	.21	.31	.19	2.45
(g) B + C/A + D	2.33	2.05	1.22	2.25	2.48
(k) 8/8 + 5	.08	.08	.05	.16	4.51**
(n) Depend.	.09	.09	.09	.16	2.83*

*$p < .05$.
**$p < .01$.

lessness, avoidance, attempts to control anxiety, or an unwillingness to offer their help to the other two members. The mothers of *Sch* and *Del* children showed greater difficulty in controlling the group process, tending to ask for suggestions rather than giving them, and also a lower index of directive control, showing a tendency toward giving fewer task-relevant opinions. The *Sch* mothers also showed a tendency toward higher dependency and asking for help, while the *Del* mothers were lowest on this variable.

As might be expected from our discussion of the R_{dev} findings, the IPA behavior of the children showed the greatest number of associations with the diagnostic grouping of the families, which was based on the diagnosis of the child. Several of the findings seem to reflect a characteristic pattern of the *Sch* children, that of making statements which are less oriented to the task and more toward emotions and social relationships, both positive and negative. The *Del* children showed a pattern of asking questions, asking the opinion of the parents regarding the TAT, and asking for help. This greater passivity of the *Del* children might be a way of avoiding committing themselves to the situation, rather than a basically greater dependence on their parents.

SUMMARY AND CONCLUSIONS

Our findings lend themselves to some speculations regarding the interrelationship of the dynamics of the family and the psychopathology of the child, and the ability of the IPA to evaluate this relationship.

One general conclusion which follows from our results is that the IPA method of evaluating intrafamily communication is more clearly related to the behavior of the child than to the behavior of his parents. A second conclusion is that this method does not differentiate between families with *Mal* children and families with *Nor* children. The observation that the *Sch* families were most clearly defined may be attributable to the fact that *Sch* children show obvious problems in the area of verbal communication, and usually speak less. Perhaps restricting ourselves in the past to studies comparing *Sch* and *Nor* children has prevented us from developing better diagnostic instruments, since the task of differentiating these two groups is too simple, and significant results are easy to come by. We need measuring instruments which can separate borderline groups, such as *Mal* and *Nor*, and which are sensitive to features of the family interaction which are not heavily weighted with the *Sch* patient's unwillingness or inability to talk, or with other factors traditionally regarded as characteristics of the individual rather than of the interaction.

What knowledge have we gained, then, by applying the IPA to our groups of families? Unfortunately, very little. In terms of interactional variables, IPA provided only minor distinctions among our diagnostic groups. The families with *Mal* children function very much like *Nor*'s. The *Sch* families generally fall at the opposite pole of pathology, largely due to the behavior of the *Sch* child. The *Sch* child is withdrawn, and measures of participation which involve him show these families to manifest unequal participation. The *Sch* families interact less, spend more time asking questions, and ask for opinions and suggestions in a dependent manner. This dependency on the opinion of others is most characteristic of the *Sch* parents, and this is congruent with Cheek's (1964, 1965) findings. The *Sch* child responds less to the reality demands of the TAT task, asking less and giving less when it comes to making up a family story. Instead, the *Sch* child devotes his comments to both positive and negative social-emotional categories, either because his emotions are less easily controlled than those of other children, because the task does not motivate him positively, or because interpersonal relations are more important than the "real" world. The mother of the *Sch* spent relatively less of her time presenting task-relevant opinions and more time giving a general orientation to the task, information, clarifying, etc., probably in an attempt to clarify the situation for her child.

The *Del* families are less clearly differentiated from the *Nor*'s than are the *Sch*'s. The *Del*'s have a low total interaction score, but this is less due to the withdrawal of the child than is true of the *Sch*'s. Inspection of the data shows that both the *Del* child and his father speak less than average, but not greatly so. The *Del* father and child ask dependent questions and ask for help in deciding what to do and how to do it. The mother also requests suggestions, but gives more help and spends time interpreting and clarifying the task (generally for her child). The *Del* family sticks more closely to the task and spends less time in emotional interactions than do the *Sch*'s. The behavior of the *Del* fathers is similar to that of the *Sch*'s; the behavior of the mothers is also similar, except that the *Del* mothers are slightly more willing to give help. The *Del* child is more task-oriented and less emotional than the *Sch* child. The observed behavior of *Del* families seemed often directed toward getting the job over with quickly without getting too involved in it, as if they were interested in minimally meeting the obligations imposed on them. The *Sch* children seemed to be unable to break out of their pattern of sticky emotional entanglements to deal with the task effectively. This interpretation is consistent with the findings of Ferreira and Winter (1965) in a decision-making test of many of these same families, in which the *Del*'s reached their decisions more quickly than the *Sch*'s, and reached more rational decisions. In fact, many of the *Del* families had unusually fast reaction times, perhaps reflecting impulsivity or lack of involvement.

Despite these interesting results, we are forced to conclude that the Bales IPA system, in its present form, is not suited for work with families. Even with presumably adequate training of raters, neither we nor Waxler and Mishler (1966) have been able to achieve reassuring reliability levels. The major difficulty seems to be that the categories are multidimensional in meaning, and the raters are required to classify the items on the basis of high-order inferences. Thus, there seems to be no easy way to achieve consistency in these interpretations. What is needed here is the development of new behavior categorization systems or modifications of the IPA which are more unidimensional in meaning. Waxler and Mishler (1966), for example, mention that they are making use of new codes which allow raters to achieve 85 percent act-by-act agreement with only two or three weeks of training. * * *

It should be pointed out that it may always be more difficult to measure interaction in families than in problem-solving groups of college students, the usual source of group dynamics data (Haley, 1964). For example, Borgatta (1965) has developed a method of factor analysis of IPA-based data which has proved successful in determining stable patterns of interaction in small group discussions of college students. However, when this method was applied to Cheek's family triads, it was found that the status positions of father, mother, and child were "not derived from the structure of the organization in an interaction sense." The factors obtained with families seemed to reflect similarity of behavior among family members, not complementary behavior. In addition to the problem of shared similarity of behavior in families, one might also mention the subtle patterns of nonverbal and verbal communication within a family, and the immensely rich contextual historical background against which a remark by one family member is judged by the others.

Some Dynamics of Laughter during Family Therapy*

*Gerald H. Zuk, Ivan Boszormenyi-Nagy,
and Elliot Heiman*

The data on which this study was based were derived from family psychotherapy sessions tape-recorded in 1961 and 1962. The technique of family psychotherapy has been described in several papers (cf. Ackerman, 1958; Bell, 1961; Jackson & Weakland, 1961). The family in this case was composed of a mother, father, and schizophrenic daughter—a white Protestant family whose social-class status would probably be described as lower-upper in level.

Twenty-three tape recordings were available to the writers. The first author joined the second as a family psychotherapist in January of 1962. The authors continued to see the family—usually at two-week intervals—over the next six months. From time to time these intervals stretched over three weeks or more because of scheduling difficulties.

The patient, now a 23-year-old girl, was admitted to Eastern Pennsylvania Psychiatric Institute (EPPI) in October 1957. Her admission diagnosis was schizophrenic reaction, paranoid type.

In the family psychotherapy sessions, the laughter of the mother could be described frequently as of the "embarrassed" sort, a kind of quavering chuckle reflecting underlying tension or anxiety. She often tagged it on to the end of a phrase or sentence in an apparent attempt to make what she had to say as socially palatable as possible. The father's laughter was heartier. At times it was also of the "embarrassed" variety, but more frequently than mother his laughter was associated with a statement—usually his own—intended to be humorous. The laughter of the schizophrenic daughter was quite bizarre. Apparently without adequate social stimulus, she would break into wild, uncontrolled laughter. * * *

The basic measure employed in this study was frequency of laughter—presumably reflecting tension or anxiety—in psychotherapy sessions. On an arbitrary basis, the thirteen most recent sessions were selected from twenty-three available tape-recorded sessions for analysis of laughing behavior. The sessions were not controlled with respect to persons

---

*Excerpted from *Family Process*, 1963, 2, 302–314, with permission of the senior author and *Family Process*.

present, and obviously the content of the sessions varied considerably. The schizophrenic daughter was usually silent. The parents did most of the talking.

In order to arrive at some index of reliability of ratings, frequency of laughter was rated independently in one psychotherapy session by the first and third authors. The comparatively greater difficulty in rating the laughter of the patient was compared with the laughter of the parents was revealed by a 79 percent agreement (27 out of 34 occasions) of the third author with the first on identifying the patient's laughter. Agreement of the third author with the first was better in the case of the mother's and father's laughter; 95 percent agreement (18 out of 19 occasions) on the laughter of the mother; 100 percent agreement (4 out of 4 occasions) on the laughter of the father. * * *

Table 1 shows the raw frequencies of laughter in the successive fifteen-minute intervals. This table served as the basis for the chi-square analyses shown in Table 2, and is to be read specifically in conjunction with Table 2 since it will establish more clearly the nature of the trends in the data. Table 2 describes five hypotheses which are examined. Chi-square test of the frequencies of the mother's laughter revealed that it was not equally distributed in the various intervals (χ^2 = 23.5, p < .001). Reference to Table 1 indicates that the mother laughed almost twice as frequently in the first fifteen-minute interval as in the second and third.

TABLE 1

RAW FREQUENCIES OF LAUGHTER OF FAMILY MEMBERS
AT 15-MINUTE INTERVALS IN THERAPY SESSIONS

FAMILY MEMBER	15-MINUTE INTERVALS			
	1	2	3	4
Mother	120 (13)	66 (13)	65 (13)	43 (10)
Patient	35 (13)	55 (13)	92 (13)	55 (10)
Father	46 (12)	25 (12)	17 (12)	17 (9)

Note: Numbers in parentheses are numbers of sessions on which raw frequencies are based.

Chi-square test of the patient's laughter revealed that it was not equally distributed in the various intervals (χ^2 = 27.5, p < .001). Reference to Table 1 indicates that the greatest frequency of laughter by the patient occurred in the third fifteen-minute interval. Chi-square test of the father's laughter showed that it also was not equally distributed in the various intervals (χ^2 = 15.6, p < .001). Reference to Table 1 indicates that the father's greatest frequency of laughter occurred (in an overall pattern that is similar to that of the mother) in the first fifteen-minute interval.

A chi-square test comparing the patterns of laughter of the mother and father reported in Table 2, showed the patterns to be similar (χ^2 = .9,

TABLE 2

CHI-SQUARE ANALYSES OF RAW FREQUENCIES OF LAUGHTER BY
FAMILY MEMBERS IN 15-MINUTE INTERVALS OF THERAPY SESSIONS

Hypothesis	Occasions of Laughter	x^2	p	Hypothesis Accepted?
Mother's laughter is equally distributed in the first three 15 min. intervals of 13 therapy sessions.	251	23.5	$<.001$	No. (More laughter in first 15 min. interval than later intervals.)
Patient's laughter is equally distributed in the first three 15 min. intervals of 13 therapy sessions.	182	27.5	$<.001$	No. (More laughter in third 15 min. interval than earlier intervals.)
Father's laughter is equally distributed in the first three 15 min. intervals of 12 therapy sessions.	88	15.6	$<.001$	No. (More laughter in first 15 min. interval than later intervals.)
Mother and father's laughter in the first three 15 min. intervals of 12 therapy sessions is similarly distributed.	326	.9	$<.05$	Yes
Mother and patient's laughter in the first three 15 min. intervals of 13 therapy sessions is similarly distributed.	433	42.3	$<.001$	No. (Patient's laughter more frequent in the third 15 min. interval; mother's more frequent in the first 15 min. interval.)

$p < .05$). Both mother and father tended to laugh most frequently in the first fifteen-minute interval of sessions analyzed and markedly less thereafter. A chi-square test comparing the patterns of laughter of the mother and patient showed the patterns to be different ($\chi^2 = 42.3$, $p <.001$). Reference to Table 1 indicates that whereas the mother tended to laugh most frequently in the first fifteen-minute interval of the sessions, the patient tended to laugh most frequently in the third fifteen-minute interval. * * *

Family Functioning as an Index of Need for Welfare Services[*]

Ludwig L. Geismar

* * * The present approach offers an approximation to the measurement of need by social functioning analysis, a technique which examines role performance in relation to familial and community role expectations. Although this method also avoids a definition of the concept of need, it operates on the basis of the seemingly defensible assumption that major needs are reflected in the degree of malfunctioning experienced by individuals and families in the home and community. A degree of standardization in the study is achieved by two means: The family is made the focus of research; the physical, social, and emotional welfare of family members and community expectations are set up as criteria for social functioning.

Brief Outline for a Standardized
Evaluation of Family Functioning

Because of the felt need to systematize and order data for evaluation, the present approach is organized around the single dimensional concept of family functioning. This is defined as all behavior, including attitudes and feelings, which has a direct bearing upon the well-being of the family group and community. Family functioning in terms of this approach is being studied from two foci. First, the sum of roles performed (role clusters) by each person who is a member of the family either as a result of his identification with the group and/or his moral and legal responsibility for the group. These roles are described and evaluated under the heading Individual Behavior and Adjustment. Second, the tasks or functions carried which are seen by society as necessary for developing and maintaining the social system called "family." These functions were divided into eight areas, each of which represents the convergence of roles or sets of activities performed by family members, with the object of achieving certain family-related objectives.

---

[*]Excerpted from *Family Process*, 1964, *3*, 99–113, with permission of the author and *Family Process*.

Individual Behavior and Adjustment as a diagnostic category has both an intrapsychic and interpsychic focus, since it covers the behavior of the individual in terms of his physical and emotional health, and his capacity to deal with his environment. The other eight areas of functioning are largely sociological in character, for they deal with the way in which socially-assigned tasks are performed by any family member or group of family members who are charged with the performance of their task. The functions rather than the functionaries are here the object of study and evaluation. The eight areas are Family Relationships and Unity, Care and Training of Children, Social Activities, Use of Community Resources, Relationship of Social Worker, Economic Practices, Health Conditions and Practices, and Household Conditions and Practices.

Groups of families included in this study were evaluated on a seven-point scale ranging from adequate to inadequate functioning in terms of (1) whether laws are violated or observed; (2) whether behavior contributes or is harmful to the physical, social, and emotional well-being of family members; (3) whether behavior is in harmony or conflict with the standards of a family's status group; (4) whether a family member's behavior is commensurate with his potential for social functioning. The conceptual scheme and the method of evaluation have been discussed elsewhere (Geismar & Ayres, 1959, 1960).

The procedure of evaluating a family's functioning is as follows: An open-ended interview schedule is used for gathering information on each one of the nine areas and 26 subareas. Interviews with the family, case records of one or more agencies, and collateral information from schools, clinics, courts, etc., are the sources for collecting the data on family functioning. Two or more judges then rate independently, with the aid of the Levels of Functioning Scheme (Geismar & Ayres, 1960), each area and subarea of family functioning. Scores are entered on a Family Profile Chart. Where inter-rater agreement is high, differences in ratings are settled by conference. Low reliability requires reexamination of data and/ or additional training of judges.

An estimate of the reliability of the evaluation technique is given in the above cited manual (Geisman & Ayres, 1960). Any claim to validity of the instrument must be at this stage based upon three arguments: (1) Internal validity of the scale is suggested by its reproducibility of .88 (Geismar, LaSorte, & Ayres, 1962). (2) There is a correspondence between the dimensions of the behavior measured by the scale and social work criteria of adequacy of social functioning. (3) In another study in which ten mothers and ten fathers were interviewed separately on their families' social functioning, the ratings of the two sets of interviews resulted in the following rates of agreement between two raters.

Population and Research Method

Groups of families who had at least one parent or parent surrogate and one child under 18 in the home were selected from five different settings for this comparative study on family functioning. A setting is defined here

TABLE 1

HUSBAND-WIFE RELIABILITY

	No. of Responses	% of Responses
Complete agreement	47	58.8
Agreement within 1 scale step	27	38.7
Disagreement—2 or more scale points apart	6	7.5
Total Ratings	80	100.0

as a service agency or project giving some form of help to clients. Families studied were randomly selected from active caseloads except in setting 5, called Reaching-Out Service, where all the 150 families were included in the research. These families had been identified earlier as being seriously disorganized. The total sample studied comprises 320 families with N's for settings ranging from 30 to 150.

The five types of service settings, arranged in descending order of average level of functioning of client population, are as follows:

1. A mental health center in New Jersey for treatment of children with adjustment problems. The center has a demonstration, teaching, and research function. Practically all the families of these children have shown a willingness to work with the agency in solving the problems of their child. Services were initiated either through self-referral or by recommendation of other social agencies and the school.

2. A public assistance program serving ADC (Aid to Dependent Children) families in urban and suburban areas in New Jersey. Service, rendered on the basis of financial need and following the establishment of eligibility, is mainly in the nature of grant allocation and, depending on size of case load and skill of worker, counseling in times of crisis.

3. A small, private family service in New Jersey. Families are referred through private (self, relatives, and friends) and professional channels (other agencies, doctors, and the school authorities). Most families studied have given evidence of readiness to be treated, as indicated by their continuance in treatment beyond the fourth interview.

4. The family care program of a public child-welfare agency in New Jersey. Families served are both self-referred and other-agency-referred, but service is most generally extended in response to a problematic situation in the home affecting the welfare of the children. Clients' responses range from cooperative to resistive.

5. A "reaching-out" service, carried on by an alliance of agencies, to multi-problem families in Minnesota. Referrals are of an authoritative or quasi-authoritative nature. Initial response of most client families was marked by resistance or apathy. * * *

TABLE 2

MEAN SCORES OF FAMILY FUNCTIONING AND STANDARD DEVIATIONS FOR CLIENT GROUPS IN FIVE
SERVICE SETTINGS

CATEGORY OF FAMILY FUNCTIONING	1. Mental Health Center (N = 30)		2. ADC Program (N = 70)		3. Private Family Service (N = 30)		4. Public Family Care Program (N = 40)		5. Reaching-out Service* (N = 150)	
	Mean	S.D.	Mean	S.D.	Mean	S.D.	Mean	S.D.	Mean	S.D.
Care and training of children	5.2	.93	5.7	0.95	4.4	0.83	4.9	1.65	3.7	1.04
Individual behavior and adjustment	4.9	.83	5.3	1.04	3.9	0.71	4.5	1.14	3.8	0.81
Family relationships and unity	4.8	.98	5.4	1.02	3.6	1.02	4.7	1.29	3.9	0.93
Relationship to social worker	5.6	.76	5.7	1.08	5.3	1.05	5.1	1.26	4.7	0.84
Use of community resources	6.1	.51	5.7	0.95	5.5	0.80	5.0	1.33	4.7	0.86
Social activities	5.6	.84	5.3	0.99	5.3	0.97	4.8	1.20	4.6	0.79
Economic practices	6.2	.87	5.8	0.77	5.8	0.80	5.2	1.65	4.8	0.88
Health conditions and practices	6.3	.66	5.9	0.99	6.1	0.83	5.5	1.53	4.9	1.06
Household conditions and practices	6.2	.92	5.8	1.23	6.4	0.87	5.4	1.84	5.1	1.42
Means of category means	5.7	0.81	5.6	1.00	5.1	0.88	5.0	1.43	4.5	0.96

SERVICE SETTINGS

*Since the scale ordering for this setting was based upon a dichotomization of scores, the means shown in this table deviate slightly from a rigidly numerical ascending order.

Table 2 shows the statistical values of levels of social functioning for the family groups in the five service settings described above.

All five profiles, allowing for some minor variations, show basic similarities in structure. Three areas of predominantly instrumental function (Economic Practices, Health Conditions and Practices, and Household Conditions and Practices) represent the relatively most adequate sets of behavior. Three areas in which expressive functioning is dominant (Family Relations and Unity) or constitutes a major component (Individual Behavior and Adjustment, and Care and Training of Children) are among the least adequate areas of social functioning. These three are also areas where functioning is to a large extent intrafamilial, i.e., the bulk of the roles evaluated have to do with relationships among family members. Three areas representing a mixture of expressive and instrumental functioning largely beyond the borders of the family group (Relationship to Social Worker, Use of Community Resources, and Social Activities) compose the middle group in terms of behavioral adequacy.

To state this differently, the functioning of families is least adequate in those areas where interpersonal relationships are key elements and most adequate in the performance of functional tasks. By and large, relationships toward the outside are managed better than intrafamilial relationships, particularly family relations and child care.

In contrast to families in setting 3, whose functioning in the nine areas spreads over 2.8 scale points, the maximum range in the lower status groups in settings 1, 2, 4, and 5 is 1.5, 0.6, 1.0, and 1.4 respectively. The Spearman rank order correlation (rho) between range in family functioning and occupational status is +.90. Thus, family groups of lower socioeconomic status appear to be more susceptible to cumulative effects of malfunctioning in all areas. Behavior problems are more likely to affect economic functioning as the family is without the financial security of the higher socioeconomic classes, and conversely, greater economic vulnerability increases the likelihood of problems in the functional task area affecting social relationships.

Family Interaction Associated with Child Disturbances: Assessment and Modification*

Barclay Martin

This report describes a preliminary attempt at both assessment and modification of a three-way family interaction involving father, mother, and preadolescent son. * * *

Assessment

Can one as a researcher sample this kind of interaction under standardized conditions? One must be able, on the one hand, to stimulate meaningful interaction which is not too artificial or game-like, and on the other hand, be able to maintain a reasonable degree of control and standardization.

The following procedure represents an attempt to strike a compromise between these two aims. In order to reduce the complexity of interaction, all siblings are excluded. Father, mother, and deviant son are asked to come to the Psychology Building, and hence the inevitable distractions of home are also avoided.

In order to separately analyze communications between different pairs of family members, it is necessary to impose some structure on the interaction. Otherwise it is very difficult to know to whom a given communication is directed. In fact, in free interaction many communications are directed to both other members. The following procedure was developed in order to force communication to just one other person at a time.

The three family members sit in chairs facing each other around a circular coffee table. A small, movable panel is attached to the right arm rest and can be rotated around to face the person. At the top of the panel are two signs that say respectively, *Talk* and *Don't Talk*. At the bottom of the panel are two switches with flat surfaces that allow for easy pushing and holding down. Above the two switches are the respective names of the

---

*Excerpted from *Psychotherapy*, 1967, 4, 30–35, with permission of the author and *Psychotherapy*.

other two family members. For example, above the son's switches would be the names "Mom" and "Dad," or whatever might be his preferred way of addressing his parents. The *Don't Talk* sign is visible at all times until the person pushes a switch. When the person pushes either switch the *Don't Talk* sign goes off, becoming invisible, and the *Talk* sign goes on, becoming visible. Members are instructed to push the appropriate switch down whenever they are talking with another person.

The main point of this procedure and accompanying instructions, as previously mentioned, is to insure that each person directs all of his expressions to one other person at a time. The procedure also permits one, by the use of voice-operated relays, to obtain exact measures of the amount of time that each person talks to each other person. The verbal content is recorded from microphones in the panels; and on a second channel of the stereo tape-recorder, a signal is recorded that indicates to whom each expression is directed.

Some time is spent at the beginning of a session helping the family members become accustomed to the switch-pushing procedure. The aim is to have the switch-pushing become as automatic as possible so that it will not interfere with their verbal interaction. Families do indeed seem to forget about the switch-pushing, though still doing it, as they become involved in important interaction.

Family members are asked first to talk among themselves and decide upon some recent incident involving disagreement or where one or more family members were upset, disappointed, hurt, or angry; second, to describe what happened, who did what, who said what; and third, to tell each other what their own feelings were in the situation. In the course of an hour session, it is usually possible to repeat the above sequence for three different incidents.

A scheme that reflects the theoretical interest is being developed for scoring the verbal content in the second two parts. At the present time raters rate each unit of speech with respect to the following categories: (1) Indirect Blaming, (2) Direct Blaming, (3) Self-Blaming, (4) Non-blaming Description of the Situation, and (5) Non-blaming Description of Own Feelings. These categories are not all-inclusive; that is, some speech units are not scored under any of these categories. A speech unit is defined as that speech bounded on either side by someone else's talking.

Direct Blaming is defined as any directly critical or fault-finding expression. There are three subcategories of Indirect Blaming: (1) questions or requests aimed at getting the other person to admit to wrong-doing, or questions in which person is asked why he did something wrong; (2) lecturing, in which the parent explains the necessity for correct behavior by emphasizing general principles and long-range consequences; and (3) self-justification involving excuses or reasons for behavior that person is being blamed for.

The following brief excerpt illustrates a chain of blame and self-justification or counter-blame. The family is talking about an occasion in which father and mother came home to find the house a mess and the three children fighting among themselves.

Father to son: "Do you feel I was justified in giving you a good scolding and whack for the shape the house was in in the hour we were gone?" (Indirect Blame)

Son to father: "Well, sort of, but Betty and Tommy [siblings], they did some of it, too." (Self-justification, a form of Indirect Blame)

Father to son: "Well, I figured you were the oldest, you were in charge, you should be able to control 'em without pounding 'em around." (Direct Blame)

Son to father: "Well, that Tommy, I tried to watch TV, and he'd just jump on me, and I'd hit him and tell him to sit in his seat, and he wouldn't and he'd keep doing it. After I hit him he'd pick up them orange peels, and he'd start throwing 'em at me . . ." (Self-justification, a form of Indirect Blame)

At present these ratings are being made from typescripts only, i.e., without the tape-recorded speech. It is desired to break the interaction into segments and mix together segments from a pre-treatment session with those from a post-treatment session, and thus keep the raters blind with regard to the pre- and post-treatment dimension. Only moderately good agreement among independent raters is being obtained at present— between 60 and 86 percent for the different categories. In time it should be possible to further objectify these measures, perhaps by changing the structure of the task itself. * * *

The modification procedures are very closely related to the assessment procedure. Basically an attempt is being made to intrude into the repetitive cue-response sequences of these families and get them to experiment with different responses that will tend to break up the original sequences. The main features of the procedure are as follows: (1) Point out to the family the salient features of their stereotyped interaction *as it occurs in the session*. (2) Encourage them to experiment with new ways of responding. For example, a father who expresses blame indirectly by directing questions to his son such as, "Why do you keep doing such and such?" or "Don't you think I am justified in punishing you in this way when you do such and such?" would be encouraged to express his criticism of his son's behavior directly. Then, he would be encouraged to express his feelings about the son's misbehavior and *his feelings*, and, if possible, without implying blame or criticism of the son. (3) Family members are encouraged to listen to the expressions of other family members. Listening responses have frequently been all but extinguished in these stereotyped interaction sequences, each person being preoccupied with his own blaming or self-justifying responses.

From time to time, after the family has become involved in an emotionally important interaction, they are requested to do the following: Person A is asked to express his feelings to B. Person B is instructed to listen. Then Person B is asked to tell Person A what he heard. Person A is given a chance to correct Person B or add to B's response. After a while the roles are reversed and Person B is asked to express his feelings to Person A and Person A is asked to listen.

The new behaviors, whether of a self-expressive or listening type, are reinforced in the session by the verbal approval of the "therapist," but perhaps most importantly by satisfaction that comes as time goes by from the experience of being understood, and relief from not being criticized. Other reinforcements for changed behavior occur outside the sessions; for example, improvement in the son's school performance tends to reinforce any changes in the parents' behavior. * * *

Family Interaction Scales*

Jules Riskin

This report describes a group of scales which have been developed in order to study family interaction. These scales enable us to make "blind" interpretations of a family's interaction. * * *

Interview

Each family, as an entire family (with the single exception of the family with the absent schizophrenic member), participates in a standardized, semistructured interview, which lasts about an hour. The scales presented in this paper focus on the analysis of a small part of the family interview. The interviewer presents the following task to them: "I would like you to plan something you could do together as a family." After saying this, the interviewer leaves the room. He gives the family about ten minutes to perform this task. Several people observe the interview behind a cne-way screen, and the interview is taped. The analysis is therefore limited to material which is available on the tape.

Scoring

The scoring, or coding, of the transcript is done on the first 76 speeches of a family's discussion of "plan something together," and also on a second block of 76 speeches starting at about the fourth minute. (The exact number of speeches is an arbitrary one.) Each group of 76 speeches usually takes a family from two to three minutes. The total amount of discussion analyzed is therefore four to six minutes. The procedure is as follows: The writer and a research assistant jointly listen "blindly" to just that portion of the tape which is to be scored, in order to make an accurate transcript, and determine *who speaks* and *to whom*. They do not discuss any intuitive impression that they might have as they listen to this section of the tape. Their version of the transcript and judgments regarding these categories are then checked by observers of the original interview. The writer then codes the speeches according to the scales discussed below.

---

*Excerpted from *Archives of General Psychiatry*, 1964, *11*, 484–494, with permission of the author and the American Medical Association.

Scales

Our goal has been to construct scales which require only relatively simple judgments by the rater. It should be noted that the scales used are derived from theoretical notions about family interaction and its relationship to personality development. These scales should, by appropriate manipulation, permit the deduction of more abstract yet significant inferences about the family relationship and individual dynamics. In other words, the variables should be bridges between the observable clinical material and theorizing. The scales used have only two (or in some cases three) positions to simplify the rating process. The scales with brief definitions, the positions in each scale, and examples are as follows.

A. *Clarity Scale*: This scale refers to whether the speech is clear to the rater, not whether it is clear to the family. It includes both verbal and nonverbal (i.e., tonal) aspects of speeches. The speech is to be given only *one* of the following scores:

1. *Clear speech*
2. *Unclear speech*

NS. *Nonscorable*, because speech is too fast, too soft, interrupted before a judgment can be made, or for other mechanical reasons.

The rater should stay at a superficial level, and avoid imputing motives. His bias should be towards *clear* rather than towards *unclear*, i.e., when in doubt, he should score *clear* rather than *unclear*.

Examples:
Clear speech:
   A: Let's go to the movies.
   B: I think that's a good idea [*said firmly and with enthusiasm*].
B's speech is *clear*.

Unclear speech:
   A: Let's go to the movies.
   B: I think that's a good idea [*said with obvious and strong sarcasm*].
B's speech is *unclear*.

NS speech:
   A: Let's . . .
   B: (*Interrupts*) I want to go to the movies.
A's speech has been interrupted before a judgment about its clarity can be made.

If a speech is scored as *unclear*, the reason it is *unclear* should be indicated. Three classes of *unclear* are used:

Incongruent—an inconsistency between what a person says and how he says it; for example: "I feel very happy," said in an obviously depressed manner.

Vague—the words in themselves, not including the tone of voice, do not make sense to the observer; e.g., "Movies are utterly heffalumpy."

Linear disqalification—a self-contradiction at the verbal level, that is, a logical inconsistency or a marked change in the direction of a speech which serves to negate its original meaning; e.g., "Let's go to the mountain but let's go to the beach."

B. *Topic Scale*: This scale refers to whether a speech stays on the same topic as the immediately preceding speech. The "topic" is the least abstract statement which describes what the speaker is talking about. It includes just the verbal aspect of a speech. The speech is to be given only one of the following scores:

1. *Same topic*
2. *Different topic.*

NS. *Nonscorable*, for same reason as indicated in the clarity scale.

The rater should stay on a superficial level. His bias should be towards *same topic* rather than *different topic*, i.e., when in doubt score *same topic* rather than *different topic*.

Examples:
Same topic:
   A: Let's go to the beach.
   B: Let's go to the mountains.
A and B are both discussing what they could do together, and B's topic is therefore the *same* as A's.

Different topic:
   A: Let's go to the mountains.
   B: Pass the ashtray, please.

If a speech is scored as *different topic*, the rater must make a further judgment as to whether the topic change is *appropriate* or *inappropriate*. Appropriateness is judged in the context of the assigned task. The rater's bias should be towards *appropriate*, rather than *inappropriate* change. The scoring is as follows:

1) *Appropriate topic-change*
2) *Inappropriate topic change*

Examples:
Appropriate topic-change:
   A. Let's go to the beach.

B. Did the interviewer want us to reach an agreement among ourselves, or just talk about something?

B's question is a legitimate request for clarification, and therefore an *appropriate change*.

Inappropriate topic-change:
A: Let's go to the beach.
B: Who won the World Series in 1923?

C. *Commitment Scale*: This scale refers to whether the speaker takes a strong stand—that is, commits himself. It includes both verbal and nonverbal aspects of a speech. The speech is to be given only one of the following scores:

1. A *commitment is made*.
2. A *commitment is avoided* when it has been asked for.
NA. The *scale is not applicable*, i.e., a commitment was neither made nor asked for.
NS. *Nonscorable*.

Examples:
Commitment is made:
A: Let's go to the beach.
B: I don't like the beach [*said firmly*].

Comment is avoided:
A: Would you B., like to go to the beach?
B: I don't know.

Scale is not applicable:
A: Let's go to the beach.
B: When would we go?

B does not commit himself, nor was he asked to commit himself.

D. *Agreement Scale*: This scale refers to whether the speaker explicitly agrees or explicitly disagrees with the person to whom he is talking. It includes just the verbal aspect of a speech. The speech is to be given only one of the following socres:

1. *Explicit agreement*
2. *Explicit disagreement*
NA. The *scale is not applicable*, i.e., neither an explicit agreement nor explicit disagreement has been made.
NS. *Nonscorable*

Examples:
Agreement:
A: I would like to go to the beach.
B: That's a good idea.

Disagreement:
A: Let's go to the beach.
B: No, Let's go to the mountains instead.

Scale is not applicable:
A: Let's go to the beach.
B: It's awfully hot in this room.

E. *Intensity Scale*: This scale refers to whether the speaker expresses an average—that is, a normal conversational—amount of affect, whether he becomes intense, or whether he withdraws affect. It includes verbal and nonverbal aspects of a speech. The speech is to be given only one of the following scores:
> *Increased affect*
> *Normal affect* (normal conversational tone)
> *Decreased affect* (withdrawn)

Examples:
Increased affect:
A: Let's go to the beach.
B: What a great idea!

Normal affect:
A: Let's go to the beach.
B: What would you like to do, Johnny? [*said casually and pleasantly*].

Decreased affect:
A: Let's go to the beach.
B: [*Mumbles an inarticulate comment.*]

F. *Relationship Scale*: This scale refers to whether the speaker expresses a friendly, neutral, or attacking attitude towards the person to whom he is speaking. It includes both verbal and nonverbal aspects of a speech. The speech is to be given only one of the following scores:
> + A *friendly speech*
> − A *neutral speech*
> 0 An *attacking speech*

Examples:
Friendly speech:
A: Let's go to the beach.
B: That's an excellent suggestion [*said with warmth, sounds quite supportive and friendly*].

Neutral speech:
    A: Let's go to the beach.
    B: That would be quite a long trip [*said casually*].

Attacking speech:
    A: Let's go to the beach.
    B: That's a ridiculous suggestion [*said quite sharply*].

In addition to the above scales, the following (nonscale) categories are also used:
1. Who speaks
2. To whom a speech is addressed
3. Interrupted speeches.

Studies of Family Interaction: Intra-Family Communication

Forcing a family to make a joint decision is an excellent way to bring about meaningful interaction, and this general paradigm underlies most interaction research. But the concept which is most useful in understanding what takes place in such decision-making is that of communication— the exchange of meaningful information. Of course, communication is broader than decision-making, but research into family communication of affection, curiosity, etc., in other than overt problem-solving contexts has not been seriously attempted. In any case, communication is a crucial concept, both theoretically and clinically, and the quality of ongoing communication is not only a cause of current family behavior, but also a result of previous events which have affected family members, and is therefore a sharp analytical tool.

Levin focuses directly on how families communicate by presenting a task which requires one member actively to transmit information to another. In previous articles (e.g., Article 11), subjects could participate passively, remain silent, and still meet the requirements of the task; but this is more difficult in Levin's paradigm. Again, this is a study of pseudo-interaction, as the communicator is not physically present (see Article 17). The greater ambiguity of communication found by Levin in abnormal families is also confirmed by Ferreira and Winter (see also Becker, Tatsuoka, & Carlson, 1965). The abnormal families tested by Ferreira and Winter exchanged fewer "informational units," spent more time in silence, and were more inefficient. The authors attempt to derive a family pathology cycle which places communication of information in a key dynamic role. Consistent with his attempts to simplify this investigation of communication, Haley placed his families in a restricted communication setting and obtained a variety of data on their efforts to solve problems, which he analyzed from the structure, process, and outcome points of view. Haley's discussion emphasizes information theory, and his results invite comparison with those of Articles 11, 12, 21, 22, 24, 25, and 32.

The article by Ravich et al. discusses one of several interesting new techniques which can be used to study family communication. For further examples the reader is also referred to the articles by Straus (1968), Reiss (1967), Singer (1966), and Usandivaras, Grimson, Hammond, Issaharoff, and Romanos (1967); and the work of Rakoff, Sanders, and Sigal (1968, abstract).

In reviewing this collection of readings, it is obvious that there has been significant research in the area of family interaction. The articles included here have shown that valuable instruments, tests, designs, and concepts have already been developed in family-interaction research. It is the editors' earnest hope that this field will continue to mature and move from correlational studies, which can only confirm hypotheses of association, to experimental studies, which can demonstrate cause-effect relationships. To date, only the studies dealing with artificial families and the effects of therapy have actually manipulated variables (see Articles 11, 13, 24, and 33). We have begun to learn the techniques—it is time to expand our horizons!

Communicator–Communicant Approach to Family Interaction Research*

Gilbert Levin

A major obstacle in family interaction research has been the complexity of the phenomena being studied. When two or more people are interacting freely the things that go on are so numerous, so complicated, and so tightly interconnected that it is nearly impossible for the human observer, together with the currently available extensions of his perceptual apparatus, to untangle what has happened in a minimally inferential way.

The purpose of this paper is to introduce a method suitable for the study of interpersonal processes in the family. Results obtained in an exploratory experiment on the etiology of schizophrenia will be used to demonstrate the promise of the method. * * *

The method being introduced here is yet another way of paring the data down to size. The event to be analyzed is greatly restricted and the complexity of family interaction is reduced by studying family members as individual interactors. The cost is that instead of observing interaction, we study an isolated segment of it. We gain, however, by being able to subject some of the elements of interaction to experimental analysis.

The essential feature of the method is that it seeks knowledge about social interaction by physically isolating the subject. In each case, the subject and experimenter are alone. The experimenter asks the subject to make a tape recording which might be played subsequently to some specific other person (in S's family) that would enable that other person to carry out some simple task. The subject is physically isolated, but in order to perform the task he must take an imagined other into account. Usually the task has been to produce a geometric figure like the following.

---

*Abstracted from *Family Process*, 1966, 5, 105–116, with permission of the author and *Family Process*.

Showing the subject a card with this figure on it, the experimenter gives the subject the following verbal instructions:

> Imagine that this microphone is a telephone and that ____ is on the other end of the line.____can hear everything you say, but____cannot see you and may not speak to you.____has only a pencil and a blank sheet of white paper. Your task is to get____to draw a figure just like the one on this card, in one continuous line. That is, without taking the pencil off the paper and *without retracing* (going back over) *any line.*
>
> You may say as much or as little to____as you think is necessary in order to get____to do this. Keep in mind that all ____knows about the task is what you will tell.

In this experimental situation, the basic elements are (1) the Communicator, who gives instructions to (2) the Communicant, who is psychologically but never physically present, (3) the Experimenter and (4) a feedback channel. Each of these elements can be varied, depending upon the particular hypothesis under investigation. For example, it is possible to study the effect upon the Communicator's behavior of variations in the identity of the Communicant. We can, for instance, tell one sample of Communicators that they are in contact with a child and another sample that they are in contact with an adult. Other possibilities would include daughter versus son, older versus younger sibling, schizophrenic offspring versus non-schizophrenic offspring, stranger versus friend, or unknown child versus unknown adult.

Similarly, many variations of Communicator identity are possible; in what respects do mothers communicate differently from non-mothers, parents from children, children with siblings from children without siblings, parents of schizophrenic offspring from parents of non-schizophrenic offspring?

Feedback can also be varied. It can be eliminated, as in our work to date, or it can be experimentally manipulated by misrepresenting a set of stimuli to the Communicator. Programmed feedback can be presented through various physical means and at any level of magnitude, ranging from zero feedback toward a seemingly totally open channel; e.g., the Communicator can be told that he will hear a tone whenever the Communicant feels he is "on the right track."

The tape recordings generated by this procedure become the experimental protocols which are later examined. The behaviors generated in this situation are surprisingly diverse. For example, here are quotations of the instructions given by two Communicators:

> A: Draw downward about an inch. Now go up at a 45 degree angle for an inch and a half. Now straight down for an inch. Now draw a straight line back to the place where you started.
> B: I want you to draw something that looks a little like a bow tie. It consists of two equilateral triangles, touching at their apex.

> You must draw it as a continuous line. That is, you must not
> take your pencil off the paper, or go back over any line.

From the many ways in which a Communicator's instructions can be
evaluated, we distinguish three separate aspects of the protocols: their
impact, their *style*, and their *formal adequacy*.

Impact, the most significant criterion, refers to the real behavior of
another subject who subsequently listens to the record. Some of the most
interesting communication hypotheses will refer to this level of analysis.
However, for practical reasons we have not made sufficient use of the
technique to dwell upon it here. We plan in the future to play selected
tapes for homogeneous groups of school children and to evaluate the
drawings produced by the children in order to determine the impact of
these recordings along the accuracy dimension.

Style refers to the quality of the Communicator's instructions, independent of whether or not they can be accurately followed. The two
examples of instructions given above are very different from one another,
and it is not difficult to characterize in a rough fashion the ways in which
they differ. We might say, for example, that A is piecemeal and B is
integrated; or that A focuses on the parts and B upon the whole figure. We
might guess that A was the product of a stimulus-response psychologist
and B was given by a gestaltist. To describe A, we want to use words like
"atomistic," "particularistic," "point-by-point." We want to say that the
person in B grasped and tried to communicate the "whole problem," or
the "structure of the problem." An essential feature of the difference
between A and B has to do with the attributing of role relations to oneself
and to the other, and with certain considerations about the transfer of
information and control. The subject has two very different choices open
to him. He may, as in A, regard himself as "strategist" and the other
person as "tactician." The explanation in A carries with it the implicit
notion that the self is the true problem-solver, who will do literally everything that is important about the problem, using the other person simply
as an extension of his writing hand and pencil. In contrast, the subject in
B is following an implicit line of reasoning something like the following:
"He (the Communicant) has all the necessary elements (pencil, paper, and
the mental capacity) for solving this problem. What he lacks is a graphic
representation of the figure and the rule about the continuous line. I will
provide this to him." In effect, the subject in B regards himself as a
transfer agent and his listener as the true problem-solver.

There are altogether twenty ways to make the geometric figure illustrated. In A, the Communicator limits the Communicant's possible
response to only one way. In B, the Communicant is free to use any out
of the twenty. Other explanations fall between these extremes of freedom
and constraint. At the present time, we are following up this matter of
Communicator style in the hope of developing a typology of Communicator style and of differential Communicant receptivity. We expect
soon to be able to pose and answer some applied questions concerning
group composition. We will want to know, for example, the effects of

mixing and matching the Communicator's style and Communicant's receptivity upon therapy dyads and therapy groups as well as upon classroom teaching groups.

Formal Adequacy of Communicator behavior is the dimension under investigation in the sample experiment being described here. We use the term "adequacy" to refer to some of the formal characteristics of the Communicator's language. At this level of analysis, we are concerned with ambiguity, vagueness, redundancy, and generality. It is important to note that a communication may contain one or more of these "negative" properties and still be effective in its impact on the receiver. Similarly, a formally adequate explanation may prove to be ineffective in its impact.

The method we adopted for evaluating Communicator adequacy was to listen to the recordings and/or to read typescripts of them, and to attempt to determine the path the Communicator intended the Communicant to take.

This study contrasts the communicative behavior of a group of schizophrenic-family members with a control group. The subjects in the experimental group consisted of 33 members of families, one of whose members was diagnosed as schizophrenic. In all, there were 7 patients, 12 fathers of schizophrenics and 14 mothers of schizophrenics. All subjects in the experimental groups were approached through the identified patient who was being treated as an inpatient at the Bronx Municipal Hospital Center.

The control group consisted of 30 subjects. About half of these subjects were personnel of a hospital psychiatry service, including nurses, aides, social workers, and doctors. The other control subjects were residents of a middle-income housing development in New York City. The experimental and control groups were of similar age and sex distribution, but they differed in that the control group was of a higher socioeconomic status.

The other independent variable, besides the subject classification, was the identity of the Communicant. Subjects performed the communication task twice. They were instructed to imagine that they were speaking to a different person each time. In the experimental group, parents "spoke to" their spouses and to the identified patient. Patients spoke to a parent and to a friend. The Controls spoke to a friend or co-worker and to an unidentified eight-year-old boy. In both groups, the order of presentation was balanced.

When the recordings were examined, all of the instructions were classified as one of two main types:

The Whole Figure Approach. Where the whole figure was to be executed by the Communicant, the Communicator might have instructed him that he was to follow the continuous line rule or he might have neglected to do so.

The Discrete Steps Approach. In this type of instruction, the Communicant was told to carry out a sequence of discrete steps which would yield the whole figure. The coding system for this type of instruction includes (1) whether the instructions were ambiguous, (2) whether they were unambiguous, (3) whether the Communicant must break the continuous line rule, and (4) whether the instructions were self-contradictory.

In the case of recordings where the task was divided into steps smaller than the whole, the Experimenter traced out all the possible paths the Communicant's pencil might travel. In doing this, once again no inferences were made about effectiveness or appropriateness. If some construction could be placed upon the Communicator's words that would imply a particular path to the exclusion of all other possibilities, then the recording was coded as "unambiguous." If possibilities could not be narrowed down in this fashion to a single path, that recording was classified as "ambiguous." Referring back to the earlier sample recordings, Example A would be coded as "discrete steps, unambiguous"; Example B as "whole figure, rule mentioned."

Two independent raters coded 86 completed explanations, categorizing them first grossly as to "whole figure approach," "discrete steps approach," or "mixed approach." They then went on to make a number of finer discriminations within each of these categories; in all, 329 decisions were made by each rater. Results: (1) all gross discriminations were identical, (2) 83 percent (71) of 86 explanations were coded identically, (3) 95 percent (313) of 329 total decisions were identical, (4) of greatest relevance to the present study are those explanations classified grossly as "discrete steps approach." Two hundred and ninety-five decisions were made regarding the precise path the Communicant's pencil was to have taken; with 10 disagreements, the agreement percentage was 95 percent.

The major dependent variable in this study was unclarity, which was measured in three ways, as follows:

1. *Initial attempt ambiguity.* The subject was first asked to instruct the hypothetical person in the task. In cases where the continuous-line rule was broken by the subject, the Experimenter intervened to clarify directions. The "Initial Attempt" refers to the response before the Experimenter intervened. Only responses which could be classified as *ambiguous* or *unambiguous* were used in making this analysis. The residual category, which was omitted from the analysis, includes responses that are probably effective as well as ineffective ones. It consists of whole-figure responses with or without mention of the continuous-line rule, responses in which the Communicant was instructed in such a way as to make it necessary to break the continuous line rule, self-contradictory responses, and incomplete responses.

2. *Initial attempt adequacy.* In this classification, the categories above were regrouped into adequate and inadequate. "Adequate" consisted of unambiguous responses and whole figure with the continuous-line rule responses. All other categories, including "ambiguous" were considered to be "inadequate."

3. *Overall ambiguity.* This classification is an index based upon both of the Communicator's attempts. If either one was ambiguous, or if one was unambiguous and the other was whole figure, he was rated "unambiguous." He was rated "figure overall" if both attempts were whole figure.

In addition to the classification of the Communicator's instructions, a correlation was done between the clarity of his responses and his "creativity" as measured by an Imagination Scale, which was given to all subjects. This is a nine-item, binary-choice, paper-and-pencil test adapted by Schutz (to be published) from the Myers-Briggs Type Indicator Test. The test had been validated previously against the criterion of "creativity" among a group of architects. As a first attempt to explore some of the factors associated with communication clarity, we wanted to find out if the imagination test would discriminate between the "controlled" and the "free" styles of communication used by the Communicators in the study.

HYPOTHESES AND RESULTS

The first two hypotheses in this study were derived from the "double bind" theory as stated by Bateson et al. (1956), which views psychopathology in general and schizophrenia in particular as a dysfunction in communication and a property of a social system or a relationship, not of an individual.

The particular hypotheses can be listed with the results obtained.

1. *The experimental group, composed of members of families containing a schizophrenic, will produce more ambiguous and less adequate explanations than the control groups.*

This hypothesis was confirmed on all three indices of unclarity. The two groups differed with respect to the ratio of ambiguous to unambiguous responses and in the number of cases to be assigned to the residual categories. It is notable that in nine instances, the instructions given by the experimental group violated the continuous-line rule, while in the control group this did not happen at all (see Tables 1, 2, and 3).

TABLE 1

PERFORMANCE OF EXPERIMENTAL AND CONTROL
GROUPS ON INITIAL ATTEMPT

	Experimental	Control
Discrete Steps Approach		
ambiguous	9	8
unambiguous	7	17
breaks rule	9	0
self contradictory	4	0
Whole Figure Approach		
figure without rule	2	0
figure with rule	2	5
Total	33	30

TABLE 2

PERFORMANCE OF EXPERIMENTAL AND CONTROL
GROUPS ON THREE INDICES OF UNCLARITY

	Experimental	Control	χ^2	p
Initial attempt				
ambiguous	9	8		
unambiguous	7	17 (41)[a]	2.36	ns
Initial attempt				
inadequate	24	8		
adequate	9	22 (63)	13.34	.0005
Overall				
ambiguous	21	12		
unambiguous	8	14 (63)	3.94	.025

[a]Sample size was reduced because subjects were omitted if either attempt was coded anything other than ambiguous or unambiguous.

TABLE 3

AMBIGUITY AND COMMUNICANT IDENTITY
(EXPERIMENTAL GROUP)

	TO SPOUSE	
	Ambiguous	Unambiguous
To "Patient"		
ambiguous	7	1 (8)
unambiguous	2	6 (8)
	(9)	(7) (16)[a][b]

[a]Sample size was reduced because subjects were omitted if either attempt was coded anything other than ambiguous or unambiguous.
[b]Includes only *parents* subsample who instructed two communicants.

2. *The parents of schizophrenics will give more ambiguous and less adequate explanations to their children than to their spouses.*
The subjects had very little disposition to switch from ambiguous to unambiguous instructions, or vice versa, between their first and second attempts (see Tables 3 and 4). In the control group there were five switches out of a total of 25 subjects. In the experimental group there

TABLE 4

AMBIGUITY AND COMMUNICANT IDENTITY
(CONTROL GROUP)

	TO CO-WORKER OR FRIEND	
	Ambiguous	Unambiguous
To "8-Year-Old Boy"		
ambiguous	5	2 (7)
unambiguous	3	15 (18)
	(8)	(17) (25)[a]

[a]Sample size was reduced because subjects were omitted if either attempt was coded anything other than ambiguous or unambiguous.

were three switches among 16 parents. Two of the three switches in the experimental group were in the direction counter to the hypothesis—parents who were unambiguous toward their child were ambiguous to their spouses. However, the conclusion that seems warranted is not that the hypothesis is disconfirmed, but rather that the experimental procedure did not produce sufficient switching of subjects between clear and unclear communications to permit it to be tested.

Other subdivisions related to characteristics of Communicants did not reveal any differences in ambiguity associated with Communicant identity.

In addition to these hypothesized results, the data revealed a negative association between imaginativeness and unclarity (see Table 5). With

TABLE 5

UNCLARITY AND IMAGINATION

	IMAGINATION			
	Low	High	χ^2	p
Uncoached attempt				
ambiguous	10	7		
unambiguous	9	15 (41)[a][b]	1.82	ns
Uncoached attempt				
inadequate	20	9		
adequate	11	20 (60)[a]	6.73	<.005
Summary				
ambiguous	17	13		
unambiguous	10	12 (52)[a]	.64	ns

[a]Sample size was reduced because subjects were omitted if either attempt was coded anything other than ambiguous or unambiguous.

[b]Three subjects in the experimental group were not administered the Imagination Scale.

respect to adequacy on the initial attempt, the association is statistically significant, although this is not the case on the other two indices of unclarity. Closer examination of these data revealed a stronger, nonlinear association between these variables. They appear to be related in a manner approximating an N-shape distribution. The psychological and theoretical significance of this finding is the subject of a separate paper (Levin & Schutz, 1965). There is impressive confirming evidence of this association. Twenty-seven out of 30 controls, and only two subjects in the experimental group, were above the median in imagination (see Table 6).

TABLE 6

PERFORMANCE OF EXPERIMENTAL AND CONTROL GROUPS ON IMAGINATION SCALE

	Experimental	Control	χ^2	p
Low	28	3 (31)		
High	2	27 (29)		
	$(30)^a$	(30) (60)	41.72	$<.0001$

[a]Three subjects in the experimental group were not administered the Imagination Scale.

In summary, one of the main hypotheses was confirmed. The experimental group was more ambiguous and less adequate than the controls, as well as less imaginative. Imagination and communication clarity were significantly associated. The fact that the parents of schizophrenics were no less effective in communicating with their schizophrenic child than with their spouses neither supports nor contradicts the view that schizophrenia is the property of a relationship.

Information Exchange and Silence in Normal and Abnormal Families*

Antonio J. Ferreira and William D. Winter

* * * It has been the consensus among therapists that in pathologic relationships there is a noticeable breakdown in communication (Bateson,
Jackson, Haley, & Weakland, 1963; Beavers, Blumberg, Timken, & Weiner,
1965; Farber & Jenne, 1963; Ferreira, 1960a, 1960b; Levy & Epstein,
1964; Miller, 1951; Ruesch, 1957, 1958; Ruesch & Bateson, 1951; Satir,
1964; Singer & Wynne, 1965a, b; Stabenau, Tupin, Werner, & Pollin,
1965; Wynne & Singer, 1963). In abnormal families, people do not seem
to talk to each other as freely, frequently, or explicitly as they do in
normal families. Instead, as experience with families in conjoint family
therapy indicates, members of abnormal families tend to withhold information from each other as to their feelings and wants. They "don't communicate," and their likes and dislikes often go unverbalized. On the basis
of these clinical impressions, it seemed reasonable to speculate that such
quantitative disturbances in intra-family communication could account
for the lower efficiency in decision-making demonstrated in abnormal
families. * * *

The taped family discussions, together with the individually completed questionnaires, constituted the basis for this present inquiry. (See
Article 11 for a fuller description of techniques of unrevealed differences
and subject pool from which this sample was drawn.) In order to assess
the assumed quantitative differences in intra-family communication, we
focused on two questions: (1) How often did family members inform
each other of their "real" likes and dislikes, i.e., the likes and dislikes
previously indicated in the individually filled-out questionnaires?
(2) What was the percentage of decision time "wasted away" in silence by
the family?

Hypotheses

There were two main hypotheses to be tested:

Hypothesis 1: *The amount of valid and explicit information exchang-*

---

*Abstracted from *Family Process*, 1968, 7, 251–276, with permission of the authors and
Family Process.

ed among family members as to what they like and dislike is significantly less in abnormal than in normal families.

Hypothesis 2: *The amount of time spent in silence is relatively greater in abnormal than in normal families.*

Method

The taped discussions of normal and abnormal families in the course of family decision-making were studied for the amount of information exchanged among family members, and for their silent time. The tapes, recorded through two microphones that fed into a stereophonic recorder, permitted a good differentiation of the voices and an easy identification of what was being said.

The Sample

The families in this study were part of a sample of 125 families which had been tested and taped as reported in Article 11. Of this pool of tested families, 75 tapes were randomly selected, corresponding to 30 normal (*Nor*), 17 maladjusted (*Mal*), 14 delinquent (*Del*), and 14 schizophrenic (*Sch*) families. A comparison of the general characteristics of these families, summarized in Table 1, revealed no significant differences (χ^2 = 31.13, df = 24) among diagnostic groups as to the age or educational level of the father, mother, and child; the occupational level of the father; or the number of children in the family.

TABLE 1

GENERAL CHARACTERISTICS OF THE FAMILIES STUDIED (MEDIAN VALUES)

VARIABLE	DIAGNOSTIC GROUPS				TOTAL
	Nor	*Mal*	*Sch*	*Del*	
Father's age (years)	45.50	42.00	47.00	47.00	45.30
Mother's age (years)	44.00	40.00	43.00	41.00	41.90
Child's age (years)	15.95	15.83	16.16	15.50	15.75
Father's education (years)	15.75	14.00	14.00	14.00	15.10
Mother's education (years)	13.90	12.36	13.00	12.00	12.94
Child's education (years)	10.77	10.00	9.00	9.00	10.50
Father's occupational level	1.44	2.10	2.16	2.10	1.89
No. children in family	3.04	2.79	2.70	3.30	2.96

The Procedure and the Variables

The selected tapes were studied from two distinct points of view: (1) the amount of explicit information exchanged among the family members, and (2) the percentage of time spent in silence by the family.

Information Exchanged. The amount of information exchanged among family members as to their respective likes and dislikes was measured by listening to the taped family discussion and tabulating the instances when a given family member was heard to say to the family, explicitly and clearly, that he (or she) liked or disliked some alternative available in the questionnaire. For this purpose a research assistant was instructed to listen (usually several times) to the tape and register on a sheet every instance when he heard an identified family member communicate to the other two that he wanted, chose, liked, preferred, etc. (or, to the contrary, that he did *not* want, choose, like, prefer, etc.) a clearly stated alternative. Criteria were established as follows.

Statements to be tabulated as expressing explicit information:

1. An explicit declaration of choice (positive or negative) made in the past tense, and disclosing the member's responses to the "private" individual questionnaire previously administered ("I chose . . . ," "I crossed off . . .").
2. An explicit choice (positive or negative) made in the present tense, and without reference to the individual questionnaire ("My first choice is . . . ," "I don't like . . .").
3. An explicit statement of preference between alternative choices, but only when the superlative was used and referred to all the alternatives available in the questionnaire ("I want . . . more than any other," "The one I want the least is . . .").
4. An explicit statement of agreement with another family member, but only when the choice(s) in question was (were) verbalized in full and stated unambiguously by the speaker ("I choose . . . also," "You and I both crossed off . . .").
5. An explicit statement of choice (positive or negative) given in an answer to a "neutral" question, that is, to a definitely "non-leading" question (*Q.* "What did you choose?" *A.* "I chose . . ."; *Q.* "Which were your cross-offs?" *A.* "They were . . .").

Statements *not* to be scored were:

1. Statements made in the third person, or in the plural, and from which the individual's choices could only be inferred ("Let's choose . . . ," "We don't want . . .").
2. Statements made as answers to conceivably leading questions (*Q.* "Do you want . . . ?" *A.* "It's okay by me." *Q.* "I put down . . . as one of my choices, did you?" *A.* "Yes, I did, too").
3. Statements of preference not in the superlative, and/or not covering all the alternatives available for the situation in the questionnaire ("Between those two, I prefer . . . ," "Of those three, I like . . . the least").
4. Statements of agreement when the choice(s) in question was (were) not verbalized by the speaking family member, or when the response might be the equivalent to a nod-of-the-head (*Q.* "How about . . . for our first choice?" *A.* "Fine." *Q.* "I chose . . . how about you?" *A.* "Me too!").

Upon tabulating the family members' informational statements, a research assistant proceeded to compare the statements so tabulated with the answers previously given by the respective family members on the occasion of their filling-out of the "private" individual questionnaires. From this comparison between what was heard on the tape and what was written on the individually administered questionnaires, a score (*Inf*) was determined as follows: One *explicit informational unit* was scored whenever a statement tabulated as explicitly information was found to be "valid," that is to say, to correspond in fact with the choice (positive or negative) indicated in writing by the individual member in his "private" answers to the questionnaire. Thus, for each family member, a score was obtained representing the number of explicit informational statements (found to be valid) that he made in the course of family decision-making in regard to those alternatives which he liked and disliked the most. For each family, then, the amount of total information available to, and exchanged among, its family members was determined by the sum total of the explicit informational scores obtained by its members.

The tapes were assigned for scoring at random. Throughout the scoring procedure, the research assistant in charge of listening to and scoring the tapes was kept in total ignorance both of the diagnosis of the family, and of the choices adopted by the respective family members in their individual questionnaires.

Questions about the reliability, validity, and internal consistency of the *Inf* scores were answered very satisfactorily. The *reliability* of the scoring procedure was measured by means of two interjudge correlations. The one based upon scores from questionnaire "situations" ($N = 35$), taken at random from as many different families, was $r = .939$; the other, based upon scores obtained by families ($N = 8$) in the whole questionnaire, was $r = .963$. An indication of the *validity* of the tabulated scores was the finding that 92 percent of the tabulated scores corresponded in fact with the family member's private choices made in the previously administered individual questionnaire. This close correspondence appears to indicate that it is the total amount of information exchanged which is most important, not its "validity," since the family members seem to have reported their choices honestly. Finally, a measure of *internal consistency* was obtained by comparing the scores on the first three questionnaire situations with the last three; for the whole data, the split-half correlation (Spearman-Brown formula) was $r = .916$. In this respect, it was very impressive to observe that, although the amounts of *Inf* varied from situation to situation, the scores achieved by the different diagnostic groups remained in their same relative positions, that is to say, practically parallel throughout.

Silence. The relative amount of time spent in silence by the family was calculated by measuring silent time as a percentage of the total decision time (*DT*). To this end, a research assistant was instructed to measure the total number of seconds of silence in the taped family discussion. No attempt was made to distinguish between the kinds of silence, whether it was a simple pause or a genuine lull in the discussion. The amount of silence was cumulated by means of a common stop watch. Despite the coarseness of the procedure, *interjudge reliability* for the percentage of silence in family discussions ($N = 8$) was extraordinarily high ($r = .993$).

RESULTS

The two preceding procedures, *Information Exchanged* and *Silence*, permitted the testing of the main hypotheses, Hypothesis 1 and Hypothesis 2, and certain subsidiary hypotheses.

Information. Hypothesis 1 was corroborated: *The amount of information exchanged among family members was significantly greater for normal than for abnormal families.* Since the questionnaire was composed of seven "situations," for each of which the family member was to mark three alternatives as "most liked" (positive choices) and three as "disliked" or "least liked" (negative choices), there was, by our procedure, a maximum of 42 valid informational statements that a family member could have made to the family. Thus the theoretical range of *Inf* scores for the individual family member was 0 to 42; and for the family triad, conceived as a sum of the three individual members' scores, was 0 to 126. The observed range, however, was 0 to 39 for individual family members, and 8 to 107 for families as a group. As indicated in Figure 2, the average *Inf* scores for the diagnostic groups were 59.57 for *Nor*, and 36.00 for *Abn* families (40.53 for *Mal*; 32.00 for *Sch*; and 37.00 for *Del*). These differences were statistically significant ($F = 5.74$, $df = 3/71$, $p < .005$). The difference between *Nor* and *Abn* families was significant ($t = 2.61$, $df = 71$, $p < .01$), as were also the specific differences between *Nor* and each of the *Abn* (*Mal, Del,* or *Sch*) subgroups of families. The observation that *Inf* scores did differentiate well between *Nor* and *Abn* families was expressed in a highly significant biserial correlation between *Inf* scores and the dichotomy normality-abnormality of the families ($r = .561$, $p < .00001$).[1]

Of particular interest here was the hypothesized correlation between the family's *Inf* scores and the choice-fulfillment (*PP*) derived from the family decision. The results fulfilled the prediction. The correlation between *Inf* and *PP*—adjusted for the level of spontaneous agreement (*SA*)—was $r = .388$, statistically significant, $p < .001$. This finding corroborated the hypothesis that, generally speaking, *the greater the amount of information exchanged among family members, the greater the choice-fulfillment the family is likely to derive from their family decision-making.* In

---

[1] The amount of "misinformation," that is to say, of statements tabulated from the tapes according to the established criteria as being explicitly informational and yet failing to correspond with the individual's private answers to the questionnaire, did not clearly differentiate among diagnostic groups. Little should be made of this finding since the number of "misinformations" was too small (as indicated before, only 8 percent of the scored statements fell into this category) to permit satisfactory statistical treatment. The mean "misinformations" per diagnostic groups were 3.70 for *Nor*, and 4.18 for *Abn* (5.06 for *Mal*; 4.21 for *Sch*; and 3.07 for *Del*), and the simple prediction that there would be more "misinformation" in *Abn* than in *Nor* families was corroborated by Median Test ($\chi^2 = 3.494$, $df = 1$, $p < .05$, one-tailed).

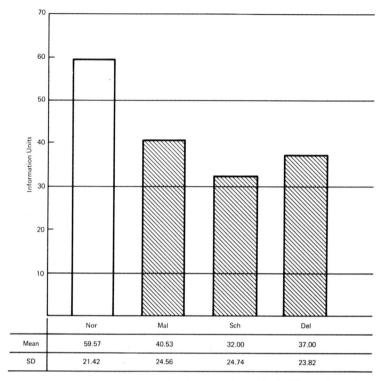

Fig. 1. Mean information (explicit informational units) exchanged in families by diagnostic groups.

other words, the more the family members explicitly tell each other about their likes and dislikes, the greater their likelihood of arriving at family decisions which better represent and fulfill the wishes of everyone concerned.

At this point in the investigation, a question of great and immediate interest was raised: Within a given family, how do family members compare in regard to the amount of information volunteered? The data show that *Abn* families exchange significantly less information than *Nor*; is it the "patient" (the child by our definition of *Abn* families) who brings down the family score by informing less than the child in comparable *Nor* families? The results were again very illuminating: *The decrease in explicit information exchanged among family members observed in Abn families appeared to be a function of the whole family, and not of any one individual family member.* This was expressed in high intra-family correlations of *Inf* scores, such as father-mother ($r = .714$, $p < .001$), and child-parents ($r = .748$, $p < .001$). It is noteworthy that, as Table 2 shows, the average score of every abnormal family member was less than the corresponding member in normal families. But perhaps even more interesting was the observation that when the data were taken as a whole, *the child seemed to have a tendency to inform more than his parents* (two-way analysis of variance, mixed model, $F = 3.700$, $df = 2/74$, $p < .05$). Only in the *Sch* group did the child appear to deviate from this rule.

Silence. The second main hypothesis in this investigation was also corroborated: *The relative amount of time spent in silence (percentage of the total decision time) was found to be significantly greater in abnormal than in normal families*. The theoretical range of percentage of silence (*Sil*) was, of course, 0 to 100 percent; the observed range for our data was 0.77 to 19.8 percent. As illustrated in Figure 4, the mean *Sil* scores for the diagnostic groups of families were 6.69 for *Nor* and 10.79 for *Abn* families (9.29 for *Mal*, 12.04 for *Sch*, and 11.26 for *Del*). These differences were statistically significant ($F = 6.42$, $df = 3/71$, $p < .001$). The difference between *Nor* and the total group of *Abn* families was statistically significant ($t = 4.11$, $df = 71$, $p < .001$), as was also the difference between *Nor* and each of the *Abn* subgroups of families (*Mal, Sch,* and *Del*). The correlation between *Sil* scores and the dichotomy normality–abnormality of the families was expressed in a biserial $r = -.547$, ($p < .00001$).

Since the variable called decision time (*DT*) can be regarded as made up of two mutually exclusive elements, silent time (*ST*) and talking time (*TT*), the question was raised as to what extent one or both of these

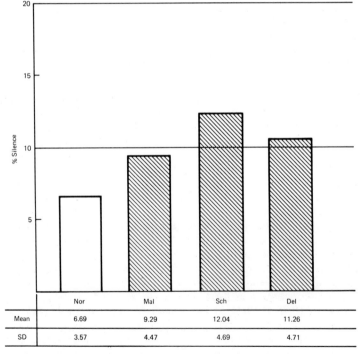

Fig. 2. Mean silence as **percentage** of decision-time in families by diagnostic groups.

components were responsible for the longer decision time observed in abnormal families. Pursuing this question, it was found that the longer decision time observed in *Abn* families reflected not only a longer silence (*ST*), but also a longer talking time (*TT*). In other words, the data showed that although a longer silence (both in a percentage and in an absolute sense) was a causative factor in the longer decision time observed in abnormal families in the process of family decision-making, this longer decision time appeared to be due also to their (absolute) longer talking time. Thus it was found that there was a remarkably high positive correlation between *ST* and *TT* ($r = .510$, $p < .0001$). The breakdown of *DT* scores into *ST* and *TT* for the diagnostic groups of families is shown in Table 3. The differences in the absolute values of *TT*, although definitely in the direction of longer times for *Abn* families, were not statistically significant ($F = 2.45$, $df = 3/71$, $p < .10$).

TABLE 2

MEAN DECISION-TIMES (*DT*) IN MINUTES, BROKEN DOWN INTO
SILENT-TIME (*ST*) AND TALKING-TIME (*TT*), BY DIAGNOSTIC GROUPS

	DIAGNOSTIC GROUPS			
	Nor	*Mal*	*Scb*	*Del*
ST	1.29	2.40	2.96	2.33
TT	17.93	23.41	21.64	18.21
ST/TT Ratio	.072	.098	.130	.116

We wondered here if, and to what extent, the variable *Sil* (i.e., relative silence) could be regarded as characteristic of a family. To this end we proceeded to compare the *Sil* scores obtained by these families in the performance of two distinct tasks. We took advantage of the fact that the same families used in this questionnaire investigation had also been studied in the task of making up "family stories" based on TAT cards. As reported elsewhere (see Article 25), measurements of the silences observed during that task had shown that *Abn* families were significantly more silent than *Nor* ones. However, this comparison of the two tasks—decision-making over questionnaire situations as described here and decision-making about stories on a family TAT—immediately revealed that the families' utilization of silence was decidedly different from one task to the other. The average percentage of silent time observed for the questionnaire was 9.13 percent, whereas for the discussions on the family TAT it was 39.91 percent. Still, in both tasks, *Abn* families were significantly more silent than *Nor* ones. In this respect, it is worth noting that a remarkably high correlation was found to exist between the family's percentage of silence (*Sil*) in the questionnaire and in the TAT situations ($r = .625$, $p < .0001$), a correlation which seems to indicate that *the rela-*

tive usage of silence may be a rather stable interactional characteristic of the family.

As expected, the two main variables in this investigation, *Inf* and *Sil*, were shown to be significantly correlated ($r = -.312, p < .001$). However, it was unclear as to whether this finding did express in fact an association between the two parameters or was simply the consequence of their heterogeneity in relation to a third common variable, in this case, the normality or abnormality of the families in question with which both *Inf* and *Sil* were known to correlate. The *Inf* and *Sil* correlations with the dichotomous variable Normality–Abnormality had to be taken into account. Using their respective biserial r's, it was found that the partial correlation coefficient between *Inf* and *Sil* was practically zero (partial $r = -.009$), indicating that in all probability their relationships to the Normality–Abnormality variable had been responsible for the false appearance that the variables *Inf* and *Sil* were related to each other.

TABLE 3

VALUES OF EXCHANGED INFORMATION (*Inf*), AND PERCENTAGE
OF SILENCE (*Sil*) FOR NORMAL AND ABNORMAL (IN-THERAPY)
FAMILIES IN A SIX-MONTH TEST-RETEST

FAMILIES	TEST		RE-TEST	
	Inf	*Sil*	*Inf*	*Sil*
Nor # a	55	6.30	43	7.17
b	18	14.44	18	10.88
c	83	12.56	78	8.65
d	45	11.98	42	5.13
e	83	3.65	77	3.97
f	50	10.78	42	6.37
g	61	9.91	46	6.36
h	59	7.78	42	2.27
k	66	3.65	81	5.42
l	39	10.61	47	11.48
Mean	55.9	9.17	51.6	6.77
Abn # m	71	8.67	67	4.95
n	51	11.50	39	5.54
o	42	12.50	27	15.00
p	49	9.39	8	11.84
q	77	9.58	75	13.46
r	68	8.20	54	4.81
s	83	12.44	52	11.33
t	77	11.56	73	13.18
u	74	7.95	81	7.80
v	24	14.12	51	9.95
Mean	61.6	10.59	52.7	9.79
Overall Mean	58.8	9.88	52.2	8.28
SD	18.8	2.95	20.8	3.54

Test–Retest. In order to assess the possible effect of time and/or therapy upon the interactional variables *Inf* and *Sil*, a test-retest experiment was undertaken. For this purpose, 20 families (10 *Nor* and 10 *Abn*), were randomly selected and retested six months later (Ferreira & Winter, 1966). The test-retest scores on the *Inf* and *Sil* variables are summarized in Table 4. The test-retest comparison revealed that virtually *no change* had occurred during the six months that elapsed between test and retest on either the *Inf* or *Sil* scores. Although during this six-month period these ten retested *Abn* families all had been receiving the benefit of conjoint family therapy, there seemed to be no "improvement" to be measured in the interactional variables under consideration. As far as exchange of information and silence were concerned, the differences between the group means on test and retest were not statistically significant for either normal or abnormal (in therapy) families. Instead, it was found that there were some remarkably high test-retest correlations for both *Inf* ($r = .729$, $p < .001$), and *Sil* ($r = .536$, $p < .01$), correlations which speak strongly for the stability of these interactional variables.

COMMENT

It was the purpose of this investigation to find an explanation for the abnormal families' relative inefficiency in decision-making (Ferreira, 1963a; Ferreira & Winter, 1965, 1968) within the general hypothesis of disturbed communication among family members. The assumed intra-family disturbance of communication was considered only in its quantitative sense. It was hypothesized that there would be less communication among members of abnormal families than among members of otherwise comparable normal families. Since a previous investigation (Ferreira & Winter, 1965) had disclosed that abnormal families' inefficient decision-making was expressed in their requiring a longer time (DT) and reaching less "fulfilling" family decisions than normal families, the general hypothesis of disturbed communication was couched in two different formulations corresponding to well-accepted clinical impressions (1) that the abnormal families' less fulfilling decisions would relate to their lower informational state; and (2) that their requiring longer time to reach family decisions would appear as a consequence of their greater time "wasted" in silence.

Both hypotheses were corroborated. Abnormal families' members were found to exchange significantly less information among themselves, and to remain silent considerably longer than normal families' members. * * *

Also in a previous investigation (Ferreira, Winter, & Poindexter, 1966), it was found that in family decision-making there was a direct relationship between percentage of silence and efficiency of performance. It was observed that during family discussions about TAT-induced stories, those families characterized by longer silences (percentagewise) were also the ones more likely to require prolongation of the allotted discussion time. This conclusion was corroborated by the findings of this study. In family decision-making, longer percentages of silence did indeed go together with longer decision times, and these related phenomena were important distinguishing features between normal and abnormal families. In comparison to normal families, abnormal families had appreciably longer silences and required more time to perform tasks involving family decision-making (TAT stories, questionnaire situations), thus appearing as more "wasteful" and less efficient in their utilization of time. To the extent that such findings may be generalized to real-life situations, we suspect that the long-range effect of such inefficiency may be quite inimical to the proper functioning of the family system. For the require-ment of a longer decision time such as observed in abnormal families is likely to result in a backlog of unmade family decisions (many of which may never get made at all), which is bound to further increase the burdens of family life and promote other pathologic and pathogenic interactional events.

The sum of our and others' investigations is sounding an encouraging chord. A few pieces of the puzzle are falling into place. With the expecta-tion that the effort to bring some of those pieces into a cohesive picture may prove worthwhile, we have attempted to outline the main variables involved and the way in which they seem to relate. The composite picture that thus emerges suggests that family abnormality is the product of a circular chain of interactional events which we could call the *family pathology cycle*.

Family Pathology Cycle. Research findings and clinical impressions have combined to indicate that in abnormal families there is a cycle of self-perpetuating events, a self-aggravating *perpetuum mobile* which, once instituted, is bound to lead the family farther afield into pathology (see Figure 5).

In order to clarify the interrelatedness of the elements involved in the family pathology cycle, we shall briefly review the relevant findings of this and other investigations. It has been observed that abnormal families, by comparison with normal families, have:

(a) *Less spontaneous agreement* (Ferreira, 1963a; Ferreira & Winter, 1965, 1968; Katz, 1965; Newcomb, 1958), which leads into and in part causes less efficient family decisions, as expressed in the observations of (b) and (c), below.

(b) *Less choice fulfillment* (Ferreira, 1963a; Ferreira & Winter, 1965, 1968) of family decisions resulting in part from (a), above, and in part from inadequate information exchange (h), and leading to (d), below.

(c) *Longer decision time* (Ferreira & Winter, 1965, 1968), which again stems in part from (a), and in part from (f), longer relative silences, and (g), prolonged talking time. It leads also to (d).

(d) *Lower individual satisfaction* (Ferreira, 1964a; Winter & Ferreira, 1965) or happiness, resulting from the frustrations inherent to (b) and (c), above, and leading to (e).

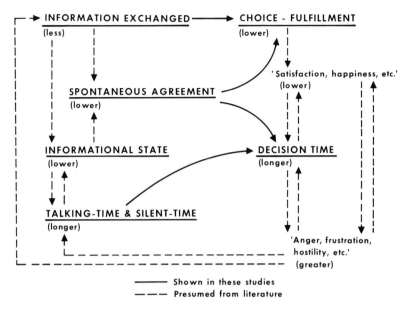

Fig. 3. Family pathology cycle.*

(e) *More anger, hostility, fear, etc.* (Ferreira, 1963b; Winter, Ferreira, & Olson, 1966) in individual family members, leading to their expression in (f), greater silences, and less self-revealing information exchanged; perhaps also to (g), longer talking times.

(f) *Longer silences* (Ferreira et al., 1966), absolutely and relatively, possibly as a result and expression of (e), greater negative feelings of anger, fear, etc., but as such leading to (c), longer decision time, and possibly facilitating less exchange of information among family members (h).

(g) *Longer talking time*, possibly with the same antecedents (reflecting the long-noticed equivalence of silence and logorrhea), and with the same consequences as (f).

(h) *Less explicit information exchanged* among family members resulting from (e), (f), and (g), and leading immediately to (b), less choice fulfillment of family decisions, and, in the long course of family life, to (a), lower spontaneous agreement.

This diagram of the family pathology cycle is proposed simply as a skeleton of the interrelated events described in the experimental and clinical observations of abnormal families. Its tenor is most emphatically quantitative. The underlying philosophy is that of the continuous nature of behavior and its pathology. Still, it must be pointed out that on this assumed continuum, families with a "schizophrenic" or "delinquent" child consistently appeared to test on the more pathologic end of the scales, that is to say, farther away from normal values than the other abnormal families. Whether this finding corresponds to some qualitative difference which specifically marks these families as schizophrenia- or delinquency-producing units, or whether, instead, it simply reflects a quantitative accentuation of the very same events or chain of events remains an open question. In either case, it is apparent that normal family decision-making and family functioning presupposes adequate communication. In this respect, it seems reasonable to postulate that, within the notion of a family pathology cycle, all forms of interactional pathology are both cause and effect to disturbances in intra-family communication, which, in the last analysis, are always quantitative.

Experiment with Abnormal Families: Testing Done in a Restricted Communication Setting*

Jay Haley

* * * Ordinarily in family research an attempt is made to obtain "natural" family behavior by letting the members talk freely and spontaneously together about some subject. This type of unrestricted behavior is exceedingly complex, since the family members communicate with each other by body movement, vocal intonations, and verbal statements containing multiple levels of meaning. Usually judgments about what family members are doing are made by raters, and the data are simplified by having the raters judge tape-recorded conversations (ignoring the body movement) or judge written transcripts (ignoring both body movement and vocal intonations). This type of reduction greatly oversimplifies the family's conversational behavior. An alternative is to simplify the data in advance by restricting the ways the family members can communicate with each other. The investigator gains measurements which are more controlled and reliable, but he risks losing the natural and typical behavior which occurs when the family converses freely. The ideal goal is to limit the interchange so that reliable measurements can be obtained, while not distorting the typical behavior one is seeking to measure.

The study reported here is one of a series which attempted to test differences between families while using the most simple and reliable measurements. The first study contrasted normal and abnormal families in which one child and the parents were talking about a neutral questionnaire, and the measurement was primarily the order in which they spoke in the conversation (Haley, 1964). The second study added a child, the identified patient in the abnormal group, as well as a sibling in the same situation (Haley, 1967). As the family members talked, impulses from throat microphones went directly to an analyzer so that speech sequence was totalled automatically. The study reported here also measured the order in which family members spoke—who spoke after whom—but also

---

*Abstracted from *Archives of General Psychiatry*, 1967, *17*, 53–63, with permission of the author and the American Medical Association.

added the measurement of who spoke *to* whom. To obtain this measure reliably, it was necessary to restrict the ways the family members could communicate with each other. If the members talk together in the same room, one cannot really say that any one person is talking *to* any other because he is being overheard by the third person. His remarks are inevitably addressed to both persons, even though he might only be looking at one of them when he speaks. Rater judgment of such a measure is also a problem. One rater may say father is speaking to the child, while another more sensitive rater might consider father to be "really" speaking to mother while looking at the child.

If the family member's communication is restricted so that any one of them can only talk to one other person at a time, with insurance that the third person cannot hear the comments, then a measure of who the person chooses to talk to is a reliable measure of who speaks to whom. A situation was therefore arranged where family members spoke from different rooms over an intercommunication network. Parents and child had to press a button to choose a person to talk with, and so the family could only talk in switching dyads. This situation is not normal for families, and so may distort the typical family processes. However, normal and abnormal groups are faced with the same stimuli in the same setting. Two different samples of families were exposed to this situation. One sample discussed a neutral questionnaire, and the behavior of normal and abnormal families was compared. An additional sample of families selected in the same way, but not including the same families, discussed a questionnaire about family problems.

The Sample

A group of 25 abnormal families composed of parents and one child were brought to the laboratory for the study using the neutral questionnaire. These families were defined as abnormal if they contained a member who had come to community attention for a problem. Included in this group were families who had sought therapy for problem children, as well as marital and family problems. The families were found through agencies, private psychiatrists, or waiting lists for treatment. Many of them were calling for treatment, and the testing was part of their evaluation for referral. The presenting problems of the families are given in Table 1 in rough categories, since some families presented a problem person but also said there were marital or family problems.

A contrast sample of 21 normal families was brought in and put through the same procedure as the abnormal group. The normal families were defined as families in which no member had come to community attention for a problem. They were randomly selected from a high-school directory; after testing, if it was found that no member had been in therapy or had been arrested, the family was placed in the normal group.

All families were middle-class, with the parents born in this country. In the normal group, the family was asked to bring in any child in the age range from 9 to 20; usually they brought in the index child from the high-school directory. The abnormal families were asked to bring in their

TABLE 1

NEUTRAL QUESTIONNAIRE

TYPE OF FAMILY	MEAN INDEX SCORE OF DEVIATION FROM EQUAL PARTICIPATION*			
	N	Voice	Button	Time
Normal	21	27.52	82.69	30.00
Abnormal	25	31.67	85.48	30.70
Type of abnormal family				
Problem father	3	22.56	81.73	20.37
Problem mother	2	41.68	103.67	36.11
Absent problem sib	2	41.84	96.28	42.83
Marriage or family problem	6	33.08	80.24	31.58
Total Non-child problems	13	Mean 28.23	86.66	28.13
Child's problem				
Psychosomatic	1	7.84	50.56	10.67
Enuretic	1	14.49	90.78	4.97
Behavior problem	2	16.70	65.56	15.05
Underachiever	1	18.88	54.86	15.39
Schizophrenic	1	39.29	80.94	42.51
Delinquent	3	54.41	108.64	56.01
Stutterer	1	66.08	122.73	66.65
Withdrawn	2	76.35	77.27	10.28
Total Child problems	12	Mean 35.84	84.20	29.92

*A score of 0 would mean the three family members participated in exactly equal pairs. The voice category refers to the sequence of speech of family members as they talked. The button category refers to whether they chose each other equally to talk with. The time category refers to whether all three pairs of the triad spent equal time talking together.

problem child if he was the presenting problem, or any child in the age range from 9 to 20 if it was a parent or family problem. The children in the two samples were not matched exactly for sex and age. Previous studies have not shown a correlation between the measurements used here and the sex and age of children (Haley, 1964, 1967), but it should be noted that there were more boys than girls in the abnormal group and more girls than boys in the normal group. The children tended to be older in the normal group, in which there were seven boys with a mean age of 19.9, and 15 girls with a mean age of 16.9. In the abnormal group there were 15 boys with a mean age of 15.5, and 10 girls with a mean age of 13.9. The total abnormal group included children with a mean age of 14.9, while for the normal group it was 17.9.

Procedure

When the three family members arrived in the laboratory, they were placed in separate rooms and asked to fill out a questionnaire. This questionnaire consisted of ten categories with seven choices in each category. The categories included choosing a type of food if one went out to dinner, choice of movies, choice of countries to visit if one went on a trip, and so on. Each family member was asked to cross off three choices he would not want at all, and then to make in order of preference three choices he would want.

After completing the questionnaires, individually, the family members learned that they were going to fill out the questionnaire again, but this time as a family. They would have to agree on the items they did and did not want. Whatever they chose all must have, and whatever they rejected none could have. The conversation became an attempt to reach compromise decisions satisfactory to all three family members. Although the questionnaire was largely neutral in nature, there was some conflict built into it since some of the items were preferable to men, some to women, and some to children rather than parents. This questionnaire was devised by Antonio J. Ferreira, M.D., and William D. Winter, Ph.D. The results have been reported elsewhere (Ferreira, 1963a; Ferreira & Winter, 1965, 1966).

The family members were also told that they were going to discuss the questionnaire under special circumstances. Each person would be in a different room talking over an intercommunication system; they would not be able to see each other, and they would not all be able to talk at the same time. Only two persons would be able to talk at a time, and when those two were talking, the other person could not hear them or be heard if he spoke. The family members were shown an intercom box which had a microphone, a headset, and two buttons. In the mother's position, the buttons were labeled "husband" and "child." If mother pressed father's button it lighted up, as did the button on *his* box, and she was in communication with him. If she pressed the child's button, that one lighted up, and she was in communication with the child. The equipment is simple to operate and the subjects were given a trial run so that they learned how to press buttons to select each other. They also learned that if two of them were talking and the third interrupted, he shut out one of them. For example, if mother and father were talking and the child pressed mother's button, he was in communication with mother, but the father was shut out. Father could no longer hear his wife, and the light went out on his box indicating he was no longer in communication with her. If he then pressed his wife's button to contact her again, the child was shut out. The conversation consisted of switching dyads, since all must reach agreement but only two could talk with each other at the same time. Each was given a copy of the questionnaire and asked to have the items all marked the same when they finished the task.

In this setting, the family must agree on points at issue in a relatively short period of time in a situation where they must solve the mechanics of communicating with each other while also resolving differences of opinion. To do the task, they must find a way of switching back and forth among the members so that all of them can converse and end up with the same choice of items. As an essential part of the task, the family must work out the organizational procedure, and the task is facilitated if someone takes a "manager's" position and organizes the conversation. Since family theory includes the idea that families with problems adapt less well to stress, one might expect that a stress situation like this would exaggerate greater differences between normal and abnormal families.

The Measurements

A variety of measurements of family behavior can be obtained in this setting.

1. A reliable measure of who chooses to speak with whom is obtained. When a family member pushes a button to speak to another, a pen is activated on the event recorder. Therefore, there is a written record of the frequency with which each person chooses another and the sequence in which this is done. Two other variables can also be examined when two people are talking: how frequently the third person intrudes into their conversation, and how often one of the two invites the third to converse.

2. The speech frequency and order of audible sounds of family members is obtained. In this study a rater judgment was made by listening to tape recordings of the conversation. It is a relatively simple judgment, since it is not necessary to determine what is said but only who spoke and who spoke next; only two people are talking at a time, so the voices of three people do not need to be differentiated.

3. There are additional measures of the time each pair of family members spend talking with each other, the number of speeches required for the total task, and the length of time to complete the task. Some content variables are also examined and reported upon, but the primary emphasis in the study is upon these simple measurements.

HYPOTHESES AND RESULTS

There are at least three possible ways to conceptualize the family for research purposes; it can be thought of: in terms of its structure and the roles of the members, in terms of the processes between the members, or as a working group which produces an outcome. These three ways of thinking about the family parallel ideas in role theory, communications theory, and information theory. The hypotheses and results of this study will be presented in each of these areas.

Structure. The usual view of family structure is derived from role theory, and implies a hierarchical organization with functional positions for the members. The stereotype portrait of families, which appears in the early family literature, suggests that in normal families the father is in the position of leader and fulfills an instrumental function, while mother is secondary in leadership and serves a more affective function. Abnormality in a family is said to stem from a role reversal; the mother in the abnormal family is reported to be dominating and intrusive, while the father is passive and withdrawn. The problem child is usually said to be either rejected or overprotected. If rejected, the parents do not include him in family decisions. If overprotected, the parents helpfully do for him what he should do himself, and include him in decisions which should be made independent of him. Often the mother is said to be interfering with the father-child relationship by intruding upon it rather than maintaining a secondary role.

Given this type of portrait, several hypotheses related to the measurements in this study logically follow:

1. Since mothers in abnormal families are more dominating, they will push buttons more actively than mothers in the normal group. They will do more managing of the conversation by inviting others to join them in conversation, and they will intrude most on the father's and child's conversation.

2. The fathers in the abnormal group, being more passive and withdrawn, will press fewest buttons, invite mother and child to converse less often, and intrude on mother and child less than the fathers in the normal group.

3. The children in the abnormal group will be more withdrawn than those in the normal group, and so will press fewer buttons than the control children and fewer than their own parents.

These hypotheses were not supported by the findings. Of the total buttons pushed in the abnormal group, the fathers were the most active button-pushers. The abnormal fathers did 48.8 percent of the pushing, while the mothers did 22.69 percent. Not only did the abnormal father rather than the mother manage the conversation by doing the most button-pushing, but the normal fathers pushed slightly less than the abnormal fathers (41.31 percent), and the normal mothers pushed exactly the same percentage as the abnormal mothers (22.43 percent) (see Table 2). When one examines who pushed which person's buttons the most, there were no differences between the normal and abnormal groups, as can be seen in Table 2.

The abnormal mother did not intrude more than the father. The fathers in both groups intruded about the same amount, and the normal and abnormal mothers had the same number of intrusions. If we examine what happened when father and mother were talking and one of them invited the child to talk, it was again the abnormal father who did more inviting than the mother. The normal and abnormal mothers invited about the same amount, and less than the children.

The abnormal children pressed slightly fewer buttons than the normal children, and intruded and invited slightly less, but the difference was not significant. The children in both groups invited their parents about equally. Although the children in the abnormal group participated slightly less than the normal children, they could not be considered passive and withdrawn since they pressed more buttons than their mothers. They also were not obstreperous and intrusive; they intruded 2 percent less than the normal children.

In summary, when one examines the button-pushing activities, the fathers in the abnormal group were not passive. They pushed the most buttons and did the most intruding and inviting. The mothers did not dominate, and in fact were less active than either fathers or children. The behavior of normals and abnormals was almost exactly

TABLE 2

NEUTRAL QUESTIONNAIRE

FAMILY TYPE	% BUTTON PUSHING BY FAMILY MEMBERS		
	Father	Mother	Child
Normal (N = 21)	41.31	22.43	36.25
Abnormal (N = 25)	48.84	22.69	28.47

	% EACH FAMILY MEMBER PUSHED BUTTON					
	Father Pushed Mother	Mother Pushed Father	Father Pushed Child	Child Pushed Father	Mother Pushed Child	Child Pushed Mother
Normal	22.11	12.20	19.20	17.26	10.23	19.00
Abnormal	25.68	11.90	23.16	13.43	10.79	15.04

	TOTAL % EACH FAMILY MEMBER INTRUDED		
	Father	Mother	Child
Normal	35.29	24.65	40.06
Abnormal	33.44	27.84	38.71
Child problem (N = 12)	41.34	22.04	36.61

	% EACH FAMILY MEMBER INTRUDED ON EACH OTHER					
	Father to		Mother to		Child to	
	Child	Mother	Child	Father	Mother	Father
Normal	12.88	22.41	9.52	15.13	24.09	15.97
Abnormal	11.71	21.73	11.88	15.96	20.37	18.34
Child problem	14.17	27.17	14.17	7.87	24.80	11.81

	TOTAL % EACH FAMILY MEMBER INVITED		
	Father	Mother	Child
Normal	42.80	22.61	34.58
Abnormal	49.92	19.25	30.83
Child problem	49.35	21.81	28.83

	% EACH FAMILY MEMBER INVITED ANOTHER					
	Father to		Mother to		Child to	
	Child	Mother	Child	Father	Mother	Father
	20.31	22.49	11.85	10.76	17.05	17.53
Abnormal	24.96	24.96	9.19	10.06	16.01	14.82
Child problem	24.77	24.58	10.35	11.46	15.34	13.49

the same in all categories, and there were no differences between the two groups of families.

It might be possible to argue that this simple measurement of button-pushing does not reflect the domination structure of the family. Perhaps the father does the most button-pushing, but mother tells him to push them. Therefore, she is covertly dominating what happens. Investigating this question requires a shift from reliable data, such as button presses recorded on an event recorder, to a judge's opinion of what happens in the family conversation. This type of rating was done on ten of the 25 abnormal family conversations. Three simple categories were devised: a person can direct someone to push, he can announce that he himself will push, or he can push a button without any comment. A statement such as "You ask Nancy now what she wants" is coded as a directive to the other to push the button. A statement such as "I'll ask Nancy if she agrees," is coded as an announcement that the speaker will push. The results in these three categories for the ten abnormal families show no indication that mother is more domineering. Of the total buttons pushed by father, he was directed by mother to push them 9.72 percent of the time. Mother was directed by father an equal amount, 9.68 percent of the time, and the child was directed by mother and father about the same number of times. Of the undirected and unannounced button-pushing, father did the most (see Table 3).

A related aspect of structure is a measure of the amount of time the various pairs spend talking together. One might expect that the abnormal mother and father are more child-oriented and also more in conflict with each other, and so would spend less time talking together than the normal father and mother. This did not prove to be so:

TABLE 3

BUTTON-PUSHING DIRECTIVES

% TOTAL PUSHES EACH WAS DIRECTED TO PUSH

Father Directed by		Mother Directed by		Child Directed by	
Mother	Child	Father	Child	Mother	Father
9.72	1.03	9.68	3.63	9.41	9.67

% TOTAL PUSHES EACH ANNOUNCED

Father	Mother	Child
36.94	31.05	20.36

% TOTAL PUSHES UNDIRECTED AND UNANNOUNCED

Father	Mother	Child
47.78	44.35	39.44

the normal parents spent 34.31 percent of the time together, and the abnormal parents 41.44 percent of the time. One might also think that abnormal mother and child would spend more time together than normal mother and child because of the overprotectiveness of the abnormal mother. This also did not prove to be so: the normal mother and child spent 28.16 percent of the time talking together, and the abnormal mother and child somewhat less, 23.42 percent of the time. Fathers and children were together about the same amount of time in the two groups: 37.63 percent of the time in the normal group and 35.14 percent of the time in the abnormal group.

It could be argued that the structural difference between the normal and abnormal families is not brought out in this setting because of the neutral nature of what they are discussing. Conversation about choice of food or a car color might not bring out the pathological role reversals in the family as would a discussion of less trivial issues. To test this possibility, a new sample of 15 normal and 10 abnormal families was selected in the same way, and talked together in the same communication network about a different conversational stimulus. The family members were first asked individually in separate rooms to make selections of possible solutions to family problem situations. There were ten family situations and five solutions for each; they included what a mother should do if her boy was caught stealing, what a daughter should do if she wished to stay out later than she had in the past, what the family should do if grandmother intruded in an overbearing way, and so on. After making their choices separately, the family members were asked to reach agreement on the solutions while talking in this network of switching dyads. Presumably, this more controversial discussion would bring out greater differences between the normal and abnormal groups.

Examining the results on the same measurements, the normal and abnormal families did not differ any more than they did in the neutral discussion. The abnormal father pushed buttons slightly more often than the normal father, while the mothers and children in the two groups pushed equally (see Table 4). One might expect that the abnormal mothers would become more intrusive when talking about family problems, but their intrusion rate dropped 1 percent. The abnormal fathers dropped from doing 48.84 percent of the pushing on the neutral questionnaire to 43.08 percent on the problem questionnaire, and the mothers increased their button pushing by 6 percent in the more controversial discussion.

These results do not support the supposed differences in the structure of normal and abnormal families. In both groups it is the father who manages the task and is most active, while the children in both groups come in second and the mothers third. If there is a structured hierarchy with dominant positions, it is not reversed in this sample of abnormal families.

A difficulty in the role theory view of dominance is that it often assumes a single hierarchy position for a family member and com-

TABLE 4

PROBLEM QUESTIONNAIRE

FAMILY TYPE	% OF BUTTON PUSHING BY FAMILY MEMBERS		
	Father	Mother	Child
Normal (N = 15)	41.40	28.81	29.79
Abnormal (N = 10)	43.08	28.72	28.20

	% EACH FAMILY MEMBER PUSHED BUTTON					
	Father Pushed Mother	Mother Pushed Father	Father Pushed Child	Child Pushed Father	Mother Pushed Child	Child Pushed Mother
Normal	21.65	14.76	19.75	14.75	14.05	15.04
Abnormal	24.20	13.09	18.87	13.81	15.65	14.39

	TOTAL % EACH FAMILY MEMBER INTRUDED		
	Father	Mother	Child
Normal	33.49	33.03	33.48
Abnormal	41.17	26.15	32.68
Child problem (N = 6)	37.83	29.73	32.44

	% EACH FAMILY MEMBER INTRUDED ON EACH OTHER					
	Father to		Mother to		Child to	
	Child	Mother	Child	Father	Mother	Father
Normal	14.42	19.07	11.63	21.40	18.60	14.88
Abnormal	13.72	27.45	8.50	17.65	22.88	9.80
Child problem	12.16	25.67	8.11	21.62	16.22	16.22

	TOTAL % EACH FAMILY MEMBER INVITED		
	Father	Mother	Child
Normal	43.90	26.83	29.27
Abnormal	43.58	29.54	26.88
Child problem	41.70	31.73	26.57

	% EACH FAMILY MEMBER INVITED ANOTHER					
	Father to		Mother to		Child to	
	Child	Mother	Child	Father	Mother	Father
Normal	21.76	22.14	14.82	12.01	14.07	15.20
Abnormal	21.06	22.52	17.43	12.11	12.35	14.53
Child problem	19.56	22.14	20.29	11.44	12.18	14.39

munication on a single level. For example, it does not include the possibility that a father can dominate a mother by being passive or by not doing what must be done so that she must do it. Dominance would seem to be a multilevel phenomenon, and the usual portrait of a hierarchy does not seem to portray the complex organizational processes in families. The study reported here tended to force the family to choose a manager by the nature of the communication structure, and the father took charge. Perhaps in other situations, particularly in family therapy where an outsider is intruding, different behavior is offered by the same families. For example, when a male therapist intervenes in a family, the father might step aside and be passive. The therapist could then easily conclude that this was typical of the abnormal family, and he would have no contrast group of normal families in the same situation for comparison.

PROCESS

The process point of view about families is most related to communication theory and emphasizes interaction, or the exchange of communicative acts between two or more family members. The unit of study from this view cannot be the individual, since it must be a process of exchange between at least two individuals. This process is multilevel and complex, since individuals communicate with more than one person at once and do so at multiple levels of body movement, vocal intonation, and words, all qualifying one another. In this study an attempt was made to reduce the complexity by forcing a conversation of only two people at once and blocking off communication by body movement. The data was examined largely in terms of the sequence of audible sounds and the sequence of button-pushing rather than the rich interchange which appears in conversational discourse.

In this view, the emphasis is not so much upon the structure of the family but upon the repeating acts interchanged by family members. There were several hypotheses examined in this area of family process.

1. *The interchange between the family members will follow patterns and not be random in nature.* Presumably, if families are organized, they must repeat certain behavior in patterned ways. This is one of the most basic questions in family research; before one can say that the patterns in two supposedly different families are different, one must first demonstrate that families follow patterns at all. This hypothesis was supported in this study, as well as in all the studies of this series. The behavior of family members in pushing buttons and speaking to each other differed significantly from a random distribution. (When one contrasts the voice order of the family members in the total group of families, it differs significantly from a random distribution of sounds. If all family members spoke randomly, as they would if they tossed a coin to determine who spoke and who spoke next, they would participate in equal pairs on an infinite

run. Taking equal participation in pairs, or random behavior, as the 0 point, randomness would be indicated by a fluctuation around 0. The total group of families deviated significantly from the 0 point; the standard deviation was 20.19. The critical ratio for the difference between the obtained mean and 0, the estimated mean of a random distribution, is 9.99. The p value for a critical ratio of this size is infinitesimally small. This might be because the hypothetical random distribution would be skewed rather than normal because it could not go below 0, but the difference is so great that it appears to support the hypothesis. The violation of the normal curve assumption here is to use a standard deviation which is too large.)

2. *The normal group of families will participate more equally in their activity together than will the abnormal group of families.* This hypothesis was derived from observation of abnormal families and from the idea that such families are more rigid in their organization. With three people in a conversation, it was assumed that the normal families would use a broader range of possible behavior than the abnormal families. When father, mother, and child were talking together, it was possible for each person to talk with either of the other two. The greatest use of the range of possibilities would be for each person to talk equally with each of the other two persons. If a family is restricted in range, one pair would talk together more than one of the other pairs; it was hypothesized that the abnormal families would follow this more restricted range. Clinical observation had indicated that in abnormal families the members do not participate equally but that two of the members tend to participate more and shut the third out of the conversation. A previous study in which parents and a child talked over this neutral questionnaire in the same room face to face showed striking differences between normal and abnormal families when a measurement was made of their speech participation in equal pairs (Haley, 1964). (In the previous study, the families were exposed to both the neutral questionnaire and three sets of TAT cards. Taking only their participation in the questionnaire discussion, the mean deviation from equal participation of the normal group was 21.85, with a standard deviation of 8.49. The two groups differed significantly at the .00003 level.)

In the study reported here, it was hypothesized that the differences between the two groups would increase with the separation of the family members during the conversation. The abnormal group was expected to participate more unequally whether one measured the order of speeches, the frequency of pushing buttons to choose each other to talk with, or the time each pair spent together. This hypothesis was not supported in the study; in fact, the two groups of families were remarkably similar on these measurements.

The calculation of equal participation in the conversation is based upon the use of a scale in which the zero point is achieved when all three family members speak after each other exactly the same number of times. Essentially this would be random behavior on an infinite run; it would be what three robots would do if each flipped a coin to determine who was to speak and then who was to speak next. Given father, mother, and child talking together, each can be followed by another, and so there are six possible categories. If they talked in equal pairs, each category would occur one-sixth of the time, or 16.66 percent. When one category is greater than 16.66 percent, and another is less, these deviations can be totalled (ignoring algebraic sign) to give the family an index score of deviation from equal participation. This is called an *R deviation* score in this study. For example, if a family deviated 1 percent from 16.66 percent in each category, they would receive an index score of 6.00 computed by totaling these deviations. The same method of computing a deviation from equal participation can be used when the measurement is frequency of pushing buttons to choose each other, or deviation from equal time together in pairs.

Examining the order of audible sounds made by the three family members as they talked together in this setting, the mean index score of deviation from equal participation by the 21 normal families was 27.52; for the abnormals it was 31.67. This difference is in the direction of the hypothesis, but it is not significant (standard deviation for the normal group is 18.32, and for the abnormal it is 21.46; $t = 0.69$). Mean index scores for the various measurements are presented below in Table 7 (p. 000).

It would seem possible that family members might not exchange an equal number of audible sounds, but each pair might spend an equal amount of time talking together. Taking equal time together in pairs as the zero point, the mean index of deviation from equal time in pairs by the normal group was 30.00, and for the abnormal group it was 30.70. This means that the pairs in the normal group of families did not spend more equal time together than those in the abnormal group.

A similar measure can be taken of the button-pressing activities of the family members. If each family member pressed each other member's call button an equal number of times, the family would be at the zero point in equality of button-pushing. Contrasting the normal and the abnormal groups, the normal families deviated from equal button-pushing by a mean score of 85.48. Once again, there was no more unequal participation in the abnormal families than there was in the normal group.

Since the lack of difference between the normal and abnormal families on these process measurements might be determined by the neutral nature of the discussion, a comparison can be made with the families talking about the problem questionnaire. Differences do not appear in this case, either; in fact, the families become more alike in their responses. In deviation from equal participation as measured by speech sequence, the index score for the normals was 23.88, and for the abnormals 24.90. The mean deviation from equal button-pushing by the normal families was 72.88, and by abnormal families it was 71.33. When we examined the deviation

from equal time in pairs, the normal score was 23.73 and the abnormal
was 25.12 (see Table 5). Whether talking about neutral matters or controversial material, the normal and abnormal families did not differ on these
measurements.

TABLE 5

PROBLEM QUESTIONNAIRE

TYPE OF FAMILY	MEAN INDEX SCORE OF DEVIATION FROM EQUAL PARTICIPATION*			
	N	Voice	Button	Time
Normal families	15	23.88	72.88	23.73
Abnormal families	10	24.90	71.33	25.12
Type of Abnormal Family				
Problem father	1	14.92	93.09	16.13
Problem mother	1	24.56	85.44	39.91
Absent problem sib.	1	12.36	65.69	15.11
Marriage or family problem	2	27.64	42.09	30.24
Mean non-child problems		21.42	65.68	26.33
Child's problem				
Behavior	1	14.16	56.36	12.25
Underachiever	1	34.50	77.78	36.89
Delinquent	2	34.45	94.20	29.46
Depression	1	24.28	46.43	16.97
Mean child problems		28.37	73.79	25.01

*A score of 0 would mean the three family members participated in exactly equal pairs. The
voice category refers to the sequence of speech of family members as they talked. The button
category refers to whether they chose each other equally to talk with. The time category refers
to whether all three pairs of the triad spent equal time talking together.

Since differences between three-person groups of normal and abnormal families were found when the families talked in the same room face to
face, but not when talking in switching dyads from separate rooms, it
seemed possible that the differences were minimized if the family members only talked in dyads. Perhaps differences would appear if family
members talked from separate rooms, but all could talk at once. In this
way the only restriction would be the elimination of communication by
body movement. A small sample was tried in this manner, with all family
members talking simultaneously about the neutral questionnaire. Seventeen normal and five abnormal families were tested; the small number of
abnormal families makes the contrast no more than suggestive. Again, it
was found that the two groups did not differ. In mean deviation from
equal speaking in pairs, the index score for the normal group was 24.27,
and for the abnormal group it was 20.17. Instead of participating more
unequally, the abnormal families participated more equally, although the

sample is too small to be representative. Comparison of the normal and abnormal groups in the switching dyad situations with both neutral and problem questionnaires, and in the open-channel situation, is offered in Table 6.

TABLE 6

PARTICIPATION IN EACH OF THREE MODES

		% SPEECHES OF EACH PAIR			Deviation from Equal Participation
	N	Father Mother	Father Child	Mother Child	
Neutral questionnaire					
Normal families	21	31.57	38.78	29.64	27.52
Abnormal families	25	39.40	35.88	24.72	31.67
Problem questionnaire					
Normal families	15	39.63	31.08	29.29	23.88
Abnormal families	10	38.99	33.31	27.70	24.90
Open channel					
Normal families	17	39.28	31.55	29.17	24.27
Abnormal families	5	39.01	33.78	27.21	20.17

OUTCOME

From this vantage point, families can be thought of as organizations which are more or less efficient: given a task, does a family accomplish it quickly with few trials and a minimum of excess activity? This way of looking at the family contains ideas derived from information theory; the group is conceived as a black box with a certain output, and there is a measurement of outcome; but what happened in the box to cause that outcome is only inferred. The questions involved passing bits of information while simultaneously minimizing noise and time for accomplishing acts.

The few positive findings in this study fall in the outcome category. Comparing the normal and abnormal families in terms of how they accomplish the task of reaching agreement on the questionnaire in this situation, the normal group takes less time, fewer speeches, and fewer button-pushings. When discussing either the neutral or the problem questionnaire, the abnormal families did more button-pushing, used more speeches, and took longer (see Table 7).

One might expect that with the problem questionnaire there would be more conflict and disagreement, reflected in increased button-pushing activity by the abnormal group compared with the normals. However, the reverse is the case. With the neutral questionnaire, the normals averaged 56.04 pushes to do the task, and the abnormals 74.00. With the problem questionnaire, the two groups were more alike; the normals pushed an average of 49.90, and the abnormals 51.40. In both cases, however, the abnormals took longer to do the task than the normals; the difference averaged nine minutes on the neutral questionnaire and eleven minutes on the problem questionnaire.

Clearly, the normal group does the task more efficiently. This point of view conceives the family as a working, task-oriented group, similar to a group of workers. Given these results, it might be inferred that the families in the normal group are better organized and have less conflict and disagreement, and that this is why they accomplish the task more quickly. However, it is also possible to infer that a family takes longer to reach agreement because the members "enjoy" the process of talking together. The outcome orientation does not tell us why families take longer, but only that they do.

TABLE 7

MEAN RESULTS ON QUESTIONNAIRES

	N	Mean No. Button Presses	Mean No. Speeches	Mean Time To Do Task
Neutral questionnaire				
Normal families	21	56.38	810.57	32.95
Abnormal families	25	74.04	906.80	41.16
Problem questionnaire				
Normal families	15	49.90	626.80	31.67
Abnormal families	10	51.40	726.10	42.00

A way to support the inference that the families who take longest to reach agreement are resolving more disagreements is to examine the correlation between agreement at the start of the task and time to complete the task. When the family members fill out the questionnaire individually in the beginning, they make choices of preferred solutions to the family problems posed, as well as solutions they would not like. One can compare these individual selections so that the amount of agreement in the family is measured before they start the family conversation. This "spontaneous agreement," as it has been termed by Ferreira, has been shown to be different for normal and abnormal families in previous studies with the neutral questionnaire (Ferreira, 1963a; Ferreira & Winter, 1965, 1966). In this study, with the problem questionnaire there is a similar finding; the abnormal families have less spontaneous agreement than the normal families (a difference significant at the .05 level), and the abnormal group also takes longer to finish the task (significant at the .05 level). Therefore, one might conclude that amount of agreement at the beginning of the task and time to complete the task are correlated. This possibility can be examined in more detail by listing the families in rank order by amount of spontaneous agreement, and examining the correlation with a rank ordering of the families in the time taken to do the task. For the total group of 25 families, the correlation between agreement and time is significant beyond the .01 level. For the two groups of families, the correlation for the abnormal group of ten families is significant at the .05 level, but for the 15 normal families there is no significant correlation.

A further breakdown is possible in this study because the amount of spontaneous agreement of each pair can be compared with the time they spent talking together. It should follow, for example, that if mother and father have chosen the most items in common, when they discuss the items they should spend the least time in conversation. If they disagreed on the most items, they should spend the most time together of any of the pairs, since they must resolve their disagreements. The results do not support this idea. There is no correlation between the pair that spends the most time or the least time talking together and the pair that has the most or the least disagreements. The results indicate that the amount of time the family members talk together in a decision-making task is related to whether they have individually agreed in their solutions prior to the conversation; but the time spent by any pair in the discussion is not related to the agreements with which they begin.

In summary, on the outcome measurements the normal and abnormal groups differ in the amount of agreement on the choices made individually, the amount of time to do the task, and the amount of activity necessary to complete the task. * * *

An Experimental and Clinical Study of
Family Decision-Making Processes*

Robert A. Ravich, Morton Deutsch, and Bert Brown

* * * This paper deals with an experimental technique for studying the interaction within families. The method employed has been adapted, not from individual psychology, but from social psychology. It is a means for studying the process of interaction between family dyads.

The method we have utilized is the two-person decision-making game developed by Deutsch and Krauss. The family members are all present in the same room, where they are presented with a road map (Figure 1) showing the start positions and destinations of two trucks, Acme and Bolt. Each truck has two routes that it may travel on. One is a main route, the other an alternate. The alternate routes are longer and by taking that path, the player will avoid any contact with the other truck, but will lose money because of the time required to complete the trip. The main route presents other problems. Specifically, one portion of the main route is a one-lane road that is common to both Acme and Bolt, but through which only one truck at a time can pass. In addition, on the main route there are two gates which can be used by each player to block the other if either or both of them decide to close their gates.

The subjects are told about the mechanics of the control panel by which they select and move their trucks. This panel also delivers certain messages telling the players when to start, where their own truck is on the selected route, when their trucks are in the head-on position on the main route, when the other player has closed his gate, and when they have completed their trip.

No specific set is given to the players as to how they should play the game. That is, they are not told whether they should compete or cooperate. They are told that both may gain money, both may lose money, or one may gain and the other lose. No restrictions are placed upon the communication between players. They can take as much time as they wish between trials to talk to each other, and are free to talk while playing.

---

*Excerpted from an unpublished paper presented before the American Orthopsychiatric Association in San Francisco in 1966, with permission of the senior author and the American Psychiatric Association.

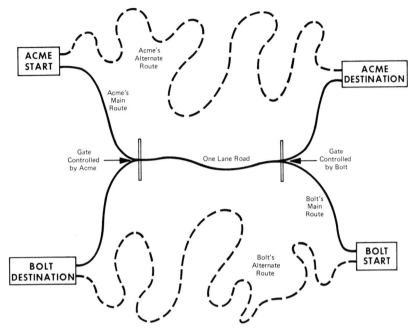

Legend: Map showing the roads at gates available to the two trucks, Acme and Bolt.

Fig. 1.

Profits and losses are based upon the time required to complete each trip, using a standard of 60 seconds. If the trip is completed in less than 60 seconds, the player gains one cent per second for each second less than 60. The fastest possible time is 35 seconds, so a maximum profit of 25 cents per trip for one player is possible. There is no limit to the loss that can be sustained if the game is played in a strict competitive way. The game is played 10 to 20 times, depending upon the number of members in the family.

We have extended our studies to whole families. If more than one child is involved, we first have the mother and father play together, then the mother plays the oldest child, after which the father plays the oldest child. Mother and second child, then father and second child play—and so forth down the line. Finally the children play each other. Because of the longer time required, each pair has 10 trials together. Again, no limit on communication is imposed.

In addition to profits and losses, we record the route taken, the number of times each one uses the gate, the time spent in the head-on position, and which player backs down how often from head-on encounters. The verbal exchange is tape-recorded.

Bibliography

Ackerman, N. W. *The psychodynamics of family life.* New York: Basic Books, 1958.

Anthony, E. G., & Bene, E. A technique for the objective assessment of the child's family relationships. *Journal of Mental Science*, 1957, *103*, 541–555.

Arnold, M. *Story sequence analysis.* New York: Columbia University Press, 1962.

Asch, S. E. Effects of group pressure upon modification and distortion of judgments. In E. E. Maccoby, T. M. Newcomb, & E. L. Hartley (Eds.), *Readings in social psychology.* New York: Holt, Rinehart & Winston, 1958. Pp. 174–183.

Astin, A. W. The functional autonomy of psychotherapy. *American Psychologist*, 1961, *16*, 75–78.

Baldwin, A. L., Kalhorn, J., & Breese, F. H. The appraisal of parent behavior. *Psychological Monographs*, 1949, *63*:4 (Whole No. 299), 1–85.

Baldwin, A. L., Kalhorn, J., & Huffman, M. H. Patterns of parent behavior. *Psychological Monographs*, 1945, *58*:3 (Whole No. 268), 1–175.

Bales, R. F. *Interaction process analysis: A method for the study of small groups.* Cambridge: Addison Wesley, 1950.

Bales, R. F., & Slater, P. E. Role differentiation in small decision-making groups. In T. Parsons & R. F. Bales (Eds.), *Family socialization and interaction process.* Glencoe, Ill.: Free Press, 1955. Chap. 5.

Bales, R. F., & Strodtbeck, F. L. Phases in group problem solving. *Journal of Abnormal and Social Psychology*, 1951, *46*, 485–495.

Ballantine, K. W. Sensitivity of alcoholic to parental censure. Unpublished Master's thesis, North Carolina State College, 1962.

Bandura, A. Social learning through imitation. In M. R. Jones (Ed.), *Nebraska symposium on motivation, 1962.* Lincoln: University of Nebraska Press, 1962. Pp. 211–269.

Barker, R. G., & Wright, N. F. *The midwest and its children.* Evanston, Ill.: Row, Peterson, 1954.

Bass, B. M. Authoritarianism or acquiescence? *Journal of Abnormal and Social Psychology*, 1955, *51*, 616–623.

Bateson, G., Jackson, D. D., Haley, J., & Weakland, J. H. Toward a theory of schizophrenia. *Behavioral Science*, 1956, *1*, 251–264.

Bateson, G., Jackson, D. D., Haley, J., & Weakland, J. H. A note on the double bind. *Family Process*, 1963, *2*, 154–161.

Baxter, J. C., & Arthur, S. C. Conflict in families of schizophrenics as a function of premorbid adjustment and social class. *Family Process*, 1964, *3*, 273–279.

Baxter, J. C., Arthur, S. C., Flood, C. G., & Hedgepeth, B. Conflict patterns in the families of schizophrenics. *Journal of Nervous and Mental Disease*, 1962, *135*, 419–424.

Beavers, W. R., Blumberg, S., Timken, K. R., & Weiner, M. F. Communication patterns of mothers of schizophrenics. *Family Process*, 1965, *4*, 95–104.

Becker, J., & McArdle, J. Nonlexical speech similarities as an index of intrafamilial identifications. *Journal of Abnormal Psychology*, 1967, *72*, 408–418.

Becker, J., & Siefkes, H. Parental dominance conflict, and disciplinary coerciveness in families of female schizophrenics. *Journal of Abnormal Psychology*, in press.

Becker, J., Tatsuoka, M., & Carlson, A. The communicative value of parental speech in families with disturbed children. *Journal of Nervous and Mental Disease*, 1965, *141*, 359–364.

Becker, W. C. The process-reactive distinction: A key to the problem of schizophrenia? *Journal of Nervous and Mental Disease*, 1959, *129*, 442–449.

Becker, W. C., & Krug, R. S. A circumflex model for social behavior in children. *Child Development*, 1964, *35*, 371–396.

Becker, W. C., Peterson, D. R., Hellmer, L. A., Shoemaker, D. F., & Quay, H. C. Factors in parental behavior and personality as related to problem behavior in children. *Journal of Consulting Psychology*, 1959, *23*, 107–118.

Behrens, M. L., & Goldfarb, W. A. A study of patterns of interaction of families of schizophrenic children in residential treatment. *American Journal of Orthopsychiatry*, 1958, *28*, 300–312.

Bell, J. E. *Family group therapy.* Public Health Monograph, No. 64. Washington, D. C.: Department of Health, Education, and Welfare, 1961.

Bell, J. E. Recent advances in family group therapy. *Journal of Child Psychology and Psychiatry*, 1962, *2*, 1–15.

Bellak, L. *Children's Apperception Test.* (2nd ed. rev.) Melbourne: The Australian Council for Educational Research, 1950.

Bender, L. Twenty years of clinical research on schizophrenic children, with special reference to those under six years of age. In G. Caplan

(Ed.), *Emotional problems of early child-hood*. New York: Basic Books, 1955. Pp. 503—515.

Bender, L., & Grugett, A. E., Jr. A study of certain epidemiological factors in a group of children with childhood schizophrenia. *American Journal of Orthopsychiatry*, 1956, *26*, 131—145.

Bene, E. The objective use of a projective technique. *British Journal of Educational Psychology*, 1957, *27*, 89—100.

Benjamin, J. D. Prediction and psychopathology in childhood. In L. Jessner & E. Pavenstedt (Eds.), *Dynamics of psychopathology in childhood*. New York: Grune & Stratton, 1959. Pp. 6—77.

Beveridge, W. I. B. *The art of scientific investigation*. New York: Random House, 1957.

Bishop, Barbara M. Mother-child interaction and the social behavior of children. *Psychological Monographs*, 1951, *65*:11 (Whole No. 328), 1—73.

Blood, R. O. The use of observational methods in family research. *Marriage and Family Living*, 1958, *20*, 47—52.

Borgatta, E. F. The analysis of patterns of social interaction. *Social Forces*, 1965, *44*, 27—34.

Bowen, M. Family psychotherapy. *American Journal of Orthopsychiatry*, 1961, *31*, 40—60.

Bronfenbrenner, U. Socialization and social class through time and space. In E. Maccoby, T. M. Newcomb, & E. L. Hartley (Eds.), *Readings in social psychology*. New York: Henry Holt & Company, 1958. Pp. 400—425.

Bronfenbrenner, U. The study of identification through interpersonal perception. In R. Tagiuri & L. Petrullo (Eds.), *Person perception and interpersonal behavior*. Stanford: Stanford University Press, 1958.

Bruner, J. S. The course of cognitive growth. *American Psychologist*, 1964, *19*, 1—15.

Caputo, D. V. The parents of the schizophrenic. *Family Process*, 1963, *2*, 339—356.

Cass, L. K. Parent-child relationships and delinquency. *Journal of Abnormal and Social Psychology*, 1952, *47*, 101—104.

Chapple, E. D. Measuring human relations: An introduction to the study of interaction of individuals. *Genetic Psychology Monographs*, 1940, *22*, 3—147.

Cheek, F. E. *Family interaction with schizophrenics*. New York: Columbia University Press, 1962.

Cheek, F. E. Exploratory study of drugs and social interaction. *Archives of General Psychiatry*, 1963, *9*, 566—574.

Cheek, F. E. The "schizophrenogenic mother" in word and deed. *Family Process*, 1964, *3*, 155—177. (a)

Cheek, F. E. A serendipitous finding: Sex roles and schizophrenia. *Journal of Abnormal and Social Psychology*, 1964, *69*, 392—400. (b)

Cheek, F. E. Family interaction patterns and convalescent adjustment of the schizophrenic. *Archives of General Psychiatry*, 1965, *13*, 138—147. (a)

Cheek, F. E. The father of the schizophrenic, the function of a peripheral role. *Archives of General Psychiatry*, 1965, *13*, 336—345. (b)

Cicchetti, D. V. Reported family dynamics and psychopathology: I. The reactions of schizophrenics and normals to parental dialogues. *Journal of Abnormal Psychology*, 1967, *72*, 282—289.

Cicchetti, D. V., & Farina, A. Relationship between reported and observed dominance and conflict among parents of schizophrenics. *Journal of Consulting Psychology*, 1967, *31*, 223.

Cicchetti, D. V., Klein, E. B., Fontana, A. F., & Spohn, H. E. The test of the censure-deficit model in schizophrenia, employing the Rodnick-Garmezy visual-discrimination task. *Journal of Abnormal Psychology*, 1967, *72*, 326—334.

Cicchetti, D. V., & Ornston, P. S. Reported family dynamics and psychopathology: II. The reactions of mental patients to a disturbed family in psychotherapy. *Journal of Abnormal Psychology*. 1968, *73*, 156—161.

Cheek, F. E. The father of the schizophrenic, the function of a peripheral role. *Archives of General Psychiatry*, 1965, *13*, 336—345. (b)

Clausen, J. A., & Yarrow, M. R. Mental illness and the family. *Journal of Social Issues*, 1955, *11*, 3—65.

Cochran, W. G. Some methods of strengthening the common X^2-tests. *Biometrics*, 1954, *10*, 417—451.

Cowen, E. L., & Tongas, P. The social desirability of trait descriptive terms: Applications to a self-concept inventory. *Journal of Consulting Psychology*, 1959, *23*, 361—365.

Dailey, C. A. The effects of premature conclusion upon the acquisition of understanding of a person. *Journal of Psychology*, 1952, *33*, 133—152.

Despert, J. L. Prophylactic aspect of schizophrenia in childhood. *Nervous Child*, 1942, *1*, 199—231.

Despert, J. L. Some considerations relating to the genesis of autistic behavior in children. *American Journal of Orthopsychiatry*, 1951, *21*, 335—350.

Drechsler, R. J., & Shapiro, M. Two methods of analysis of family diagnostic data. *Family Process*, 1963, *2*, 367—370.

Dunbar, F. Effect of the mother's emotional attitude on the infant. *Psychosomatic Medicine*, 1944, *6*, 156—159.

Dunham, R. M. Sensitivity of schizophrenics to parental censure. Unpublished Ph.D. dissertation, Duke University, 1959.

Dunham, R. *Ex post facto* reconstruction of conditioning schedules in family interaction. In I. M. Cohen (Ed.), *Family structure, dy-*

namics, and therapy, Psychiatric research reports of the American Psychiatric Association, No. 20, 1966. Pp. 107–114.

Edwards, A. L. *The social desirability variable in personality assessment and research*. New York: Dryden, 1957.

Ellison, E. A., & Hamilton, D. M. The hospital treatment of dementia praecox: Part II. *American Journal of Psychiatry*, 1949, *106*, 454–461.

English, H. B., & English, A. C. *A comprehensive dictionary of psychological and psychoanalytical terms*. London: Longmans Green, 1958.

Epstein, S. Comments on Dr. Bandura's paper. In M. R. Jones (Ed.), *Nebraska symposium on motivation, 1962*. Lincoln: University of Nebraska Press, 1962. Pp. 269–273.

Erikson, E. H. *Childhood and society*. New York: Norton, 1950.

Eysenck, H. J. The effects of psychotherapy: An evaluation. *Journal of Consulting Psychology*, 1952, *16*, 319–324.

Eysenck, H. J. (Ed.). *Handbook of abnormal psychology: An experimental approach*. New York: Basic Books, 1961.

Farber, B., & Jenne, W. C. Family organization and parent-child communication: Parents and siblings of a retarded child. *Monograph on Social Research and Child Development*, 1963, *28*, 3–78.

Farina, A. Patterns of role dominance and conflict in parents of schizophrenic patients. *Journal of Abnormal and Social Psychology*, 1960, *61*, 31–38.

Farina, A., & Dunham, R. M. Measurement of family relationships and their effects. *Archives of General Psychiatry*, 1963, *9*, 64–73.

Ferguson, J. T., McReynolds, P., & Ballachy, E. L. *Hospital adjustment scale*. Stanford: Stanford University Press, 1953.

Ferreira, A. J. The "double-bind" and delinquent behavior. *Archives of General Psychiatry*, 1960, *3*, 359–367. (a)

Ferreira, A. J. The semantics and the context of the schizophrenic's language. *Archives of General Psychiatry*, 1960, *3*, 128–138. (b)

Ferreira, A. J. Empathy and the bridge-function of the ego. *Journal of the American Psychoanalytic Association*, 1961, *99*, 91–105.

Ferreira, A. J. Decision-making in normal and pathological families. *Archives of General Psychiatry*, 1963, *8*, 68–73. (a)

Ferreira, A. J. Rejection and expectancy of rejection in families. *Family Process*, 1963, *2*, 235–244. (b)

Ferreira, A. J. Interpersonal perceptivity among family members. *American Journal of Orthopsychiatry*, 1964, *34*, 64–70. (a)

Ferreira, A. J. On silence. *American Journal of Psychotherapy*, 1964, *18*, 109–114. (b)

Ferreira, A. J., & Winter, W. D. Family interaction and decision-making. *Archives of General Psychiatry*, 1965, *13*, 214–223.

Ferreira, A. J., & Winter, W. D. Stability of interactional variables in family decision-making. *Archives of General Psychiatry*, 1966, *14*, 352–355.

Ferreira, A. J., & Winter, W. D. Decision-making in normal and abnormal two-child families. *Family Process*, 1968, *7*, 17–36.

Ferreira, A. J., Winter, W. D., & Poindexter, E. Some interactional variables in normal and abnormal families. *Family Process*, 1966, *5*, 60–75.

Fisher, S., Boyd, I., Walker, D., & Sheer, D. Parents of schizophrenics, neurotics, and normals. *Archives of General Psychiatry*, 1959, *1*, 149–166.

Fisher, S., & Mendell, D. The communication of neurotic patterns over two and three generations. *Psychiatry*, 1956, *19*, 41–46.

Flint, A. A., & Ryder, R. G. Interpersonal disagreements in marriage: The stereognosis test. Paper delivered at the Annual Meeting of the American Psychiatric Association, 1963.

Flugel, J. C. *The psychoanalytic study of the family*. London: Hogarth Press, 1948.

Foa, U. G. Empathy or behavioral transparency? *Journal of Abnormal and Social Psychology*, 1958, *56*, 62–66.

Foulds, G. A. The reliability of psychiatric and the validity of psychological diagnoses. *Journal of Mental Science*, 1955, *101*, 851–862.

Frank, G. H. The role of the family in the development of psychopathology. *Psychological Bulletin*, 1965, *64*, 191–205.

Franks, C. M. (Ed.). *Conditioning techniques in clinical practice and research*. New York: Springer, 1964.

Garmezy, N., Clarke, A. R., & Stockner, C. Child-rearing attitudes of mothers and fathers as reported by schizophrenic and normal patients. *Journal of Abnormal and Social Psychology*, 1961, *63*, 176–182.

Garmezy, N., & Rodnick, E. H. Premorbid adjustment and performance in schizophrenia: Implications for interpreting heterogeneity in schizophrenia. *Journal of Nervous and Mental Disease*, 1959, *129*, 450–466.

Geismar, L. L., & Ayres, B. A method for evaluating the social functioning of families under treatment. *Social Worker*, 1959, *4*, 102–108.

Geismar, L. L., & Ayres, B. *Measuring family functioning*. St. Paul: Family Centered Project, 1960.

Geismar, L. L., LaSorte, M., & Ayres, B. Measuring family disorganization. *Marriage and Family Living*, 1962, *24*, 52–56.

Gerard, D. L., & Siegel, J. The family background of schizophrenia. *Psychiatric Quarterly*, 1950, *24*, 47–73.

Glueck, S., & Glueck, E. *Unraveling juvenile delinquency*. Cambridge: Harvard University Press, 1950.

Goffman, E. *Asylums*. New York: Anchor Books, 1961.

Goldman-Eisler, F. Speech analysis and mental processes. *Language and Speech*, 1958, 1, 59–75.

Goldstein, A. P., & Carr, A. C. The attitudes of the mothers of male catatonic and paranoid schizophrenics toward child behavior. *Journal of Consulting Psychology*, 1957, 20, 185–190.

Goodrich, D. W., & Boomer, D. S. Experimental assessment of modes of conflict resolution. *Family Process*, 1963, 2, 15–24.

Gordon, J. E. The validity of Shoben's Parent Attitude Survey. *Journal of Clinical Psychology*, 1957, 13, 154–156.

Gottschalk, L., Gleser, G., & Springer, K. Three hostility scales applicable to verbal samples. *Archives of General Psychiatry*, 1963, 9, 254–279.

Greenbaum, W. Influence of certain maternal attitudes on the behavior of rejected children. Unpublished Ph.D. dissertation, University of Florida, 1954.

Hafner, J., & Kaplan, A. Hostility content analysis of the Rorschach and TAT. *Journal of Projective Techniques and Personality Assessment*, 1960, 24, 137–144.

Haggard, E. A., Brekstad, A., & Skard, A. On the reliability of the anamnestic interview. *Journal of Abnormal and Social Psychology*, 1960, 61, 311–318.

Haley, J. Family Experiments: A new type of experimentation. *Family Process*, 1962, 1, 265–293.

Haley, J. Research on family patterns: An instrument measurement. *Family Process*, 1964, 3, 41–65.

Haley, J. Speech sequences of normal and abnormal families with two children present. *Family Process*, 1967, 6, 81–97.

Hamblin, R. L. Group integration during a crisis. *Human Relations*, 1958, 11, 57–76. (a)

Hamblin, R. L. Leadership and crisis. *Sociometry*, 1958, 21, 322–325. (b)

Handel, G. Psychological study of whole families. *Psychological Bulletin*, 1965, 63, 19–41.

Harris, J. G. Validity: The search for a constant in a universe of variables. In M. Rickers-Ovsiankina (Ed.), *Rorschach psychology*. New York: Wiley, 1960. Pp. 380–439.

Hartwell, S. W., Hutt, M. L., Andrew, G., & Walton, R. E. *The Michigan Picture Test*. Chicago: Science Research Associates, 1953.

Haskell, R. Relationship between aggresive behavior and psychological tests. *Journal of Projective Techniques and Personality Assessment*, 1961, 25, 431–440.

Heilbrun, A. B. Perception of maternal child-rearing attitudes in schizophrenia. *Journal of Consulting Psychology*, 1960, 24, 169–173.

Heinicke, C., & Bales, R. F. Developmental trends in the structure of small groups. *Sociometry*, 153, 16, 7–39.

Helper, M. M. Learning theory and the self-concept. *Journal of Abnormal and Social Psychology*, 1955, 51, 184–194.

Herbst, P. G. Family living-patterns of interaction. In O. A. Oeser & S. B. Hammond (Eds.), *Social structure and personality in a city*. New York: Macmillan, 1954. Chap. 12.

Herron, W. G. The process-reactive classification of schizophrenia. *Psychological Bulletin*, 1962, 59, 329–343.

Hetherington, E. M. A developmental study of the effects of sex of the dominant parent on sex-role preference, identification, and imitation in children. *Journal of Personality and Social Psychology*, 1965, 2, 188–194.

Hoffman, L. W., & Lippitt, R. The measurement of family life variables. In P. H. Mussen (Ed.), *Handbook of research methods in child development*. New York: Wiley, 1960. Pp. 945–1015.

Hollingshead, A. B. *Two-factor index of social position*. New Haven: Yale University Press, 1957.

Hollingshead, A. B., & Redlich, F. C. *Social class and mental illness: A community study*. New York: Wiley, 1958.

Hovey, H. B. The questionable validity of some assumed antecedents of mental illness. *Journal of Clinical Psychology*, 1959, 15, 270–272.

Howells, J. G., & Lickorish, J. R. *Family Relations Indicator*. Edinburgh: Oliver & Boyd, 1968.

Inkeles, A. Industrial man: The relation of status to experience, perception, and value. *American Journal of Sociology*, 1960, 66, 1–31.

Jackson, D. D. The question of familial homeostasis. *Psychiatric Quarterly* (Suppl.), 1957, 31, 79–90.

Jackson, D. D. Family interaction, family homeostasis and some implications for conjoint family psychotherapy. In J. H. Masserman (Ed.), *Science and psychoanalysis: Individual and familial dynamics*. Vol. II. New York: Grune & Stratton, 1959.

Jackson, D. D., Block, J., Block, J., & Patterson, V. Psychiatrists' conceptions of the schizophrenogenic parent. *Archives of Neurology and Psychiatry*, 1958, 79, 448–459.

Jackson, D. D., & Weakland, J. Conjoint family therapy: Some considerations on theory, technique, and results. *Psychiatry*, 1961, 24, 30–45.

Jackson, L. Emotional attitudes towards the family of normal, neurotic, and delinquent children. *British Journal of Psychology*, 1950, 41, 35–51.

Jackson, W., & Carr, A. C. Empathic ability in normals and schizophrenics. *Journal of Abnormal and Social Psychology*, 1955, 51, 79–82.

Jayaswal, S. R., & Stott, L. H. Persistence and change in personality from childhood to adulthood. *Merrill-Palmer Quarterly*, 1955, 1, 47–56.

Kagan, J. The concept of identification. *Psychological Review*, 1958, *65*, 296–305.

Kagan, J. Acquisition and significance of sex typing and sex role identity. In M. L. Hoffman & L. W. Hoffman (Eds.), *Review of child development research*. New York: Russel Sage, 1964. Pp. 137–169.

Kasanin, J., Knight, E., & Sage, P. The parent-child relationship in schizophrenia: I. Overprotection-rejection. *Journal of Nervous and Mental Disease*, 1934, *72*, 249–263.

Katz, M. Agreement on connotative meaning in marriage. *Family Process*, 1965, *4*, 64–74.

Kendall, M. G. *Rank correlation methods*. London: Hafner, 1948.

Kenkel, W. F. Influence differentiation in family decision making. *Sociological and Social Research*, 1957, *42*, 18–25.

Kohn, M. L., & Carroll, E. E. Social class and the allocation of parental responsibilities. *Sociometry*, 1960, *23*, 372–392.

Kohn, M. L., & Clausen, J. A. Parental authority behavior and schizophrenia. *American Journal of Orthopsychiatry*, 1956, *26*, 297–313.

Koos, E. L. *Families in trouble*. Morningside Heights, N.Y.: King's Crown, 1946.

Korkes, L. The impact of mentally ill children upon their families. Unpublished Ph.D. dissertation, New York University, 1959.

Kreinik, P. S. Parent-child themes and concept attainment in schizophrenics. Unpublished Ph.D. dissertation, Duke University, 1959.

Kreitman, N., Sainsbury, P., Morrissey, J., Towers, J., & Scrivener, J. The reliability of psychiatric assessment: An analysis. *Journal of Mental Science*, 1961, *107*, 887–908.

Leary, T. *The Interpersonal Check List*. Berkeley, Calif.: Psychological Consulting Service, n.d.

Leik, R. Instrumentality and emotionality in family interaction. *Sociometry*, 1963, *26*, 131–145.

Lennard, H. L., Beaulieu, M. R., & Embrey, N. S. Interaction in families with a schizophrenic child. *Archives of General Psychiatry*, 1965, *12*, 166–183.

Lerner, P. M. Resolution of intrafamilial conflict in families of schizophrenic patients. I. Thought disturbance. *Journal of Nervous and Mental Disease*, 1965, *141*, 342–351.

Leton, D. A. A study of the validity of parent attitude scales. *Child Development*, 1958, *29*, 507–514.

Levin, G., & Schutz, W. C. A complex relationship between imagination and communication clarity in a pathological and control sample. Paper presented at the Annual Meeting of the Eastern Psychological Association, Atlantic City, 1965.

Levin, H., & Sears, R. R. Identification with parents as a determinant of doll play aggression. *Child Development*, 1956, *27*, 135–154.

Levinger, G. Supplementary methods in family research. *Family Process*, 1963, *2*, 357–366.

Levy, J., & Epstein, N. An application of the Rorschach Test in family investigation. *Family Process*, 1964, *3*, 344–376.

Lewin, K. Behavior and development as a function of the total situation. In L. Carmichael (Ed.), *Manual of child psychology*. New York: Wiley, 1946. Pp. 791–844.

Lidz, T. *The family and human adaptation*. New York: International Universities Press, 1963.

Lidz, T., Cornelison, A. R., Fleck, S., & Terry, D. The intrafamilial environment of the schizophrenic patient. *Psychiatry*, 1957, *20*, 329–342. (a)

Lidz, T., Cornelison, A. R., Fleck, S., & Terry, D. The intrafamilial environment of schizophrenic patients. II. Marital schism and marital skew. *American Journal of Psychiatry*, 1957, *114*, 241–248. (b)

Lidz, T., & Fleck, S. Schizophrenia, human integration, and the role of the family. In D. D. Jackson (Ed.), *The etiology of schizophrenia*. New York: Basic Books, 1960.

Lidz, T., Fleck, S., Alanen, Y. O., & Cornelison, A. R. Schizophrenic patients and their siblings. *Psychiatry*, 1963, *26*, 1–18.

Lindquist, E. F. *Design and analysis of experiments in psychology and education*. Boston: Houghton Mifflin, 1953.

Loveland, N. T. The Relation Rorschach: A technique for studying interaction. *Journal of Nervous and Mental Disease*, 1967, *145*, 93–105.

Loveland, N. T., Wynne, L. C., & Singer, M. T. The family Rorschach: A new method for studying family interaction. *Family Process*, 1963, *2*, 187–215.

Lubin, B., Levitt, E. E., & Zuckerman, M. Some personality differences between responders and non-responders to a survey questionnaire. *Journal of Consulting Psychology*, 1962, *26*, 192.

McClelland, D. C., de Charms, R., & Rindlisbacher, A. Religious and other sources of parental attitudes toward independence training. In D. McClelland (Ed.), *Studies in motivation*. New York: Appleton-Century-Crofts, 1955. Pp. 389–397.

McCord, W., & McCord, J. *Psychotherapy and delinquency*. New York: Grune & Stratton, 1956.

McCord, W., Porta, J., & McCord, J. The familial genesis of psychosis. *Psychiatry*, 1962, *25*, 60–71.

McGraw, M. B., & Molloy, L. B. The pediatric anamnesis: Inaccuracies in eliciting developmental data. *Child Development*, 1941, *12*, 255–265.

McKeown, J. E. The behavior of parents of schizophrenic, neurotic, and normal children. *American Journal of Sociology*, 1950, *56*, 175–179.

McNemar, A. *Psychological statistics.* New York: Wiley, 1962.

Madow, L., & Hardy, S. E. Incidence and analysis of the broken family in the background of neurosis. *American Journal of Orthopsychiatry*, 1947, *17*, 521–528.

Mahl, G. F. Exploring emotional states by content analysis. In I. D. S. Pool (Ed.), *Trends in content analysis.* Urbana: University of Illinois Press, 1959.

Matarazzo, J. D., Hess, H. F., & Saslow, G. Frequency and duration characteristics of speech and silence behavior during interviews. *Journal of Clinical Psychology*, 1962, *18*, 416–426.

Matarazzo, J. D., Saslow, G., & Matarazzo, R. G. The interaction chronograph as an instrument for objective measurement of interaction patterns during interviews. *Journal of Psychology*, 1956, *41*, 347–367.

Matarazzo, R. G., Matarazzo, J. D., Saslow, G., & Phillips, J. S. Psychological test and organismic correlates of interview interaction patterns. *Journal of Abnormal and Social Psychology*, 1958, *56*, 329–339.

Meehl, P. E. *Clinical versus statistical prediction.* Minneapolis: University of Minnesota Press, 1954.

Meissner, W. W. Thinking about the family psychiatric aspects. *Family Process*, 1964, *3*, 1–40.

Meyers, D. F., & Goldfarb, W. Studies of perplexity in mothers of schizophrenic children. *American Journal of Orthopsychiatry*, 1961, *31*, 551–564.

Mishler, E., & Waxler, N. Family interaction and schizophrenia. *Archives of General Psychiatry*, 1966, *15*, 64–74.

Mishler, E., & Waxler, N. *Interaction in families.* New York: Wiley, 1968.

Miller, Daniel R., & Swanson, Guy E. *Inner conflict and defense.* New York: Holt, Rinehart & Winston, 1960.

Miller, G. A. *Language and communication.* New York: McGraw-Hill, 1951.

Mills, T. M. Power relations in three-person groups. In D. Cartwright & A. Zander (Eds.), *Group dynamics: Research and theory.* Evanston, Ill.: Row, Peterson, 1960. Chap. 40.

Morris, G. E., & Wynne, L. C. Schizophrenic offspring and parental styles of communication. *Psychiatry*, 1965, *28*, 19–44.

Morris, W. W., & Nicholas, A. L. Intrafamilial personality configuration among children with primary behavior disorders and their parents. *Journal of Clinical Psychology*, 1950, *6*, 309–319.

Mottola, W. C. Family therapy: A review. *Psychotherapy*, 1967, *4*, 116–124.

Moustakas, C. E., Siegel, I. E., & Schalock, H. D. An objective method for the measurement and analysis of child-adult interaction. *Child Development*, 1956, *27*, 109–134.

Mowrer, H. O. *Learning theory and personality dynamics.* New York: Ronald Press, 1950.

Murrell, S. A., & Stachowiak, J. G. The family group: Development, structure, and therapy. *Journal of Marriage and Family Living*, 1965, *27*, 13–19.

Newcomb, T. M. The cognition of persons as cognizers. In R. Tajiuri & L. Petrullo (Eds.), *Person perception and interpersonal behavior.* Stanford: Stanford University Press, 1958.

Nuffield, E. J. A. The schizophrenic mother. *Medical Journal of Australia*, 1954, *2*, 283–386.

Olden, C. Notes on the development of empathy. In R. Eissler (Ed.), *Psychoanalytic study of the child.* New York: International Universities Press, 1958. Pp. 505–518.

Olson, J. Differentiation of clinical and normal families via thematic apperception test analysis. Unpublished Master's thesis, San Jose State College, 1964.

Oltman, J. E., McGarry, J. J., & Friedman, S. Parental deprivation and the "broken home" in dementia praecox and other mental disorders. *American Journal of Psychiatry*, 1952, *108*, 685–694.

O'Neal, P., & Robins, L. N. Childhood patterns predictive of adult schizophrenia: A thirty-year follow-up study. *American Journal of Psychiatry*, 1958, *115*, 385–391.

Parsons, T. Family structure and the socialization of the child. In T. Parsons & R. F. Bales (Eds.), *Family, socialization and interaction process.* Glencoe, Ill.: Free Press, 1955. Ch. 2.

Parsons, T., & Bales, R. F. *The social system.* Glencoe, Ill.: Free Press, 1951.

Parsons, T., & Bales, R. F. (Eds.). *Family, socialization and interaction process.* Glencoe, Ill.: Free Press, 1955.

Parsons, T., Bales, R. F., & Shils, E. A. *Working papers in the theory of action.* Glencoe, Ill.: Free Press, 1953.

Phillips, J. S., Matarazzo, R. G., Matarazzo, J. D., & Saslow, G. Relationship between descriptive content and interaction behavior in interviews. *Journal of Consulting Psychology*, 1957, *25*, 260–266.

Phillips, L. Case history data and prognosis in schizophrenia. *Journal of Nervous and Mental Disease*, 1953, *117*, 515–525.

Phillipson, H. *The object relations technique.* London: Tavistock Publications, 1955.

Pittluck, P. The relationship between aggressive fantasy and overt behavior. Unpublished Ph.D. dissertation, Yale University, 1950.

Prout, C. T., & White, M. A. A controlled study of personality relationships in mothers of schizophrenic male patients. *American Journal of Psychiatry*, 1950, *107*, 251–256.

Pyles, M. K., Stolz, H. R., & Macfarlane, J. W. The accuracy of mothers' reports on birth and developmental data. *Child Development*, 1935, *6*, 165–176.

Rabkin, L. Y. The disturbed child's perception of parental attributes. Unpublished Ph.D. dissertation, University of Rochester, 1962.

Rabkin, L. Y. The disturbed child's perception of his parents. *Journal of Individual Psychology*, 1964, *20*, 172–178.

Rabkin, L. Y. The patient's family: Research methods. *Family Process*, 1965, *4*, 105–132.

Rakoff, V., Sanders, S., & Sigal, J. Perception of parental voices by emotionally disturbed children. *Abstracts of the Proceedings of the American Psychiatric Association*, 1968.

Redl, F. The psychology of gang formation and the treatment of juvenile delinquents. In O. Fenichel, *et al.* (Eds.), *The psychoanalytic study of the child*. Vol. I. New York: International Universities Press, 1945. Pp. 367–377.

Reichard, S., & Tillman, J. Patterns of parent-child relationships in schizophrenia. *Psychiatry*, 1950, *13*, 247–257.

Reiss, D. Individual thinking and family interaction. *Archives of General Psychiatry*, 1967, *16*, 80–93.

Riessman, Frank. *The culturally deprived child*. New York: Harper & Row, 1962.

Robbins, L. C. The accuracy of parental recall of aspects of child development and of child rearing practices. *Journal of Abnormal and Social Psychology*, 1963, *66*, 261–270.

Rodnick, E. H., & Garmezy, N. An experimental approach to the study of motivation in schizophrenia. In M. R. Jones (Ed.), *Nebraska symposium on motivation, 1957*. Lincoln: University of Nebraska Press, 1957. Pp. 109–184.

Roman, M., & Bauman, G. Interaction testing: A technique for the psychological evaluation of small groups. In M. Harrower, *et al.* (Eds.), *Creative variations in the projective techniques*. New York: Charles C Thomas, 1960.

Rosenthal, A., Behrens, M., & Chodoff, P. Communication in lower-class families of schizophrenics. *Archives of General Psychiatry*, 1968, *18*, 464–470.

Rosenzweig, S., & Rosenzweig, L. *The children's form of the Rosenzweig Picture-Frustration Study*. St. Louis: 1948.

Ruesch, J. *Disturbed communication*. New York: Norton, 1957.

Ruesch, J. Synopsis of the theory of human communication. *Psychiatry*, 1958, *16*, 215–243.

Ruesch, J., & Bateson, G. *Communication: The social matrix of psychiatry*. New York: Norton, 1951.

Ryler, R. Two replications of color matching factors. *Family Process*, 1966, *5*, 43–48.

Sanua, V. D. Sociocultural factors in families of schizophrenics. *Psychiatry*, 1961, *24*, 246–265.

Sanua, V. D. The sociocultural aspects of schizophrenia: A comparison of Protestant and Jewish schizophrenics. *International Journal of Social Psychiatry*, 1963, *9*, 27–36.

Saslow, G., & Matarazzo, J. D. A technique for studying changes in interview behavior. In E. A. Rubenstein & M. B. Parloff (Eds.), *Research in psychotherapy*. Washington, D. C.: American Psychological Association, 1959. Pp. 125–159.

Satir, V. *Conjoint family therapy*. Palo Alto: Science and Behavior Books, 1964.

Schachter, S. *The psychology of affiliation*. Stanford: Stanford University Press, 1959.

Schaeffer, E. S., & Bell, R. Q. Development of a parental attitude research instrument. *Child Development*, 1958, *29*, 339–361.

Schafer, R. *Psychoanalytic interpretation in Rorschach testing*. New York: Grune & Stratton, 1954.

Schooler, C. Birth order and schizophrenia. *Archives of General Psychiatry*, 1961, *4*, 117–123.

Schooler, C. Birth order and hospitalization for schizophrenia. *Journal of Abnormal and Social Psychology*, 1964, *69*, 574–579.

Schooler, C., & Long, J. Affiliation among chronic schizophrenics: Factors affecting acceptance of responsibility for the fate of another. *Journal of Nervous and Mental Disease*, 1963, *137*, 173–179.

Schooler, C., & Scarr, S. Affiliation among chronic schizophrenics: Relation to intrapersonal and birth order factors. *Journal of Personality*, 1962, *30*, 178–192.

Schreiber, F. R. The psychological factors affecting the development of speech in the early years. In D. A. Barbara (Ed.), *Psychological and psychiatric aspects of speech and hearing*. Springfield, Ill.: Charles C Thomas, 1960. Pp. 42–69.

Schulman, R. E., Shoemaker, D. J., & Moelis, I. Laboratory measurement of parental behavior. *Journal of Consulting Psychology*, 1962, *26*, 109–114.

Schutz, W. C. *The school administrator*. To be published.

Selltiz, C., Jahoda, M., Deutsch, M., & Cook, S. W. *Research methods in social relations*. (Rev. ed.) New York: Holt, Rinehart, & Winston, 1959.

Shoben, E. J., Jr. The assessment of parental attitudes in relation to child adjustment. *Genetic Psychology Monographs*, 1949, *39*, 101–148.

Siegel, S. *Nonparametric statistics for the behavioral sciences*. New York: McGraw-Hill, 1956.

Singer, J. L. Projected familial attitudes as a function of socioeconomic status and psychopathology. *Journal of Consulting Psychology*, 1954, *18*, 99–104.

Singer, M. T., & Wynne, L. C. Differentiating characteristics of parents of childhood schizophrenics, childhood neurotics, and young adult schizophrenics. *American Journal of Psychiatry*, 1963, *120*, 234–243.

Singer, M. T., & Wynne, L. C. Thought disorder and family relations of schizophrenics: III. Methodology using projective techniques.

Archives of General Psychiatry, 1965, *12*, 187—200. (a)

Singer, M. T., & Wynne, L. C. Thought disorder and family relations of schizophrenics: IV. Results and implications. *Archives of General Psychiatry*, 1965, *12*, 201—212. (b)

Singer, S. Family interaction with schizophrenics and their siblings. *Journal of Abnormal Psychology*, 1966, *71*, 345—353.

Solomon, L., & Zlotowski, M. The relationship between the Elgin and Phillips measures of process-reactive schizophrenia. *Journal of Nervous and Mental Disease*, 1964, *138*, 32—37.

Sperber, Z. Rigidity and conformity tendencies of judges and their utilization of autobiographical material in making predictions. *Journal of Consulting Psychology*, 1962, *26*, 144—148.

Sperling, M. The neurotic child and his mother: A psychoanalytic study. *American Journal of Orthopsychiatry*, 1951, *21*, 354—364.

Spiegel, J. P. The resolution of role conflict within the family. *Psychiatry*, 1957, *20*, 1—16.

Spiegel, J. P., & Bell, N. W. The family of the psychiatric patient. In S. Arieti (Ed.), *American handbook of psychiatry*. New York: Basic Books, 1959. Vol. I, pp. 114—149.

Srole, L., Langner, T. S., Michael, S. T., Opler, M. R., & Rennie, T. A. C. *Mental health in the Metropolis: The mid-town Manhattan study*. Vol. I. New York: McGraw-Hill, 1962.

Stabenau, J. R., Tupin, J., Werner, M., & Pollin, W. A comparative study of families of schizophrenics, delinquents, and normals. *Psychiatry*, 1965, *28*, 45—59.

Straus, M. A. Communication, creativity, and problem-solving ability of middle- and working-class families in three societies. *American Journal of Sociology*, 1968, *73*, 417—430.

Strodtbeck, F. L. Husband-wife interaction over revealed differences. *American Sociological Review*, 1951, *16*, 468—473.

Strodtbeck, F. L. The family of a three-person group. *American Sociological Review*, 1954, *19*, 23—29.

Strodtbeck, F. L. Family interaction values and achievement. In D. C. McClelland, *et al.* (Eds.), *Talent and society*. Princeton, N. J.: Van Nostrand, 1958. Pp. 177—178.

Sullivan, H. S. *Conception of modern psychiatry*. Washington, D. C.: William Alanson White, 1947.

Swanson, G. E. A preliminary laboratory study of the acting crowd. *American Sociological Review*, 1953, *18*, 522—533.

Terrill, J., & Terrill, R. A method for studying family communication. *Family Process*, 1965, *4*, 259—290.

Tharp, R. G. Psychological patterning in marriage. *Psychological Bulletin*, 1963, *60*, 97—118.

Tietze, T. A study of mothers of psychiatric patients. *Psychiatry*, 1949, *12*, 55—65.

Titchener, J. L., D'Zmura, T., Golden, M., & Emerson, R. Family transaction and derivation of individuality. *Family Process*, 1963, *2*, 95—120.

Toms, E. C. Personality characteristics of mothers of schizophrenic veterans. Unpublished Ph.D. dissertation, University of Minnesota, 1955.

Usandivaras, R., Grimson, W., Hammond, H., Issaharoff, E., & Romanos, D. The marbles test. *Archives of General Psychiatry*, 1967, *17*, 111—118.

Vidich, A. Methodological problems in the observation of husband-wife interaction. *Marriage and Family Living*, 1956, *18*, 234—239.

Walton, D. A children's apperception test: An investigation of its validity as a test of neuroticism. *Journal of Mental Science*, 1959, *105*, 359—370.

Warner, W. L., Meeker, M., & Eells, K. *Social class in America*. Chicago: Science Research Associates, 1949.

Waxler, N., & Mishler, E. G. Scoring and reliability problems in interaction process analysis: A methodological note. *Sociometry*, 1966, *29*, 28—40.

Wechsler, D. *Wechsler Intelligence Scale for Children*. New York: Psychological Corporation, 1949.

Wechsler, D. *The measurement and appraisal of adult intelligence*. (4th ed.) Baltimore: Williams & Wilkins, 1958.

Westly, W. Emotionally healthy adolescents and their family backgrounds. In I. Galston (Ed.), *The family in contemporary society*. New York: International Universities Press, 1958. Pp. 131—147.

Wiener, N. *The human use of human beings*. New York: Doubleday, 1954.

Wiese, von. *Systematic sociology*, 1932. (Translated by H. Becker.)

Winter, W. D., & Ferreira, A. J. Story sequence analysis of family TAT's. *Journal of Projective Techniques and Personality Assessment*, 1965, *29*, 392—397.

Winter, W. D., & Ferreira, A. J. Talking time as an index of intrafamilial similarity in normal and abnormal families. *Journal of Abnormal Psychology*, in press.

Winter, W. D., Ferreira, A. J., & Olson, J. L. Story sequence analysis of family TAT's. *Journal of Projective Techniques and Personality Assessment*, 1965, *29*, 392—397.

Winter, W. D., Ferreira, A. J., & Olson, J. L. Hostility themes in the family TAT. *Journal of Projective Techniques and Personality Assessment*, 1966, *30*, 270—274.

Wynne, L. C. The study of intrafamilial alignments and splits in exploratory family therapy. In N. W. Ackerman (Ed.), *Exploring the base for family therapy*. New York: Family Service Association of America, 1961. Pp. 95—116.

Wynne, L. C., Ryckoff, I. M., Day, J., & Hirsch, S. I. Pseudo-mutuality in the families of schizophrenics. *Psychiatry*, 1958, *21*, 205–220.

Wynne, L. C., & Singer, M. T. Thought disorder and family relations of schizophrenics: I. A research strategy. *Archives of General Psychiatry*, 1963, *9*, 191–198. (a)

Wynne, L. C., & Singer, M. T. Thought disorder and family relations of schizophrenics: II. Classification of forms of thinking. *Archives of General Psychiatry*, 1963, *9*, 199–206. (b)

Wynne, L. C., & Singer, M. T. Thinking disorders and family transactions. Paper presented to the American Psychiatric Association, Los Angeles, 1964.

Yarrow, M. R., Campbell, J. D., & Burton, R. V. Reliability of maternal retrospection: A preliminary report. *Family Process*, 1964, *3*, 207–218.

Zuckerman, M., Ribback, B. B., Monashkin, I., & Norton, J. A., Jr. Normative data and factor analysis in the parental attitude research instrument. *Journal of Consulting Psychology*, 1958, *22*, 165–171.

Zunich, M. The relation between parental attitude toward child rearing and child behavior. *Journal of Consulting Psychology*, 1962, *26*, 197.